Throughout the siege of Altavilla, Kelly proved to be one of the toughest fighters. He took an exposed position in an upper-story window and rained fire down on the attackers. He wore out one BAR, the barrel warping from the intense heat.

By the next afternoon the defenders had run out of hand grenades. The attackers swarmed into the courtyard. Kelly then performed an experiment that his basic training instructors had forbidden. Holding a 60-mm mortar shell in his hand, he pulled the pin and the safety lock, tapped the shell on the window sill to remove the secondary pin, then lobbed it down on the Germans.

A deafening blast resulted. The GIs thought a big artillery shell had hit them. Then someone said, "It's only Kelly dropping mortar shells from upstairs."

Kelly's shells did the trick, killing twenty Germans. The rest retreated. . . .

HEROES
OF WW II

Edward F. Murphy

BALLANTINE BOOKS · NEW YORK

Unless otherwise stated, all incidents of heroic action mentioned here resulted in the award of the Medal of Honor to the person involved.

Copyright © 1990 by Edward F. Murphy

All rights reserved under International and Pan-American Copyright Conventions. Published in the United States of America by Ballantine Books, a division of Random House, Inc., New York, and simultaneously in Canada by Random House of Canada Limited, Toronto.

No part of this book may be reproduced or utilized in any form or by any means, electronic or mechanical, including photocopying, recording, or by any information storage and retrieval systems, without permission in writing from the Publisher. Inquiries should be addressed to Presidio Press, 31 Pamaron Way, Novato, CA 94949.

Library of Congress Catalog Card Number: 90-7959

ISBN 0-345-37545-9

This edition published by arrangement with Presidio Press

All photographs not otherwise credited are from the author's collection.

Manufactured in the United States of America

First Ballantine Books Edition: December 1991
Second Printing: July 1992

To Kay, Thanks again.

Contents

1
* * *

Medal of Honor History

The Medal of Honor is America's highest award for combat valor. Since its birth in the Civil War only 3,398 people have earned the august award. Its stature is so high President Harry S Truman, a World War I veteran with a deep understanding of the horrors of combat and the need for extraordinary heroism to overcome them, once told a gathering of World War II recipients, "I'd rather have this medal than be president." Gen. George S. Patton, an outstanding combat soldier who had also a clear grasp of combat bravery, told one recipient as he placed the coveted medal around the hero's neck, "I'd give my immortal soul for that medal."

Only an act of the most conspicuous gallantry and intrepidity, far above and beyond the call of duty, in the presence of an armed enemy merits the Medal of Honor. The deed must involve a clear risk of life. It must be the type of voluntary act which, if the hero did not do it, would not subject him to undue criticism. In addition, at least two eyewitnesses must attest to the deed. By adhering to these strict criteria the armed forces have reserved the Medal of Honor solely for the "bravest of the brave."

But the guidelines weren't always that clear.

When Iowa senator James W. Grimes introduced a bill in Congress in December 1861 "to promote the efficiency of the navy," he had little idea of the far-reaching impact of one of its minor provisions. That paragraph authorized a "medal of honor" for sailors and marines who distinguished themselves by their gallantry in action. President Abraham Lincoln signed

1

the bill, and the Medal of Honor, into law on December 21, 1861.

Not to be outdone, the army prevailed upon Massachusetts senator Henry Wilson to introduce a similar bill for it in February 1862. The law establishing an army Medal of Honor was signed into effect on July 12, 1862.

Originally, both pieces of legislation reserved the medal for enlisted men and limited it to the "present insurrection." Additional legislation in 1863 extended the life of the medal beyond the Civil War. Also, army officers were declared eligible for the medal; the navy continued to restrict its medal to enlisted men until 1915. The army limited its medal to combat heroism, while the navy allowed noncombat heroism, such as saving a man from drowning, to be rewarded with the medal.

The decoration was designed by a Philadelphia silversmith firm, Wm. Wilson & Son. In a letter to the War Department in May 1862 they described the medal as:

A five-pointed star, one point down. On the obverse the foul spirit of Secession and Rebellion is represented by a male figure in crouching attitude holding in his hands serpents, which, with forked tongues, are striking at a large female figure representing the Union or Genius of our country, who holds in her right hand a shield, and in her left, the fasces. Around these figures are thirty-four stars, indicating the number of states in the Union.

Both medals hung from identical ribbons—a blue horizontal top band above alternating vertical stripes of red and white— with only the suspension devices differing. The navy's medal connected to the ribbon with a rope-fouled anchor; the army's via an eagle, wings spread, astride crossed cannon and cannon-ball stacks.

Since that beginning 3,398 recipients have earned 3,417 medals. Nineteen Americans have earned the Medal of Honor twice. Heroic acts performed during the Civil War account for 1,520 medals, nearly half of all those awarded. But there were no other medals then. It was the Medal of Honor or nothing. In too many cases, it was the Medal of Honor.

Actually, the number of medals awarded would be much greater, and the corresponding dignity lesser, if the army had not convened a special board in 1916 to review all its awards made up to that time. It rescinded 911 medals, 864 of which had gone to members of the 27th Maine Infantry for voluntarily extending their enlistments for two days during the Gettysburg campaign in July 1863. The volunteers saw no action; they remained in reserve in Washington, D.C., but received the medal anyway.

To avoid future abuses of the Medal of Honor, the board further recommended the creation of additional awards to honor deeds of valor not warranting a Medal of Honor. The result would be an elevating of the Medal of Honor to the pinnacle of a so-called pyramid of honor. Lesser decorations would reward varying degrees of heroism and meritorious service. Each medal would have its own unique eligibility criteria to ensure a proper level of recognition.

During World War I the army adopted the recommendations of the 1916 board and created several new decorations. The Distinguished Service Cross (DSC) would rank immediately below the Medal of Honor, honoring combat heroism not justifying the Medal of Honor. Below the DSC was the Silver Star. The navy introduced the Navy Cross, equivalent to the DSC, and also used the Silver Star. These new decorations assured that only the top heroes of the American Expeditionary Forces in France would receive the Medal of Honor.

Today, the Medal of Honor is the most prestigious of all decorations. A strict review process ensures that the medal will not be conferred on unworthy candidates. The standards are so high over fifty-five percent of the medals awarded since World War I have been posthumous. For the Korean War and the Vietnam War nearly seventy percent of the Medals of Honor went to heroes whose bravery resulted in their death. Those who wear the Medal of Honor are truly a special breed.

Army Lt. Bernard J. D. Irwin performed the earliest deed for which a Medal of Honor was awarded. On February 14, 1861, the young surgeon volunteered to lead a relief expedition to the aid of a patrol of cavalrymen trapped by Indians at Apache Pass, Arizona. Fighting Apaches and a raging blizzard, Irwin broke the siege, saving the beleaguered command from certain death.

The first Medals of Honor actually awarded went to six soldiers from Ohio who survived the legendary "Great Locomotive Chase" through Georgia in April 1862. Twenty-one volunteers under the command of civilian spy James J. Andrews set out from Shelbyville, Tennessee, with the mission of capturing a Confederate locomotive near Atlanta. Once they had the train they'd run it north to Chattanooga, burning bridges and cutting telegraph wires along the way. The resulting confusion would prevent the Confederate Army from reinforcing Chattanooga during an upcoming Union attack.

Unfortunately, bad weather and the dogged persistence of the Confederate train's conductor spoiled the mission. All of the "engine thieves" were captured. They languished in prison for almost a year, during which time eight of the band, including Andrews, were tried, then executed by their captors. Eight more men escaped a few months later, eventually making their way back to Union lines. In March 1863 the remaining six were repatriated at City Point, Virginia.

They arrived in Washington, D.C., on March 25 with orders to report to the judge advocate general so they could revise and qualify evidence concerning the raid. When Secretary of War Edwin M. Stanton heard they were in the capital, he sent for them.

After listening to the group recite the horrors of their imprisonment, Stanton praised their courage and devotion to duty. Then he said, "Congress has recently created a special medal to honor the brave defenders of the Union. None have yet been awarded. I have the honor of presenting you the first." He pinned the first medal to the tunic of the group's youngest member, nineteen-year-old Jacob Parrott. The others receiving medals that day were William Bensinger, Robert Buffum, Elihu Mason, William Pittinger, and William H. Reddick.

A few days later the navy awarded its first medals. They held no formal ceremony for their heroes, though. Instead, the medals were forwarded to the intended recipient's commanding officer who handled the presentation ceremony on an individual basis.

When the Civil War ended in April 1865, 1,196 soldiers, 307 sailors, and 17 marines had performed deeds of valor that brought them the Medal of Honor.

Both the army and navy continued to award the Medal of Honor after the Civil War. Medals went to soldiers who fought Indians as America expanded westward, 423 in all. Sailors and marines were cited primarily for heroism involved in rescuing drowning men, although a handful of medals were awarded to men for combat heroics in isolated skirmishes around the world. Between the Civil War and the Spanish-American War, the navy awarded 128 medals to gallant sailors and marines.

As America pursued world trade and began establishing herself as a global power, the men filling the ranks of her armed forces were called upon to exhibit new heights of courage and daring. Medals of Honor went to brave men who stormed San Juan Hill, to sailors who faced the Spanish cannon at Manila Bay, and to those heroic men who marched to relieve Peking from the hordes of religious fanatics surrounding the capital in 1900. While the circumstances might have changed in the years since the Civil War, the need for heroic action had not diminished.

In 1904 the army adopted a new design for its Medal of Honor. The change was prompted by various veterans groups issuing membership badges that closely resembled the Medal of Honor. Horace Porter, ambassador to France and a Civil War recipient of the Medal of Honor, commissioned the Parisian jewelry firm of Messrs. Arthur, Bertrand, and Berenger to prepare several designs for a new medal. One was approved by both the members of the Medal of Honor Legion and the secretary of war. On November 22, 1904, a patent was issued to protect the new medal.

The chief feature of the old medal, the five-pointed star, was retained in the new design. At its center appears the head of Minerva. The words "United States of America" surround this. An open laurel wreath, enameled in green, encircles the star. Green oak leaves fill the prongs of the star. Above the star is a bar bearing the word "VALOR." An eagle with wings spread sits atop the bar.

The new ribbon for the medal was a light blue, watered-silk material spangled with thirteen white stars representing the original colonies. Initially, the medal was worn on the recipient's left breast. Later, a neck ribbon was added, although the version with the breast ribbon continued to be awarded throughout World War II.

Because the navy awarded its Medal of Honor for both combat and noncombat heroism, it adopted a second Medal of Honor to be reserved for combat heroism. In 1919, the navy introduced a gold cross, pattée-style medal designed by the New York City jewelry firm, Tiffany & Co. The old five-pointed star was kept for noncombat heroism. The two-medal system proved too cumbersome, though, and the navy dropped it in 1942, going back to just the original Medal of Honor design.

The introduction of new decorations during World War I ensured that the Medal of Honor would be reserved only for those doughboys exhibiting the highest degrees of heroism. So exacting were the standards that only 118 members of the AEF received the Medal of Honor: 90 army, 21 navy, and 7 marines (five of whom also received the army Medal of Honor for the same deed). For the first time posthumous awards accounted for a large percentage of the total. Thirty-one of the heroes died performing the act which earned them the award.

In the years following the Great War both the army and the navy awarded the Medal of Honor for exceptional heroism. Most of the navy's went to men who bravely fought fires aboard ships. Others went for exceptional accomplishments, the most notable being the army award to Charles A. Lindbergh for his epic flight across the Atlantic.

It was in World War II that the Medal of Honor achieved the prominence it holds today. To assure that only the most deserving heroes received this ultimate recognition, both the army and navy created internal decorations boards to review recommendations for awards. There were various levels of boards each recommendation had to pass, beginning at the division level. The higher the proposed medal, the longer the review process. Recommendations for the Medal of Honor went all the way back to Washington, D.C., where senior, combat-tested officers reviewed the supporting documentation. They, as well as any of the intermediate boards, could downgrade the Medal of Honor recommendation to a lesser award, or conversely, upgrade a recommendation for another award to the Medal of Honor.

While this was a lengthy, time-consuming process, it did uphold the highest traditions of the Medal of Honor. Over thirteen million men served in the military during World War II. Only 433 received the Medal of Honor (294 army, 57 navy, 81 marines, and 1 lone coastguardsman). For the first time posthumous awards outnumbered awards to living heroes—only 190 men survived to have their medals placed around their necks.

Because of the enhanced prestige of the Medal of Honor more effort was made during World War II to present the award with an appropriate ceremony. Unlike World War I when most Medal of Honor presentation ceremonies were conducted at the headquarters of Gen. John J. Pershing at Chaumont, France, whenever possible the living hero of World War II was brought back to Washington, D.C., where the president made the presentation. The families of deceased heroes usually received the award from a local unit commander.

Like heroes of earlier wars, those men whose gallantry during World War II was recognized by the Medal of Honor came from nearly all walks of life. They range from a president's son to sharecroppers' sons. They came from large cities and small towns. Some were rich, others poor. Some never saw the inside of a high school classroom, while others held graduate degrees. There were differences in their backgrounds, yet they all shared a common trait: the ability to overcome their fear in the face of overwhelming odds and respond with a courage above and beyond the call of duty. A courage worthy of the Medal of Honor.

2

* * *

Attack on Pearl Harbor

At 6:00 A.M., Sunday morning, December 7, 1941, at sea 230 miles north of Oahu, Hawaii, six Japanese aircraft carriers turned into a steady eastern wind. Although the southern seas were running high, causing the carriers' bows to dip fifteen degrees, a signal from the flagship *Akagi* confirmed the launching of the torpedo planes, dive bombers, horizontal bombers, and fighter planes comprising the Pearl Harbor striking force. To the accompanying cheers of the gathered crewmen Comdr. Mitsuo Fuchida, the leader of the strike force, sent his fighter plane thundering down the careening deck of the *Akagi*. Within minutes the rest of the fighters roared skyward.

While they circled protectively above the flotilla, the torpedo planes, then the dive bombers followed. The launching continued without a flaw until all 183 planes of the first wave of the striking force were airborne, maneuvering into formation. As they headed south, the crews of the six carriers began preparing the 270 planes of the second wave, scheduled for launching at 7:15 A.M.

Above a thick carpet of clouds Commander Fuchida homed in on an early-morning Honolulu radio program. He was worried that the cloud cover might prevent an accurate attack on the American fleet. He had started to consider his options when the clouds began breaking up. Fuchida would have no problem carrying out the original plans.

At about 7:40 A.M. the Pearl Harbor striking force was streaking down the west coast of Oahu. Off to their left front the U.S. Navy's Pacific Fleet anchorage at Pearl Harbor came into view. Commander Fuchida quickly counted the huge U.S. battleships anchored around Ford Island. There were eight. He could hardly believe his luck.

For the first weekend since July 4, all the battleships of the fleet were in Pearl Harbor. Usually they alternated spending weekends on maneuvers with one task force or another, but not this weekend.

A message warning of a possible Japanese attack on "the Philippines, Thai, or Kra Peninsula or possibly Borneo" had been received a week earlier. As a result, the carrier *Enterprise* was taking a squadron of Marine Corps fighter planes to reinforce the small U.S. garrison at distant Wake Island. Because of their slower speed the battleships that normally accompanied this task force stayed put. Similarly, the Pacific Fleet's other carrier, the *Lexington*, ferried planes to Midway Island, at the western end of the Hawaiian chain. In the meantime, the crews of the battleships enjoyed a rare weekend in port.

All across the wide harbor men on duty and off prepared to enjoy a leisurely Sunday. Aboard the cruiser *Honolulu* a boatload of sailors prepared to go ashore to attend Mass. Crewmen of the cruiser *San Francisco* got ready for a swimming outing at Waikiki Beach. Members of the crew of the battleship *Nevada* prepared for a tennis tournament. The marine detachment aboard another battleship warmed up for a softball match. Less ambitious seamen simply loafed on deck, enjoying the warm morning sun.

None of the sailors or marines in Hawaii expected to be at war in a short time. To be sure, other parts of the world were embroiled in conflict, but they were mostly in Europe. The United States was doing its best to avoid that arena. The U.S. would stay on its side of the ocean, the Germans, Italians, and Japanese on theirs. That way there would be no trouble.

Besides, who would want to fight the powerful United States of America anyway?

SAMUEL G. FUQUA

Like many other officers that serene morning, Lt. Comdr. Samuel G. Fuqua, aboard the battleship *Arizona*, was relaxing after a pleasant Sunday morning breakfast. He had just put down his coffee cup when he heard a faint explosion. He dismissed it as an accident but was startled to hear another KARUMPF. Seconds later, the wail of sirens pierced the morning air.

Fuqua glanced at his watch. 7:55. Pretty darn early for an air-raid drill, he thought. But not unlike the navy, he reflected. In his twenty-one years of naval service he had witnessed more than a few bizarre surprises.

A native of Laddonia, Missouri, where he was born on October 15, 1899, Fuqua graduated from the U.S. Naval Academy in 1923. Though promotion was excruciatingly slow in the years between the wars, Fuqua endured the routine assignments of a naval officer, taking great pride in his shipboard duties. He was particularly pleased with his assignment to the *Arizona*. She was known as a taut ship, with a crew that took great pride in her operation. As far as they were concerned she was the ''best ship in the whole damned fleet.''

Now Fuqua reached for the phone to make sure the antiaircraft battery was manned for the drill. He was puzzled when no one answered. The noise outside confirmed the drill was still in progress. He decided to go topside for a look.

Fuqua emerged on the quarterdeck just as a Japanese fighter plane bore down on the *Arizona*, its wing guns blazing. In an instant Fuqua took it in: the *Arizona* was under attack! He broke into a run for the Number 4 turret. Halfway there he was slammed to the steel deck as two Japanese torpedoes ripped into the ship. He lost consciousness.

When he came to a few minutes later hell was raging all around him. Overhead, Japanese planes seemed to fill the blue sky. On the *Arizona*, the repair ship *Vestal* moored next to her, the *Nevada* behind her, and the other battleships to her front, guns fired away at the attackers. Great columns of smoke rose from everywhere. The noise was deafening.

One man ran by shouting, ''The Japs are bombing us! The Japs are bombing us!'' Another yelled, ''The Japs are here. This is the real thing.''

Reacting with a professional coolness born of his long years of service and raw courage, Fuqua quickly set up his damage control station. He directed his crew in fighting the fires and rescuing and treating the many injured.

Fuqua had nearly gotten the fires under control when a tremendous explosion rocked the entire ship. To those watching, it appeared as if the *Arizona*'s bow rose completely into the air, shuddered, then slammed back into the water. She started sinking immediately. Many witnesses thought a bomb had gone straight down her stack, exploding the boilers. Later examination disproved that theory. More than likely a bomb landed alongside the second turret, crashed through the forecastle, then erupted in the forward magazine.

Regardless of the cause, a huge ball of fire shot five hundred feet into the air. It was not a bang as much as it was a terrific WHOOM. Yet the concussion was tremendous. It blew men off the neighboring ships *Nevada* and *Vestal*. All across the harbor men fighting the Japanese attackers paused in stunned silence.

Aboard the *Arizona* over one thousand men died instantly. The commander of Battleship Division 1, Rear Adm. Isaac C. Kidd, and the commanding officer of the *Arizona*, Capt. Franklin Van Valkenburgh, disappeared as the blast engulfed them on the bridge. For courageously discharging their duties in the face of the devastating enemy attack both men would receive posthumous Medals of Honor.

This massive eruption slammed Fuqua to the deck again. Staggering from the blow, he somehow managed to reorganize the fire-fighting party. But it quickly turned into a futile effort. Flames grew everywhere. The entire ship seemed to be on fire. The water, too, was ablaze from oil seeping from the mortally wounded ship. Fuqua continued to lead his men, undaunted by the raging infernos that threatened to engulf them.

"I saw men on fire, burning to death," he recalled years later, "but still they fought on until they fell dead at their battle stations. When we picked them up, their flesh fell off their bodies into our hands."

Fuqua knew he had to save as many of the wounded as he could. He rounded up another group of able-bodied sailors and had them evacuate the wounded to lifeboats that took them ashore to Ford Island.

Alternating his time between supervising the fire fighters and evacuating the wounded, Fuqua's calm, cool, professional manner greatly inspired those around him. His intrepid actions were credited with saving numerous lives.

After nearly an hour of superhuman efforts to save the wounded and his ship, Fuqua realized he was fighting a losing battle. Although it pained him deeply, as the senior surviving officer he issued the dreaded order, "Abandon ship."

Fuqua himself stayed on the quarterdeck, where he directed

the movement of personnel off the ship. He made a hazardous journey through accessible portions of the *Arizona*, searching for any survivors. Only when he was satisfied he had done all he could did Fuqua climb aboard the final lifeboat. Tears filled his eyes as he pulled away from the ship on which he had begun his naval career two decades earlier.

Of the 1,553 men aboard the *Arizona*, only 289 survived.

The Medal of Honor was presented to Fuqua on March 19, 1942, in a ceremony at his new duty station at the Naval Training Base, Newport, Rhode Island. Fuqua later returned to the Pacific for another combat tour. He retired as a rear admiral in 1953, earned his master's degree at Stanford University in 1957, then taught high school mathematics before retiring again in 1970. He died on January 27, 1987.

When the *Arizona* blew up, Comdr. Cassin Young, of the repair ship *Vestal*, tied to her port side, was sent flying into the harbor. Amazingly, he survived uninjured. After he disappeared, though, the executive officer ordered the *Vestal* abandoned. While men leapt from the little ship, Young swam back to her, pulled himself aboard, and stood sopping wet at the top of the gangplank. Even though bombs and flying debris from the *Arizona* had left the *Vestal*'s deck a shambles, Young was not about to quit. He shouted down to the swimmers, "Come back! We're not giving up the ship yet!"

Most of the crew returned, and Young ordered them to cast off. Ignoring the tongues of flames licking at the *Vestal* from the *Arizona*, men hacked away at the thick hawsers connecting the two ships. Oblivious to the bombs and machine-gun bullets from strafing Japanese planes, Young directed fire-fighting crews to battle the fires, then ordered his ship under way. With the help of a passing tug, Young conned the *Vestal* away from the dying *Arizona* and into the open water.

Though he had hoped to save her, Young realized the damage to the *Vestal* from Japanese bombs and the concussion from the *Arizona*'s explosion was too severe. Reluctantly, he ordered her beached near Aiea Landing, where she sat out the rest of the attack.

Other vessels among the fleet were also taking merciless poundings. Two berths ahead of the *Arizona*, the *Oklahoma* was tied outboard of the *Maryland*. In that exposed position she suffered a terrific beating. In the opening minutes of the sneak attack no less than five torpedoes crashed into her port side, ripping huge gashes in her armor plating. An unknown number of aerial bombs smashed into her deck, sending death and destruction everywhere. She never really had a chance.

Slowly, ponderously, like a huge whale, the *Oklahoma* rolled onto her port side. As one observer said, ''It was as if she were tired and wanted to rest.'' The mighty ship continued her roll, stopping only when her masts and superstructure jammed into the mud. She was bottoms up, finished.

But not her crew. Two of them deliberately sacrificed their own lives so others could live. Ens. Francis C. Flaherty, a twenty-two-year-old native of Charlotte, Michigan, who was in the navy to get enough money to return to medical school, and S1c. James R. Ward, twenty years old from Springfield, Ohio, both ignored orders to abandon ship. Instead, they remained in their turret holding flashlights so the remainder of the turret crew could see to escape. By the time the others were free, water had filled the turret.

The last ship in the line on Battleship Row that morning was the *Nevada*. At precisely 8:00 A.M. the ship's band, ignoring the crash of bombs on Ford Island, broke into the ''Star Spangled Banner'' for the morning flag-raising ceremony. Even when a Japanese torpedo plane's machine gunner sprayed the after-deck area where they stood, the band played on, never missing a note. Another strafer roared overhead, bullets ripping up the deck. This time, the conductor paused briefly as wood splinters showered the band, then quickly resumed the beat. Not a man broke formation until the final note drifted away, lost in the noise of exploding bombs and torpedoes. Then every man ran wildly for cover.

By a stroke of good fortune two of the *Nevada*'s boilers were fired up that morning, giving her enough steam to get under way. Forty-five minutes after the attack began, in spite of one torpedo and two aerial bomb hits, and the fact that her commanding officer and executive officer were ashore, the *Nevada* started moving. Enlisted men and junior officers assumed leadership roles for which they had no training, but they got the battleship moving anyway. Normally, four tugs were needed to move the ship from her berth, but this time the helmsman did it strictly on experience.

BMC Edwin J. Hill led his line-handling detail off the *Nevada* and onto the wharf. Under heavy enemy gunfire and with bombs exploding on the pier, the small party of men cast off the mooring lines. Immediately, the battleship started moving with the tide. After twenty-nine years in the navy, Hill wasn't about to be left behind. Yelling "Wait for me!" he dove into the water and swam after his ship.

The *Nevada* pulled into the channel, intent on making the open sea. Her movement quickly attracted the attention of the Japanese planes. Swarms of them descended on the battleship while her gunners fired skyward trying to ward them off.

Halfway to the open sea it became obvious the damage inflicted by the Japanese was too much. The helmsman headed her into shore near the navy hospital. The wind and current caught the drifting ship, turning her completely around. Chief Hill rushed forward to drop the anchor so the ship wouldn't smash up on the rocks. A wave of dive-bombers zeroed in on the helpless *Nevada*, moving in for the final kill. Three bombs landed near the bow. Hill vanished in the blast. The last anyone saw of him, he was still working on the anchor gear instead of seeking cover.

Now that the *Nevada* was isolated from the protective firepower of her sister ships, two more flights of Japanese planes singled her out for more punishment. That she was able to fight back was largely due to the gallant efforts of one man.

DONALD K. ROSS

While he stood shaving that morning, Warrant Machinist Donald K. Ross was mentally making plans for his thirty-first birthday the next day. He had been courting his current girlfriend, a graduate student at the University of Hawaii, for over a year, and he wanted to do something special for the occasion. His thoughts were interrupted by the crunch of exploding bombs. He peered out the porthole, saw three planes with the red "meatballs" of the Japanese Navy flying low over Ford Island, and at once knew what was happening.

A quick wipe of his face with a towel and Ross was on his way to his duty station in the forward dynamo room, a control point for the electrical generators. For the next hour, while torpedoes slammed into his ship, with Japanese bombs raining from the sky, and while the *Nevada* made her gallant sortie down the channel, Ross remained at his station providing power for the guns, fire-fighting equipment, and communications equipment.

The flight of Japanese bombers that killed BMC Hill was followed soon after by another. Four bombs fell earthward. Three exploded harmlessly in the water alongside the *Nevada*. The fourth tore through the bridge's superstructure, exploding in the stack, blowing back through the ventilation system.

In the forward dynamo room Ross stood directly under the ventilation duct. The explosion hit him full in the face, blinding him. The room quickly filled with thick, acrid smoke.

Realizing that the ship must have power to fight, but that no one could survive for long in the choking smoke, Ross ordered the others to escape. "Everybody out," he yelled. He would stay behind, feeding power to the guns until the after dynamo room took over the load.

He groped his way to a telephone and called the after dynamo room. "Take the load," he stammered, barely able to breathe. "I'm almost finished."

Fifteen minutes passed. Fifteen long, agonizing minutes during which Ross balanced the electrical demands against the power generated. Working the switches and instruments with a practiced touch developed during years of experience, Ross maintained power where it was needed, enabling the wounded *Nevada* to continue fighting.

At last the telephone rang. "We've got the load, Mr. Ross. We're going to cut you off."

Fighting unconsciousness, Ross somehow made his way to the main electrical panel. With his last ounce of strength he tripped the generator switches. Then he collapsed.

Above deck a telephone talker who had been monitoring Ross's conversation tried to raise him. No answer. He dropped the phone and raced to the forward dynamo room. There he pulled Ross to safety. Corpsmen administered first aid, reviving Ross.

Still partially blind, but determined to complete the securing of the forward dynamo, Ross shrugged off restraining hands and made his way back to the room. Though the temperature exceeded 140 degrees, Ross managed to secure the final trip switches. Now, at last, the power was completely transferred and the forward dynamo room shut down. Ross made his way to fresh air.

Later that morning, when word came that smoke was filling the after dynamo room Ross volunteered to help save the men stationed there. Years later, Ross explained his actions: "Someone went for me, so I went for them."

Still without his full vision, Ross felt his way along the corridors to the room. There he hoisted a shipmate to his shoulders. Somehow, he got his charge to safety before passing out again.

When he came to the second time the ship's doctor ordered him ashore to the hospital. En route, Ross found chaos on the dock. Someone was needed to organize the flotilla of small boats ferrying supplies to the ships in the harbor and returning with wounded and dying sailors. What the heck, Ross thought, he couldn't see well, but he could still talk.

For the next two and a half days Ross sat on the dock organizing, telephoning, and directing the rescue crews. He brought order to the confusion that followed the attack. If two officers from the *Nevada* hadn't stumbled across him Ross would have spent a week there. They ordered him to report to the hospital.

Ross's sight returned under treatment, and he reported back aboard the *Nevada* ten days after the attack. On January 7, 1942, he married his girlfriend. Three months later, on April 18, 1942, he received his Medal of Honor from Adm. Chester W. Nimitz.

Ross remained in the navy after the war, retiring as a captain in 1956.

On the other side of Ford Island the old battleship *Utah*, converted to a target ship, attracted an unusual number of Japanese planes. With her deck covered by six-by-twelve-inch planks to cushion the fall of practice bombs, she fooled the Japanese into thinking a carrier was in port. Nearly helpless against the onslaught, the venerable ship shuddered as two torpedoes hit her early in the attack. Other Japanese planes dropped bombs on her as a target of opportunity. The *Utah* listed heavily to port.

PETER TOMICH

A watertender was charged with maintaining the proper pressure of steam and the proper level of water in the boilers and the intricate network of pipes that crisscrossed the interior of the engine room. Too much of one, or too little of the other, and a ship's boilers could be damaged beyond repair. Or they could explode, sending lethal live steam onto the engine room crew.

One of the best watertenders in the fleet was Chief Watertender Peter Tomich of the *Utah*. No one seemed to understand the maze of steam lines and complexity of boilers as he did. Few men could coax as much from an old boiler as he could. He knew, and some said loved, his boilers. So great was the respect for Tomich's talent that if a problem with another ship's power plant could not be solved, he was sent for.

And it wasn't surprising, considering his twenty-two years of naval service. Born in Prolog, Austria, on June 3, 1893, he emigrated to America in his teens. When the United States entered World War I in 1917 Tomich enlisted in the army. He saw no overseas service, but did become a U.S. citizen.

A few days after his honorable discharge in January 1919, Tomich enlisted in the navy. It wasn't long before he realized he had found a home. His natural affinity for machinery soon displayed itself. As a result, he advanced quickly through the ranks. In just eleven years he earned the stripes of chief watertender—unheard of progress in the peacetime navy.

His assignment to the *Utah* proved beneficial to both the navy and Tomich. The navy was not going to spend much of its limited funds on the maintenance of an old target ship. So Tomich called upon his considerable talents to keep the ship's boilers operating.

The long hours he put in did not bother him. In fact, he enjoyed the arduous work. He had no family; he had never married, and as far as anyone knew, he had no living relatives. The navy was his home, the young men of his engine room crew his family.

Tomich demonstrated his concern for his crew that brutal December morning.

When the *Utah* started her list, water seeped into the engineering plant. Tomich knew danger was imminent. He had to secure the boilers before they blew. He knew that. He also knew that those who stayed to perform the time-consuming tasks were doomed. The rising water would trap them. Tomich made his decision.

"Get out!" he yelled to his men. "Get topside. The ship's going over."

The crew was his family. He'd save them and do what he could to save his ship from a deadly internal explosion. As the last of the crew scrambled up ladders to safety, they saw Tomich calmly turning valves, setting gauges, and opening petcocks. It was the last anyone saw of him.

Tomich's sacrifice was not in vain. Because of his actions an explosion of the boilers and the attendant loss of life were avoided. For his deliberate self-sacrifice he was awarded the Medal of Honor. But the navy could not award it. They looked in vain for a relative of Tomich's to accept the decoration. None could be found.

When a destroyer escort was named for the deceased hero in 1944 the ship's commanding officer accepted the posthumous award on his crew's behalf. Upon the ship's decommissioning after the war, the medal was returned to the Navy Department.

On May 25, 1947, in an impressive candlelight ceremony, the governor of Utah declared Tomich an honorary citizen of that state. He then accepted Tomich's medal from the Navy Department as part of a permanent memorial at the state capital honoring the men who had lost their lives aboard the *Utah*.

Peter Tomich was home at last.

Not all of the Japanese efforts on December 7th were focused on Pearl Harbor. Flights of horizontal bombers and fighter planes attacked Schofield Barracks and Wheeler Field at the center of the island, Ewa Marine Air Base west of Pearl Harbor, and the army air corps base at Hickam Field adjacent to Pearl Harbor. Kaneohe Naval Air Station, on the windward side of Oahu and the home of thirty-three amphibious PBY patrol aircraft, received special attention.

Within minutes of the opening attack thirty PBYs were burning; the other three were fortuitously out on patrol and missed the destruction. Hangars were ablaze. Strafers shot at everything in sight. Bullets ripped into buildings, planes, trucks, cars, and people.

Only one gun fired back during the entire attack. Chief Aviation Ordnanceman John Finn, a thirty-two-year-old Californian, set up a .50-caliber machine gun on an instruction stand at the far end of the parking ramp for the PBYs. When the strafers came in to shoot up the twenty-six amphibs neatly parked along the ramp, Finn hammered away at them with his machine gun.

Shrapnel hit him several times, but that didn't deter him. Again and again the Japanese planes dove down, but somehow he survived all the lead thrown his way.

Finn got one Japanese Zero fighter plane in his sights and accurately tracked it on its strafing run. He triggered a burst from the machine gun. A smile broke across his face when smoke trailed out from behind the plane. Seconds later it crashed behind a group of hangars. It was the only Japanese plane shot down at Kaneohe that day.

Finn's stubborn insistence at remaining at his exposed post for over two hours brought him a well-deserved Medal of Honor.

At just past 10:00 A.M. that morning the Japanese withdrew back to their carriers. The destruction they left behind was nearly complete. Of ninety-six ships present at Pearl Harbor that morning, eighteen were sunk or severely damaged. Among them were nine battleships.

Of 394 army, navy, and marine aircraft on the island, 188 were destroyed, another 159 damaged. At Kaneohe Naval Air Station only 1 plane out of 82 was able to fly after the attack.

Over 2,300 military personnel died. More sailors, 2,008, died in this single two-hour attack than had fallen in all America's previous wars combined.

Fifteen men earned Medals of Honor during the attack. Five survived.

The Japanese attack galvanized America into action. On December 8, 1941, President Franklin D. Roosevelt declared war on Japan. The next day a similar declaration was made against Germany and its chancellor, Adolf Hitler. And, ultimately, America would prevail. But there were many dark months ahead. Months that saw the fall of Wake Island, Guam, Singapore, the East Indies, and other Pacific bastions once believed invincible. And, perhaps worst of all, months that included the destruction of the American forces in the Philippine Islands.

3

★ ★ ★

Defeat in the Pacific

In the 1920s U.S. Army staff officers developed a plan for the defense of the Philippines in the event of a Japanese invasion. Dubbed War Plan *Orange*, it called for the armed forces to withdraw into Bataan Peninsula, on the western side of Manila Bay, and to Corregidor Island, which sat in the entrance to Manila Bay off the southern tip of Bataan. Here the Americans and Filipinos were expected to hold out for as long as six months before American reinforcements relieved them.

When he assumed command of the U.S. Army forces in the Far East in July 1941 Gen. Douglas MacArthur discarded War Plan *Orange*. His plan would stop the Japanese on the invasion beaches. To prepare his army for such an eventuality MacArthur set a furious training pace throughout the fall months of 1941. Over seventy-five thousand raw Filipino recruits had to be whipped into shape. Supplies had to be ordered and stockpiled. Defensive sites had to be prepared. A million tasks had to be completed, but there just wasn't enough time.

Within hours of the Pearl Harbor attack, Japanese infantry of Lt. Gen. Masaharu Homma's Fourteenth Army began landing on northern Luzon and Mindanao, at the southern end of the archipelago. The Japanese followed their initial landings with a major amphibious assault at Lingayen Gulf, on Luzon's northwestern shore, beginning on December 22. The overwhelming superiority of the Japanese forces led MacArthur to abandon his plans to fight the Japanese on the beaches. He hastily implemented War Plan *Orange*.

Maj. Gen Jonathan M. Wainwright's North Luzon force fought a valiant delaying action down the length of the island, allowing

MacArthur's troops to reach Bataan safely. Wainwright's force did not enter the peninsula until January 6, 1942.

Only thirty miles long and fifteen miles wide, Bataan was covered with mountains, thick jungles, and was crisscrossed by streams and impassable ravines. Two extinct volcanoes dominated the peninsula: Mount Nabid in the north, four thousand feet high, and Mount Bataan in the south, nearly five thousand feet high. Only two roads existed on all of Bataan. Route 110, a paved road, ran down Bataan's eastern shore to its tip, where it curved back north, running about two-thirds of the way up the western coast. A cobblestone road ran the width of the peninsula in the broad valley between the two volcanoes.

By the time all the troops had made the withdrawal some one hundred thousand people crowded the peninsula. About eighty thousand were military, the rest were civilian refugees. MacArthur only had enough food to feed everyone for thirty days. He immediately ordered half rations. As a result, the combat troops received less than two thousand calories per day. By the end of March that would be cut in half.

From his headquarters deep in the security of Malinta Tunnel on Corregidor, MacArthur created two new commands to defend the peninsula: I Philippine Corps under General Wainright manned the western half; II Philippine Corps under Maj. Gen. George M. Parker held the eastern. The defensive line was established about one-third of the way down the peninsula, with both generals anchoring their respective flanks on the slopes of Mount Nabib. The Japanese did not wait long before testing the line.

On the afternoon of January 9, Lt. Gen Akira Nara sent his 65th Brigade straight down Route 110 toward the defenders of Abucay, a small town on Bataan's east coast. For two days they advanced against punishing artillery fire from Parker's II Corps batteries. On the 11th the Japanese clashed with the elite 57th Infantry, Philippine Scouts. Near midnight that night they launched a vicious banzai attack against Company I, 3d Battalion, 57th Infantry (PS). Wave after wave of screaming, fanatical Japanese threw themselves against the barbed wire entanglements fronting the company's positions. The defenders were forced to give ground. The regimental commander threw in a reserve company to plug the line. That stalled the attack. At first light the reserve company's commander, Capt. Ernest Brown, counted over 250 Japanese bodies littering the battlefield. He and his men began the task of mopping up dozens of enemy infiltrators.

ALEXANDER R. NININGER

His friends called him "Sandy," because of his wavy, dark blonde hair. Born October 30, 1918, at Gainesville, Georgia, Nininger graduated sixth in his class of 450 at West Point in June 1941. But he was not the typical hard-boiled career infantry officer. Sandy Nininger possessed a fondness for art, music, and good books. As one of his class's top graduates Nininger had his choice of assignments. He never hesitated. He wanted to go where the action was likely to be. He chose the Philippines.

Following advanced infantry officer training at Fort Benning, Georgia, 2d Lt. Nininger arrived in Manila in October 1941. He became a platoon leader in Company A, 1st Battalion, 57th Infantry (PS), one of three regiments assigned to the Philippine Division. Nininger easily adapted to the rigorous training schedule. This was exactly what he had studied and trained for over four years to do. He quickly developed a reputation as an indefatigable and resourceful officer, always willing to go a little further than the others to complete his mission.

After the initial Japanese attacks, the Philippine Division guarded Clark Field. Next, they built defensive positions along Subic Bay, at the top of Bataan's western shore. As soon as MacArthur ordered War Plan *Orange* implemented, the Philippine Division became part of Parker's II Corps.

When General Nara sent his brigade toward Abucay, Nininger's battalion was in reserve several hundred yards behind the main line. Throughout the frenzied banzai attack Nininger waited restlessly. When Captain Brown's company was called forward, Nininger requested permission to accompany him. It was denied. He was to stay with his platoon.

On the morning of January 12, when Brown realized there were far more infiltrators than his weakened company could handle, Nininger and two squads from his platoon were released from their reserve position to help him. Quickly moving to the area held by Brown's Company K, Nininger found that the Japanese occupied the Allied foxholes they had overrun the previous night. Their presence threatened the integrity of the entire sector.

Nininger loaded himself down with grenades, slung a captured Japanese light machine gun over his shoulder, and began a one-man assault on the enemy positions. Over and over he attacked them in their foxholes. He'd toss in a grenade and follow the blast with rapid bursts from his machine gun. Dogged by persistent sniper fire he ignored it to continue his attack.

Soon, the art-loving young second lieutenant was far ahead of his comrades. Completely on his own, he pressed forward into the dense jungle. Suddenly, a Japanese rifle slug plowed through his shoulder. He staggered, then caught himself and moved on, wiping out still another enemy foxhole. When he ran out of machine-gun ammo, he pulled out his .45 pistol.

Hit a second, then a third time, Nininger ignored the pain and fought on. As he moved in on still another Japanese-occupied foxhole, three enemy soldiers suddenly fell on him, stabbing him from behind with their bayonets. Whirling around, Nininger killed all three at point-blank range with his .45 before collapsing on the jungle floor.

No one ever knew for sure how many Japanese the sensitive art and music lover had killed, but his valiant actions greatly bolstered the courage of the Filipinos. Inspired, they raced forward, wiping out the infiltrators and restoring the torn line. Nininger's actions had bought Bataan's desperate defenders a few more days.

In a solemn ceremony on February 10, 1942, at McDill Army Air Base, Tampa, Florida, Nininger's father accepted his son's posthumous Medal of Honor. Sandy Nininger was the army's first Medal of Honor hero in the war.

Reinforced by fresh troops, General Nara intensified his attack against the Abucay Line. Though the Americans and Filipinos counterattacked several times, they were unable to stop the well-supplied enemy. On January 16, thirty-four-year-old Filipino mess sergeant Jose Calugas joined the ranks of America's greatest heroes when he ignored the crashing explosions of Japanese artillery rounds to go to the aid of an injured gun crew in his Battery B, 88th Field Artillery (PS). He sprinted across a thousand yards of open ground to the howitzer, rounded up a few volunteers, righted the gun, and soon had it sending shells back at the enemy. For four hours Calugas crewed the weapon, then the Japanese pulled back.

The general order announcing Calugas's Medal of Honor was read in front of his entire assembled battery on February 24, 1942. He would have to wait until the Philippines were recaptured to receive the actual medal, though. In the intervening three years he would survive the Bataan Death March, have his skull split wide open by a frenzied prison guard, and fight the Japanese as a guerilla. He remained in the U.S. Army, retiring in 1957 as a captain.

The heroic efforts of men such as Calugas were not enough. Groggy from constant fighting, disease, and hunger, the Allied infantrymen could no longer resist the Japanese. A number of Filipino regiments had been so debilitated by casualties they ceased to exist as fighting units. After hearing the facts, MacArthur authorized a pullback on January 22 to the secondary defense line, the cobblestone road bisecting the peninsula.

On the west side of Bataan, Wainwright's corps, weak, hungry, and riddled with casualties, prepared for the anticipated renewed Japanese attack. They had a two-day respite as Nara rested his troops and absorbed replacements. He began his attacks anew on January 25.

Against Wainwright's line Nara threw his strongest troops. The Allies held them back at all points but one. Near the center of the line one thousand Japanese broke through the thinly spaced Filipino defenders. They advanced south for nearly a mile, completely undetected by the Allies. At a junction of two important trails, deep in the nearly impenetrable jungle, the Japanese commander skillfully emplaced his men. Not until three days passed did Wainwright realize the extent of his threat to his rear. He sent a battalion of the 45th Infantry (PS) to deal with the well-entrenched foe. When they took heavy casualties over several days he ordered in Company A, 192d Tank Battalion, to help reduce the pocket.

As four tanks of the company rumbled up the jungle trail, 1st Lt. Willibald C. Bianchi, Company D, 45th Infantry (PS), volunteered to accompany them. The twenty-six-year-old from New Ulm, Minnesota, fell in behind the lead tank. When heavy rifle and machine-gun fire erupted from a well-concealed enemy strongpoint, Bianchi quickly returned fire with his rifle. Two enemy rifle bullets smashed into his left hand, shattering it and his rifle. He pulled his pistol from its holster and went after the machine gun alone. He destroyed it with two well-placed grenades.

When a second enemy machine gun opened fire on the lead tank a few minutes later, Bianchi boldly mounted the vehicle's rear deck. There he grabbed the tank's .30-caliber machine gun. Before he could fire, the enemy machine gun barked. Two bullets buried themselves in Bianchi's chest. But he didn't stop. He fought on until a direct hit on the tank by a Japanese artillery round knocked him from his exposed perch. His actions so inspired the nearby soldiers they rallied to overwhelm the enemy.

Bianchi spent a month in the hospital, then rejoined his company as a newly promoted captain and a proud recipient of the Medal of Honor. Taken captive after the surrender of Bataan, Bianchi survived the infamous Death March and two years as a prisoner of war only to die when American planes sank the Japanese freighter taking him and thousands of other Allied POWs to Japan in December 1944.

Though the defenders of Bataan fought bravely, they were doomed. Unknown to all but a handful of senior American officers, American and British military planners had adopted a joint war plan in February 1941. Known as *ABC-1*, it affirmed that in the event of war with both Germany and Japan, the U.S. and Great Britain would concentrate the majority of their efforts on defeating Germany. The European theater would have priority on money, men, and material. Officially, the garrison of Americans and Filipinos had been condemned to death or imprisonment.

As early as December 14, 1941, Gen. George C. Marshall, chief of staff of the U.S. Army, had decided the beleaguered garrison, in spite of *ABC-1*, had to be encouraged to resist as long as possible. That would buy time to send available resources to Australia and begin the drive to defeat Japan. Also he determined it must not appear to anyone that the Philippines were being abandoned.

On New Year's Eve 1941, President Roosevelt sent a stirring message around the world, pledging "the entire resources of the United States" to the defenders of the Philippines. This was exactly what they needed to hear. It motivated them to fight harder and longer. But the information was wrong.

The deception was continued when MacArthur had all commanders read a cheerful message of his own to the troops on

January 15. "Help is on the way from the United States," he assured them. "Thousands of troops and hundreds of planes are being dispatched. . . . It is imperative that our troops hold until these reinforcements arrive."

Many of the Americans jeered at MacArthur's words; they were beginning to suspect the truth. But to the Filipinos the speech was a bright ray of hope and inspiration. They intensified their effort, fighting the Japanese to a stalemate all along the line. Through the rest of February and into March the two armies sat behind their respective battle lines, patrolling in the no-man's-land between them much like the combatants of World War I. Morale took a great leap forward. Some of the men even began believing they might hold out until help did arrive. Then, MacArthur left the islands.

DOUGLAS MACARTHUR

Few men in history have been more destined to command other men in war than Gen. Douglas MacArthur. His father, Arthur MacArthur, earned the Medal of Honor in the Civil War, then remained in the army to rise to the rank of major general and become military governor of the Philippines. Douglas was born at the old cavalry post of Fort Dodge, Little Rock, Arkansas, on January 26, 1880. The romance of frontier military life was a part of him from the moment of his birth. He would later say his "first recollection is that of a bugle call." Life among the rugged cavalrymen of the Old West was as idyllic as imaginable for a youngster who dreamed of a military career.

Though he worshipped his father and strove throughout his life to please him, the greatest influence on MacArthur was his mother, Mary Pinkney Hardy, the daughter of an aristocratic Virginia family. She so doted on young Douglas that she dressed him in skirts and kept his hair in long curls until he was eight. When he left for West Point in 1899 she accompanied him on the journey, then moved into a nearby hotel suite that gave her a view of his barracks room. She stayed there for his entire four years at West Point.

At West Point MacArthur established a remarkable record. Not only did he finish first in his class, he did it by setting an academic record exceeded by only two others in West Point history. As an athlete he displayed a passion for baseball that surpassed his ability, yet he still earned his varsity letter in his junior year, an accomplishment he would boast of long after he wore the five stars of a general of the army.

Upon graduation in 1903 MacArthur was sent to the Philippines. There he had his first taste of combat, killing two insurgent ambushers. His next combat experience came in Mexico in 1914 when, as a captain, he made a solo reconnaissance of the Mexican railroad in order to judge its usefulness in case war broke out between the two countries. War did not develop, but MacArthur's exploits behind the Mexican lines did earn him his first recommendation for the Medal of Honor. It was turned down by an awards board, which led MacArthur to believe certain factions of the army hierarchy were jealous and out to get him.

At the start of World War I MacArthur joined the 42d "Rainbow" Infantry Division as a full colonel and its chief of staff. By the time the war ended he was a brigadier general commanding the division. Along the way he led the 84th Infantry Brigade through some of the bloodiest fighting of the war. He earned twelve U.S. decorations, including the Distinguished Service Cross twice, the Distinguished Service Medal, seven Silver Stars, and two Purple Hearts. Allied nations awarded him seventeen decorations. Recommended once again for the Medal of Honor, he blamed "certain members of Pershing's staff" when it was turned down. Regardless, Secretary of War Newton Baker called MacArthur the "greatest fighting front-line officer" of the American Expeditionary Forces. It was obvious to all who knew him that MacArthur was going places in the postwar army.

The first place MacArthur went was to West Point as its superintendent. After helping to bring that institution into the twentieth century, he returned to the Philippines in 1922. Three years later he received his second star and returned to the States. In 1930 he was elevated over several more senior general officers to receive the four stars of the army's chief of staff.

Controversy followed MacArthur throughout his career, but rarely more so than during his tenure as chief of staff. Much of his time was spent fighting for funds for his small army; it was the sixteenth largest in the world, trailing both Portugal and Greece. His battles with the budget-conscious depression-era Congress earned him few friends.

Perhaps his greatest scandal involved sending soldiers charging into the destitute World War I veterans encamped in Washington in an effort to persuade Congress to grant them a bonus. On July 28, 1932, MacArthur personally led army troops in evicting the veterans from their encampment on the Anacostia River. He was convinced the Bonus Expeditionary Force's ranks were filled with communists and criminals, not legitimate veterans. Even though President Herbert Hoover ordered MacArthur not to invade the camp, he did so anyway. Under his leadership the soldiers drove the veterans off with tear gas, then torched their shanties. Two babies died in the melee and a seven-year-old boy was bayonetted in the leg. It was not MacArthur's finest hour.

MacArthur left the service in 1937. As a civilian, he served as military advisor to the newly formed Commonwealth of the Philippines. He still held that position when recalled to active duty in July 1941.

As the situation in the Philippines continued to deteriorate in early 1942, President Roosevelt, on February 23, personally ordered MacArthur to evacuate Corregidor Island. Much pressure had been brought to bear on him to save MacArthur. Influential members of Congress, Secretary of State Cordell Hull, Secretary of War Henry L. Stimson, and General Marshall all felt MacArthur had to be saved. If he were killed or captured, it would be a tremendous blow to American morale. It would also provide Japan with incredible propaganda ammunition. Further, no better American general existed to lead the drive to recapture the Philippines.

Though initially he refused, MacArthur finally radioed President Roosevelt his agreement to abide by the order. He, his wife, their young son, and seventeen staff officers departed Corregidor on the night of March 12. Four worn PT boats commanded by navy Lt. John D. Bulkeley (who had already earned a Medal of Honor for his fearlessness in attacking Japanese warships during the previous three months) carried the party south. They arrived on Mindanao on March 14. Two days later B-17 bombers ferried them to Darwin, Australia. Once they landed safely there MacArthur held a brief press conference. He said, ''The president of the United States ordered me to break through the Japanese lines . . . for the purpose, I understand it, of organizing the American offensive against Japan, a primary object of which is the relief of the Philippines. I came through and I shall return.''

In Berlin, Germany, Nazi Propaganda Minister Josef Goebbels derided MacArthur as a ''fleeing general.'' Italian dictator Benito Mussolini called him a ''coward.'' In Tokyo, Japanese newspapers had a field day, referring to MacArthur as a ''deserter,'' who had ''fled his post.'' To counter this barrage of propaganda Marshall proposed that MacArthur be given the Medal of Honor. Though the medal was supposed to be reserved for extraordinary personal heroism above and beyond the call of duty, in actual combat with the enemy, Marshall rationalized that the award would give America a desperately needed morale boost.

Marshall forwarded a recommendation to Roosevelt, who approved it. The medal was presented to MacArthur on March 26, 1942, at a dinner given in his honor by the Australian prime minister.

When word of the award reached the troops still locked in battle on Bataan, many greeted it with derision. The words of the citation, ''His utter disregard of personal danger under heavy fire . . . ,'' implied MacArthur had been actively involved in the defense of the peninsula. In actuality, he had visited Bataan but once. On January 10 he spent less than eight hours on Bataan, never venturing closer than five miles to the front lines. He never again made the short boat ride from Corregidor to Bataan.

In fact, for a combat-tested soldier decorated numerous times for personal bravery, his absence from the front lines was perplexing. Once MacArthur ordered the retreat onto Bataan he spent nearly all his time deep in the bombproof Malinta Tunnel on Corregidor, tending to the administrative side of the war. As a result, the troops began referring to him as ''Dugout Doug.''

For the rest of his life MacArthur would remain a controversial and enigmatic character. Throughout his brilliant successes in the western Pacific, his governing of occupied Japan, his defense of Korea, and his relief by President Truman, MacArthur would generate loyalists and detractors. Few would ever really know him. Fewer still would lack an opinion. And only a handful of men have ever had so much influence on a nation. He died on April 5, 1964.

* * *

On the night of March 9, 1942, before he left Corregidor, MacArthur sent word through his chief of staff for his I Corps commander, Maj. Gen. Jonathan M. Wainwright, to report to him at Malinta Tunnel the very next morning. MacArthur had selected his successor.

JONATHAN M. WAINWRIGHT

Like Douglas MacArthur, Jonathan M. Wainwright had deep roots in America's army. His father, too, was a senior military man, a graduate of West Point who served many years as a cavalryman at frontier posts in the west. The senior Wainwright later served on the staff of Maj. Gen. Arthur MacArthur in the Philippines.

Jonathan Wainwright arrived at West Point in June 1902. Like MacArthur three years before him, Wainwright graduated in 1906 with the highest honor possible: first captain of cadets. Unlike MacArthur, he excelled not only militarily, but socially as well. He was a popular figure, well liked and respected by his fellow cadets and teachers. Blessed with a thin, gangly six-foot frame, Wainwright earned the moniker "Skinny" at West Point. He liked it, and it stuck with him throughout his life.

Newly commissioned 2d Lt. Wainwright followed his father into the cavalry. He served at a succession of isolated western posts before being sent to the Philippines in 1909. Like MacArthur, Wainwright first experienced combat against the Moro rebels in the islands. He, too, received his superiors' praise for his coolness under fire.

During World War I Wainwright served in France as a staff officer with the 76th and 82d Infantry Divisions. Although his actual combat experience was limited, he made it a practice to visit the front lines every chance he had. He ended the war as a lieutenant colonel with the Distinguished Service Medal pinned to his tunic.

Following the war Wainwright held a number of routine assignments, including a tour in the Plans Division of the War Department. While there he took a major role in formulating War Plan *Orange*, which he would help execute twenty years later.

In 1934 Wainwright was promoted to colonel. Three years later he made brigadier general, taking command of the ceremonial 3d Cavalry at Fort Myer, Virginia. From there he normally would have been put out to pasture except for the impending world war. Gen. Marshall wanted to defer from active command all general officers over age fifty. However, he made a few exceptions. One was for George S. Patton. Another was for Jonathan Wainwright. Wainwright was too old for a stateside command, Marshall reasoned, but he did have need of a seasoned brigadier general in the Philippines. In October 1940, Skinny Wainwright arrived in Manila to take command of the Philippine Division.

One year later MacArthur appointed Wainwright commander of the North Luzon force, the most important of the island commands. When the Japanese invasion came, Wainwright had the onerous task of holding them back. When MacArthur ordered the retreat into Bataan, Wainwright's extraordinary leadership talents made it possible. In command of the I Corps on Bataan Wainwright again proved his mettle by doing all he could to stem the Japanese attack.

Wainwright was a true front-line general. He believed in sharing the dangers faced by his men. During his time on Bataan he was repeatedly taken under fire by enemy troops. On one occasion he grabbed a rifle and blazed away at five Japanese soldiers intent on infiltrating American lines. On another, he personally led a ragtag collection of headquarters personnel on an assault against a Japanese roadblock. More than once men on either side of him were killed or wounded in action.

Wainwright's constant visits to the front line, his concern for the welfare of his troops, and his leadership style—personal, intense, informal—earned him a considerable measure of respect from his men. One of his officers later said, "We just loved the guy."

Soon after Wainwright moved over to Corregidor the Japanese launched a major offensive on Bataan. Fifty thousand fresh Japanese troops stepped off on April 3, 1942. Though the remaining Americans and Filipinos fought as valiantly as they could with the limited supplies at their disposal, it was all in vain. On April 9, against Wainwright's express orders, Bataan's commander, Maj. Gen. Edward P. King, surrendered his forces to General Homma.

When Wainwright learned of the move he visibly slumped at his desk. He wired the sad news to MacArthur and Marshall. On Bataan the brutal Death March began. About seventy thousand men began the trek from Bataan to Camp O'Donnell, ninety miles away. Only fifty-four thousand completed the trip. Nearly ten thousand men died at the hands of the merciless Japanese on the Death March. Another six thousand managed to escape along the route.

Corregidor held out for another month. Subjected to savage daily artillery bombardments, it is amazing the troops resisted as long as they did. When the Japanese landed on Corregidor on May 5, Wainwright knew it was over. The next day he reluctantly sent a message to President Roosevelt: "It is with broken heart and head bowed in sadness but not in shame, that I report to Your Excellency that I must go today to arrange terms for the surrender of the fortified islands of Manila Bay."

Three and a half years as a prisoner of the Japanese lay ahead for Wainwright. He would be beaten, starved, and humiliated. He was so convinced he'd eventually be court-martialed for his decision to surrender, he remained severely depressed for much of his captivity.

MacArthur was, of course, furious over Wainwright's actions. At first he refused to accept the surrender, but later was forced to acknowledge it. His fury remained so high, though, that when General Marshall proposed a Medal of Honor for Wainwright on July 30, 1942, MacArthur vehemently opposed it.

After reviewing the recommendation, MacArthur wired Marshall:

> The citation proposed does not repeat does not represent the truth. I am recommending General Wainwright and a number of other officers for the DSM and Legion of Merit but I do not repeat not recommend him for the Medal of Honor. In order to avoid the inclusion of my adverse observations and opinion and certain facts into his record which would now serve no useful purpose I am not including in this message an enumeration of these circumstances which could properly preclude such an award but will do so if it is your desire. It was my complete knowledge of this officer's past in the Philippine campaign that impelled me to prepare upon my departure a command set-up which would have limited his responsibilities.
>
> As a relative matter award of the Medal of Honor to General Wainwright would be a grave injustice to a number of other

general officers of practically equally responsible positions who not only distinguished themselves by fully as great personal gallantry thereby earning the DSC but exhibited powers of leadership and inspiration to a degree greatly superior to that of General Wainwright thereby contributing much more to the stability of the command and to the successful conduct of the campaign. It would be a grave mistake which later on might well lead to embarrassing repercussions to make this award.

Rarely had such a damning letter been written by one senior officer against another. Not only was MacArthur implying that Wainwright was solely responsible for the loss of his beloved Philippines, he was clearly suggesting that reports of Wainwright's personal bravery were exaggerated. Further, his veiled reference to "certain facts" was inexcusable. Those who read the message felt MacArthur was referring to Wainwright's well-known preference for alcohol. But alcohol had not interfered with Wainwright's ability to lead the gallant defense of the Philippines.

MacArthur had repeatedly demonstrated confidence in Wainwright throughout the hard campaign. After all, he had selected Wainwright to take the most important command in Luzon at the start of the war. Later he depended on Wainwright's leadership to hold the Japanese at bay while the troops withdrew into Bataan. And he had personally chosen Wainwright to follow him as commander on Corregidor. Now many felt MacArthur was simply reluctant to share the spotlight with Wainwright. After all, MacArthur was the hero of Bataan. Skinny had given it up.

Whatever MacArthur's motive, Marshall shelved the recommendation.

Wainwright was repatriated from a Japanese POW camp in Manchuria on August 19, 1945. The emaciated general arrived in Yokohama, Japan, on August 31. There a now-jubilant MacArthur greeted him. The two men embraced for the news photographers. MacArthur's animosity toward Wainwright was apparently in the past. Two days later Wainwright stood aboard the U.S.S. *Missouri* in Tokyo Bay to witness the formal surrender ceremony of the Japanese.

Much to Wainwright's surprise his return to the United States a few days later resulted in joyous celebrations wherever he went.

When he arrived in Washington, D.C., on September 10, General Marshall met him at the airport. After a tearful reunion with his wife, Wainright visited the Capitol where the Senate and the House gave him a standing ovation. From there Wainwright's procession headed down Pennsylvania Avenue to the White House.

In the Oval Office President Truman rose from his desk to greet Wainwright and his entourage. After chatting a few minutes the president suggested they step into the Rose Garden. About one hundred people and a large corps of reporters and photographers were waiting there. President Truman stepped to the microphone. He pulled a piece of paper from his pocket and began to read: "At the repeated risk of his life above and beyond the call of duty . . ."

At that moment Wainwright knew he was about to receive the highest accolade any soldier could aspire to. After he read the citation President Truman draped the blue ribbon of the Medal of Honor around General Wainwright's neck.

Just five days earlier General Marshall had revived his original Medal of Honor recommendation for Wainwright. After carefully reviewing the documents, Marshall concluded MacArthur's objections of three years earlier were without foundation. He approved the award. President Truman concurred.

In January 1946 General Wainwright assumed command of the Fourth Army in San Antonio, Texas. One and a half years later, on August 31, 1947, Skinny Wainwright retired from the army he loved so dearly and had served so well. He was the last of his West Point class to leave the army.

Wainwright served on several corporate boards of directors after his retirement. He availed himself of nearly every request to speak before veterans' groups. He never harbored any bitterness toward MacArthur for his actions in the Philippines. Indeed, when it appeared MacArthur might be nominated for president at the 1948 Republican National Convention, Wainwright stood ready to make the nominating speech. He was that kind of a man.

The last of America's fighting generals died on September 2, 1953, after lapsing into a coma following a stroke on August 13. Thousands attended the funeral services in San Antonio and at Arlington National Cemetery. MacArthur was not among them.

* * *

While the U.S. Army fought so desperately to stave off the inevitable Japanese victory in the Philippines, the remnants of the U.S. Navy's Asiatic Fleet also battled futilely for survival. Composed of a few auxiliary ships, thirteen old destroyers, two light cruisers, and the heavy cruiser *Houston*, the Asiatic Fleet held out against the Japanese in the Dutch East Indies as long as they could. In a series of sharp clashes the *Houston*-led task force even managed to briefly turn back the Japanese.

Houston's commanding officer, Capt. Albert Rooks, a fifty-year-old Naval Academy graduate from Seattle, Washington, consistently fought his ship with incredible skill and bravery against overwhelming odds. In a three-week period in February 1942, culminating in the Battle of the Java Sea, Rooks repeatedly fought off Japanese sea and air attacks. At the Battle of the Java Sea, Rooks was credited with seriously damaging two Japanese heavy cruisers. But the *Houston* sustained serious wounds herself.

While maneuvering through the Sunda Strait, at the west end of Java, on the night of February 28–March 1, bound for Australia and a repair yard, the *Houston* and the H.M.S. *Perth* were ambushed by a large Japanese fleet comprised of three light cruisers and twenty-three destroyers. The enemy cruisers pumped shell after high-explosive shell into the two Allied cripples. *Perth* went down first. The Japanese destroyers then closed in, their smaller guns raking the *Houston* from stem to stern. The badly battered cruiser desperately fought back, scoring numerous hits on her foes.

With the *Houston*'s steam lines cut by torpedoes and her deck a mass of wreckage, Rooks gave the order to abandon ship. Enemy gunfire killed him shortly afterwards. Soon after that the *Houston* went down. Of her complement of 1,011 men, 651 died in this battle. Seventy-six of the survivors would later die as POWs of the Japanese.

Captain Rook's posthumous Medal of Honor was presented to his son by President Roosevelt on June 24, 1942. A few weeks earlier, on Memorial Day, in a patriotic gesture designed to show that the *Houston* and her crew had not been lost in vain, one thousand young men were sworn into the navy in an impressive candlelight ceremony on a downtown Houston street.

Elsewhere on the Java Sea that brutal night another American ship was sent to the bottom. An old four-stack destroyer, the U.S.S. *Pope*, was escorting the battle-damaged H.M.S. *Exeter* to Australia for repairs. They were intercepted by a Japanese flotilla far from their goal and sunk.

RICHARD N. ANTRIM

The executive officer of the *Pope*, Lt. Richard N. Antrim, was the senior officer among the 150 survivors who floated on the blue water the next morning. Antrim assumed command of the group, organizing the men and carefully distributing the meager rations. Under his direction all the men survived until a Japanese destroyer pulled them from the sea a week later.

They were taken to a POW camp at Makassar on the island of Celebes. Like all prisoners of the Japanese, the men at Makassar found themselves at the mercy of sadistically cruel prison guards. Because the Japanese military culture allowed no room for surrender they considered their Allied prisoners to be subhuman for having been captured. Beaten or tortured for the slightest infraction of the camp's many petty rules, the POWs lived in constant fear of the Japanese guards.

One day in April 1942, a naval officer broke one of the camp's rules when he failed to bow low enough to a guard. Infuriated at this supposed insult, the guard went into a frenzy. Grabbing his swagger stick he began beating the officer. Again and again the club swished through the air, tearing human flesh.

Antrim, watching the beating with the others, finally had enough. In the preceding weeks he had seen too much cruelty, too much death. Something had to be done to halt the carnage. "Stop!" he commanded, stepping forward.

Later, he wasn't sure who was more stunned at this bold move, the guard or the other prisoners.

By using Pidgin English and sign language Antrim convinced the guard to discuss the charges against the officer, now huddled nearly unconscious at their feet. Soon, the entire Japanese prison force assembled in the open yard of the compound. The twenty-seven hundred Allied POWs stood silently by, unable to believe the events unfolding before them.

Antrim argued the officer's case to the Japanese. The officer meant no insult, he told them. He explained that Americans were not used to bowing. They needed more time to learn Japanese customs.

The camp commandant was unmoved by Antrim's pleas. With the prisoners waiting nervously in the tense atmosphere, he ordered the helpless officer punished with fifty lashes.

Fifteen vicious blows with a length of heavy hawser rained down on the man, driving him into unconsciousness. Three of the enlisted guards, intoxicated by the bloody body, began kicking the unconscious form along the ground.

Antrim was unable to control his fury and disgust. He stepped forward. In a bold, clear voice, he said, "I'll take the rest."

A stunned silence fell over the entire prison camp. The Japanese were amazed at Antrim's maneuver. He repeated his offer. "I'll take the rest of the lashes."

At that moment a robust, spontaneous roar erupted from the assembled prisoners. Antrim's actions were the bravest they had ever witnessed.

The Japanese didn't know what to do. After conferring among themselves the commandant indicated the unconscious officer could be carried to the dispensary. He then bowed slightly to Antrim, saluting his willingness to sacrifice his own life for another. The POWs again roared their approval. Antrim's actions did not completely end the Japanese cruelty at the prison camp, but they did earn the POWs a respite from the senseless beatings, as well as bringing them new respect from their guards.

A native of Peru, Indiana, Antrim entered the U.S. Naval Academy in 1927, graduating in 1931. His commissioning as an ensign was followed by a series of routine shipboard assignments over the next nine years. In 1940 Antrim had the unusual distinction of qualifying as a dirigible pilot. He then joined the *Pope* as her executive officer.

Once the POWs were liberated in September 1945, Antrim's gallant conduct quickly became known. The Medal of Honor was presented to him on January 30, 1947. He already wore the Navy Cross earned by his heroism at the time the *Pope* was sunk.

Antrim remained on active duty until ill health caused by his years as a prisoner forced his early retirement in April 1954 as a rear admiral. He died on March 8, 1969.

Not all of the U.S. Navy's activities in the early months of 1942 were defensive in nature. The Pacific Fleet's new commander, Adm. Chester W. Nimitz, knew it was important to bring a new vitality and optimism to a badly dejected navy. To bolster his command's spirit he organized several offensive, carrier-oriented task forces to carry the war to the Japanese. One, under Adm. William F. Halsey, took the carriers *Enterprise* and *Yorktown* on a raid to the Marshall Islands, two thousand miles southwest of Hawaii.

Another task force, centered on the carrier *Lexington*, under the command of Vice Adm. Wilson Brown, was designated to penetrate more deeply into Japanese-controlled waters than any other Allied surface vessels up to that time. The Japanese were making the port of Rabaul, on the northeast coast of the island of New Britain, which sat off the east coast of New Guinea, into a major base for their offensive operations in New Guinea and the adjacent Solomon Islands. Admiral Brown proposed to launch a surprise air raid on Rabaul, thus relieving pressure on the Allied supply base of Port Moresby, on New Guinea's south coast.

On the morning of February 20, 1942, the *Lady Lex* plowed her way through smooth seas some four hundred miles east and north of Rabaul. At about 9:30 the ship's nerve-racking klaxon sounded its strange wail. A Japanese flying boat had been spotted shadowing the task force. *Lexington's* commander, Capt. Frederick C. Sherman, ordered four F-4F Wildcats up to intercept and destroy the intruder. They did. But the Japanese plane had fulfilled her mission of spotting and reporting to its headquarters the position of the American task force.

Later that afternoon nine Mitsubishi twin-engine Betty bombers came looking for the *Lexington*. A squadron of Wildcats tore into the precise formation. Meeting the enemy bombers head-on, the Wildcats shot down eight and drove the ninth away.

Much to their horror the *Lexington's* radar operators now detected a second formation of nine Betty's approaching on an attack course from another direction. Because of the previous air battle only two fighters were in a position to intercept this new threat.

EDWARD H. O'HARE

As the two Wildcats raced to gain altitude to intercept the Bettys, the guns on one jammed, leaving only one fighter to face the enemy: a lone Wildcat piloted by twenty-eight-year-old Edward H. "Butch" O'Hare. Though this was his first combat, O'Hare, a 1937 Naval Academy graduate, reacted like a seasoned pro. He zipped through the bomber formation, pivoted steeply on one wingtip, and attacked the formation of three three-plane vees from above and behind, focusing on the two trailing ships in the rearmost vee.

"I had fired at the starboard engine on each ship and kept shooting 'til they jumped out of their mounts," O'Hare later said. Both enemy planes yawed sharply to starboard before beginning dark, smoky trails to the sea below.

O'Hare then sideslipped his fighter to the other side of the formation. Though under continuous machine-gun fire from the crown turrets on the bombers, he resolutely bore in amidst the steady stream of tracers, zeroing in on a third bomber.

"I fired at the port engine of that plane," O'Hare said, "and saw it jump out." He pulled away while this third bomber skidded violently, then fell away. He then went back in and attacked a fourth bomber. The same thing happened: He poured a stream of bullets into the port engine, it left its mounts, and the bomber headed down. Seconds later he downed another bomber. He went after the next one, but he was out of ammo.

Incredibly, in just four brief, hectic minutes, Butch O'Hare had shot down five Japanese bombers to save his ship and become the navy's first ace of World War II. It was an outstanding feat of airmanship.

Soon after he flamed the fifth bomber a flight of Wildcats reached the melee. They quickly smoked two more bombers and sent the remaining two diving for cover in the nearby clouds.

On board the *Lexington* Admiral Brown, Captain Sherman, all the plane-handling crews, and many others had witnessed O'Hare's single-handed attack. They knew they owed their lives to his superb airmanship and cool courage.

In recognition of his valor, O'Hare, a St. Louis native, received his Medal of Honor from President Roosevelt on April 21, 1942. Because of his heroic conduct O'Hare was jumped two grades to lieutenant commander and given command of Fighting Squadron 6, flying the new F-6F Hellcats. Back on duty in the Pacific he added to his score in a battle near Wake Island, downing a Zero and two bombers.

On the night of November 26, 1943, while conducting the navy's first night-fighter operation near the Gilbert Islands, O'Hare was lost following a successful attack on a Japanese bomber formation. His Hellcat was last seen with its lights on, diving for the ocean. What happened that night has never been determined. No wreckage of his plane was ever found.

The memory of the navy's first World War II ace is preserved at the nation's busiest airport—O'Hare Field, Chicago, Illinois.

4
* * *

Pacific Turning Point

In the rough seas of the Pacific Ocean 650 miles east of Japan on April 18, 1942, a sixteen-vessel U.S. Navy convoy plowed headlong through the crashing waves. Operating under strict radio silence, the convoy was still 150 miles from its destination off the coast of Japan. Once there, sixteen U.S. Army Air Corps B-25 bombers would take off from the deck of the navy's newest aircraft carrier, the *Hornet*, on a retaliatory air raid against the Japanese empire's capital, Tokyo.

The idea for a raid on Tokyo originated with President Roosevelt. Two weeks after Pearl Harbor he told General Marshall he wanted to hit back at Japan at the earliest possible moment. A strike would not only bolster the morale of America and her allies, but would prove Japan was vulnerable. Marshall passed the president's idea to the air corps's chief of staff, Gen. Henry H. ("Hap") Arnold.

Arnold's staff, working closely with the staff of Adm. Ernest J. King, chief of naval operations, developed a plan within several weeks. According to their figures the B-25 bomber was the only plane in the army's inventory that would work. It couldn't land on the carrier, but it could take off, complete with extra gas tanks and a two-thousand-pound bomb load.

Next, Arnold needed to select someone to oversee the needed modification of the bombers, train the crews, and select the targets. Arnold would have to choose a man who was used to doing the impossible with airplanes. Not only should this man be an experienced pilot, but he would also have to have an aeronautical engineer's understanding of airplanes. And he had to be able to inspire others by example.

41

Fortunately, just the man worked right down the hall from General Arnold at the Pentagon. Arnold later described his candidate: "He was fearless, technically brilliant, a leader who not only could be counted upon to do a task himself if it were humanly possible, but could impart that spirit to others." General Arnold summoned the man to his office to discuss the problem.

JAMES H. DOOLITTLE

If ever there was a man and a mission made for one another it was Jimmy Doolittle and the Tokyo bombing raid. America's premier aviator, he had almost single-handedly pioneered aviation from a daredevil county fair attraction to a major national transportation mode. He held more flying records than any man alive. Doolittle was the first person to fly across the continental United States in less than twenty-four hours; he was the first to fly an outside loop; he set the then world record for speed; he held dozens of racing trophies; and, perhaps most importantly for the advancement of aviation, he was the first person to take off, fly a prescribed course, and land completely on instruments, without any reference to the outside horizon.

Born on December 14, 1896, in Alameda, California, Doolittle's formative years were spent in Alaska during the rough and tumble days of the Gold Rush. Following her wanderlust-stricken husband, Frank, to Nome in 1900, Rosa Doolittle and four-year-old Jimmy lived a primitive existence until the harsh conditions and limited educational facilities there forced the family to move to Los Angeles in 1908.

It was in high school that Doolittle's interest in aviation blossomed. He built his first glider from plans he found in an old *Popular Mechanics* magazine. It promptly crashed. But that didn't discourage Doolittle. He next built a motorized glider, which winds wrecked before he could test it. In 1917, during his junior year at the University of California, Doolittle enlisted in the aviation section of the Signal Corps so he could learn to fly properly.

Much to his chagrin, Doolittle's skill as a pilot kept him out of World War I; he served stateside as an instructor. He remained in the service until 1930 when he resigned his commission to accept a position with Shell Oil Company as the head of their new aviation department. He came very well qualified. In addition to his numerous aviation records, Doolittle had earned his master's degree in aeronautical engineering from the Massachusetts Institute of Technology in 1924, then completed his doctorate degree there in the same discipline the next year.

Doolittle voluntarily returned to active duty in July 1940. He helped Detroit's automotive industry convert to wartime production, then joined Arnold's staff in January 1942.

Twenty-four hours after General Arnold summoned Lieutenant Colonel Doolittle to his office to discuss the Tokyo raid, the bantamweight aviator was back to announce that the mission was risky but feasible. Arnold assigned Doolittle to head the project.

Doolittle tackled the assignment with all the enthusiasm he could muster. Volunteer bomber crews were recruited from the 89th Reconnaissance Squadron at Columbia Air Field, South Carolina. The next weeks passed in a frenzy of hectic activity. At an isolated air strip at Eglin Army Air Force Base, Florida, the bomber pilots, used to taking off on runways thousands of feet long, learned to do it in less than five hundred feet. It demanded the most exacting flying skills, but after the volunteer pilots witnessed Doolittle do it, they bore down and were soon able to coax the thirty-one-thousand-pound bombers into the air with room to spare.

After three weeks of intense training Doolittle briefed General Arnold on the group's progress. When he was done describing the various problems and how he had solved them Doolittle presented Arnold with a point that had been bothering him. "Hap," he started, using Arnold's nickname, "I know more about this mission than anyone else. I'd like your permission to lead the mission myself."

Arnold protested, "I need you here on my staff."

Doolittle persisted in his argument. "I never got overseas in the last war, Hap. I've just got to get into this one!"

Finally, Arnold said, "Okay. If it's okay with General Harmon, the chief of staff, it's okay with me."

"Thanks, Hap," said Doolittle.

With that he quit talking and left Arnold's office. Once in the hallway he ran down to Gen. Millard Harmon's office. He burst in and announced, "Hap says it's okay with him if I lead this mission if it's okay with you. Do I have your permission?"

As Doolittle had hoped, Harmon was caught off guard. "Sure,

Jim," Harmon said. "Whatever is all right with Hap is all right with me. Go ahead and go."

Harmon's desk intercom buzzed as Doolittle left the office. It was General Arnold. Standing outside the door Doolittle heard Harmon plead, "But Hap, I just gave him my permission since he said it was okay with you."

With that, Doolittle beat a hasty retreat, hoping General Arnold wouldn't be angered at his ploy and order him off the mission. He didn't.

The plan called for the B-25s to depart the *Hornet* beginning at 4:00 P.M. on April 18, from a point of five hundred miles off Japan. Arriving over Tokyo at nightfall, the planes would unload their bombs, head west across the China Sea, and land at Chu Chow Airfield in China. The bombers would be left with the Chinese, and the crews would be ferried home.

It was a sound plan and probably would have worked satisfactorily except that the task force was spotted by a Japanese picket boat at dawn on the 18th. Rather than risk having the entire task force attacked by Japanese planes, Halsey ordered the bombers launched immediately. Since they were 150 miles farther east than planned, they'd be bombing Tokyo in broad daylight and have little chance of reaching China, but Doolittle and the fifteen crews never hesitated. They raced to their waiting planes.

In the lead plane Doolittle started his engines and warmed them up. When he was ready he looked to the carrier's signal officer. The signal officer raised his checkered flag. Doolittle advanced the bomber's throttles, his brakes fighting the screaming horsepower. At the instant the carrier's deck started an upward movement on the back of a swell, the signal officer dropped the flag. Doolittle released his brakes.

Slowly at first, then faster, the bomber moved forward. Doolittle held the control wheel completely back, pulling the nose gear off the deck. As the plane passed the ship's superstructure, or "island," the two main wheels lifted off. Doolittle was airborne! It was 8:20 A.M.

The watching bomber crews and the ship's crew breathed a collective sigh of relief. Doolittle circled the carrier once, then set course for Tokyo, flying just two hundred feet above the water. Behind him the remaining B-25s departed the *Hornet* without incident.

The five-hour flight to Japan went according to schedule, except that stronger-than-expected head winds cut the B-25's range. Doolittle crossed the Japanese coast eighty miles north of Tokyo. He had a brief encounter with five Zeroes, but lost them by flying at treetop level. Then the metropolitan area of Tokyo popped into view. Still flying just above the ground Doolittle climbed to fifteen hundred feet. Soon their target, a munitions factory, loomed in their windshield. "Open bomb bay doors," Doolittle commanded.

The bombardier tracked the target in the bomb sight. When it was lined up, he barked, "Bombs away!" The plane jumped upward as the four five hundred-pound incendiaries fell earthward. Doolittle pushed the bomber's nose down, again seeking safety near the ground. Behind them they could hear the muffled KARUMPFs of their exploding bombs. It was 1:30 P.M.

Over the next three hours, while Doolittle's bomber raced across Japan, the fifteen remaining B-25s appeared over Tokyo. All but one hit their targets. All then headed west for China.

Doolittle's B-25 attracted occasional bursts of antiaircraft fire as it flew west, but none did any damage. Once over the open sea the plane's navigator estimated the strong head winds would cause them to run out of gas 135 miles from China. The crew calmly prepared for the expected ditching. Halfway across the China Sea they ran into foul weather. Thick clouds blotted out the horizon. Heavy rain sloshed the windshield. Fortunately for them, the storm provided a much-needed tail wind.

About 8:45 P.M. Doolittle's tail-gunner, S. Sgt. Paul J. Leonard, spotted land through a brief break in the clouds. "There she is," he yelled into his intercom. Doolittle climbed to eight thousand feet, hoping to break through the soupy clouds. He didn't, but could occasionally see dim lights on the ground. Unsure of his location, he tried to radio Chu Chow, but had no luck. Finally, with only a few minutes' fuel left in his tanks, Doolittle announced to his crew they were going to have to abandon the plane.

One by one the crew members jumped through the escape hatch. Fearful of a rough landing, Doolittle was relieved when his parachute plopped him down in the middle of a soggy rice paddy.

Covered with thick, gooey mud and shivering from the damp cold, Doolittle spent the night in an abandoned building. The next morning a friendly farmer led Doolittle to the local National Chinese Army headquarters. After convincing the skeptical major in charge that he was an American pilot who had just bombed Japan, Doolittle received a warm welcome, a meal, and a much-appreciated hot bath. The next day he was reunited with his crew members; all were okay. Over the next two days occasional bits of news about the other crews reached Doolittle. As far as he could learn, all the bombers were lost.

For Doolittle, it was the absolute low point of his life. In his mind, the mission had failed. Not only had he lost sixteen B-25 bombers, he worried deeply about the fate of the other crews. He heard that at least one man was dead and several others had been captured by the Japanese. He told Sergeant Leonard he thought he'd end up in the military prison at Fort Leavenworth, Kansas, for his foolhardiness.

"No, sir," said Leonard. "They're going to make you a general."

Doolittle smiled weakly at the sergeant's attempts to lift his spirits.

The sergeant spoke again. "And, they're going to give you the Congressional Medal of Honor."

Doolittle didn't believe him, but the sergeant was more prescient than he realized. When Doolittle arrived in Chungking a few days later, a telegram from General Arnold awaited him. He had been promoted to brigadier general, skipping the rank of colonel.

During his stay in Chungking, definite information on the other crews reached Doolittle. Fifteen of the B-25s either crashed on landing in China or had been abandoned in the air. One, against specific orders, landed at Vladivostok, Russia, where the crew was immediately interred. Of the eighty men comprising the Doolittle raiders, three were dead and eight had been captured. Of those eight, three were later executed by the Japanese, and one starved to death in a Japanese prison.

From the raid itself, little physical damage to the targets was actually realized. Only ten of the bombers managed to hit their primary targets; five struck secondary targets. One plane jettisoned its bombs without hitting any target area.

The real damage to Japan was psychological. Up until the time Doolittle's raiders appeared in the blue skies over Tokyo, the Japanese people had been fed a steady diet of propaganda touting the invulnerability of the Japanese home islands. As word of the raid spread among the population, they began to question the honesty of their government. Some wondered if the government had lied about other things, too.

The Japanese military hierarchy reeled from the raid. Naval commander in chief Adm. Isoroku Yamamoto took the raid as a personal affront to his military judgment. Because Japanese naval intelligence believed the raiders had originated on Midway Island, at the western end of the Hawaiian Islands, they prepared a plan for its capture. Yamamoto quickly approved the plan. It was a fortuitous decision that sealed the fate of the Japanese.

For the American public, the raid provided a morale lift desperately needed after five months of bitter defeat. Coming just a week after the fall of Bataan, the raid promised that America was going on the offensive, that it would be able to avenge Pearl Harbor.

When Doolittle arrived back in Washington, General Arnold told him he was to receive the nation's highest honor. Doolittle didn't feel he deserved the Medal of Honor. "Hap, I lost sixteen planes and eleven men. I honestly don't believe I deserve the medal."

"You deserve it," General Arnold told him.

In the Oval Office on May 19, 1942, President Roosevelt pinned the Medal of Honor to General Doolittle's shirt. Doolittle's wife of twenty-four years, Jo, stood nearby with General Marshall, smiling proudly. Doolittle told the president, "I'll spend the rest of my life trying to earn this."

A few months later Doolittle assumed command of the Twelfth Air Force in North Africa. A year later he took over the Fifteenth Air Force in Italy, then became the commanding general of the famed Eighth Air Force in England in 1944. At the war's end Lieutenant General Doolittle was on Okinawa, still in command of the Eighth Air Force, waiting to once again bomb Tokyo.

Following his retirement as a four-star general after World War II, General Doolittle continued an active life. He served on a variety of presidential boards and commissions, as well as maintaining a vice-presidency with Shell Oil Company and holding directorships on nearly a dozen corporations.

When General Doolittle finally retired for good he settled in his native Alameda, California, still "the world's greatest aviator."

* * *

In early April 1942 U.S. naval intelligence, having broken the Japanese Navy's code, uncovered a Japanese plan to strengthen their hold on New Guinea by attacking the Allied base at Port Moresby. From there it would be an easy step to the Solomon Islands, which would give the Japanese control over the vital sea and air links between the United States and Australia.

Adm. Chester W. Nimitz dispatched the carrier *Lexington* to reinforce the carrier *Yorktown*, already operating in the Coral Sea northeast of Australia. Admiral Halsey's *Hornet* and *Enterprise* would sail for the Coral Sea once they were replenished after their journey to Japan.

On May 3, 1942, a Japanese task force, with two carriers, the *Shokaku* and *Zuikaku*, established a base on Tulagi Island in the Solomons. This task force then sailed into the Coral Sea to support the amphibious landing at Port Moresby. The Port Moresby attack force, protected by the carrier *Shoho*, left Rabaul on May 4. Both fleets operated on a tight schedule. They were needed to support the impending June 1 invasion of Midway Island. The American fleet commander, Rear Adm. Frank J. Fletcher, sent planes from the *Yorktown* against the new Japanese seaplane base at Tulagi on May 4. The pilots reported numerous Japanese ships sunk, but their claims were wildly exaggerated. Only three vessels were actually sunk, but the raid did force the Japanese to temporarily abandon the base.

Fletcher, now joined by the *Lexington*, next headed north to engage the Port Moresby invasion fleet on May 7. Unknown to Fletcher, who had earned a Medal of Honor at Vera Cruz, Mexico, in 1914, the carriers *Shokaku* and *Zuikaku* were futilely searching for him less than one hundred miles away.

The opposing forces launched their planes at dawn on May 7. The Americans flew north to turn back the *Shoho*; Japanese planes from the *Shokaku* and the *Zuikaku* went south to attack a reported U.S. carrier and cruiser. In actuality, the ships were the oil tanker *Neosho* and its escorting destroyer, *Sims*, which Fletcher had ordered to remain behind in a safe area while he sailed off to battle.

The *Sims* fought off the first wave of Japanese planes, but then three waves of dive-bombers attacked her simultaneously. Ripped in half by exploding bombs, she sank in less than sixty seconds. The *Neosho* took seven bomb hits. With flames belching forth huge clouds of thick, dark smoke the Japanese pilots gave her up for dead.

Chaos reigned aboard the *Neosho*. Fire fighters battled the hot, searing flames, finally bringing the fires under control. Below decks, damage control parties worked desperately to save their ship. Forty-two-year-old Chief Watertender Oscar V. Peterson, though badly burned, led one such party. Under his expert guidance, garnered during nearly twenty-five yeas of naval service, his repair party extinguished the flames threatening the boiler rooms. Then, though he knew the risk was high, Peterson volunteered to close the bulkhead stop valves, which would reduce pressure in the boilers and prevent a fatal internal explosion. He did so, but sustained additional severe burns which resulted in his death.

The *Neosho*, partly as a result of Peterson's self-sacrifice, stayed afloat for four days until she was found by a rescue destroyer. The crew of the *Sims* spent ten days afloat in the Coral Sea before being rescued, an ordeal only sixty-eight men survived.

Far to the north Fletcher's aircraft spotted the Port Moresby invasion fleet just before noon. Torpedo bombers from the *Lexington* and dive-bombers from the *Yorktown* swooped down on the *Shoho*. The Japanese carrier and her escorts responded with a wall of antiaircraft fire, but the Americans were too numerous. They badly damaged the *Shoho*. A second wave of American planes sent her to the bottom. The pilots excitedly radioed back to Fletcher, ''Scratch one flattop!''

The decisive battle came in the Coral Sea on May 8. One hundred twenty-six American planes attacked the *Shokaku* and *Zuikaku*. The two carriers, heavily protected by cruisers and destroyers, proved to be much tougher foes than the *Shoho*. Only a few hits were scored on the *Shokaku*; the *Zuikaku* escaped unscathed. It was a costly battle for the Americans: the Japanese shot down forty-three planes.

At nearly the same time the Americans were attacking the Japanese carrier, Japanese planes struck the *Lexington* and *Yorktown*. They suffered far more damage than the Japanese carriers. The *Lexington* received fatal injuries and went down that night. The *Yorktown* took her share of punishment, too. One bomb killed sixty-six men when it pierced four decks to explode beneath the hangar deck. A twenty-eight-year-old engineer officer from Baltimore, Maryland, in the compartment directly above the explosion, was mortally wounded by the blast. Immediately recognizing the severe threat to his ship, Lt. Milton E. Ricketts ignored his painful wounds to organize a damage control party from those around him still able to function. Under his inspiring guidance the enlisted men began beating back the deadly flames. Ricketts himself picked up a fire hose and directed a heavy stream of water at an intense fire before he collapsed and died at his post. HIs courageous efforts were directly responsible for containing the fires and materially contributed to saving the *Yorktown*.

By early afternoon of May 8 the fight was over. The opposing forces disappeared over the horizon, trailing columns of smoke from their damaged ships. When the final tally was posted the Japanese had clearly won a tactical victory. The Imperial Navy had lost 77 planes, 1,074 men, and the carrier *Shoho*. The U.S. Navy lost 66 aircraft, 543 men, a tanker, a destroyer, and one carrier, plus another carrier badly damaged. Yet it was a strategic victory for the U.S. Admiral Fletcher's forces had checked the Japanese plan to advance southward and dominate the Coral Sea and the approaches to Australia. With the Japanese invasion fleet scurrying for home, Port Moresby was safe.

Four months later, during a major radio speech to the nation on the progress of the war, President Roosevelt took the unprecedented step of announcing the award of the Medal of Honor to one of the pilots at the Battle of the Coral Sea. He told his audience, "I wish that all the American people could read all the citations for various medals recommended for our soldiers, sailors, and marines. I am picking out one of these citations which tells of the accomplishments of Lt. John J. Powers during the battle with Japanese forces in the Coral Sea." He then related the circumstances that brought Powers this high honor.

JOHN J. POWERS

During the May 4 raid on Tulagi, Lt. John J. Powers, a dive-bomber pilot, scored a direct hit on a Japanese gunboat, sinking that vessel. He also received credit for two close misses. This was remarkable airmanship for a pilot who had earned his wings less than two years earlier.

Powers was born in New York, New York, on July 13, 1912. The son of a Spanish-American War navy veteran, Powers entered the Naval Academy in 1930. Four years later, after establishing a name for himself as a feisty boxer, Powers graduated.

With the shiny gold bars of an ensign on his collar, he was posted to the cruiser *Augusta*, then the flagship of the Asiatic Fleet in Shanghai. Two years' duty aboard the battleship *West Virginia* preceded Powers's acceptance to naval flight school at Pensacola, Florida, in 1940. As a youth Powers had never shown much interest in flying. In fact, his family was somewhat surprised at his decision to enter flight training. He later told them that witnessing Japanese bombing attacks on Chinese cities convinced him air power would be the controlling factor in the impending global war.

After flight school Powers was accepted in dive-bombing school, then was posted to Bombing Squadron 5, aboard the *Yorktown*. For several months after Pearl Harbor the *Yorktown* sailed throughout the central and southern Pacific, harassing Japanese installations in the Marshall and Gilbert Islands, but causing no real damage. When the *Yorktown* received orders to head for the Coral Sea, it looked as though the opportunity Powers and his fellow pilots had been itching for for over four months had finally arrived.

Bombing Squadron 5 launched from the *Yorktown* just after dawn on May 7. When the *Shoho* was sighted torpedo planes from the *Lexington* tore into her. High above the sea the *Yorktown*'s dive-bombers circled impatiently. Finally it was their turn. Powers fearlessly lead his section of three Dauntless dive-bombers straight down. Heavy enemy antiaircraft fire peppered the sky around Powers's plane. Normally, the dive-bomber releases its missile several thousand feet above the target, giving the pilot sufficient altitude in which to recover from his steep, stomach-churning plummet.

This time, though, Powers carried his dive to below one thousand feet. Risking death and near certain damage to his plane, Powers was much more concerned with destroying the Japanese carrier. Down he went, planting his bomb right on the *Shoho*. The hit was witnessed by many American pilots, who were amazed not only at the low release point, but the amount of destruction caused by the accurate hit.

That night, back aboard the *Yorktown*, Powers, as squadron gunnery officer, lectured on point-of-aim and diving technique. He clearly advocated an abnormally low release point as the only way to ensure a hit. At the same time, based on his experience that afternoon, Powers stressed the inherent risks in his approach. Not only was the bomber exposed to enemy fire for a longer time and at a lower altitude, he said, but there was considerable danger of the plane being caught in its own bomb blast and damaged by its bombs' fragments.

At the prelaunch briefing early the next morning, Powers again stressed his low-bombing techniques. Then he emphasized the need for accuracy. "Remember," he said, "the folks back home are counting on us. I am going to get a hit if I have to lay it on their flight deck."

The barrage of antiaircraft fire thrown skyward by the *Shokaku* and *Zuikaku* was much more formidable than the Americans had anticipated. In addition, a tough screen of protective Japanese fighters challenged the American planes at every turn. But they didn't matter in the end. Powers was too intent on getting an enemy carrier.

From eighteen thousand feet he led his section down toward the *Shokaku*. Completely disregarding the normal safe altitude and without concern for his own survival, he plunged downward until the carrier filled his plane's entire windshield. As his section mates watched in awe, Powers dove nearly to the deck of the *Shokaku*. Only when he was assured of a hit did he release his bomb. It ripped through the wooden flight deck to explode deep inside the enemy carrier.

A great column of flame, smoke, and debris filled the air around the *Shokaku*. From the unbelievably low altitude of two hundred feet Powers struggled to regain control of his damaged Dauntless. As the other pilots watched helplessly, Powers's plane was engulfed by his bomb's explosion.

When President Roosevelt announced her son's Medal of Honor, Powers's mother responded to reporters with typical maternal pride. "With us it's not a matter of feeling proud all of a sudden," she said. "What he's done all his life has made us proud."

For his decisive blow against Midway Island, Admiral Yamamoto assembled an armada that dwarfed the Pearl Harbor invasion fleet: 8 carriers, 11 battleships, 20 cruisers, 60 destroyers, 15 submarines, 30 auxiliary ships, and 16 troop transports. His air arm consisted of more than seven hundred planes. Yamamoto was determined to finish off the U.S. Navy once and for all and emerge victorious in the Pacific.

Yamomoto's plan called for dispersing his great fleet in a wide arc across the Pacific. His northern force would attack and occupy two Alaskan islands, Attu and Kiska. This would not only give the Japanese a foothold in North America, but would draw off American reactionary forces as well.

Meanwhile, planes from the four carriers of the First Carrier Striking Force, under Vice Adm. Chuichi Nagumo, who had led the Pearl Harbor attack, would smash Midway's defenses. Once that was accomplished, five thousand Japanese troops steaming up from Saipan, in the Marianas chain, would land and consolidate the Japanese grip on the Hawaiian Islands. Finally, when the remnants of the U.S. Pacific Fleet set sail from Pearl Harbor to challenge the Midway invaders Yamomoto, lying in wait several hundred miles from Midway, would pounce and wipe them out.

It was an excellent plan, except it overlooked several important factors. First, the Japanese believed they had sunk both the *Lexington* and the *Yorktown* in the Coral Sea. In reality, the *Yorktown* had survived and was already undergoing a massive repair effort in Pearl Harbor. Second, Yamomoto thought the U.S.'s two other carriers, *Hornet* and *Enterprise*, were still in the area of the Solomon Islands. Actually, they had arrived in Pearl Harbor on May 26, were quickly replenished, and sent west. Third, and most importantly, the U.S. Navy's ability to read the Japanese's coded messages bared the master plan to the Americans. They had plenty of time to prepare their defenses and assemble their forces.

The opening gambit came early on June 4. As the first faint streaks of dawn lay on the horizon, 108 Japanese planes left the carrier *Akagi* bound for Midway. When Midway's radar picked them up ninety miles out, twenty-six old marine Brewster Buffalo fighters rose to meet them. At the same time, the twenty-seven dive-bombers of Scout-Bombing Squadron 241, under the command of Maj. Lofton R. Henderson, took off after the *Akagi*. For nearly all the dive-bomber pilots this would be their first taste of combat. For eleven of them it also would be their last.

RICHARD E. FLEMING

One of the untested pilots in Henderson's squadron was twenty-four-year-old Capt. Richard E. Fleming. Born in St. Paul, Minnesota, on November 2, 1917, Fleming had enlisted in the Marine Corps Reserve in 1939 and immediately applied for flight training. He earned his wings on November 13, 1940.

Fleming survived the Pearl Harbor attack, but was frustrated that he hadn't been able to get in the air that day to fight back at the attackers. When he and his squadron were sent to Midway ten days later, Fleming was afraid he'd been sent to the war's backwaters. The squadron spent the next six months patrolling the waters around Midway without making any contact. When word of the Japanese invasion fleet reached them they bristled with excitement at being able to at last tangle with their enemy.

Because the marine fighters stayed behind to fight the approaching Japanese planes, Fleming and the rest of the dive-bombers had to go after the Japanese carrier without fighter protection. Nevertheless, Henderson led his men in the attack. Through an intense barrage of antiaircraft fire the twenty-seven little planes started down toward the *Akagi*.

In the first few moments of the bombing run Fleming watched in horror as Henderson's plane disappeared in a ball of flame from a direct hit. Undaunted, Fleming pressed on. The shrapnel was so thick from the exploding airbursts, Fleming's gunner told his squadron mates that night that it sounded like "a bucket of bolts" being thrown into the propeller.

Fleming's bomb just missed the carrier's deck. Disappointed, he recovered from the steep dive and headed back to Midway. He and his gunner both were wounded by shrapnel, but not severely enough to be grounded. Fleming's ground crew counted 179 holes in his Vindicator.

The marine dive-bombers scored no major hits on the *Akagi*, but their sacrifices were not in vain. The appearance of these land-based bombers convinced Admiral Nagumo to launch a second strike against Midway. He ordered his waiting torpedo planes rearmed with high explosive bombs. That took about one hour. Before they could take off, Nagumo received word that the American carriers lay within striking distance. He ordered his planes rearmed with torpedoes. Another hour went by. As the planes finally lifted off the *Akagi*, the ship's lookouts screamed, "Dive-bombers!"

For the next several hours over 200 carrier-based American planes assaulted the Japanese carriers. In a vicious battle that cost over 150 planes, the brave U.S. pilots ripped gaping holes in the carriers *Akagi*, *Soryu*, and *Kaga*. The flames on the ships soon reached stored bombs, torpedoes, and fuel tanks. All three carriers were destroyed.

The fourth Japanese carrier, *Hiryu*, though, was still very much alive. She sent twenty-five bombers and fighters against the *Yorktown*. They severely wounded the mighty ship. The next day a Japanese submarine caught her with a torpedo as she was being towed back to Pearl Harbor. The *Yorktown* sank on June 6.

While the *Hiryu*'s planes swarmed over the *Yorktown*, dive-bombers from the *Enterprise* appeared above the *Hiryu*. No less than four bombs crashed through her deck, turning her into a mass of flames. Seven hours later the *Hiryu* slipped beneath the waves.

When it became obvious that Midway was not going to fall, Admiral Yamamoto ordered his occupation forces to return to Saipan. As the convoy turned back south, the U.S. submarine *Tambor* spotted it and was in turn spotted by the Japanese. Racing to attack the *Tambor* two Japanese cruisers, *Mogami* and *Mikuma*, collided. The *Tambor* radioed Midway to scramble bombers to finish off the two damaged cruisers.

The remnants of Fleming's squadron, twelve planes, rushed to the scene. Though he had slept only four hours the night before after attacking the *Akagi* and flying numerous patrols off Midway the rest of the day, Fleming led the second division of his squadron in the attack. He repeated his action of the day before, piloting his bomber into a screaming dive toward the *Mikuma*.

Suddenly, Fleming's plane rocked wildly from a direct hit from an antiaircraft round. Another pilot thought surely the plane would explode, but it soon righted itself and continued down under control. At the incredibly low altitude of 350 feet, Fleming released his bomb. Then he followed it straight down to the Japanese cruiser.

A terrific double explosion erupted from the stern of the *Mikuma*. The skipper of the *Mogami* witnessed Fleming's last seconds. "I saw a dive-bomber dive into the last turret and start fires," he said after the war. "He was very brave."

Fleming's heroic actions did not sink the *Mikuma*, but did cripple her so badly she was easy prey for the *Enterprise*'s dive-bombers the next day. They sank her in a mass of flames.

Captain Fleming was the only person to earn the Medal of Honor at the Battle of Midway. He stands as a proud symbol of all the gallant pilots who faced the formidable Japanese foe in that decisive encounter. His medal was awarded on November 24, 1942. Several years later the town fathers of St. Paul voted to name their airport in memory of the gallant aviator.

The Japanese Navy would never recover from the beating it took at Midway. Japan would never again go on the offensive, would know no more conquests; instead, she would only know the desperation of defense. Yamamoto's move into the waters of the Hawaiian Islands cost him dearly. Resting on the bottom of the Pacific were 4 Japanese aircraft carriers, 1 cruiser, 322 planes, and the bodies of more than 3,500 Japanese fighting men, including over one hundred irreplaceable first-rate pilots.

It was not a cheap victory. The Americans had lost 1 carrier, a destroyer, 150 planes, and 307 men. But the victory avenged the disaster of Pearl Harbor. And, more importantly, it set the stage for the Americans to go on the offensive.

5

★ ★ ★

Attack in the Solomon Islands

With Midway and the rest of the Hawaiian Islands finally secure, the Allied strategic focus shifted back to New Guinea and the Solomon Islands, where the enemy still posed a threat to Australia. The huge Japanese air and sea base at Rabaul, New Britain, constituted the nucleus of their expansion efforts in the southwest Pacific. After establishing bases at Lae and Salamaua on New Guinea's northeast shore in preparation for throwing the Allies out of New Guinea, the Japanese turned again to the Solomons. In June they reestablished their seaplane base on the island of Tulagi, then began construction of an airfield on a grassy plain at Lunga Point on the north coast of neighboring Guadalcanal Island.

Evidence of the new air base had a chilling effect on Admiral Nimitz's staff in Hawaii. An enemy air base on Guadalcanal would be more crucial than the one at Rabaul. From Guadalcanal Japanese bombers could reach Allied bases in the New Hebrides Islands, New Caledonia, the Fijis, and Samoa. If they conquered those bases the Japanese would own the South Pacific. Guadalcanal had to be captured before the airfield was completed.

The task of taking Guadalcanal fell to the 1st Marine Division, an untried unit, a division in name only. In June 1942 the division was scattered over half the Pacific Ocean. The 5th Marine Regiment was in New Zealand, the 1st Marines were en route from San Francisco, and the 7th Marines garrisoned Samoa. Further, a large percentage of the marines were inexperienced, just barely out of boot camp, having flocked to the recruiters in the weeks after Pearl Harbor. Most of the junior officers were products of officers candidate school, ninety-day wonders, not much older than the eighteen- and nineteen-year-old enlisted men they commanded. A large number of the senior officers and enlisted men were reservists who had attended one meeting a month and two weeks' annual summer camp. Here and there, sprinkled throughout the division, were veterans of the marine campaigns in the Caribbean and an occasional veteran of World War I.

The division commander, Maj. Gen. Alexander A. Vandegrift, thought he'd have six months to prepare his men to go on the offensive. He got six weeks. By working around the clock Vandegrift had his division ready on time.

Before the marines landed on Guadalcanal, little was known of the island or the rest of the Solomons. Guadalcanal was about one hundred miles long and varied from thirty-five to fifty miles in width. It was covered with thick jungle vegetation that thrived on the heavy rainfall normal in this southern latitude. The northern coast was relatively flat, but a short distance inland the hills and mountains began, culminating in the domineering fifteen-hundred-foot peak of Mount Austen.

Vandegrift planned to make five separate landings. The main body, the 1st and 5th Marines, would land on Guadalcanal's northern shore, move inland, and capture the airfield. The 1st Marine Raider Battalion and a battalion from the separate 2d Marines would hit Tulagi, twenty miles across the water to the north. Just behind Tulagi, the parachutists of the 1st Marine Parachute Battalion and another battalion of the 2d Marines would assault Gavutu and Tanambongo, two smaller islands, and larger Florida Island.

A garrison of about eight hundred Japanese marines held Tulagi, Gavutu, and Tanambongo. Another fourteen hundred construction laborers made the daily crossing to Guadalcanal from Tulagi to work on the airfield. Only a few hundred Japanese actually lived on Guadalcanal.

On the night of August 6, 1942, the nineteen transports carrying the marines and their escort of cruisers and destroyers under Adm. Frank J. Fletcher rounded Cape Esperance on Guadalcanal's northwest coast. Past Savo Island they steamed in the soggy night air to positions off Lunga Point and Tulagi. The opening bombardment was scheduled to begin at 6:00 A.M. August 7. Hundreds of marines crowded the transport's open decks, nervously awaiting their baptism of fire. Far to the north, B-17 bombers attacked Rabaul in a supporting mission designed to suppress Japanese response to this, the first Allied offensive landing in World War II.

Capt. Harl Pease, Jr., a native of Plymouth, New Hampshire, piloted one of the B-17s. Since being chased out of the Philippines with the rest of the 93d Bombardment Squadron, 19th Bombardment Group, in January, he had grown tired of running from the Japanese. Since arriving at Port Moresby in June Pease and his crew, a combination of Americans and Australians, volunteered for every possible mission. They didn't care if it was against the enemy at Lae, Rabaul, or in the Solomons, they went. They volunteered for the strike against Lae on August 6, part of a two pronged attack designed to draw Japanese fighter planes away from the Guadalcanal landings.

Much to his dismay, Pease's B-17 developed engine trouble right after takeoff. Because there were no facilities at Port Moresby to make the needed repairs to his defective engine, Pease opted to fly to Townsville, Queensland, where they'd be able to do the work. Bad news awaited him there, too. The plane couldn't be repaired. Because he'd missed the Lae strike, Pease became determined to make the run against Rabaul the next day.

Pease and his crew went to work to make another grounded B-17 flyable. Against all odds they made the necessary repairs, then flew back to Port Moresby, arriving there at 11:00 P.M. The crew slept for three hours, then attended the prestrike briefing. Then it was off to Rabaul.

Less than eleven miles from the target, Zeroes jumped the flight of bombers. Pease's B-17 took a brutal beating, but his gunners flamed three Zeroes in retaliation. Pease stayed in formation all the way through the bombing run, dropping his bombs on the target. The Zeroes chased the B-17s back toward Port Moresby. Mechanical problems with the worn B-17 forced Pease to break formation. He lagged farther and farther behind, Zeroes making passes at him one after another. Pease was seen to drop a flaming bomb bay fuel tank. Then the other B-17s lost sight of him.

For his indomitable courage in volunteering for this dangerous mission in a barely airworthy aircraft, and for his high devotion to duty, valor, and complete contempt for personal danger, Pease was awarded the Medal of Honor on December 2,

1942. The citation accompanying the award said, "It is believed that Capt. Pease's airplane and crew were subsequently shot down in flames, as they did not return to their base."

Harl Pease was dead when his Medal of Honor was awarded, but he hadn't died as a result of his plane being shot down. Pease bailed out of his crippled bomber with at least one other crew member. They were both captured. Taken to Rabaul, Pease languished in a POW camp until October 8, 1942. On that date Pease, three other Americans, and two Australians were taken into the jungle by their guards. They were forced to dig their own grave, then beheaded.

The Japanese bitterly contested the landings on Tulagi and the other outlying islands. Only two dozen of them survived the fighting. For the marines it was a brutal introduction to three long years of island warfare. The capture of the islands cost the marines over 300 casualties, including 145 dead.

On Guadalcanal, the Japanese fled into the jungle at the first sign of the landing craft, abandoning the airfield. The marines suffered no combat casualties during this landing. They quickly went to work consolidating their positions and landing supplies. It was a respite that would not last long.

On the second day ashore General Vandegrift received some bad news. The carriers supporting the landing were being withdrawn because Admiral Fletcher felt they were vulnerable to Japanese bombers from Rabaul. As a result, even though over one thousand marines and half the supplies remained aboard, the transports were pulling out, too. The marines would be isolated for several days. Only a small force of six American and Australian cruisers and six destroyers would remain behind to provide some protection.

It wasn't much. That very night a large Japanese naval force attacked them off Savo Island. In a vicious forty-minute engagement the Japanese sank two cruisers and severally damaged two more. The Battle of Savo Island cost over one thousand Allied dead—a greater loss than the total number of marines who would die on Guadalcanal—and over seven hundred wounded.

Though Fletcher's departure deprived the marines of most of their construction equipment, by using abandoned Japanese equipment they finished the airfield on August 19. They named it in honor of Maj. Lofton R. Henderson, killed at Midway. The first contingent of marine fighter planes, nineteen Wildcats, arrived the very next day. The soon-to-be famous "Cactus Air Force" was in business. And none too soon. The first of many Japanese attempts to retake Henderson Field was already under way.

The Japanese command at Rabaul greatly underestimated the marines' strength on Guadalcanal. Instead of the sixteen thousand men actually ashore, the Japanese thought no more than two thousand garrisoned the airfield. So, they sent a thousand soldiers of the Japanese 28th Infantry Regiment to attack Henderson Field. At 3:00 A.M. on August 21 they hit the eastern flank of the marines' perimeter. In a suicidal attack that lasted until dawn, over eight hundred of the Japanese were slaughtered by the rookie marines.

The next major effort by the enemy to reclaim Henderson Field came on the night of September 13–14, 1942. Six thousand additional Japanese troops had been brought to Guadalcanal via fast, nighttime destroyer runs. These runs were made down the Solomon's main channel that divided the islands to the north from those to the south. The channel was promptly dubbed "the Slot," the nighttime destroyer runs the "Tokyo Express."

Thirty-five hundred Japanese hit Henderson Field's south perimeter near midnight on September 13. They ran smack into the 1st Marine Raider Battalion dug in on the top of a grassy ridge. The raiders' commander, Lt. Col. Merritt A. Edson, a Navy Cross veteran of the marine's 1925 Nicaraguan intervention, spent most of the night at the front lines. Fighting more as a platoon leader than a battalion commander, Edson urged his men onward. When the Japanese rushed at them in human wave assaults chanting "Banzai! Banzai!" Edson directed the fire of his machine guns into their ranks, killing them by the score. When some marines broke and ran under the intense combat, Edson braved the carnage to chase them down and push them back into the fighting.

Forced to give ground under the heavy pressure, Edson called artillery in on his former position. The barrage caught the enemy in the open and helped slow their attack. Edson roamed back and forth across his battle line, oblivious to the threat of death all around him, encouraging, exhorting. His raiders held. When dawn came more than a thousand Japanese bodies littered the landscape in front of Bloody Ridge. The surviving Japanese fled into the jungle.

General Vandegrift sent battalion-sized patrols west from his perimeter to catch the fleeing Japanese and others reported to be in the area. When the marines became heavily engaged on the east bank of the Matanikau River, about ten miles west of Henderson Field, Vandegrift sent two companies to make an amphibious assault behind the Japanese. Unfortunately, instead of landing behind the Japanese they landed right in the middle of them. Before they had moved five hundred yards inland an intense barrage of mortar fire rained down. The expedition leader was killed. Japanese infantry moved in, forcing the marines back to the beach. They were in real danger of being annihilated. They had to be pulled back. A call went out for help.

DOUGLAS A. MUNRO

The call reached the destroyer *Ballard*, which was supporting the landing. Deadly fire from its five-inch guns held the Japanese back. The *Ballard* signalled the flotilla of landing craft which had put the marines ashore to move in and begin the evacuation.

The sailor in charge of the Higgins boats, more commonly known as Landing Craft, Vehicle, Personnel (LCVP), Signalman 1st Class Douglas A. Munro, U.S. Coast Guard, ordered his nine boats to stay put while he drove his own boat shoreward to reconnoiter the scene. Though Japanese machine-gun fire peppered his boat, Munro went into the beach area anyway to pull off thirty wounded marines. After he transferred them to another boat he led three boats back to the beach. While they loaded up wounded men, Munro deliberately placed his boat in a position to draw enemy fire away from the evacuation.

While the able-bodied marines fought off the advancing Japanese, the landing boats loaded the wounded. Increased machine-gun fire fell on the boats. The Japanese were determined not to let the marines escape. Dozens of marines were wounded making their way to the boats.

When the loaded boats began to pull away, Munro noticed one had grounded on the jagged coral. The crew worked vainly to free it. Munro instantly ordered his boat alongside. A line was tossed to the stranded vessel. Munro pulled it free and into deeper water. At that moment the Japanese set up a machine gun right on the beach. They took the boats under fire. Two of Munro's crew fell wounded.

Munro and one of his crewmen, signalman Raymond Evans, jumped to their boat's machine guns. They exchanged gun fire, then Munro's bullets found the machine gun and silenced it. As the firing ended Evans turned to his longtime friend. He found him slumped at the base of his gun mount. Japanese bullets had cut him down.

Evans knelt by his friend's side. Munro opened his eyes. In a voice so weak Evans had to bend over to hear, Munro asked, "Did we get them all off?"

Evans answered, "Yes." Munro smiled, then died. Through his efforts five hundred marines had been saved to fight another day.

Douglas Munro was born in Vancouver, British Columbia, on October 11, 1919, but grew up in Cle Elum, Washington. He completed one year at Central Washington University, then enlisted in the Coast Guard in 1939. He spent eighteen months aboard the *Spenser* in the Atlantic before transferring to the West Coast. He served on the *Hunter Ligget* during the Guadalcanal landings before being assigned to the landing boat pool.

Munro's mother, Edith, accepted her son's posthumous Medal of Honor from President Roosevelt on May 24, 1943. She then enlisted in the Coast Guard, serving two years as an officer.

Douglas A. Munro is the only coastguardsman to earn the Medal of Honor.

The arrival of the nineteen Wildcats of Marine Fighter Squadron 223 at Henderson Field on August 20 meant the difference between success and failure in the Solomons. Up until then the Japanese had had virtual control of the skies over Guadalcanal. Not only could, and did, their bombers harass the desperately needed transports, they also made daily forays over the marines' perimeter. There, the enemy bombs caused casualties and created havoc for the crews trying to complete Henderson Field.

The Grumman F-4F Wildcat flown by the pilots of VMF-223 was the best the marines had in their inventory at the time, but that wasn't saying much. Originally designed as a biplane, it had been converted to a stubby-wing monoplane with retractable landing gear after the navy had already accepted it. As a result, it was difficult to fly.

Armed with six .50-caliber machine guns, the Wildcat carried more armament than its main enemy, the fabled Zero. But that was about the only advantage it had. The Zero could outclimb, outturn, and outmaneuver the Wildcat. Only the skill of its young pilots would defeat the Zero.

Though much maligned and greatly overshadowed by the superior fighters of the later war years, namely the Corsair and Mustang, the Wildcat would make quite a name for itself in the battle for the control of the Solomons.

JOHN L. SMITH

The first Wildcat to touch down at Henderson Field was piloted by the squadron commander, Capt. John L. Smith. A native of Lexington, Oklahoma, Smith had joined the Marine Corps in 1936 as a twenty-two-year-old graduate of the University of Oklahoma. After two years as an artillery officer he applied for flight training. He flew as a dive-bomber first, then transferred to a fighter squadron being sent to Wake Island. However, Wake Island fell before Smith's squadron arrived. They were diverted to Midway Island.

Smith spent six boring, routine months on Midway developing his skills as a fighter pilot. With not much else to do he put in a lot of time at the controls of his plane. His finely developed flying habits and well-deserved reputation as an innovative fighter tactician did not escape his superiors' notice. Just before the Battle of Midway, Smith was tapped to go to Pearl Harbor and organize the newly created VMF-223.

A tough, moody disciplinarian, Smith recognized that the only way his fledgling pilots could compete with the more experienced Japanese pilots was through a hard regime of training. Smith provided it. He drove his men without letup. Those who didn't muster up to his exacting standards were quickly replaced. In fact, just days before VMF-223 loaded aboard the carrier *Long Island*, he swapped eight of his pilots for eight more experienced men from another squadron.

Smith wasted no time establishing himself as a superb combat airman. On the day after he landed Smith scrambled four of his Wildcats in response to a report of Japanese Betty bombers on their way down the Slot. Over Savo Island, at fourteen thousand feet, Smith spotted six Zeroes five hundred feet higher and on a reciprocal heading. Smith quickly climbed to meet the unsuspecting Zeroes head-on. He opened fire on the lead Zero as the two machines roared toward each other at a combined speed of over six hundred mph. The Japanese pilot flinched first. He pulled up, his belly exposed to Smith's six cannons. Smith stitched a stream of tracers into his foe. The Zero fell off on a wing. Two more Zeroes jumped on Smith's tail. He lost them by diving into a cloud. Smith's kill was the first over Guadalcanal.

By the time eight more days passed Smith was the Cactus Air Force's first ace. On August 30, he added four more to his score.

After receiving a report of a flight of enemy bombers and fighters headed to Guadalcanal from Rabaul, Smith led his remaining seven F-4Fs and seven army P-40s skyward. He leveled off at fifteen thousand feet. The P-40s stayed at twelve thousand because they lacked oxygen. Below them clouds built rapidly, obscuring their vision.

Thirty minutes into the patrol a scared voice shouted over Smith's radio, ''Zeroes on us! Jumping us! We're just north of the field.'' Six Zeroes had dropped out of the clouds to pounce on the P-40s. Four of them went down in minutes. The others raced for the protection of the antiaircraft guns around Henderson Field.

Smith and his wingman raced downward to the enemy at better than three hundred fifty miles per hour. Ordering his men to pick a target and stay with it, Smith pivoted on his left wing and lined up behind one of a flight of four Zeroes. The unsuspecting Zero banked slowly to the left through the thick clouds. Smith narrowed the gap between them. At seven hundred feet the Zero filled Smith's gun sight. He pressed the trigger button on his control stick. The red tracers converged on the Zero. Pieces of the plane flew off into the air. Smith fired again. A yellow ball of fire filled the sky in front of Smith's windshield.

So complete had been the surprise attack, all four Zeroes were flamed within seconds of one another. Smith's squadron had added four victories to its total in less than sixty seconds.

Smith next put his Wildcat into a climb, searching for more Zeroes. A speck in a cloud caught his eye—a Zero trying to hide in the fluffy cumulus. In seconds Smith had the Zero in his sights. A quick press on the trigger and the Zero exploded. A piece of the plane bounced off Smith's canopy but caused no damage.

Once again Smith scanned an empty sky, looking for targets. Before he could spot one his wingman yelled over the radio, "Bandit ahead!" A dark silhouette crossed in front of him, partially obscured by the clouds. Smith slipped his finger up on the trigger button. He hardly had to change course. He squeezed the button. A murderous stream of fire flew across the sky. Smoke erupted from the Zero. Seconds later, a flicker of flame burst from under its cowling. The Zero pulled up sharply, then fell off to the sea below.

The sky was now clear of Zeroes. The clouds closed in, cutting visibility even more. Smith began a spiral down to six thousand feet. The scud was so thick he lost his wingman on the way down. Smith continued down alone, hoping to break out of the clouds. At eight hundred feet above the jungle he leveled off. Ahead of him two planes moved at a right angle to his course. Visibility was still limited so Smith couldn't easily identify the planes. He closed to five hundred feet. Zeroes! But they hadn't seen him.

Smith maneuvered behind the closest Zero, who was still oblivious to his presence. He pressed his trigger. The six guns roared. The Zero literally staggered under the blow. The pilot pulled straight up. Smith followed, maintaining his fire on the Zero. Suddenly the Zero nosed over into a dive. Smith watched it crash into the jungle, now only a few hundred feet below him. When he looked back the other Zero had disappeared.

When Smith landed at Henderson Field his ground crew greeted him at the tie-down. One of them yelled to Smith over the engine noise, "How many?" With a big smile covering his face Smith held up four fingers. Everyone cheered.

By the time Smith rotated off Guadalcanal on October 11, 1942, he wore the oak leaves of a major and was the Marine Corps' leading ace with nineteen kills. He, along with several other marine aces, went on a War Bond–selling tour, attending rallies and dozens of public receptions. His picture appeared on the cover of *Life* magazine. He met with President Roosevelt on February 24, 1943, to receive a well-deserved Medal of Honor. The citation noted his "bold tactics and indomitable fighting spirit" in rendering the enemy's attacks "ineffective and costly."

Smith wanted to return to combat duty, but was told, "Not until you have trained 150 John Smiths." He finally went overseas again in 1944 as executive officer of Marine Air Group 32 with duty in the Philippines, but never again saw combat.

Smith remained in the marines following the war. He served primarily in staff positions before retiring as a full colonel in 1961. He then worked as an executive in the aerospace industry. Despondent at being laid off during a slowdown, Smith took his own life on June 9, 1972.

With the arrival of forty-two hundred fresh men of the 7th Marines on September 18, General Vandegrift's hold on Guadalcanal became less tenuous. He could now construct a stronger defensive ring around Henderson Field. Every point on the perimeter was defended. And he could send stronger patrols on more frequent forays deeper into the interior of Guadalcanal. Skirmishes and pitched battles with the Japanese were an everyday occurrence. Though they had been stymied so far, the Japanese were not giving up on Guadalcanal.

In fact, they were nearly obsessed with it. It had long since overshadowed their attempt to capture Port Moresby. The Japanese continued to feed men into Guadalcanal. Some nine hundred troops a night arrived via the Tokyo Express. But they were never quite enough. The marines were chopping them up into little pieces. The Japanese command decided it was time for a bold move.

The entire Sendai Division under Lt. Gen. Masao Maruyama was sent to Guadalcanal. Maruyama developed a bold plan that would once and for all throw the hated marines off Guadalcanal. He would send two thrusts into the American lines from the west. While the marines reeled under these crushing blows, a surprise attack from the south would seal their fate. This attack would fall on the same Bloody Ridge defended by Red Mike Edson a month earlier.

The results would be the same as before. Only this time, much of the credit would go to an intrepid machine-gun section leader.

JOHN BASILONE

One of the marines who came ashore with the 7th Marines was a colorful sergeant in the heavy weapons company known to one and all as "Manila John" Basilone. Born November 4, 1916, in Buffalo, New York, Basilone grew up in Raritan, New Jersey, where his father, Salvatore, was a tailor. As one of ten children

Basilone knew intimately the tough life of a depression-era family. His parents struggled financially to send all their children to parochial school because Salvatore believed in education. But when he finished the eighth grade at age fifteen, John Basilone went to work to help the family.

He got a job driving a laundry truck. It wasn't much money, but it helped his parents. Then, in 1934, he was laid off. Unwilling to hang around on the street corner with others of his age, Basilone enlisted in the army. After basic training he was sent to the Philippines.

Basilone fell in love with Manila. A big kid with dark, handsome features, he was a hit with the girls in the bars along Dewey Boulevard. The dark-eyed Filipino girls reminded him of the Italian girls he used to date back in Raritan. It was a fun-filled two years for the young soldier.

After his three-year hitch ended Basilone took his honorable discharge and went home to a job in a chemical plant in Raritan, but he never forgot Manila. Three years of civilian life were all he could take. In 1940 he reenlisted. This time, though, he joined the marines; he thought he might get back to Manila quicker with them.

To a Marine Corps rapidly expanding with eighteen- and nineteen-year-old recruits, Basilone was a godsend. His previous military experience earned him rapid promotion. And his many tales of his love-filled adventures in Manila quickly got him tagged "Manila John." Soon everyone, even his officers, called him by that name.

Like the others of the 7th Marines Sergeant Basilone was disappointed to be left on Samoa while the rest of the 1st Marine Division landed on Guadalcanal. When word came they were embarking for Guadalcanal Basilone was pleased. It put him that much closer to Manila.

The three companies of Lt. Col. Lewis B. Puller's 1st Battalion, 7th Marines, occupied tight defensive positions on Bloody Ridge on the night of October 24, 1942. Manila John's water-cooled .50-caliber machine guns supported Company C, smack in the middle of the line. Earlier that day a Japanese officer was spotted looking over the marines' lines through binoculars. Everyone knew the Japanese were going to hit that night.

Thick sheets of rain fell in the pitch-black moonless night. The marines huddled under ponchos, trying to keep their weapons, and themselves, dry. Just past 9:30 P.M. an outpost provided the first news that Maruyama's troops were beginning their assault. "Colonel," the scared private reported to Puller, "there are about three thousand Japs between me and you." Puller alerted his line companies.

Seconds later, the Japanese came pouring out of the rain-soaked jungle. High-pitched voices yelled, "Blood for the Emperor! Marine, you die! Banzai!"

Ferocious fire from Basilone's machine guns mowed down the first wave. With a slight decline in front of him forcing the Japanese to expose themselves as they made for his position, Manila John had no trouble picking out targets. He fired full trigger—250 rounds per minute streaking out of his weapon. Japanese bodies dropped by the dozens in front of him.

The heavy rain made it very difficult to see. An occasional lightning flash or a bursting mortar round provided the only illumination. Fanatical groups of screaming Japanese rushed forward, hurling grenades, firing rifles. They overwhelmed two machine guns to Basilone's right.

At about that time Basilone's guns started running low on ammo. He knew there were probably Japanese infiltrators between him and the ammo dump back at the command post, but if they were going to hold the enemy he had to have more ammo.

"I'm going back for ammo," he yelled to his crew. He pulled off his mud-caked boots so they wouldn't weigh him down and took off down the mud-slickened trail. Scurrying into the CP he grabbed several belts of ammo and some needed parts, then turned and headed back to the front.

Back at his gun pit a runner slid in next to him. "They got the guns on the right," the man sputtered. Basilone swore. Without those heavy weapons to stop them the Japanese would soon be pouring through the lines. He headed for the abandoned weapons. He jumped into the silent pit and found both guns jammed. He ran back to get one of his own.

At his pit Basilone seized a machine gun and threw it across his shoulder. "Follow me," he shouted to a crew, then raced up the slippery trail. His men came behind him, overtaking him just as he bumped into half a dozen Japanese infiltrators. The marines killed them and ran on.

Once in the pit Basilone hurriedly set up the new machine gun. While his crew fired that one, Manila John lay in the mud, frantically working on one of the jammed weapons. Below them the Japanese formed for another charge. Finally, Basilone had the jam cleared. He fed a belt into place and fired away.

Basilone's fire piled up so many bodies in front of his gun he had to send his men out to push them down to clear the fire lane. Several more times during the night Basilone raced back to the CP for ammunition. With his bare torso covered with heavy ammo belts and glistening with sweat and rain in the artillery flashes, Basilone was stopped on one trip by the battalion executive officer. Manila John calmly answered the major's questions about the fight then excused himself. "My men need the ammo," he calmly explained.

All through the night Maruyama's men came at the marines. No less than eight separate attacks were sent against the Americans. A few Japanese broke through; most died on Bloody Ridge. They finally stopped coming around 7:00 A.M., October 25. They had no more troops to send forward.

Manila John Basilone surveyed the battlefield through the still-falling rain. Mounds of Japanese bodies were everywhere. An accurate count of Maruyama's casualties could not be made, but it was estimated over twelve hundred Japanese died that night. Probably a quarter of them were killed by some of the twenty-five thousand rounds of ammo Manila John and his men fired that night. He had played a major role in stemming this savage Japanese attack.

Eight months later, on June 23, 1943, while recuperating with the rest of the survivors of the 1st Marine Division in Australia, newly appointed Gy. Sgt. John Basilone received his Medal of Honor during a division review. He was the first enlisted marine in World War II to earn this decoration.

When he returned to the States in September Basilone received a tumultuous welcome. Raritan held a "Basilone Day" and met the hero at the train station with a blaring brass band. He spent several months touring the States on a War Bond drive. On the tour he met and married in July 1944 a lady marine, Sgt. Lena Riggi. Later, the Marine Corps offered Manila John a lieutenant's commission, but he turned it down. "I'm a plain Marine—I want to stay one," he told them.

Most of the Marine Corps thought Manila John had done enough fighting for his country—but he didn't. He yearned to get back to soldiering. His repeated requests for a transfer back to a line unit were turned down. Finally, the marine corps said yes. In the fall of 1944, Gy. Sgt. John Basilone joined the newly formed 5th Marine Division training in Hawaii.

On February 19, 1945, Manila John's company landed in the first assault wave on the hellhole called Iwo Jima. After he wiped out a stubborn machine-gun pillbox, a mortar shell exploded at his feet. Basilone was killed instantly. His valor brought him a posthumous Navy Cross.

The army's 182d Infantry Regiment arrived on Guadalcanal on November 11, 1942, their transports escorted by a small task force under Adm. Daniel Callaghan. The Americans still held only a small part of Guadalcanal and needed more reinforcements to combat the ever-present Japanese. Enemy planners on Rabaul still hoped to wrest Henderson Field from the marines and regain control of the Solomons. Even though thousands of Japanese soldiers had already died in the brutal war of attrition the Tokyo Express rarely halted its nightly run down the Slot.

In fact, American naval intelligence uncovered yet another plan by which the Japanese hoped to retake Henderson Field. The Imperial Army's 38th Division would land on November 13 covered by a major sea and air bombardment. Two Japanese carriers, four battleships, five cruisers, and some thirty destroyers were already reported to be on their way to bombard Henderson Field.

To stop them the Americans had the five cruisers and eight destroyers under Admiral Callaghan. At 1:45 A.M. on November 13, 1942, Callaghan's fleet met the Japanese armada north of Guadalcanal. In what would be the largest and fiercest surface ship engagement of the entire war, the two flotillas joined battle. To witnesses, the battle scene resembled Armageddon. Huge flashes of light from massive guns ripped through the hot, humid night. The turbulent wakes of speeding ships crisscrossed with the thin lines of deadly torpedoes. The crashes of huge shells on the armor plating of ships filled the night with dreadful screams. And above it all, the wailing of painfully wounded men reached an unbelievable crescendo.

In the opening minutes of the battle between the two massive fleets, a full salvo from the fourteen-inch guns of the battleship *Hiei* fell on the bridge of Admiral Callaghan's flagship, *San Francisco*. Callaghan, the ship's commander, Capt. Cassin

Young, who had earned the Medal of Honor at Pearl Harbor, and nearly everyone else on the bridge died in the explosion. A second salvo crashed into the *San Francisco*, wounding her further.

Fires raged throughout the ship. Smoke filled nearly every compartment and passageway. Twisted metal and dead bodies were strewn all about. Out of this disaster two men responded with tremendous courage and skill to save the heavily damaged cruiser.

On the bridge, Lt. Comdr. Bruce McCandless, the communications officer, found himself the senior officer alive. Reacting instantly, he first sent a message to the other ships, advising them of Callaghan's death. Then he barked out orders, establishing himself as the new commanding officer. He fought the ship through the remainder of the battle. Under his control the turret guns fired salvoes at the enemy ships until they retreated. McCandless, a thirty-one-year-old Naval Academy graduate from Washington, D.C., then busied himself with guiding the *San Francisco* to safety.

Below decks Lt. Comdr. Herbert E. Schonland, the damage control officer, had his hands full fighting fires and repairing the crippled vessel. The second deck was flooded. The communications system had been knocked out. And the ship's steering and engine controls had been severely damaged by an exploding shell.

Schonland set up a series of seamen to relay steering instructions from McCandless on the bridge. He then turned his attention to his two main problems: fires and seawater. To fight the fires he organized crews from the uninjured, several times personally leading them into dangerous areas. To pump out the excess water he manhandled heavy pumps through waist-deep water. It took careful planning to remove the water so he wouldn't disturb the ship's stability.

Schonland, a forty-three-year-old Naval Academy graduate from Portland, Maine, struggled through the night to save his ship. He won. At dawn the *San Francisco* joined up with two other survivors of the sea battle. Together the three ships limped into the naval base at Espiritu Santo. After temporary repairs, the *San Francisco* sailed to Pearl Harbor. From there she headed to San Francisco for an extensive overhaul.

The two heroes received their medals from President Roosevelt on December 12, 1942, just one month after they earned them.

Elsewhere that fearsome night, the Japanese fleet pounded other U.S. ships. The cruiser *Atlanta* with her gallant commander, Adm. Norman Scott, went down. The *Juneau* was badly wounded and would be sunk by an enemy torpedo later that morning. Four of the escorting destroyers were sunk. Only one escaped injury.

Just twenty-four minutes after the gunfire began it was over. Though he had lost only two destroyers the Japanese admiral turned back north, abandoning his part of the invasion. The U.S. Navy's burning ships littered the sea. Over one thousand U.S. sailors were dead. The surviving Allied ships moved southward.

The deaths of so many Americans in the waters north of Guadalcanal were not in vain. When the twelve transports carrying twelve thousand men of the invading Japanese 38th Division arrived off Guadalcanal on November 14, they were met by the dive-bombers and fighters of the Cactus Air Force. While the Wildcats tangled with the Zeroes flying cover, the dive-bombers went to work. When they'd dropped their bombs, the fighters flashed down, strafing the remaining ships. Without the covering antiaircraft fire of the cruisers and destroyers the Japanese troops were slaughtered by the marine flyers. Seven transports went down. The five survivors beached on Guadalcanal. Less than five thousand Japanese soldiers survived the bombing and strafing. Most of those were later taken aboard destroyers and returned north.

The victory was stunning, and nearly complete. If it hadn't been for the loss of one of the marine's leading aces, it would have been. Lt. Col. Harold W. "Indian Joe" Bauer, skipper of VMF-212, had earned a Medal of Honor on October 16. Bauer had been in the landing pattern at Henderson Field that afternoon when nine Japanese Val dive-bombers were spotted lining up for an attack on the transport *McFarland*, which was loaded with Guadalcanal wounded. Though his fuel tanks were nearly empty, Bauer went after the Vals. He shot down four before returning to make his landing.

All together Bauer destroyed eleven Japanese aircraft over the Solomons. An utterly fearless pilot, who showed complete disdain for the enemy, Bauer was downed in the wild melee over the Japanese transports. One of Bauer's best friends, a cigar-chewing South Dakota farmer, saw Bauer swim clear of his sinking Wildcat and wave up at him. He flew off for help. By the time he returned with an amphibious scout plane Bauer was gone. It was a sad day for the South Dakotan, Joe Foss.

JOSEPH J. FOSS

The first American fighter pilot to equal the record of World War I ace Capt. Eddie Rickenbacker, who destroyed twenty-six German planes over France, was Marine Corps Capt. Joseph J. Foss. He arrived at Henderson Field as executive officer of VMF-121 on October 9, 1942, just three days before Capt. John Smith, then the leading ace, headed home. By November 19 Foss had destroyed an incredible twenty-three enemy aircraft! Three more were added on January 15, 1943. Foss would finish the war as the marine's second-ranking ace.

Born April 17, 1915, Foss grew up on the family's farm near Sioux Falls, South Dakota. It was a hard life, filled with long hours of backbreaking work, few rewards, and even fewer luxuries (even in 1943 the Foss farmhouse lacked electricity). Farming was never easy, and it got harder after Foss's father died in a 1933 car accident.

The growing seasons of 1935 and 1936 were disasters for the widow Foss and her three sons. Drought conditions destroyed the crop both years. The little income the family had came mostly from Joe's job. A big, strapping Norwegian youth of six feet and 175 pounds, Foss spent most of his hours after high school pumping gas and repairing cars at a local gas station. Many times he talked to his mother about quitting school to work full time, but she always gave an emphatic no. She wanted her boys to have an education so they wouldn't have to depend on the farm for a living.

Foss saw his first airplanes in 1932 when a Marine Corps squadron put on an air show at the local fair. Three years later he plunked down five hard-earned dollars for his first ride. He was hooked. In 1937 he paid for his first flying lesson. When he graduated from the University of South Dakota in 1939 he already had his pilot's license. The next year he enlisted in the Marine Corps's aviation program. He earned his wings in March 1941. He was such a talented pilot, the navy kept him at Pensacola, Florida, for a year as an instructor. After more training stateside, Foss shipped out for Guadalcanal at the end of August 1942.

On October 13, Foss downed his first Zero during an enemy bombing attack on Henderson Field. Jumped from behind while climbing to intercept the bombers, his attacker came in too fast, flying by Foss's Wildcat. Foss pressed his trigger button, and the Zero exploded. Then three more Zeroes closed in on Foss. They shot up his plane, forcing him to make a deadstick landing back at Henderson. "That was close," he told his crew chief.

October 25, 1942, was a good day for Foss. Since his first kill two weeks before, he had downed four more and was amassing an enviable record for brilliance in the sky. After Maruyama's abortive attack on Bloody Ridge, Japanese bombers and fighter planes filled the sky above Guadalcanal throughout the day in what was their portion of a coordinated sea, air, and land attack. The heavy rains had turned Henderson Field into a mud pit, but Foss and a few other Wildcats managed to get airborne. In an attack on sixteen enemy medium bombers and escorting fighters, Foss knocked four Zeroes out of the sky. With the four Zeroes he'd shot down on October 23, he had a remarkable three-day total of eight Zeroes.

On the morning of November 7, 1942, a Japanese cruiser and ten destroyers were spotted in the Slot about one hundred miles north of Guadalcanal. Seven dive-bombers and three torpedo planes, escorted by twenty-three Wildcats under Captain Foss, headed after them. The bombers hit the cruiser twice and damaged a destroyer. The covering force of Zeroes tangled with Foss and the other pilots.

In the wild dogfight Foss shot down three of the nine Japanese planes destroyed that day. His own Wildcat, though, had been badly shot up. He streaked for home in the damaged plane, but two Zeroes cornered him over the island of Malaita. They forced him down in the water.

Foss spent nearly twelve hours trying to swim to Malaita through the tricky currents before a missionary and local natives in a dugout canoe rescued him. He spent one night in their peaceful village before being picked up by a PBY amphibious plane and returned to Guadalcanal. Two days later he was back in the air, shooting down Japanese planes.

On November 13, he led his flight of Wildcats on a strafing run against the fleeing Japanese ships that had shot up the *San*

Francisco and sunk six other ships. At one point he flew so close to the battleship *Hiei* he thumbed his nose at the white-clad officers lining the bridge.

That same day he lost his friend "Indian Joe" Bauer. When Bauer waved at him from the water Foss felt confident the two would be sharing a cold beer that night back at Henderson Field. But it was not to be. For several weeks Foss hoped that Bauer might have made it to the safety of a nearby island. But when no word of his survival came from any of the missionaries or coast watchers, Foss had to accept that Bauer was gone.

Foss knocked down his twenty-third enemy plane on November 15. That same night he awoke shaking violently from a severe malaria attack. He was evacuated to a hospital near Sydney, Australia. After six weeks rest he returned to Guadalcanal on New Years Day 1943, fully recovered.

The Marine Corps finally decided Foss had had enough combat after he downed three more planes in January. He went home. A massive hero's welcome awaited him. He was feted everywhere he went, and after he received his Medal of Honor on May 18, 1943, his picture graced the cover of *Life* magazine.

Foss served a year's duty in Washington, then returned to the Pacific in mid-1944. He flew numerous combat missions, but targets were rare. He did not add to his score. He took his discharge in December 1945.

Foss's war record propelled him into South Dakota politics. After several terms in the state legislature he successfully ran for governor in 1954. He served one four-year term, then became commissioner of the American Football League in 1959. He held that position until the AFL merged with the NFL in 1966, then produced an outdoors television program for several years.

In 1986 Foss became the president of the National Rifle Association.

Major General Vandegrift passed control of operations on Guadalcanal to the U.S. Army on December 9, 1942. The last weeks of November and early days of December had been relatively quiet. The Japanese had tapered off their reinforcements. The last Tokyo Express ran on November 30. Enemy planes were disappearing from the skies over Guadalcanal in the face of a Cactus Air Force that had grown from the original 31 aircraft to more than 150.

It was now time to give the 1st Marine Division a rest. They had suffered over twenty-one hundred casualties, and another fifty-six hundred Marines had developed malaria and other unique jungle diseases. Now they were going to Australia for rest and recuperation before beginning the next campaign.

For General Vandegrift the end of the Guadalcanal campaign meant a Medal of Honor and, eventually, the commandantcy of the Marine Corps.

The army troops arriving on Guadalcanal faced several more months of fighting before organized Japanese resistance ended, and it would be well over a year before the rest of the Solomon Islands were secure.

6

★ ★ ★

Action in the South Pacific

The defeat of the Port Moresby invasion fleet in the Coral Sea in May 1942 did not thwart the Japanese desire to conquer New Guinea. They still wanted the island as a springboard for attacks on Australia. Accordingly, they devised a daring plan to land a force on New Guinea's north coast and advance overland through the formidable Owen Stanley Mountains to fall on Port Moresby from its rear.

On July 22, 1942, thirteen thousand Japanese troops landed at Buna, on New Guinea's northeast coast, and began moving down the Kokoda Trail. No more than a mere footpath, the trail snaked its way back and forth up and into the Owen Stanleys. It tunneled between trees so overgrown with moss and creepers that sunlight could barely penetrate to the muddy trail.

Vastly outnumbered Australian troops fought gallantly against the invaders. Not until they were reinforced by troops of their own 7th Division in September did the Australians fight the Japanese to a draw.

Because of reverses suffered in the Solomon Islands, the Japanese had no reinforcements for their campaign in New Guinea. Just thirty miles short of Port Moresby they were ordered to withdraw to the north coast villages of Buna and Gona. There they would hold out until the forces committed to the recapture of Guadalcanal could be freed to aid in a renewed drive on Port Moresby.

General MacArthur wasn't going to let that happen. Early in October 1942 transport planes from Gen. George Kenney's Fifth Air Force began landing troops of the 32d Infantry Division, a Wisconsin–Michigan National Guard unit, at makeshift airfields south of Buna. By the third week of November they were ready. While the 7th Australian Division operated against Gona, the 32d would drive north to capture Buna.

Initial intelligence reports indicated Buna was lightly held. The 32d's commander, Maj. Gen. Edwin F. Harding, said Buna would be "easy pickings" for his National Guardsmen. In actuality, over forty-five hundred determined Japanese occupied the little village.

Using tree trunks, steel, concrete, and earth, the Japanese constructed a mutually supporting network of bunkers, machine-gun nests, and connecting tunnels to defend their beachhead. The 32d's advance began on November 19 in a drenching rain. Within minutes of starting, the Americans ground to a halt, stopped by a wall of machine-gun and rifle fire that erupted from the dense jungle. Every time the GIs tried to move they were met with fire from cleverly camouflaged bunkers. They withdrew.

Two days later they went back. Again the attack ground to a halt. The stubborn resistance and bloody, hand-to-hand fighting, combined with the constant eighty-five percent humidity and ninety degree heat, quickly wore down the green combat troops. After two weeks of terrible fighting, the Americans had gained only a few hundred yards.

The delay infuriated MacArthur. He ordered Harding to take Buna "regardless of cost." Harding tried a flanking movement which came to naught as GIs found themselves floundering in leech-infested, waist-deep swamps where they became easy targets for Japanese snipers.

On November 30, Harding's GIs finally penetrated the outskirts of Buna. One American platoon leader described the brutal fighting: "Machine gun tracers lit the entire sky, and our own rifle fire made a solid sheet of flame. Everywhere men cursed, shouted, or screamed. Order followed order. Brave men led and others followed. Cowards crouched in the grass frightened out of their skins."

Embodied with superhuman courage, the GIs overran the outposts and crossed an open field of jungle grass to seize a cluster of buildings that served as the Japanese headquarters. They were in Buna, but the fighting was not over.

In spite of such gains MacArthur was still not satisfied. He replaced Harding with Lt. Gen. Robert L. Eichelberger. Mac-

Arthur told Eichelberger, "Go out there, Bob, and take Buna, or don't come back alive."

Eichelberger took over the 32d on December 1. After a two-day respite he put the 32d back on the offensive. Within hours he realized it would take many more days of murderous, hand-to-hand fighting to capture Buna.

As they were driven into a smaller and smaller salient, their backs to the sea, the Japanese defenders became more stubborn, more desperate. They even used corpses to bolster fortifications, the living firing over the bodies of their dead comrades. It was combat at its absolute worst. By Christmas Eve the GIs had eliminated all but the most heavily fortified bunkers. The ocean lay but six hundred yards away.

KENNETH E. GRUENNERT

Two days before Christmas 1942, Company L, 127th Infantry Regiment, returned to the front lines at Buna. After two weeks of heavy fighting and severe casualties, the company had been given twenty-four hours' rest. They couldn't have any more; the fighting was too desperate to allow more than a casual break from its horrors.

Leading one of its squads was twenty-year-old Sgt. Kenneth Gruennert. He had been a member of Company L since February 1939, enlisting when he was but sixteen. Though underage, Gruennert possessed a skill badly needed by the local National Guard unit. He was a star athlete on his hometown Helenville, Wisconsin, high school baseball team. When the National Guard team found itself in need of a catcher they simply recruited Gruennert. In the days before World War II the National Guard served as a community social club as much as a patriotic one, so young Gruennert's recruitment was not unusual.

The social aspect ended when Company L was federalized in June 1940 as part of the 32d Infantry Division. Following extensive training, the 32d left for Australia in April 1942. By that time, though only nineteen, Gruennert wore the stripes of a sergeant. His promotion was a measure of his hard work and determination.

In the weeks of fighting around Buna, Gruennert saw too many of his hometown buddies die in the brackish jungle swamps. It was a tough way for a youngster to grow up.

Christmas Eve found Gruennert's platoon holding the left flank of the assault line. A dawn artillery barrage crashed down on the jungle-covered enemy emplacements. When it ended, 1st Lt. Fred Matz, Gruennert's platoon leader, shouted, "Let's go!"

To a man the platoon rose and moved forward toward its objective, the wooden Buna mission house, only a few hundred yards away through the torn foliage. Suddenly, machine-gun fire from two pillboxes split the air. Matz went down, hit hard by the Japanese slugs. Gruennert and the others dove for cover.

Determined to destroy the positions holding up the attack, Gruennert said to the man lying closest him, "I'm going after those pillboxes. Keep shooting at their slits and give me all the covering fire you can."

Without another word the former high school baseball star wormed his way through the undergrowth. Snipers in the grass took him under fire, but miraculously he made it to within throwing distance of the first emplacement. He hurled a grenade into the pillbox. With the explosion he dashed forward, thrust his M-1 rifle through an opening, and fired off a clip. Three Japanese died.

When others from his platoon joined him they found Gruennert propped against the side of the pillbox, crudely bandaging a badly bleeding shoulder wound. One of them said, "Go on back, Sarge. You've had enough for today."

"No," replied Gruennert. "I'm not through."

He quickly wriggled out of sight.

As the weary infantrymen anxiously waited they heard three quick explosions. Gruennert's expert throwing arm had pegged a barrage of grenades into the second pillbox. He killed the survivors with rifle fire as they fled the smoldering ruins.

The crackle of gunfire brought the others forward. When they reached Gruennert he was dead, shot by a sniper. Aroused by Gruennert's courage and death, the surviving platoon members stormed the mission house, finally taking it that afternoon. By that evening they had fought their way to the beach, the first unit to split the enemy position.

Word of Gruennert's posthumous Medal of Honor reached his parents, Arthur and Belva, at their tidy frame house in Helenville on September 10, 1943. They were invited to the White House on October 6 to receive the medal from President Roosevelt.

Instead of packing their bags Mr. and Mrs. Gruennert, after much reflection, sent the following letter to the War Department:

> We feel honored indeed to receive a Medal of Honor for our departed son, to be delivered to us personally by the President. Under present conditions, however, we cannot help but give expression to some of the following thoughts which race through our minds day and night. We are now in the midst of the Third War Bond drive. We believe every cent of money subscribed should be used to supply our boys with the necessities of war and not spent for trips that do not directly help the war effort.
>
> Only this last week, thousands of other parents lost their loved ones on the battlefields of Italy; all brave boys that were loved by their parents as much as we loved our son. These parents cannot converge on Washington, and because of the common bond we have with them we feel we shouldn't either. The loss of our brave boy is still too fresh in our memory to make this trip, even though it would be in his honor.

The War Department and President Roosevelt honored the brave parents' request, mailing them the Medal of Honor. Secretary of War Henry Stimson included a letter that said, in part, "We stand humble in the face of such a demonstration of patriotism as yours."

Buna fell January 3, 1943. By the end of the month the Australians conquered Gona. The campaign in that part of New Guinea was over at last. But much hard fighting remained ahead as General MacArthur prepared to leapfrog his forces along the northern coast. Once he captured the key ports there he could turn his attention to Rabaul. From there he could move to recapture his beloved Philippines.

Meanwhile, American forces in the Solomons were finalizing the capture of Guadalcanal before moving farther up the chain to squeeze Rabaul from that side. Maj. Gen. Alexander M. Patch, commander of the XIV Corps, consisting of the 25th and the Americal Infantry Divisions, decided to eliminate the Japanese still holding out on Mount Austen. Located just six miles south of Henderson Field, the fifteen-hundred-foot peak gave the Japanese a clear view of the airfield and of ship and troop movements everywhere in the Lunga Point area. General Patch sent elements of Maj. Gen. J. Lawton Collins's 25th Infantry Division to begin the move up Mount Austen on January 6, 1943.

Mount Austen was actually a jumbled series of ridges, steep and rocky, with grassy areas scattered among dense jungle. The Japanese had firmly entrenched themselves in natural caves and man-made dugouts. Each had to be blasted out with grenades and sheer courage.

On January 12, a unit of the 25th Division, the 2d Battalion, 27th Infantry Regiment, found themselves at grips with the enemy on Mount Austen. A series of four ridges, all held by the Japanese, stood between the tired infantrymen and their final objective, Hill 53. By noon, two companies of the battalion, on its first combat operation, had mowed down the Japanese holding the first two ridges. But the two companies took heavy casualties, reducing their already depleted ranks to about 120 men. When they reached the base of the third ridge they reported back to the battalion command post that heavy enemy fire from above had stymied their advance. And enemy fire now blocked their route to the rear.

The battalion commander drew up a plan of attack for his two companies. At this point his executive officer stepped forward. "I'll take it up front, sir," he volunteered.

CHARLES W. DAVIS

Battalion executive officers do not ordinarily enter combat; their duties are more administrative. But Capt. Charles W. Davis wasn't an ordinary officer. He had been chosen as the executive officer, though just a captain, because he had consistently demonstrated his organizational skills and leadership abilities during eighteen months as a platoon leader and company commander. He would soon prove the wisdom of that choice.

Born February 21, 1917, in Gordo, Alabama, Davis had been commissioned a second lieutenant through the University of Alabama's ROTC program in July 1940. After training at Fort Benning, Georgia, and a tour with the 2d Infantry Division in Texas he joined the 25th Infantry Division at Schofield Barracks, Hawaii. There he witnessed the Japanese sneak attack on Pearl Harbor.

Davis and the rest of the 25th arrived on Guadalcanal in late December 1942 as part of the contingent relieving the exhausted marines. Before the marines left Davis gathered as much information from them as he could about the fighting tactics of the enemy, their snipers, bunkers, mortars, grenades, and rifles. By the time the 2d Battalion took over a section of the front lines Davis was well-versed about his foe.

Accompanied by two second lieutenants, Davis started his mission by trekking through two hundred yards of sniper-infested jungle. A sniper killed one of the junior officers. When he reached the pinned-down companies Davis immediately saw the inexperienced men could not execute the attack plan. Instead, he took up a position on the side of the ridge that gave him a view of the enemy. In his quiet southern drawl he called in artillery and mortar barrages on the Japanese positions. Davis remained in the exposed position throughout the night, his effective fire keeping the Japanese pinned down. Davis didn't have to spend the night on the slope, but he did. He felt he could be helpful if he stayed. And he remembered a comment General Collins had made during a meeting on the troopship bringing them to Guadalcanal. "Remember," the general told the assembled officers, "in a stalemated action, the victory often goes to the side that initiates some positive action."

Davis decided to take that action. At daybreak he conferred with his battalion commander, who had come forward during the night. Davis would take a few volunteers and go to the top of the ridge. It seemed like suicide, but he felt a small group had a better chance of catching the Japanese off guard.

Davis was surprised at the four men who volunteered to go with him. They were not trained infantrymen. Instead, they were a supply sergeant, two cooks, and a clerk, all of whom had been pressed into service as infantrymen.

Davis led his small team up a shallow draw he had spotted the night before. The men kept low, crawling on all fours through the tangled undergrowth. When they reached a small rise in the draw Davis halted. Cautiously, he raised up. A second later he dropped back down.

"Get your grenades out," he whispered. "There's a bunker just thirty feet ahead."

Less than a minute later five grenades sailed up the hillside. Without waiting for the explosions each man threw another grenade. Before they could erupt a heavy object plopped onto the ground near Davis. Just six inches away from his head lay a Japanese grenade.

Instinctively, he turned away, wondering how it felt to have your head blown off. The seconds slowly ticked by. After what seemed like forever Davis turned back. The grenade was a dud.

"All right, men. I guess it might as well be now," he announced.

With a yell the five men jumped up. Triggering quick bursts from their rifles, and throwing grenades, they ran up the hill.

Startled by the bold charge, a dozen Japanese broke from cover. Davis fired his M-1 from the hip, dropping two or three. Others fell from his men's fire. Davis sighted on another enemy and pulled his rifle's trigger. Nothing. The M-1 was jammed. He transferred it to his left hand while he pulled his pistol from its holster with his right. He fired. The Japanese soldier crumpled in a heap.

Continuing up the hill, the five soldiers fired at every target, wiping out each Japanese position they encountered. Within minutes they had crested the ridge.

Sixty yards below them, their brave charge stirred the two companies. They arose en masse, killing any enemy stragglers they found as they moved up the hill.

In a few more minutes the ridge was firmly in American hands. But Davis didn't stop there. Still carrying his rifle in his left hand and his .45 in his right, Davis waved his arm to the men around him and yelled, "Let's go!"

Without waiting to see if anyone followed, he broke into a trot, headed down a slope to the fourth ridge. Down he ran, firing his pistol at the Japanese fleeing before him. He bravely led the way the whole 250 yards to the top of the fourth ridge. The entire Japanese defense collapsed before Davis and the two companies. A short time later they stood victorious on Hill 53.

Unknown to Davis, General Collins had witnessed his gallant charge through binoculars from a rear position. When the action was over Collins told an aide, "Get me the name of that man carrying the rifle and pistol." He wanted to reward the soldier for his daring.

The reward came on July 30, 1943, during a division review on Guadalcanal. The commanding general of the army forces in the South Pacific, Lt. Gen. Millard F. Harmon, placed the blue ribbon of the Medal of Honor around Davis's neck. It was a proud day for Davis, now a major and in command of the 27th Infantry's 3d Battalion.

The day after the ceremony the 25th Infantry Division sailed for the invasion of New Georgia, farther up the Solomon Island chain. Davis fought there for six weeks before returning to the States. He later attended the Command and General Staff College at Fort Leavenworth, Kansas.

Davis remained in the army after World War II. He saw further combat as a deputy corps advisor in the Mekong Delta during the Vietnam War. He retired as a full colonel in 1972.

One of the vital links in America's plans for conquering Japan was the U.S. Navy's submarine force. In the days immediately following Pearl Harbor the submarines were the only practical weapon capable of carrying the war to Japan. But the boats were few, far between, and woefully inadequate for the task before them.

Only fifty-five subs were assigned to the Pacific in 1942. Of these, twelve were World War I–vintage boats, and another eleven were unavailable for combat service for various reasons.

Further, this small force was plagued by a wide variety of problems. Their tactics were obsolete. The submarine service had no combat tradition—during World War I they had not sunk a single enemy ship. The subs' equipment and weapons were scandalously poor. During the first two years of the war they fought the enemy with a torpedo with a failure rate of nearly sixty percent. Not until 1943 would the U.S. submarines go to sea with a torpedo that worked.

In spite of a multitude of problems the "silent service" carried the offensive to the enemy with deadly results. In World War II American subs sank over two hundred Japanese warships, totaling over half a million tons. Even more importantly, 1,113 enemy merchant ships, totaling over 4,700,000 tons of shipping, were sunk by U.S. subs. The effect of this massive loss of supply and troop carrying vessels on Japan's war efforts was immeasurable.

Not all of the submarines' efforts were offensive in nature. They also ran a variety of special missions: hauling munitions, transporting troops, rescuing agents from behind enemy lines, snatching downed pilots from under the enemy's very noses, and scouting and reconnaissance missions.

Service aboard submarines carried extreme risks. For their vital achievements the silent service paid a dreadful price. During the war 52 subs and 3,505 submariners were lost; this was a casualty rate of sixteen percent for the officers and thirteen percent for the enlisted men.

The members of the submarine service were a close-knit fraternity whose shared dangers created a bond few men ever know. Within that closed society tales of heroism inspired others to greater effort. A handful of submariners earned their country's highest honor and immortal glory.

HOWARD W. GILMORE

One of the first heroes of the silent service was the skipper of the *Growler*. Born September 29, 1902, in Selma, Alabama, Comdr. Howard W. Gilmore was a relative rarity: a former enlisted man who had qualified for the Naval Academy through tough competitive exams and then risen to the coveted command of a submarine.

A fine officer by anyone's standards, Gilmore had had more than his share of bad luck. His throat bore the scars left from a knife attack by Panamanian thugs. His first wife had died of a debilitating disease. And when Gilmore left for war, his second wife lay unconscious from injuries suffered in a fall down a flight of stairs.

Adversity did not dampen Gilmore's aggressiveness. During a patrol in Alaskan waters in mid-1942 he attacked three Japanese destroyers off Kiska. In a rare stroke of good luck all his torpedoes worked. One destroyer sank and the other two had to be towed back to Japan for repairs. Late in 1942 the *Growler* sank four Japanese ships totaling fifteen thousand tons in the East China Sea.

On January 10, 1943, the *Growler* left her base at Brisbane, Australia, on her fourth war patrol. Her hunting grounds were the hostile waters around Rabaul. Within days of her arrival, the *Growler* sank a six thousand-ton merchant vessel.

After sunset on February 7, Gilmore ordered the *Growler* to the surface. He had carefully surveyed the surrounding sea through the periscope. Nothing was visible. The moon hid behind a nearby squall. He decided he had enough time to recharge the sub's batteries and give the crew a breath of fresh air before dawn forced him to dive.

At 1:10 A.M. Gilmore was on the bridge with six of his crew. The radar operator suddenly reported a surface contact a scant two thousand yards away. Gilmore ordered his crew to battle stations. Seconds later the enemy ship changed course, heading straight for the *Growler* at full speed. She was going to ram the sub.

"Left full rudder," shouted Gilmore. But it was too late. The *Hayasaki*, a nine hundred-ton patrol boat, and the *Growler* collided. The sub rolled fifty degrees, sending men sprawling. Heavy Japanese machine-gun fire poured down into the *Growler*'s bridge, killing an officer and an enlisted lookout. Two other lookouts and Gilmore lay wounded.

At the foot of the bridge ladder in the conning tower *Growler*'s executive officer, Lt. Comdr. Arnold Schade, heard Gilmore's shouted order above the chatter of the machine gun, "Clear the bridge!" The two unwounded men dropped through the hatch, pulling the wounded lookouts behind them. Gilmore did not appear. Instead, Schade heard him shout the command that would save the *Growler* and seal his own fate: "Take her down!"

Schade hesitated. He hated to leave his wounded skipper, but his orders were clear. Schade's duty was to save the *Growler*. He closed and dogged the hatch, then spoke tersely, "Take her down. Dive! Dive!"

The *Growler* went under, leaving Gilmore still clinging to a bridge frame. *Growler* limped out of the area, taking water through bullet holes in her hull and her smashed bow. Once clear of Rabaul Schade surfaced and set a course for Brisbane.

For sacrificing himself so his crew might live, Gilmore was posthumously awarded the Medal of Honor on July 13, 1943, the first submarine officer so recognized. American submariners would never forget Gilmore's last words: "Take her down!"

General MacArthur and Admiral Halsey met in Brisbane, Australia, on April 15, 1943, to coordinate their respective offenses aimed at Rabaul. The campaign worked out between the two senior officers commanding adjoining areas of operation called for MacArthur's troops to continue their effort against the Japanese on New Guinea. Once he had seized control of that large island, MacArthur could jump across to New Britain itself.

Beachheads on the western end of that island would allow fighter planes to accompany heavy bombers on their raids on Rabaul.

At the same time, Halsey's forces would move up the Solomons chain, capturing islands that lay between Guadalcanal and Rabaul. Three islands were keys to Halsey's strategy: New Georgia and Kolombangara in the central Solomons, and Bougainville at the chain's western end. By the time he captured Bougainville Halsey's forces would be within 250 miles of the Japanese fortress at Rabaul.

The campaign, dubbed *Cartwheel*, kicked off on June 30. MacArthur's forces landed at Nassau Bay just sixty miles south of the Japanese base at Lae on New Guinea. Within a month the GIs had battled their way half the distance to Lae.

On the same day Halsey landed the 43d Infantry Division on New Georgia. The objective of the New England National Guard unit was Munda, on the island's southwest tip, the site of an airfield. Halsey expected the campaign to last two weeks. He underestimated two factors: the jungles of New Georgia and the tenacity of the Japanese defenders.

The terrain between the assault beaches and Munda was totally patternless, a thick matting of dense jungle vegetation, dank, fetid, and seemingly endless. Visibility was sometimes measured in inches. Deep-running streams cut the jungle in random flows. It rained nearly every day, turning the jungle trails into greasy slides under the booted feet of the American soldiers. Huge clouds of mosquitoes constantly filled the air, contributing to the men's misery and spreading disease.

Into this inhospitable jungle Maj. Gen. Nabor Sasaki, the resourceful Japanese island commander, sent his troops to construct defensive positions around the airfield. Gun emplacements were dug five feet into the earth, piled high with logs and dirt, then skillfully camouflaged. Sasaki was content to let the Americans hurl themselves at his Munda fortifications, so he only sent out skirmish patrols to harass the advancing GIs.

His scheme worked well. The green American troops faltered in the jungle. Japanese snipers and night infiltrators played havoc with the GIs. Morale plunged. Every day close to a hundred soldiers were pulled off the line due to combat fatigue. One regiment lost twenty-five percent of its troops to war neuroses. The American advance ground to a halt.

By mid-July Halsey was forced to feed two more full divisions, the 25th and 37th Infantry Divisions, into the battle. The offensive against Munda resumed on July 25. The Americans stood only three thousand yards from the airfield. Against an estimated three Japanese battalions the Americans had twelve on line, with more coming. The GIs also had tanks, flame-throwers, artillery batteries, naval gunfire, and air support. Still, progress was measured in inches.

By July 27 the 145th Infantry Regiment, 37th Division, had fought its way to the base of Horseshoe Hill, which protected one of the main approaches to Munda. Japanese machine guns, encased in log-covered emplacements, fired down on the Americans. Knee mortars[1] rained down on them, felling men in thunderous explosions.

There were cries of anguish: "I'm hit!" "Medic! MEDIC!"

Pfc. Frank J. Petrarca, a medic from Cleveland, Ohio, grabbed his medical bag and rushed to the aid of three wounded men. He quickly bandaged two and sent them to the rear. The third man was too badly wounded to move. Knowing the man would soon die, Petrarca nevertheless stayed with him, using his own body to shield the casualty from the bursting mortars and sniper rounds.

Two days later the regiment again found itself the victim of a furious mortar barrage. One round buried a sergeant in his fox-hole. Unhesitatingly, Petrarca raced forward. Completely exposed to enemy fire he dug the man out, revived him, and hauled him to the rear.

On July 31, a mortar round dropped on two GIs huddled in a foxhole only twenty yards from the Japanese line. Against warnings from his buddies, Petrarca went to their aid. A target for the murderous Japanese fire, Petrarca made his way to within two yards of the men. Then a mortar round fell at his feet. He died just inches from his objective. It was his twenty-fifth birthday.

The 172d Infantry Regiment, 43d Infantry Division, also bogged down in front of a hilltop salient fronting Munda on July 27. First Lt. Robert S. Scott, from Santa Fe, New Mexico, took

[1] Knee mortars were a Japanese light mortar, about 50-mm, also sometimes considered a grenade launcher. Because of its curved base plate it was thought the weapon was braced against the user's knee, but in fact it was not.

a squad from his platoon straight up the hill. Halfway up, and only seventy-five yards from the Japanese, a counterattack stopped them. Enemy riflemen, throwing grenades, emerged from their dugouts. Their bold attack threw the exhausted GIs off the hill.

Except for Lieutenant Scott.

He ducked behind a wide tree stump. Blasting away from his position, Scott broke up the charge. From behind the stump he had a rare unobstructed view of nearby Japanese bunkers. Over the next half hour he threw some thirty grenades at the enemy, completely disrupting their attack and opening the way for the GIs to take the hill. He was wounded twice, had his rifle shot from his hands, but never quit until the enemy withdrew. Later, twenty-eight Japanese dead were counted in the bunkers he wiped out.

On July 31, a few hundred yards north of where Pfc. Petrarca died, the 148th Infantry Regiment, 37th Infantry Division, made a wide sweep through the jungle, outflanked the entire Japanese line, and advanced to within a thousand yards of the airfield. Then it was cut off. The GIs turned to fight their way back to safety. Company B had almost made it when a hidden Japanese machine gun barked. Several men fell. The others dove for cover. They were pinned down. Something had to be done.

RODGER W. YOUNG

The one man who crawled forward to do something did not fit the stereotype image of a combat soldier. Pvt. Rodger W. Young was a little guy who wore big glasses that gave him an owly, scholastic look. But what he lacked in stature he more than made up for in determination and drive.

Born April 28, 1918, one of five children, Young grew up in Green Springs, Ohio. He had two interests as a youngster: music and sports. He could play the harmonica, banjo, and guitar. With his musically inclined siblings, Young put together a combo that frequently played at neighborhood gatherings.

But it was sports—any team game: baseball, football, and basketball—that was Young's true passion. Though not a great athlete, he possessed a lot of team spirit. Too small for football, he put his considerable energy into baseball and basketball. He played second string on his freshman basketball team, usually playing in scrub games. But once in a while the coach put him in a real game. Young provided the enthusiastic spark for some of the other, better players who did not possess his spirit.

It was a basketball game that nearly ruined Young. While going up for a long shot an opposing player clipped his legs out from under him. Young's head smacked against the hardwood floor with a sickening thud.

Two hours later he came to in the local hospital. The doctor pronounced him okay and sent Young home. But within a few months he became slightly deaf and developed bad headaches. His eyesight weakened. He started wearing glasses. The following year he dropped out of school, going to work in a nearby factory.

But he never lost his love of sports. He read the sports page religiously. It was a family joke that he'd spent his last nickel on a paper for the sports news rather than buy food.

For the extra money it paid, Rodger and his older brother joined their local National Guard unit in 1939. A year later they were federalized as part of the 37th Infantry Division.

By the time the 37th sailed for the Pacific, Young was a sergeant, leading a rifle squad. In spite of his bad eyes and weakened hearing, his enthusiasm for the military and his expertise with a rifle marked him as a leader. Young took great pride in his stripes. At the training areas on Guadalcanal few NCOs were more conscientious in training their men for combat than Young. He volunteered them for night maneuvers and extra time on the rifle range. Thanks to his diligence, Young's squad would be ready when they entered combat.

As he progressed through training Young grew increasingly aware that his hearing was getting worse. Aware of the danger this posed for his men, he volunteered to take a reduction to private and sacrifice the rank he had worked so hard to obtain. His company commander, knowing Young's request came as a result of his devotion to duty, reluctantly granted the request. He also allowed Young to stay with his old squad.

During the fighting on New Georgia, Young proved himself a resourceful, nearly fearless combat soldier. When bigger and stronger men collapsed under the strain, Young shrugged off the adversity and continued soldiering.

On the muddy trail near the Munda airfield the enemy machine gun spoke again. Seventy-five yards away Young's shoulder suddenly felt as if it had been hit hard by a baseball bat. He rolled over, blood pouring from the wound.

A buddy said, "You're hit!"

Rodger grimly answered, "Yes, but I see the gun."

Without another word he started crawling for the gun.

His buddy yelled, "Rodger, come on back!"

Maybe Young didn't hear him. Maybe he had already made up his mind to get the gun regardless of the cost. Whatever the reason he continued forward. Every few yards he'd stop, fire at the machine gun, then start forward again.

While the rest of the platoon provided covering fire Young crept to within fifteen yards of the enemy nest. The Japanese gun pivoted, fired. Young's body shuddered under the impact of the red-hot rounds.

Determined to complete his suicidal mission he painfully worked a grenade free from his webbed harness. He threw it. Then a second. And a third.

The grenades destroyed the enemy machine-gun nest. The company was released from the trap. And Rodger Young lay dead on the jungle trail.

His parents accepted his posthumous Medal of Honor on January 17, 1944. In an unusual tribute to the fallen hero, songwriter Pfc. Frank Loesser penned a song in his honor. "The Ballad of Rodger Young" played on jukeboxes around the country in 1945.

Over a thousand Americans died fighting to capture the Munda airstrip. Though expensive in human lives the battle for New Georgia moved American forces two hundred miles closer to Rabaul. Within days of its fall several Marine Corps fighter squadrons took up residence at Munda Airfield. From there, they began escorting heavy bombers on the run to Rabaul and battling Japanese fighters in the skies over the northern Solomons.

Next on Halsey's list was Kolombangara, northwest of New Georgia. American intelligence estimated that over ten thousands Japanese troops garrisoned the island. Halsey was wary of another slugfest and the attendant casualties. But if he wanted Rabaul he needed Kolombangara's airfield.

Then his staff came up with a surprisingly simple and irresistible solution. They would bypass Kolombangara. Just to the northwest of Kolombangara lay the island of Vella Lavella. It offered relatively flat areas where an airfield could be built, and, most importantly, it was lightly defended. Halsey agreed.

American troops landed on Vella Lavella on August 15. Within three weeks an airfield was operational. A short time later a revived Tokyo Express began nightly runs to evacuate the Japanese from Kolombangara. The leapfrog strategy had worked. It would remain a basic strategy for the rest of the Pacific campaign.

MacArthur's turn came next. He needed to capture northeast New Guinea's Huon Peninsula, which thrust east toward New Britain. To do so he had to take the airfield and anchorage held by the enemy at Lae, on the peninsula's south side. To aid the troops struggling toward Lae from the south, MacArthur landed Australian troops twenty miles east of Lae on September 4, while an American airborne regiment parachuted down twenty miles to the west. This phase of the New Guinea campaign went surprisingly well. By September 25 Lae was in Allied hands. The next operation would not be quite so easy.

Five thousand Japanese held Finschafen, at the eastern end of the peninsula. Australian troops landed on September 22. Two weeks of brutal fighting raged before Finschafen fell on October 2. Japanese troops counterattacked on October 16, nearly throwing the Australians out of the town. Only the timely arrival of reinforcements prevented a disaster. Several more weeks of heavy fighting loomed ahead of the Allied forces before Huon Peninsula was cleared of Japanese.

Admiral Halsey's last major operation in the Solomons began on November 1, 1943, against Bougainville, at the chain's northwestern edge. Stretching for more than 125 miles, the island's narrow beaches were bordered by extensive swamps and a jungle-covered mountainous interior. Once again the terrain would prove to be as formidable a foe as the Japanese.

Because the Japanese heavily guarded their four airfields at Bougainville's southern tip, Halsey elected to put his troops ashore at Empress Augusta Bay. Halfway up the island's west coast, Empress Augusta Bay had no airfield—the Seabees would have to hack one out of the jungle—but there were also less than a thousand Japanese defending the area.

Spearheading the invasion was the untried 3d Marine Division, to be followed ashore by the army's 37th Infantry Division.

Halsey's landing completely fooled the Japanese. They never expected a landing at Empress Augusta Bay. This proved fortunate, for the leading assault waves found eighteen well-camouflaged pillboxes that enfiladed the beach. If they had been manned they would have devastated the landing craft.

As it was, the landing boats had to pass right under the nose of a heavily defended 75-mm gun. It pummeled the boats, destroying several and causing numerous casualties. Ashore, the marines desperately tried to wipe out the gun, but two mutually supporting bunkers hampered their efforts.

Sgt. Robert A. Owens, 1st Battalion, 3d Marines, decided to go after the emplacement. The twenty-three-year-old Greenville, South Carolina, native picked four men to provide covering fire, then began crawling forward. When he was past the two bunkers he suddenly rose to full height and charged straight into the mouth of the cannon.

He dove right through the firing port, firing his M-1 as fast as he could. The Japanese fled in terror out the rear door. There, other marines cut them down.

When the marines entered the emplacement they found Owens mortally wounded. His actions prevented many casualties and allowed the invasion to succeed.

The marines quickly pushed inland, expanding their beachhead. Behind them Seabees set to work building the airstrip. In spite of extremely adverse conditions they had the field operational by December 1st. By the middle of the month two more fields were completed. American fighters were now just a little over two hundred miles from Rabaul.

Sporadic fighting would rage into the next spring, but Bougainville had been effectively neutralized as Operation *Cartwheel* came full circle at the end of 1943.

7

* * *

Mediterranean Operations

The first U.S. offensive operation in the European theater began shortly after 1:00 A.M., November 8, 1942, when more than 107,000 men hit the beaches at nine points along the northwestern shore of Africa. Their main objectives were three French North African port cities: Casablanca in Morocco, Oran and Algiers in Algeria. After securing these supply bases, the troops would race east into Tunisia to keep the ports of Tunis and Bizerte from falling into the hands of the famed German general, Erwin Rommel, and his Afrika Corps.

The planners of the North African landing, code-named Operation *Torch*, recognized that their first big hurdle would be of French making rather than German. Though defeated at home, the French still retained control of their colonies. The opinions of the French military officers in charge of these colonies toward the Allied cause varied widely. Some were openly pro-American, others anti-British, and still more were swayed by the fact that German troops occupied France.

Regardless of their personal opinions, the French officers were officially responsible to their superiors in Vichy, the seat of the government established to rule that part of France not actually occupied by the Germans. In return for being allowed to govern a portion of France, and retain their overseas possessions, Hitler had extracted a pledge from the Vichy government to defend those possessions in the event of an Allied invasion.

How sincerely the French in North Africa took that pledge was of major concern to the planners of *Torch*. Discreet diplomatic inquiries by the Americans failed to resolve the question completely but did seem to indicate the French would not seriously resist the American landing. This element of doubt led the Allied supreme commander, Lt. Gen. Dwight D. Eisenhower, to authorize a daringly unique plan to reduce the potential for unnecessary bloodshed. Several teams of American military officers, acting as Eisenhower's emissaries, would land with the first wave of assault troops, penetrate the enemy lines, find the French commanding officers, and ask for an armistice.

DEMAS T. CRAW
PIERPONT M. HAMILTON

The team that came ashore at Mehdia Plage, a resort town seventy miles north of Casablanca, consisted of two army air force officers, Col. Demas T. Craw and Maj. Pierpont M. Hamilton. Craw, a forty-two-year-old native of Traverse City, Michigan, was a career officer who had graduated from West Point in 1924 after serving in World War I as an infantryman. He learned to fly in 1929, then transferred to the army air force. As an observer with the Royal Air Force in Egypt in 1939, Craw gained firsthand experience with the Nazis when he flew several combat missions against them. Later, he was on duty in Athens when the Nazis overran Greece. After a short period of internment, he was released and sent to neutral Turkey. From there he made his way back to Washington.

Hamilton, born in Tuxedo, New York, on August 3, 1898, and a direct descendant of Alexander Hamilton, served in World War I as a flight instructor. Between the wars he had a successful career as an international banker. In March 1942 he was recalled to active duty.

Both men were assigned to the Western Task Force due to invade Morocco. When the call for volunteers went out for the behind-the-lines mission Craw and Hamilton volunteered. They would go ashore with the first wave of the 9th Infantry Division. Once on land they would proceed to Port Lyautey, five miles inland, and the site of the headquarters of the local French commander.

After they landed, the two officers, with their enlisted driver, boarded a jeep and started through the resort town. Shells from destroyers and cruises offshore crashed around them as they navigated the town's narrow streets. Answering fire from French artillery batteries added to the din. Just past the town they drove through a company of native Moroccan troops taking up positions in the predawn darkness. The three Americans held their breath, expecting a burst of fire any second. Instead, the Moroccans simply waved at them. The Americans drove on.

The next hurdle came when the jeep drove into the midst of a battery of French artillery. Feeling absurdly like a lost Sunday driver, Hamilton asked for directions to Port Lyautey. The young French officer obligingly pointed the way.

A mile down the road the jeep crested a small hill. A sudden blast of machine-gun fire shattered the early morning calm. Craw slumped in his seat, his chest torn apart by the bullets. Hamilton and the driver were taken prisoner by the French infantry patrol.

Escorted to Port Lyautey, Hamilton demanded to see the French commander. After explaining his mission of peace, he asked the colonel to issue a cease-fire order. He declined, saying he did not have the authority. Hamilton urged the man to convey the message to his superior. The Frenchman telephoned his general at Mekness, sixty miles farther inland. The general refused to take the responsibility, but promised to contact the next higher headquarters. Hamilton and his driver were made POWs and confined.

Two days passed during which Hamilton persisted in his efforts to induce the French to agree to an armistice. Back on the beach the fighting was not over. Oran and Algiers had capitulated fairly easily. In Morocco, after tough fighting, the U.S. troops had finally secured the beachheads north and south of Casablanca. But Casablanca itself was another matter. Enemy resistance stiffened as U.S. troops closed on the city. Rather than risk large casualties the onshore American commander, Maj. Gen. George S. Patton, decided to bomb Casablanca into submission. At daybreak on November 11, he planned a massive land, air, and naval bombardment of the city. A follow-up ground attack would force the city's surrender.

On the night of November 10, the French general finally recontacted Hamilton to agree to the cease-fire. Released from confinement, the two Americans reclaimed their jeep and headed toward the beach. A short distance past the airport Hamilton came upon an American tank unit. He used the platoon leader's radio to relay news of the French agreement. Word reached Patton at 6:48 A.M., just in time to call off the attack on Casablanca. "It was a near thing," he later said. "The bombers were over their targets and the battleships were in position to fire."

At 8:00 A.M. the armistice was signed. A significant loss of life was spared on each side.

For their incredible courage on this daring mission Craw and Hamilton received the Medal of Honor. Colonel Craw's widow accepted her husband's award from President Roosevelt in March 1943.

Major Hamilton remained with the American forces throughout the rest of the North African campaign before returning to Washington and a staff position at the Pentagon. He received his Medal of Honor on February 19, 1943. He retired from the air force in 1952 as a major general. His last years in uniform were spent in a senior air force policy-making position with NATO. He died on March 4, 1982.

Though Eisenhower hoped to exploit his quick victory in North Africa, it was not to be. A rejuvenated Afrika Corps halted the British Eighth Army eighty miles outside of Tunis on November 25. The armies clashed again just before Christmas, but the Allies did not have the staying power to overcome the Nazis. Eisenhower reluctantly ordered a withdrawal on Christmas Day.

Rommel renewed the attack on February 14, 1943. His panzers forced the Americans out of Tunisia. On February 19, his armored forces crushed the Americans at Kasserine Pass, sending them reeling back into Algeria.

Surprisingly, Rommel did not exploit his victory. Worried about the British threatening his rear from their positions in Libya, he pulled his Afrika Corps back through Kasserine Pass and headed southeast. On March 6 he met the British near Medenine. There the British won a stunning victory, destroying over fifty panzers. Three days later Rommel was removed from his command.

At about the same time, the demoralized Americans received a much-needed morale boost with the appointment of Major General Patton as the commander of the beaten II Corps. A tough, no-nonsense, profane man, Patton whipped his troops into shape through a rigid campaign of discipline and harsh training. To add punch to his armored divisions, Patton demanded some of the new Sherman tanks armed with 75-mm guns. At last the Americans had a tank that was a match for the feared Panzer IV.

At dawn on March 16, Patton launched an all-out attack against the western flank of the German line near El Guettar, Tunisia. With their new tanks blasting a path through the well-entrenched German positions, the II Corps easily rolled over the Germans. With Montgomery's Eighth Army exerting tremendous pressure from the south, the Germans had no choice but to withdraw.

The new Afrika Corps commander, Gen. Jurgen von Armin, established his defensive line along a ragged 130-mile arc that stretched from a point twenty-five miles west of Bizerte on Tunisia's north coast to the little town of Enfidaville, on the east coast about fifty miles south of Tunis. Here the Germans had to hold against the Allies or lose Africa.

The two-pronged attack against the Nazis began on April 19, 1943. The British drove on Enfidaville, soon running into stubborn resistance from a well-entrenched foe. The American II Corps, now under Maj. Gen. Omar Bradley since General Patton had been detached to work on the plans for the impending Sicilian invasion, moved toward Bizerte.

Vicious and bloody fighting exploded all along the line. The Nazis defended their key terrain positions with all the tenacity of bulldogs. At times, they even launched counterattacks. One such local counterattack came at a ridge called Djebel Dardys, northwest of the little town of Sedjenane a few miles inland from the Mediterranean Sea, on April 24. The three battalions of the 60th Infantry, 9th Infantry Division, had been battling the Germans for two days for this bit of ground.

At daybreak on the 24th deadly German 88-mm howitzer shells exploded among the American positions with brutal efficiency. The GIs burrowed deep into their holes, seeking protection in the earth. Behind the barrage several companies of Afrika Corps infantry, accompanied by a dozen tanks, moved steadily forward. A forward observer from the 60th Infantry's heavy weapons company saw that if he could break up the enemy infantry attack, the tanks would be left unprotected and be forced to withdraw.

Sgt. William L. Nelson, a twenty-five-year-old Delaware draftee, grabbed his radio and raced forward. Through the intense artillery barrage and under small arms fire, Nelson crawled up the slope to a position that looked down on the attacking Germans. He called down mortar shells on the Nazis, radioing corrections back to his mortar battery. He picked out one particular group of Germans, clustered behind a tank. With a skill born of hours of practice Nelson called in mortars right in their midst. German bodies flew through the air. The tank rolled forward a few yards, then turned back to its own lines.

Since he was concentrating fully on the Germans in front of him, Nelson didn't see the enemy soldier who crept up and tossed a grenade at him. The blast severely wounded him. Rather than seek medical attention, though, he moved from his hiding spot to a position only fifty yards away from the Germans. Completely exposed to their fire, Nelson ignored it to radio further firing instructions to the mortars. Before he died he knew his efforts had broken up the counterattack. More than 130 Germans lay sprawled on the slopes of Djebel Dardys, many of them killed by Nelson's mortar shells.

Four days later Company A, 6th Armored Infantry, 1st Armored Division, spearheaded an attack on German positions near Medjez-el-Bab, in the center of the German line. Suddenly, a machine gun opened up on Company A's left flank, driving the men to cover. Before the company could organize a response a Polish-born World War I veteran, Pvt. Nicholas Minue, rose to his feet. Ignoring the enemy fire that threw up dirt at his feet, Minue charged forward, right into the center of the German position. Pulling the trigger of his M-1 and using the razor-sharp bayonet mounted on its end, he quickly waded through the ten Germans manning the machine-gun nest. Then, as his stunned buddies watched in awe, Minue climbed out of the nest and went after other nearby enemy positions. He killed several more Germans before he was struck down. Inspired by Minue's daring attack the rest of Company A rose to its feet and rushed forward, sweeping the Germans before them.

In the face of such incredible heroism the Afrika Corps had no chance. It was only a matter of time before they collapsed. AT 3:30 A.M., May 6, 1943, the final Allied attack began. British troops fought their way into the outskirts of Tunis by noon. American GIs entered Bizerte on the afternoon of May 7. The final surrender of the famed Afrika Corps came on May 13. The Allies now possessed the ports necessary to support the first attack on a part of Fortress Europe herself: Sicily.

* * *

The decision to invade Sicily had been made at the January 1943 conference between President Roosevelt and Prime Minister Churchill at Casablanca. Though there were strategic differences between the Allies—the U.S. preferring a massive force making a bold crossing of the English Channel to open the Second Front Russian Premier Josef Stalin had been demanding for a year, and the British preferring to nibble away at the periphery of Hitler's empire until an opportunity developed to launch a decisive blow—logistical shortcomings precluded an immediate attack on France. Instead, the Allies agreed to maintain the momentum of the North Africa landings. They would assault and capture Sicily.

The tactics approved for Operation *Husky* called for Field Marshal Montgomery's Eighth Army to land four full divisions on the southeast coast of Sicily. General Patton's Seventh Army, consisting of the 1st, 3d, and 45th Infantry Divisions, several battalions of rangers and paratroopers, and the 2d Armored Division would go ashore on the south central shore. *Husky* would be the largest amphibious operation in history.

The heavily laden landing boats of Patton's Seventh Army began their run to the assault beaches at 2:00 A.M., July 10, 1943. So far, there had been no sign that the Germans and Italians knew any invasion fleet lay off their southern shore. The American commanders hoped it would stay that way.

Then a smoke pot burst into flames in the hold of LST (Landing Ship, Tank) 375. It was on a Higgins boat filled with high explosives, detonating fuses, and ammo. If the smoke pot lit off the explosives not only would many American die, but the eruption would prematurely announce the fleet's presence to the enemy.

Ens. John J. Parle took immediate action. Undaunted by the thick, acrid smoke filling the landing craft, he entered it, snuffed out an ignited fuse, and tried to put out the smoke pot. When he couldn't do so, he picked up the burning pot in both hands and carried it to the ship's rail. He dropped it overboard. The LST, and the invasion fleet, were safe. Parle collapsed on the deck, his lungs filled with black smoke. The twenty-three-year-old from Omaha, Nebraska, died one week later.

The landings went smoothly. Only sporadic resistance greeted the invaders. Within ninety minutes of landing some units had moved over one mile inland. At sea, the successive assault waves raced shoreward, adding depth to the initial punch. Throughout the day occasional counterattacks by German and Italian infantry and armor tried to stem the flow of Allied forces into Sicily, but were unsuccessful. By nightfall the Allied beachheads were very much intact.

The invasion troops began expanding their beachhead on July 11. In the 3d Infantry Division's area all three of its combat infantry regiments moved out against varying degrees of resistance. Company L, 15th Infantry, found itself pinned down by fierce enemy machine-gun fire near the village of Favarotta. One at a time three company officers tried to make their way around the gun's flanks, but all were hit.

Second Lt. Robert Craig, who had been drafted out of his Toledo, Ohio, home less than a year before, now crawled forward. With the aid of a squad leader he made his way to a boulder only thirty-five yards from the machine gun. One of the Germans saw him and shouted a warning. Before the gunner could swing his gun around Craig leaped from behind his rock, carbine blazing. He reached the gun, stood over it, and fired the rest of his clip into the three Germans. The company arose and moved forward.

A few hours later Craig was leading his platoon down the forward slope of a small ridge devoid of cover. Halfway down, one hundred Germans in concealed positions at the ridge's base opened fire. The men frantically looked for cover. There was none. Seeing this, Craig ordered his platoon to pull back over the ridge's crest while he moved forward. All alone, the sole target for a hundred Germans, Craig boldly ran down the slope, drawing the enemy's fire so his platoon could reach safety. When only twenty-five yards from the enemy's positions, and with no hope of survival, he knelt down and brought his carbine to his shoulder. He squeezed off a full clip, killing five and wounding three before he fell, riddled with German bullets.

The next major objective for the 3d Division was Agrigento, a sizable coastal town northwest of Licata. Over the twisted, potholed mountain roads the GIs overcame numerous strong points, and entered the town from the east. Sporadic street fighting broke out, but by 3:00 A.M. on July 17 Agrigento was in American hands. A few hours earlier a platoon from the 3d Reconnaissance Troop had been given a mission to locate a ranger patrol missing in the mountains north of Agrigento.

DAVID C. WAYBUR

The man who volunteered to locate the ranger patrol was a twenty-three-year-old platoon leader from Piedmont, California. David Waybur had enlisted in the army before Pearl Harbor. Because he had spent a lot of time on his mother's family's ranch near Red Bluff, California, it was only natural he ask for an assignment in a cavalry unit. Unfortunately, the army was phasing out its horse units. So, after basic training, Waybur found himself in a medical detachment.

Dissatisfied with that duty he applied for, and was accepted at, officer candidate school. Two weeks after Pearl Harbor he received his gold bars and an assignment to the 3d Infantry Division's reconnaissance troop then in training at Fort Lewis, Washington.

The recon unit was a handpicked outfit of 190 enlisted men and 7 officers. Divided into three platoons and a headquarters section, the troop's mission was simple—in jeeps and half-tracks they would explore ahead of the infantry, keeping the pressure on a retreating enemy and relaying current information about them to the infantry.

Waybur's platoon, like the others, consisted of two sections, each with four jeeps and a half-track, all mounting .30- or .50-caliber machine guns. In addition, he also had command of an 81-mm mortar squad, a 37-mm gun, and a demolition squad.

Waybur's unit landed near Licata on D-Day + 1. They were immediately sent to the front, charged with finding the enemy. For three days his platoon roamed the mountain roads north and west of Licata, fighting the Germans wherever they found them.

After helping the 7th Infantry Regiment move into Agrigento on the night of July 16, Waybur and the other two platoon leaders were called to their headquarters. There their commander, Capt. A. T. Netterblad, addressed them. "We're looking for a lost ranger patrol. They got through enemy lines at Agrigento. They're somewhere in the vicinity of Port Empodocle."

Port Empodocle lay ten miles beyond Agrigento. Since the rangers hadn't been heard from in over twenty-four hours it would be necessary to locate them, then leave them a radio so they could keep in touch with their headquarters. Netterblad asked for a volunteer. Waybur, though he'd been fighting for forty-eight hours spoke up. "I'll take it, sir." Netterblad nodded his approval.

Back at his platoon's position Waybur had no trouble rounding up volunteers. He had enough men for five jeeps and one half-track. In the moonlight he led his patrol out of Agrigento, past the infantrymen setting up their night outposts.

The narrow road to Port Empodocle ran through a steep-walled, rocky canyon. It was like moving down a narrow corridor. If they met the enemy, there'd be no place to turn around. They would only be able to back up.

A short distance past Agrigento the recon unit came upon a small cluster of houses. Waybur had the half-track and one of his jeeps remain there while he went on ahead with the others to reconnoiter the dark road.

The three-jeep patrol coasted slowly down a long incline, rounded a corner in the canyon, then approached a deep ravine, cut by a mountain stream. The bridge over it had been blown by the retreating Germans. It was about 3:00 A.M., July 17.

While he stood at the edge of the ravine trying to see a way across in the dark, Waybur heard a muffled rumble behind him. Thinking his half-track had come forward, Waybur hurried back to his jeeps. Just as he reached them two Italian tanks came around the bend in the road, the moonlight reflecting off their armor. Somehow, probably from a secondary road Waybur had missed in the dark, the tanks had moved in behind him.

Waybur looked for an escape route. The sides of the canyon were too steep. There was no cover on the slopes, no culverts or gullies in which to seek refuge. In front of him was the gorge. He was trapped.

He shouted orders to his men. The jeeps moved apart, making themselves more difficult targets and allowing more than one machine gun to bear on the tanks. At the same time two more enemy tanks clanked around the bend.

Waybur yelled, "Open fire!"

The .30- and .50-caliber machines burst into life. Ricocheting tracer rounds bounced off the tanks' armor, skyrocketing into the night. At that instant the lead tank fired its 27-mm cannon. The round slammed into Waybur's jeep.

His driver screamed "I'm hit!" and slumped down.

The gunner leaped off the burning jeep. Behind them the second jeep took a round from the tank's cannon. Two more of Waybur's men went down.

Waybur himself took a machine-gun round in each thigh. A

27-mm round exploded behind him, driving a piece of red-hot shrapnel into his back, dangerously close to his spine. He dropped to one knee. He yelled to his men, "Take cover! Get off the road!"

As they scrambled to obey, Waybur staggered to his jeep. With the lead tank now not more than thirty yards away, he grabbed his .45-caliber tommy gun from the vehicle. Standing in the bare road, in the bright moonlight, he poured a stream of bullets into the open ports of the tank, killing the driver. Out of control, the tank rumbled off the road and tumbled into the streambed below.

He then turned his attention to the three remaining tanks, but they retreated up the road, out of Waybur's range, but still able to keep the Americans pinned down. Waybur joined his men at the road's edge. He called one of the unwounded to him.

"Make your way down the streambed to our lines," he told the man. "Bring up the half-track and we'll squeeze these Italians between us."

The enlisted man made it to the rear and brought up not only the half-track and the other jeep, but a detachment of infantry as well. Meanwhile, Waybur and the rest of the troop spent two hours under fire from the tanks, periodically shooting back to convince the tanks it was still too unhealthy to come forward.

When the rescuing infantry arrived they found the tanks deserted. Apparently the Italian crews had heard them coming and took to the hills.

While he was being evacuated to the hospital, his men spread the tale of Waybur's David versus Goliath action. "Just three jeeps," the story went, "three jeeps took on four tanks. And the lieutenant knocked out one all by himself." The image of a bold young lieutenant standing smack in front of an enemy tank blazing away with a tommy gun inspired the men of the 3d Division to new heights in their fight against the Nazis.

Waybur spent several months in a hospital in North Africa recovering from his wounds. He then rejoined the 3d Recon Troop in Italy for more combat. After receiving his Medal of Honor from the Fifth Army commander, Gen. Mark Clark, on December 2, 1943, Waybur went back to the States for a much-needed rest and an emotional reunion with his family.

He could have stayed in the States, doing bond tours, taken a cushy desk job, but that wasn't Waybur's way. The cherub-faced hero requested a return to duty with the 3d Recon Troop. His request was granted.

While fighting deep in Germany on March 28, 1945, Waybur was killed in action.

A considerable rivalry had developed between the British and American commanders as they crossed the mountainous island. Each thought the other was seeking headlines at the expense of cooperation between the two forces. General Patton fueled the controversy when he made a bold, headlong dash to capture Palermo, the island's largest city situated on the north coast. Foot soldiers of the 3d Infantry Division entered the city on July 22, after racing across fifty-four rugged miles in one thirty-six-hour stretch.

On the eastern half of the island, Montgomery fought a methodical, measured campaign toward the main prize of Messina, on the northeast tip of Sicily. The field marshal preferred a slower approach to war, massing his men behind heavy artillery barrages before overwhelming an objective, as opposed to the Americans', or Patton's, bolder, direct frontal assaults.

As a result of the rivalry, Patton viewed the capture of Palermo as merely a stepping stone toward the prize of Messina. He turned his army east and told his commanders, "This is a horse race in which the prestige of the U.S. Army is at stake. We must take Messina before the British."

Patton leapfrogged his I Corps along the northern coasts in a series of behind-the-lines amphibious landings. His II Corps, under General Bradley, advanced along an interior highway that curved along Mount Etna's northern slope to the island's east coast. Besides the Germans and Italians Bradley's men also had to fight the terrain. The roads in mountainous northern Sicily were narrow, twisting, and steep, punctuated by tunnels and bridges easily defended then effortlessly blown up by a few Germans left behind with an automatic weapon. The only way to knock out these rearguard positions was the hard way: outflank them and kill the Germans with rifle fire and grenades.

On Bradley's right flank the 1st Infantry Division advanced along a mountain road. Progress was slow. The road was typical of the area, heavily mined and fiercely defended by fanatical Germans. On July 31, 1943, an advance element of the division's recon unit came up against a particularly stubborn position.

GERRY KISTERS

That morning, a company of the 91st Reconnaissance Squadron was bivouacked in the mountains near Nicosea. Their mission was to scout the road ahead for any sign of the Germans. Three bantams—three-quarter ton, low-slung armored vehicles mounting .50-caliber machine guns—headed out at first light. A short time later they returned. They had traveled two miles without seeing any Germans. The company commander decided to explore farther. He called for his first platoon leader, 2d Lt. Orsell C. Price. "Take another patrol up the road and don't stop until you meet some Germans."

Price organized three bantams. In the first vehicle rode a squad leader, Sgt. Gerry Kisters, in addition to the driver and a gunner. The other two vehicles each carried three men.

The patrol drove up the steep road, pausing frequently to examine any likely ambush sites before cautiously proceeding. The dirt road consisted of a series of sharp hairpin turns, with a cliff on the left and rugged slopes of various pitches to the right. At 2.7 miles from their starting point Kisters motioned the column to a halt. He jumped down and walked forward to examine a roadblock. The Germans had blown a large hole in the road. It would have to be filled before the patrol, and those behind them, could continue. Kisters reported the information to Price. The lieutenant radioed back to the company for a demolition truck and a bulldozer to come forward.

While the rest of the patrol relaxed, Kisters eyed the slopes above him suspiciously. He thought it was odd the Germans had prepared a roadblock and not defended it. Kisters reported his concerns to Price.

"If the Jerries are around here, they're probably over there," he said, pointing to a stone farmhouse a few hundred yards away to their right.

The two men decided to investigate.

Making their way through the rock-strewn terrain as carefully as they could, the two were surprised when they suddenly stumbled on four Germans relaxing in a machine-gun emplacement at the base of a large boulder.

Kisters and Price whipped their rifles up. Before they could say anything the Germans had their hands in the air. "Kamerad!" they shouted.

The Americans ordered the Germans away from their guns.

While Price covered him Kisters began disarming the men. He had just begun when the deadly chatter of machine gun erupted from above them. Kisters, Price, and the four German prisoners hit the ground. The second machine gun, not more than twenty-five yards uphill, sent a torrent of bullets snapping overhead. Kisters made a decision.

He turned to Price, "You stay here and guard the prisoners. I'll go up and get the gun." Before Price could respond Kisters crawled out of the nest. He had only his carbine and one fifteen-round clip.

He could see the gun, hidden behind some brush, its barrel spitting flame as it raked the area with fire. Kisters later said the bullets were passing so close to him he could feel their heat.

Behind the brush he detected movement. He fired. Every time he saw movement he fired. Meanwhile, German snipers farther up the slope took him under fire.

The first round to hit him ricocheted off a rock, then buried itself deep in Kisters's left leg just above the ankle, ripping muscles and tendons. Kisters thought he'd been hit by a sledgehammer.

Within seconds six more bullets ripped into his damaged leg. Still he lay there firing into the brush. At last the machine gun stopped. A lone figure burst from the undergrowth and started up the hill. Later, three dead Germans were found sprawled in the empty machine-gun nest.

Kisters fired his final rounds at the fleeing German. As he did so a seventh bullet slammed into him. This one tore into his right arm, just above the elbow, destroying the nerves and leaving the arm numb and useless.

With that final shot the snipers pulled out. Silence fell over the hillside. Kisters, bleeding profusely from his seven wounds, yelled down to Price, "Bring those prisoners up. I'm hit."

Price quickly bandaged Kisters's wounds, then had the prisoners carry him to the road. From there a bantam raced him to an aid station. Surgeons worked frantically to save his life. They succeeded. He spent a few more days in the hospital before being sent back to North Africa.

Before he left, Lt. Price visited Kisters in the hospital. "I'm putting you in for a commission," he said. "And a little something to go with what you got in Tunisia."

Price was referring to the Distinguished Service Cross Kisters had earned on May 7, 1943, near Ferryville. On that day he single-handedly knocked out a German 88-mm artillery piece and its crew, saving the lives of his squad. The award had just been approved on July 26, and had not yet been awarded.

Born March 29, 1919, in Salt Lake City, Utah, Kisters grew up in Bloomington, Indiana. After he graduated from high school in 1937, he joined his father in the family fur business. Drafted in January 1941, Kisters joined the newly organized 91st Recon Squadron, training with it in California and Texas before heading to North Africa in December 1942.

Kisters received his promised battlefield promotion to second lieutenant on January 28, 1944, while he was a patient at Nichols Army Hospital, Louisville, Kentucky. At the same time he learned he would receive the Medal of Honor for his gallantry on Sicily.

On February 8, 1944, General Marshall pinned the DSC to Kisters's tunic, then escorted him to the White House where President Roosevelt personally pinned the Medal of Honor next to the DSC.

It would be another year before Kisters was recovered enough from his wounds to return to active duty. He spent his final months in uniform in an administrative slot. After the war he returned to his fur business in Bloomington.

He died on May 11, 1986.

Three more weeks of hard fighting remained after Kisters's gallant action before Sicily was secure. Patton won the race to Messina; the vanguard of the American troops cautiously entered the city on August 17. A week earlier, the German commander, Field Marshal Albert Kesselring, had given the order to begin the evacuation of troops and equipment across the narrow Strait of Messina to Italy. Nearly forty thousand Germans and seventy-five thousand Italians made good their escape.

For the Americans, the thirty-eight-day fight for Sicily provided a valuable preview of the fighting that lay ahead in Italy. The battle for the Italian peninsula would prove to be an eighteen-month struggle with numerous opportunities for extraordinary heroism.

8

* * *

Invasion of Italy

The Allied campaign for Italy was a creature of improvisation. It did not spring forth from the mind of a military genius—it simply grew. General Eisenhower received instructions in May 1943 to "plan such operations" after Sicily "as are best calculated to eliminate Italy from the war and to contain the maximum number of German forces."

Eisenhower needn't have worried about getting Italy out of the war. After two decades of Fascist rule and five years of war the Italian people were weary. Not only was the country's military posture weak, its economy was a shambles. When it became obvious Sicily would fall and nothing could prevent the Allies from invading Italy, King Victor Emmanuel III acted. On July 25, 1943, he replaced the dictator Mussolini with Field Marshal Pietro Badoglio.

Badoglio immediately pledged his country's undying loyalty to the Axis camp. But, by July 31, he had sent emissaries to the Allies to negotiate a separate peace. The Allies accepted his overture. Eisenhower and Badoglio simultaneously announced Italy's surrender on September 8. The next day Allied forces landed at Salerno, Italy.

Lt. Gen. Mark Clark's Fifth Army controlled the Salerno invasion force. The VI Corps, comprised of the U.S. 36th and 45th Infantry Divisions, would go ashore on the southern beaches. The northern beaches belonged to the two British infantry divisions of the X Corps.

Salerno was selected for the invasion site because it not only offered good beaches for the landing craft, but had good harbor facilities for the future landing of supplies. Not far inland ran a railroad and the main coastal highway running from Salerno to Naples and, eventually, Rome.

Salerno had several disadvantages. Enemy artillery emplaced in the mountains surrounding the beaches could do severe damage to the invaders. In fact, the German commander, Field Marshal Albert Kesselring, called the commanding heights, "God's gift to the gunners." And once the beachhead was consolidated, the Allies would have to move toward Naples through the formidable Sorrento hills, in which there were only two narrow, easily defended gorges.

GIs from the 36th Infantry Division began landing at Salerno at 3:30 A.M., September 9. The Texas National Guardsmen of Maj. Gen. Fred L. Walker's division were well trained and brave, but had no combat experience. They would learn quickly. Formidable German resistance greeted them as they leaped from the landing boats onto Salerno's sandy beaches. Enemy tanks backed by heavily defended machine guns fired on the GIs, sending them scrambling for cover behind dunes, rocks, and patches of scrub. German artillery shells erupted in geysers of sand and water among the boats and clusters of infantrymen.

Despite the stiff enemy resistance, by 7:00 A.M. the Texans had pushed inland nearly one thousand yards. Then German tanks, aided by machine guns spotted along a four-foot-high stone fence, suddenly counterattacked the 141st Infantry Regiment. They fired point-blank at the American infantrymen strung out along the flat terrain. Voluntarily exposing himself to the tanks' fire, Sgt. James M. Logan, a Texas oil field wildcatter, shot three Germans rushing through a break in the wall.

Logan then dashed across two hundred yards of open ground, his path traced by a stream of machine-gun bullets. When he reached the wall, he crawled along its base until he came to a machine gun. Jumping up, he shot the two German gunners, hurdled the wall, and seized the gun. He swung it around, then opened fire on the Germans crouched along the wall. After he had cleared the area of the enemy he smashed the gun on the rocks. Later, he captured a Nazi officer and private who were trying to sneak away.

The gallantry of Sergeant Logan, who would later earn a DSC to wear along with his Medal of Honor, and other brave 36th Division soldiers quashed the German attack by noon. The division moved four miles inland, capturing its objectives, including a long portion of the main highway.

The next day the 36th Infantry Division, reinforced by two regiments of the 45th Infantry Division, began a push into the hills west of Salerno. Their main objectives were Hill 424 and the village of Altavilla, both of which held commanding views of the Salerno beachhead.

Resistance proved tough, but the GIs were tougher. Both targets fell after bitter fighting. Unwilling to concede the Salerno beachhead so easily, Kesselring organized a counterattack. Two German divisions, the elite Hermann Goering Division and the 15th Panzer Grenadier Division, rushed south from their rest camp north of Naples. On September 13, they hit Hill 424 and Altavilla with a furious attack. The fight to hold Altavilla produced one of the most celebrated heroes of World War II.

CHARLES E. KELLY

Cpl. Charles E. Kelly's combat career began with a splash. While running across the beach at Salerno he sought refuge in a drainage ditch. He dropped his Browning automatic rifle (BAR) in the slimy water. It took him several frantic minutes to retrieve the weapon from the oozy bottom and another half hour to clean it. Then he raced off to find his buddies. They took great delight in Kelly's predicament. It was just another typical problem for Kelly, one of the company's malcontents.

Born on September 23, 1920, Kelly grew up in the gritty tenement area of Pittsburgh's tough north side. The Kelly family lived in a dilapidated shack in an alley behind a rundown apartment building. They had no electricity; kerosene lanterns provided light. They had no bathroom; the eleven Kellys shared a smelly outhouse with several other alley families.

After finishing grade school Kelly worked as a paperhanger's helper for ten dollars a week. He wanted to be a truck driver, but there was little work in the depression. When work slowed down Kelly, a tough youngster, roamed the streets with the local gangs. A slender, wiry youth with a mop of wavy black hair, he had several arrests for gang brawls but no convictions. In those neighborhoods the beat cops often administered their own justice. They knew Kelly well.

A few days after Pearl Harbor Kelly enlisted in the army, volunteering for the infantry. The day before he left for basic training he swaggered up to the cops on the beat and bragged, "I'll go fight this war while you 4-Fs guard the vegetable wagons." Then he strutted away.

Kelly did not take well to army discipline. His bunk often lay rumpled, his uniform was unkempt, and his shoes rarely carried a shine. Though he shot expert on the rifle range he had an unorthodox way of aiming. He sighted with his left eye instead of his right. That caused no end of harassment from the drill instructors.

Kelly did demonstrate an unnerving curiosity about explosives. He would unscrew the cap of a hand grenade and pour the powder out. At other times he'd pull the fuse from a 60-mm mortar shell then shake it to see if anything inside rattled. "God, Kelly," a sergeant yelled one day. "Do you want to blow us all up?"

After basic Kelly volunteered for the paratroopers. The tough training suited him just fine, until he visited a sick friend in the base hospital. The sight of all the airborne trainees recuperating from broken arms, legs, and backs shook Kelly. He didn't want to end up like that. Depressed, he went AWOL.

Back home Kelly told his folks he was on leave. But after three weeks they began questioning him. Rumors spread through the neighborhood that he was a coward.

One night he casually strolled into an alley. Two cops hemmed him in. "You're AWOL," growled the oldest officer. "But now you're going back, aren't you?" Their threats worked.

At his court-martial Kelly entered a plea of guilty. He received a twenty-eight-day restriction and a fine of one month's pay. Then he was shipped out to the 36th Infantry Division, staging at Camp Edwards, Massachusetts, for overseas movement.

It was a strange outfit for a city boy, but Kelly soon found himself at home among the boisterous Texans. They were just as cocky as he and even more eager for a fight, and his sergeants didn't care which eye he used to aim. They just wanted him to hit what he aimed at.

After the bloody beach fighting at Salerno Kelly and his company pushed inland, headed for Altavilla. The little village sat atop a vine-covered, terraced mountain six miles from the beach. Late on September 13, Kelly's company entered the enemy-occupied town. Mortar shells exploded on the streets while machine guns chattered ominously from the rooftops. Enemy snipers were everywhere.

The company took up positions in a three-story house, filling the place with arms and ammunition. The Germans poured artillery on them from nearby hill positions, the shells crashing into the thick stone walls, filling the house with smoke and dust. Soon, nearly half of the one hundred original GIs were casualties. Later that night Kesselring's counterattack struck. American reinforcements tried but were unable to reach Altavilla. The Americans there were surrounded.

Throughout the siege Kelly proved to be one of the toughest fighters. He took an exposed position in an upper-story window and rained fire down on the attackers. Every time he detected movement he sent a deadly stream of bullets tearing into the night. He wore out one BAR, the barrel warping from the intense heat. He then picked up a tommy gun and used that to mow down a squad of Germans entering the house's courtyard.

Kelly especially liked to shoot the fanatical SS troopers. They attacked with a cold-blooded fury. Scrambling across the stone wall they would run up to the house's windows and spray away with their "burp" guns. Whenever they came Kelly would be there, firing into the courtyard, his green eyes cold and expressionless above his weapon. Soon the courtyard was littered with gray-clad bodies.

By the next afternoon the defenders had run out of hand grenades. The attackers swarmed into the courtyard, screaming and firing their weapons. Kelly then performed an experiment that his basic training instructors had forbidden. Holding a 60-mm mortar shell in his hand, he pulled the pin and the safety lock, tapped the shell on the windowsill to remove the secondary pin, then lobbed it down on the Germans gathered below.

A deafening blast resulted. The other GIs thought a big artillery shell had hit them. Then someone said, "It's only Kelly dropping mortar shells from upstairs."

Kelly's shells did the trick. He threw at least a half-dozen, killing twenty Germans. The rest retreated.

By nightfall only thirty GIs remained unwounded. The company commander wisely ordered a withdrawal. They would leave in groups of six. Those too badly wounded to walk would be left behind.

Before the first group left, Kelly sauntered up to his commanding officer. "I'll cover the rear," he volunteered.

"OK, Kelly," said the officer. "Good luck."

As the men began pulling out Kelly again stationed himself at the window, a bazooka across his shoulder. The tremendous back-blast from the first round knocked him off his feet, so he gave up on that weapon. He grabbed a BAR and went to work, firing at the Germans darting around in the night.

When the last group filtered out through the alley Kelly hid in the shadows behind the house, his BAR at his hip, waiting for the Germans to come through the house and out the back door. As they filled the doorway Kelly stepped forward, his finger holding the trigger back. The weapon bucked heavily, leveling everyone in the doorway. After emptying his last two clips into the crowd of Germans, he tossed the smoking gun aside and took off. It had been a great fight while it lasted, but now it was time to get out.

After Altavilla more tough fighting loomed ahead of Kelly. He took forty-four men across the bloody Rapido River. Eight came back. At Cassino his company took such heavy casualties that Kelly, by then a sergeant, was the highest ranking man left alive.

On March 11, 1944, while the 36th Division was in a rest camp near Naples, Kelly received the Medal of Honor for his actions at Altavilla. Four days later he went back into battle, the Medal of Honor stuffed in his pocket.

A few weeks later Kelly, now dubbed "Commando" by war correspondents, received the greatest reward of them all: He was going home. Pittsburgh threw a huge parade for the former gang member. The mayor gave him a key to the city. Kelly wore a neat and tidy uniform, but he still had a haughty swagger in his walk.

Besides the fame, the Medal of Honor brought financial reward to Kelly. A publisher gave him $40,000 for his story. A Hollywood producer paid him $25,000 for the rights to a movie about his war experience. Kelly used some of the money to buy his parents a house with electricity and indoor plumbing. He used the rest to buy a gas station.

The postwar years were not good to Kelly. He preferred to remain out of the limelight, but his fame was too great. People pestered him constantly to tell his story. More often than not, well-meaning questioners rewarded him with a drink. Then his first wife died in 1951, leaving him with two small children and a mountain of bills. He lost his gas station. He moved to Louisville, Kentucky, where he did well with a contracting business until a strike shut him down. The war hero couldn't find work and, since he was ineligible for unemployment compensation, was forced to go on welfare to feed his family. For awhile he lived in government housing.

Kelly eventually found work as a house painter, moving his second wife and their six children first to California, then Washington, D.C. After a hit-and-run driver ran him down on a Washington street, breaking both his legs, word of his plight reached veterans' groups in Pittsburgh. They raised enough money to bring him back to Pittsburgh and give him an apartment. He got a job as a maintenance man in a senior citizens' complex.

When Commando Kelly died on January 11, 1985, his brother, Howard, said of the pressures Kelly faced as a well-known war hero, "He couldn't handle it as well as somebody else might have been able to. He moved around a lot, never settled down. I never knew what he was looking for."

Kesselring's counterattack came perilously close to driving the Allies from Salerno. Only the timely arrival of reinforcements stemmed the onslaught. But the Germans were not defeated. Their withdrawal into the rugged Apennine Mountains was part of Kesselring's master plan to make the Allies pay dearly for every square foot of Italian soil.

Through the jagged ridges and valleys of the Apennines the GIs pursued the Germans north toward Naples. Combat in the mountains of Italy was worse than in Sicily. There was little flat land for deployment of armored vehicles. Italy would be an infantryman's war.

It took two more weeks of heavy fighting before Naples fell to the Allies. Within six more days Allied troops had advanced to the Volturno River, twenty miles north of Naples, where exhaustion and a stubborn German defense brought them to a halt.

While the Americans regrouped preparatory to crossing the Volturno, Kesselring rushed to complete a series of defensive positions designed to slow their movement toward Rome. First came the Barbara Line, seven miles north of the Volturno. Here

Kesselring hoped to hold the Allies while defenses behind it were strengthened. Next came the Bernhard Line, developed in depth along a series of fortified mountain positions. Finally, there was the Gustav Line. Anchored on a superb natural fortress, Monte Cassino, Gustav was the strongest of all.

Two American infantry divisions, the 3d and 34th, crossed the Volturno River on the night of October 12–13, 1943. One hundred and fifty feet in width and ranging from three to six feet in depth, the Volturno was well protected by strongly defended German emplacements on its north side. By the night of October 13, the Americans were across the Volturno in sufficient strength to have driven the Germans off several strategic hills.

During the crossing Capt. Arlo L. Olson, Company F, 15th Infantry Regiment, 3d Infantry Division, knocked out one German machine gun with a pair of hand grenades. While guiding his company to their positions on the north side of the river he went after two more enemy positions. He killed eight Germans, captured six, and wiped out two more machine guns. Over the next two weeks the GIs fought their way north, meeting their enemy on every hillside and in every village. Throughout the entire two-week period Captain Olson consistently demonstrated a fearlessness and courage that inspired his men to overcome every obstacle the Germans threw at them.

At noon on October 27, north of San Felice, the South Dakota–raised infantry officer charged headlong into an enemy strongpoint blocking Company F's advance. Armed only with a pistol, Olson took one of his platoons right into the German position. When the gun smoke cleared, twelve Germans lay dead and seven were headed to the rear as prisoners.

The next objective lay two thousand yards north. Under Olson's valiant guidance Company F quickly overran it. He had begun organizing his company for an anticipated counterattack when a German mortar shell fell on his small command group. A lieutenant, a radio operator, and Olson were all fatally wounded. While being carried by mule train to an evacuation hospital several ridge lines to the south, Captain Olson died.

The heroism of men like Captain Olson carried the Americans through Kesselring's Barbara Line. By the end of October, the 3d and 34th Infantry Divisions stood poised at the southern entrance of the formidable Mignano Gap. A narrow, six-mile-long, north-south corridor dominated by numerous sharp peaks, including Mount Rotundo, Mount Lungo, Mount Camino, and Mount Cesima, the Mignano Gap led straight to the Benedictine monastery atop Monte Cassino, along the flooded Rapido River. Before the Americans could claim the grand prize of Rome, all this ground had to be captured. The Germans knew it and prepared their defenses accordingly.

In early November, accompanied by the thunder of massed artillery pieces, American troops began their push through the Mignano Gap. German resistance was fierce. Enemy forces on the hilltops brought accurate fire to bear on the attackers with an intensity rarely seen in World War II. Even after the GIs managed to struggle to the top of a hill, the Nazis frequently counterattacked, trying to throw the Americans off their newly won real estate. A former professional football player leading Company L, 30th Infantry, 3d Division, found himself in that precarious position on November 10, 1943.

MAURICE L. BRITT

Because he wore a size 13½ shoe Maurice L. Britt carried the nickname "Footsie." As a star end for the University of Arkansas Razorbacks and the Detroit Lions, Britt used those big feet to break up plays in the opposing backfields. It was a habit he took to war.

Born June 29, 1919, at Carlisle, Arkansas, Britt played both basketball and football at the University of Arkansas. The six-foot, three-inch, 220-pound end received an honorable mention all-American in 1939 and 1940. When he graduated in 1941 with a degree in journalism Britt signed on with the Lions.

He played one season, then on December 5, 1941, because he held a reserve commission through ROTC, answered the call to active duty. Britt spent his entire military career with Company L, 30th Infantry Regiment. He landed in Africa as a platoon leader, battled Rommel in Tunisia, made the initial and four more of the amphibious landings in Sicily, then came ashore at Salerno.

When his company commander was evacuated from wounds suffered in the fighting north of Salerno, Britt assumed command. On September 22, 1943, in the drive toward Naples, Britt earned a Silver Star by knocking out a German tank with an antitank rifle grenade. That same day he picked up his first

Purple Heart when an exploding German mortar drove shrapnel into his arm.

In the fighting north of the Volturno on October 29, 1943, a German sniper's shot knocked one of Britt's officers to a ledge on a cliff face. Rather than wait for the safety of night, Britt disregarded the enemy fire, climbed down the rocky cliff, retrieved the wounded man, then carried him to safety. This deed earned Britt a Bronze Star.

In the Mignano Gap Britt's company, whittled down to just sixty-five men, struck the east side of Mount Rotundo on November 8, 1943, catching the Germans by surprise and throwing them off the hill. The counterattacks started almost immediately and continued in mounting intensity for forty-eight hours. By the morning of November 10, only fifty-five men remained in Company L. They were thinly spread across nine hundred yards of Mount Rotundo's eastern slope. To add punch to the defense the battalion heavy-weapons company placed a machine gun on Company L's south flank. Britt sent four riflemen to protect it.

Just after 8:30 A.M. that day, a German counterattack overran the isolated machine gun. As a shield, the Germans made the four captured American riflemen walk in front of them as they came up the hill. Britt spotted the ruse when they were fifty yards away. "Take off!" he called out to the captive GIs. "They can't hurt you. We're going to open up!"

When the four captives broke for cover, Britt and the GIs around him loosed a barrage of rifle fire downhill. One of the men crouched near Britt watched in fascination as the husky officer ran back and forth across the little defensive line, firing his carbine at every sight and sound from the Germans.

Suddenly, Britt barked "Ow!" and grabbed his side. Blood seeped through his grimy fingers. Instead of seeking help, though, Britt simply tossed aside his empty carbine and grabbed an M-1 rifle from a badly wounded man. He also picked up some hand grenades and went out into a wooded area ahead of the position looking for Germans. A few minutes later his men saw him throwing grenades, disregarding machine-pistol bursts hitting all around him.

For more than two hours Britt defended the heart of his sector against the determined enemy. His men credited him with personally knocking out one machine-gun nest and killing no less than eight Germans. His actions prevented the fragile line from cracking.

Though wounded several times by mortar fragments during the action, Britt refused to be evacuated. "I've got to get back up on the hill to help my boys," he told the battalion surgeon.

For his actions on Mount Rotundo Britt would receive the Medal of Honor at an impressive ceremony held at Razorback Stadium, Fayetteville, Arkansas, on June 5, 1944. But before that happened he had a lot of war left to fight. In mid-November, the 3d Infantry Division was pulled out of the line for rebuilding before storming ashore at Anzio, south of Rome, on January 22, 1944. Four days later Britt, now a captain, led his company in an attack on a vital crossroads at Della Crucetta. The Germans were absolutely determined not to yield this strategic bit of ground. They reinforced it with tanks, flak wagons, and ground troops.

It was a brutal battle. Neither side asked or gave any quarter. Vicious hand-to-hand fighting raged across the battleground. Americans and Germans lay sprawled in death just inches from one another. One particular German machine gun played havoc with the GIs. To force the machine-gun nest to reveal itself, Britt actually stood up in full view of the enemy. Twice he clapped his hands above his head, as if he were doing a "jumping jack" exercise. When he spotted the gun he fell back to the ground. He radioed the nest's location back to the mortars. Seconds later he grinned with satisfaction as the lethal rounds fell from the sky, destroying the gun. Britt had just earned the DSC.

In mid-February Britt was in his command post at the rear of a stone farmhouse. While he talked over the field telephone to a nearby artillery battery a German tank rumbled up the road outside. At point-blank range the panzer fired its cannon into the farmhouse. The armor-piercing shell passed through three stone walls before it exploded in Britt's small room. The blast hurled him against the wall, ripped his right arm off at the elbow, and fractured his leg. Dazed, Britt retrieved his severed arm from the debris with his left hand. "This is it," he said. Then he passed out.

Britt spent several months in stateside hospitals recovering from his painful wounds. After receiving his Medal of Honor Britt went on a War Bond drive. In ceremonies on the steps of the New York Public Library on Pearl Harbor Day, 1944, Britt received the DSC for his Anzio heroism. When that medal was pinned to his tunic, he became the first person in history to earn America's four highest valor awards.

Following his discharge on December 27, 1944, Britt returned to the University of Arkansas to study law. Before he graduated he went to work for a local firm. In 1966 he successfully ran for lieutenant governor of Arkansas. He served two terms, then became director of the Arkansas Small Business Administration.

The successes of the gallant GIs of the 3d Infantry Division were not enough to break through Kesselring's formidable defenses at Mignano. On November 15, General Clark called a halt to the offensive operations. For the next two weeks his Fifth Army would rest and refit for a renewed attack.

On November 20, Montgomery's Eighth Army, on Italy's east coast, pushed off on a new offensive. Initially, considerable ground was gained, but the British soldiers bogged down after Kesselring shifted a division eastward from the Mignano area. Quick to detect a thinning of the German lines, General Clark renewed his offensive on December 1. A British division under his command fought for five days to clear Monte Camino, on the Mignano Gap's left side. The U.S. 36th Infantry Division had two battalions chewed up in the fighting for the mountain village of San Pietro. The die-hard Nazi defenders did not relinquish their hold on San Pietro until December 16.

The new Allied offense had been under way for two weeks and still had not yet reached the halfway point to the main German defensive line at Cassino. To all outward appearances the Italian campaign was stalemated. It might have remained so had not Prime Minister Churchill revived a cancelled plan for an amphibious landing behind German lines.

A two-division, end-run amphibious landing behind the German lines at Anzio, just twenty miles south of Rome, had been considered in November. The failure of the Allies to punch through the Mignano Gap had cancelled the idea. At the Big Three conference at Teheran in early December Churchill convinced Roosevelt and Stalin of the benefits of the plan. Though they were reluctant, the notion of quickly ending the stalemate in Italy and capturing Rome swayed the two leaders.

The January 22, 1944, assault at Anzio would be preceded by yet another renewed offensive by the Fifth Army. During the first two weeks of January the battle-worn GIs put forth an extraordinary effort and, at an alarmingly high casualty rate, overcame the last strong points before Cassino and the Gustav Line. Clark's army now stood at the entrance to the heavily defended Liri Valley.

Clark's plan called for the capture of the high ground on either side of Cassino, then a crossing of the Rapido River into the center of the valley's mouth. Once a bridgehead had been established across the Rapido, an armored division would make a headlong dash to link up with the Anzio forces.

The Rapido River did not appear formidable. Only twenty-five to fifty feet wide, it flowed between steep banks four feet high. But its waters ran ice-cold, fast, and ten feet deep. All trees on both sides of the river had been cut down, giving the Germans an unobstructed field of fire. They had also opened upriver dams, turning the ground for nearly a mile on both sides of the river into a marsh. Thousands of mines had been strewn throughout the approaches to the river. Since no roads led to the river the assault troops would have to carry their boats and rafts two miles to the crossing sites. And because the Germans had artillery and mortars zeroed in on the approaches, the 36th Infantry Division would make the crossing at night.

THOMAS E. MCCALL

The attack began at 8:00 P.M. on January 20. A heavy fog cut visibility to a few yards. General Walker planned to put his 141st Infantry Regiment across the river upstream of the ruined town of San Angelo; the 143rd Infantry would cross downstream. With bayonets fixed to their rifles, the infantrymen lugged their four hundred-pound, twelve-man wooden assault boats across the mile-wide marsh. Before they were halfway across, German artillery shells started dropping among them. Entire squads of men disappeared in brief flashes of fire.

One of the men working his way toward the hell of the Rapido River was a machine-gun section leader in Company F, 143d Infantry. S. Sgt. Thomas E. McCall, born May 9, 1916, at Burton, Kansas, grew up on a farm near Veedersburg, Indiana. A member of the Indiana National Guard, McCall found himself transferred to the 36th Infantry Division while that unit was staging at Camp Edwards, Massachusetts.

McCall made the initial landing at Salerno, earning a Silver

Star a few days later. By the time of the Rapido crossing McCall was one of the few remaining original members of his company. Fate had been kind, sparing him while others around him were cut down, but his luck would soon run out.

When McCall's company reached the river nearly half of its boats had already been destroyed or abandoned. Under heavy fire engineers desperately worked to erect portable bridges. McCall, ignoring the bombardment around him, hustled his men into the remaining boats. "Let's get at it," he said. "The fighting's over there."

Across the ice-choked Rapido the infantrymen paddled their clumsy boat. McCall knelt in the bow, firing his M-1 into the darkness ahead. On the opposite bank he quickly dispersed his remaining men, directing their fire on German positions.

Only about a thousand men from the 143d Infantry made it across the river. As dawn broke they came under even heavier fire directed by enemy observers from heights on both flanks. Sensing annihilation, the battalion commander ordered a withdrawal. By 10:00 A.M. McCall, and all the others who were able to do so, had made their way back across the Rapido.

Late that afternoon, under a heavy smoke screen, the 143d Infantry tried again. Earlier, McCall's company commander had called him aside.

"Wait until dark," the lieutenant said. "Then take your machine guns across the one footbridge that's still up. If you make it, set up a gun on each side of the road and shoot anyone that moves down it. Got it?"

"Yes, sir," McCall answered simply.

In the darkness before the bridge McCall turned to the men around him. "You ready?" He didn't wait for an answer. "Let's go!"

McCall jumped onto the bridge, took two steps, and went sprawling. A thin layer of ice coated the wooden structure. He swore under his breath. German artillery shells smashed into the water on either side of the bridge. If he stayed there he would die.

Staggering to his feet he started running across the bridge. Slipping and sliding, he zigzagged across the bridge. Somehow, he made it to the other side. Behind him a handful of his men ran across the bridge. The rest were gone, killed or wounded.

McCall flopped down behind a small mound of frozen dirt to

escape the grazing machine-gun fire and survey the land. Several hundred yards of flat ground lay between him and the road. It was suicide to move forward, but his guns were needed to support the GIs crossing the river behind him.

He started toward the road. Bending low and firing his M-1, McCall led his men across the exposed terrain in a zigzag path. When he stopped he had five men and two machine guns with him. He put one gun in a shallow depression alongside the road, then led the remaining three men across it. He stayed with them long enough to ensure the gun was sighted properly, then started back across the bullet-swept road. A scream warned him of an incoming artillery round. As he flung himself flat the shell exploded, covering him with snowy dirt.

When he looked back at the gun he had just left he recoiled in horror. "My God!" he muttered. The shell had exploded right next to the position. The gunner, bleeding heavily, lay on the ground, writhing in pain. One look at the assistant gunner and McCall knew he was beyond help. The third man lay unconscious where the blast had thrown him. The gun was ruined.

Unmindful of the danger, McCall crawled back to them. He managed to stop the flow of blood gushing from the gunner's wound, then pulled him to safety into a ditch. He yelled across the road to his other gun, "Fire! Knock out that damn machine-gun nest."

There was no answer: no sound except the staccato burst of the enemy gun a few hundred feet up the road. McCall called out again. Still no answer.

Frustrated at his inability to get the gun into action, McCall disregarded the stream of lead flying across the ground to dash back across the road. He found both men dead, killed by shrapnel from another exploding shell. McCall was the only man still on his feet!

McCall realized the German machine gun in front of him was preventing the men behind him from expanding the bridgehead. If he could knock it out. . . .

Reaching down, he grabbed the .30-caliber machine gun, the ammo belt dangling on the frozen ground, and ran forward—directly toward the Nazi machine gun.

The enemy gunners tried to cut McCall down, but in their shock and fear missed him. Seconds later, McCall stood over them, his legs spread wide. He opened fire. He didn't miss. His raking fire killed the gun's crew.

A second enemy machine gun now fired on McCall from his left. The sergeant, moving as if his anger and frustration had hypnotized him, turned and charged this gun, too. Still firing from the hip, he riddled the German crew and silenced that weapon.

A third machine gun, fifty yards behind the second, next opened fire. When last seen, McCall was boldly walking toward that gun, firing his weapon in short, measured bursts. He disappeared in the roar of an exploding artillery shell.

To McCall's rear the battle raged on through the night and into the next day. Most of the pontoon bridges the engineers had built were destroyed one by one throughout the day. Small groups of shaken and wounded men made their way back to the river. Many of them drowned trying to swim to safety. As night fell again, the sound of American weapons firing on the far bank grew fainter, then stopped completely. By 11:00 P.M. on January 23, every American on the German side was either dead or a prisoner. In an action lasting just over forty-eight hours nearly seventeen hundred men were lost without making a dent in the German defenses.

One of the prisoners of the Germans was S. Sgt. Thomas McCall. After his liberation in 1945, McCall explained what happened. "After I started toward the third nest an artillery shell landed near me and tore me up pretty good. When I awakened I was in a German aid station. An English-speaking German officer told me that my war was over. I told him to go to hell and the next day I was on my way to a POW camp."

McCall left the army after the war, but he found life on the family farm in Indiana too quiet for him. He reenlisted. He went to Korea when fighting broke out there. He lasted five days before being wounded and evacuated. When he recovered he went on recruiting duty for the army. He planned to retire in June 1966, twenty-six years after he first enlisted.

He almost made it. On the afternoon of September 18, 1965, McCall and his eight-year-old son were fishing on the Susquehanna River near Fort Meade, Maryland. Without warning the locks on a nearby dam were opened. The onrushing waters swamped the small boat.

The sergeant kept his son afloat until onlookers threw the boy a line and pulled him to safety. Exhausted by his ordeal, McCall slipped beneath the water. His body was recovered downstream a few days later.

While Sgt. McCall fought his last desperate fight at the Rapido the Allies made their landing at Anzio. As conceived, Operation *Shingle* called for the British 1st Infantry Division and the U.S. 3d Infantry Division to establish a strong beachhead, then push inland twenty-five miles to seize the Alban Hills and cut Highways 6 and 7, the Germans' main supply and escape route. Thus entrapped, the Nazis would be forced to withdraw from the Gustav Line, opening the way to Rome.

The Allies began their landing at 2:00 A.M., January 22, 1944. Enemy resistance was light. Only two weakened German battalions opposed the landing. By noon the British had pushed two miles inland, the Americans three. By the end of the day over thirty-six thousand troops were ashore.

Field Marshal Kesselring reacted swiftly to this new threat. By nightfall three fresh German divisions were headed south from northern Italy. Elements of four more divisions were withdrawn from around Cassino. To Kesselring's surprise the Allies made no major advances on the second day. On the third and fourth days the Allies made only minor moves that deepened their beachhead to ten miles. By the end of the fourth day Kesselring had nearly eight divisions ringing Anzio. Five more were on their way.

Maj. Gen. John P. Lucas, commander of the VI Corps at Anzio, was intent on getting more men and supplies ashore before beginning offensive actions. His delay in moving toward the Alban hills not only allowed the Germans to build up their forces, but resulted in a four-month-long battle reminiscent of the trench warfare of World War I.

Warfare at Anzio consisted of a constant series of seesaw battles for the shattered small towns that dotted the landscape. The Allies would push into a ruined village, suffering frightful casualties, only to be driven out within hours by determined German counterattacks. Several times the Germans launched massive attacks designed to throw the Allies into the sea, only to be stopped by desperate men fighting for their lives.

Allied casualties at Anzio would exceed thirty thousand, with some units, most notably the 1st and 3d Ranger Battalions, being completely destroyed. Twenty men earned Medals of Honor in the fighting at Anzio. Though General Lucas would not open his drive on the Alban Hills until January 30, the first Medal of Honor action came on January 28, during an attempt to eliminate an enemy pocket near the town of Cisterna.

In preparation for Lucas's first drive the 3d Battalion, 30th Infantry Regiment, 3d Infantry Division, set off to eliminate a stubborn pocket of Germans guarding an approach to Cisterna. Behind a heavy artillery barrage, the battalion stepped off at noon. The Germans responded with a dense concentration of artillery, mortars, and machine-gun fire. While the main elements of the 3d Battalion swept into Cisterna, Company I encountered stubborn resistance on its left flank. A twenty-four-year-old cook, who frequently volunteered for combat missions, went after the Germans threatening his company.

Tech. 5 Eric G. Gibson, born in Sweden but raised in Chicago, Illinois, led his squad into an irrigation ditch paralleling their line of advance. Proceeding ahead of his men, Gibson fearlessly attacked a German automatic weapon emplaced along the ditch. With his tommy gun cradled in his arms, he wiped out the crew with a quick burst of fire. A short distance down the ditch he took on another enemy machine gun. Again, his bold, single-handed attack destroyed the weapon, killed one German, and captured another.

Farther up the ditch a third German machine gun opened up on the little band of men. After ordering his squad to lay down a base of covering fire, Gibson left the relative safety of the ditch and began crawling across an open field toward the enemy position, 125 yards away. Thirty-five yards from the gun he threw two grenades. Even before the second erupted, Gibson was on his feet, charging the position. He killed two more Germans and captured another.

Gibson turned his prisoners over to another soldier, then rejoined his squad in the ditch. Twenty-five yards away the ditch curved sharply. The cook told his men he'd go forward alone to reconnoiter. A few minutes later the tensely waiting squad heard a brief exchange of fire. They rushed around the bend. They found two bodies—a German soldier's and Gibson's, his fingers still gripping his tommy gun.

General Lucas's first major push against the Alban hills failed. Though American troops came within yards of reaching Highway 7, they had no flank protection and were forced to with-draw. After three days of fighting, in which the Allies suffered fifty-five hundred casualties, General Clark ordered Lucas to stop trying to break out of the beachhead. Instead, he was to dig in behind a perimeter of mines and barbed wire.

General Clark, in the meantime, would attempt to break the stalemate at the Gustav Line by attacking north of Cassino and going around behind it, thus pinching off the bastion without having to fight for it. At his disposal Clark had American, British, French, Indian, New Zealander, Italian, and Polish troops. All would eventually be thrown into the maelstrom that would become known as the Battle of Cassino.

It took the 34th Infantry Division more than two weeks to secure a crossing of the Rapido River and move into the mountains beyond it. Two infantry regiments drove into the mountains, while the division's third regiment moved into the town of Cassino. Located below the seventeen-hundred-foot-high Monte Cassino and its famous monastery, the town was heavily fortified by Germans dug in among its rubble.

For three frightful weeks the 34th fought as desperately and as bravely as any division in World War II. The division suffered twenty-two hundred battle casualties in this three-week period. Some rifle companies lost eighty percent of their strength.

A company of the 133d Infantry was assigned the task of eliminating the Germans holding Hill 175, northwest of Cassino. No less than fifty Germans, in three strong pillboxes supported by automatic weapons, held the position. As the company moved forward at dawn on February 3, 1944, every man knew a tough fight awaited them.

LEO J. POWERS

The GIs in his company called Pfc. Leo Powers ''Pop.'' Born on April 5, 1909, at Anselmo, Nebraska, Powers was at least ten years older than his buddies. He didn't mind the nickname; he knew it came good-naturedly.

Though born in Nebraska, Powers grew up in Montana where he earned his living as an honest-to-goodness cowboy. He worked on a number of larger ranches before being drafted in September 1942. Following basic training he joined the 34th Infantry Division in Italy as a replacement.

When Powers's company started up Hill 175 the Germans

instantly reacted by sending a blizzard of automatic weapons fire flying downhill. In seconds eight men fell. The survivors jumped for safety, scurrying behind piles of rocks. Two men behind Powers didn't cover themselves well enough. German bullets whizzed by Powers's head, killing them.

Aware that something had to be done or else his company would be wiped out, Powers started crawling uphill. While his buddies called for him to return he crept to within fifteen yards of the first pillbox. In order to pitch his grenades in to the pillbox, Powers had to stand up in full view of the Nazi gunners. Unmindful of the danger, he tossed his grenades through a small opening in the roof. The explosion killed or wounded all the occupants.

The center of the line now cleared, Powers's company again started forward. Immediately, the second pillbox opened fire. Once again Powers moved over the rocky landscape, ignoring the bullets seeking him. For a second time Powers lobbed grenades into the pillbox, this time killing one enemy soldier and wounding four more.

When the third pillbox was spotted Powers repeated his tactics. Somehow he snuck to within ten yards of this strong point, all the while under machine-pistol and rifle fire. Out of ammo for his M-1, Powers tossed his last two grenades into the pillbox. The terrific explosions killed two more Germans and wounded four. These four staggered out of the smoking concrete structure to surrender to Powers. ''Pop'' pointed his empty rifle at them and herded them downhill.

Powers's incredible action broke the backbone of the heavily defended hilltop position and allowed his company to make its way into Cassino itself, the first unit to do so.

Powers, a diminutive, mild-mannered man, was asked by a reporter after receiving his Medal of Honor from President Roosevelt on January 10, 1945, why he performed such a feat.

''I was just mad, I guess,'' Pfc. Powers said.

Mad, he said, at the Germans who had killed ten of his comrades in minutes. Mad at the battalion commanding officer, a major, with whom he'd had an argument that morning. And mad at his sergeant who refused to leave his position of safety behind a stone wall. But most of all, mad at the situation. He was fed up with twenty-five days of constant combat, of being pinned down time and time again. The madder he got, the more he wanted to do something.

"Pop" Powers went back to cowboying after his discharge in 1945. He rode the range for ten years before taking a job as a foreman at a local copper company. He had been retired for several years when a sudden heart attack felled him on July 14, 1967.

Despite heroic acts such as Pfc. Powers's, the Germans were not driven from Cassino. General Clark fed new units into the line, but the Germans chewed them up. Convinced German artillery observers were using the fourteenth-century Monte Cassino monastery to bring their lethal weapons to bear on the Allies (in fact, they were not), General Clark ordered the structure destroyed by aerial bombardment. On February 16, 600 tons of high explosives fell from U.S. heavy and medium bombers.

The monastery was all but destroyed, but still the ground troops could not take it or the town of Cassino. Foul weather postponed further attacks for three weeks, but even then the Gustav Line resisted the best General Clark threw at it. Finally, following four weeks of massive preparation, the Fifth Army launched an all-out, determined attack. Beginning on May 11, tens of thousands of Allied soldiers hit the Gustav Line.

Slowly, foot by bloody foot, the Germans were pushed back. By May 17, British troops had pushed far enough into the Liri Valley to flank Cassino and the monastery. The Germans withdrew. On May 18, Monte Cassino fell to Polish troops. By May 23, Kesselring's Tenth Army was in retreat all along the main battlefront.

At Anzio, the U.S. VI Corps's commander, Maj. Gen. Lucian K. Truscott (General Lucas's timidity had brought his relief on February 22), launched a massive effort to break out of the beachhead. At 5:30 A.M. on May 23, six hundred Allied guns opened fire from the beach. Four of the seven divisions at Anzio advanced against fierce resistance. Their objective was Valmontone, astride Highway 6. If they could cut that road, they would block the escape of the Germans fleeing from the Cassino area.

Eleven men earned Medals of Honor during the two-day breakout from Anzio. Among them was 2d Lt. Thomas W. Fowler of the 1st Armored Division. He personally cleared a path through a seventy-five-yard-deep mine field by digging the explosives out of the ground with his bare hands. Then, though a tank commander, he took two leaderless infantry platoons through the mine field. He led them in taking their objectives, cleaning out several enemy emplacements himself. With several German Mark VI tanks bearing down on a burning Sherman tank, Fowler ignored their concentrated fire to pull the tank's injured crew members to safety. Ten days later he was killed in action on the road to Rome.

When two German machine guns held up the advance of S. Sgt. George J. Hall's company of the 34th Infantry Division, he volunteered to knock them out. A veteran of the entire Italian campaign, he crawled sixty yards down a furrow in an open field, all the while under constant enemy fire. Thirty yards from the first gun he hurled four grenades. When the smoke lifted, two dead Germans occupied the position. Using German "potato masher" grenades found in the first nest, he moved toward the second. A vicious grenade duel followed. Finally, the Germans yelled "Kamerad!" Hall sent the five Nazis crawling to the rear.

While he was on his way to attack yet a third position, an exploding German artillery shell tore up Hall's left leg and nearly severed his right. Though suffering excruciating pain he tried to crawl the seventy-five yards back to his platoon. The pain was too much. "I lay there and rested awhile and gathered my wits," he said afterwards. "I was still under fire and I knew I'd have to do something. I studied it for awhile and then pulled my sheath knife and cut through the two tendons that were holding my right leg on. I was able to crawl after that." Complications from his grievous wounds caused Hall's death on February 16, 1946.

The long-awaited, and very costly, linkup between the VI Corps at Anzio and the II Corps pushing up the Liri Valley came on May 25. General Clark then sent most of his men toward Rome. The 3d Infantry Division stayed behind to capture Valmontone, thus securing the Allies' eastern flank. The mission of scouting the Valmontone area fell to the Battle Patrol, 15th Infantry, a composite scouting unit made up of volunteers from the entire regiment.

At 11:00 P.M. on June 2, an element of the Battle Patrol moved across Highway 6, then turned north searching for enemy dispositions. By 1:00 A.M., June 3, the patrol had covered fifteen hundred yards. Halfway across a wide clearing the Germans opened up. Three enemy tanks pumped 20-mm slugs and machine-gun fire on the men. Three other machine guns supported by sixty riflemen raked the Americans from both flanks and the front. The Germans had sprung a trap. GIs fell everywhere. The only way out lay to the rear.

The patrol leader, from a prone position, ordered the survivors to pull back. Two men, Pvt. Herbert Christian of Byersville, Ohio, and Pvt. Elden Johnson of East Weymouth, Massachusetts, elected to sacrifice themselves so their buddies could escape. On their own initiative they leaped to their feet and started moving directly toward the enemy.

Almost at once, a 20-mm slug hit Christian just above the right knee, completely severing his leg. Blood gushed from the shredded stump. Instead of calling for help, Christian took his tommy gun and made his way forward on one knee and his bloody stump, firing his weapon as rapidly as possible.

Near him, Johnson also elected to draw the enemy's fire on himself so the patrol members could escape. Using his BAR with deadly effectiveness he killed the crew of the closest enemy machine-gun nest. He slammed another magazine into his smoking weapon, then coolly turned to a squad of German infantry. He fired the full clip at them, killing all four.

As Johnson loaded a third clip, a burst of enemy machine-gun fire caught him full in the chest. He slumped forward. Somehow he found the strength to rise back up, balance himself on his knees, and kill one more German. Then he pitched forward on his face, dead.

Meanwhile, Pvt. Christian had hobbled forward to within ten yards of the Germans' positions. Intent on covering his comrades to the last, he emptied his tommy gun into a German soldier. He reloaded one more time and was still firing at the enemy when the full fury of the German fire knocked him down for the last time.

The deliberate self-sacrifice of these two men allowed their fellow GIs to reach safety. The patrol leader then called artillery in on the Germans, driving them from the ambush site.

Kesselring realized he could no longer stem the ever-growing flood of Allied troops. He declared Rome an open city and withdrew to the north. At 9:00 P.M., June 4, 1944, the last German convoy pulled out of Rome. Within sixty minutes American tanks entered the city. The next day, Clark officially declared Rome in Allied hands.

9

* * *

Air War over Europe

Less than three months after Pearl Harbor Brig. Gen. Ira C. Eaker, U.S. Army Air Force, arrived in England to set up headquarters for the newly formed Eighth Air Force. Along with Eaker came a controversial bombing strategy.

The Royal Air Force preferred nighttime area bombing. By flying at night they reduced the threat from German fighter planes and antiaircraft guns. Area bombing not only destroyed factories and plants but also hit workers' housing, public transportation, and utilities. The peripheral damage often had a greater impact on a factory's return to war production than the bombing of the factory itself.

General Eaker favored daylight precision bombing for several reasons. First, he felt the two main American heavy bombers—the B-17 Flying Fortress and B-24 Liberator—were better armed than their British counterparts. Each carried at least ten protective .50-caliber machine guns. Both were also equipped with the very accurate, top secret Norden bombsight. Further, Eaker believed that precision bombing could cripple Germany's industrial capacity faster and more efficiently while causing fewer civilian casualties.

Between August 17, 1942, and the end of the year, Eighth Air Force bombers flew twenty-seven missions against targets in occupied Europe. Though losses amounted to just two percent of the planes, the results were disappointing. Eaker's daylight strategy seemed doomed. Prime Minister Churchill began a campaign to persuade the Americans to abandon their strategy and join the RAF in their nighttime area bombings.

General Eaker personally met with Churchill at Casablanca

in January 1943 to change his mind. Among his arguments Eaker proposed that "by bombing the devils around the clock, we can prevent the German defenses from getting any rest."

That, more than anything, convinced Churchill of the advantages of the American strategy. On January 21, 1943, President Roosevelt and Prime Minister Churchill formally endorsed around-the-clock bombing of Germany. The Casablanca Directive listed target priorities and defined the objectives of the aerial bombardment campaign for the men who would conduct it. "Your primary object," read the directive, "will be the progressive destruction and dislocation of the German military, industrial, and economic system, and the undermining of the morale of the German people to a point where their capacity for armed resistance is fatally weakened."

On January 27, 1943, the Eighth Air Force launched its first attack inside Germany. Ninety-one B-17s and B-24s attacked Wilhelmshaven, the submarine-building center on the North Sea. Bad weather and attacking Luftwaffe fighters made bombing accuracy difficult, but the mission was still considered a success.

The next major target was the submarine yards at Vegesack, Germany. Taking part in the raid were the B-17s of the 359th Bombing Squadron. The bombers that took off for Vegesack on March 17, 1943, were equipped with a flight instrument being used for the first time. The automatic flight control equipment provided a link between the bombardier and the plane's automatic pilot. This gave the bombardier control of the plane during the crucial bombing run. He flew the plane by lining up the cross hairs of his Norden bombsight. The overwhelming success of the raid on Vegesack was due not only to this new gadgetry but to the heroism of the lead bombardier.

Less than a minute before he was due to release his bombs an antiaircraft shell exploded in the nose compartment housing 1st Lt. Jack Mathis. Red-hot shrapnel tore a gaping hole in the Texan's side, nearly severed his right arm, and knocked him nine feet backwards. Determined to complete his vital task, Mathis ignored his excruciating pain to crawl forward to his bombsight. Against the strong wind howling through the huge hole in the B-17's skin, Mathis pulled himself over his sight. When the cross hairs lined up on the target, he called, "Bombs away!" then died at his post. Mathis's gallantry allowed the entire flight to accurately drop their bombs on the target.

In announcing the destruction of seven U-boats and severe damage to the shipyard, General Eaker said, "This is a successful conclusion to long months of experimentation in daytime, high-level precision bombing. After Vegesack comes a new chapter."

Lt. Jack Mathis became the first in a long line of airmen to earn the Medal of Honor over Europe.

The ten-man crew of a B-17 was a highly trained, well-coordinated team. Four officers—pilot, copilot, navigator, and bombardier—and six enlisted men—radio operator, flight engineer, and four gunners—trained together and usually flew all their missions together. Not only was each crew member a specialist, but each was also trained to perform at least one other job. Like a finely tuned engine, the crew coordinated all their activities so their missions would be successful.

The versatility of the crew was best demonstrated when enemy fighter planes attacked. The navigator and bombardier manned a pair of machine guns in the nose, the flight engineer took up the machine gun in the top turret, the radio operator had a machine gun that fired through a port in the top of the fuselage, and the other gunners fired waist guns, the tail gun, and the low-slung belly turret machine gun.

The belly gunner had to assume the position of a contortionist in order to take his place in the turret. Scrunched into a near-fetal position, the belly gunner hung about two feet below the B-17's fuselage, completely exposed to enemy fire in his Plexiglas bubble. The position required men short in stature and tall in courage.

MAYNARD H. SMITH

When S. Sgt. Maynard "Snuffy" Smith dropped himself into the ball turret of his B-17 on the morning of May 1, 1943, it was with more than the normal amount of excitement. After eight months of training Smith was going on his first combat mission.

Born May 19, 1911, in Caro, Michigan, Smith received his summons to military service on August 31, 1942. While in basic training Smith heard about a program that would make him a staff sergeant in just nine weeks: aerial gunnery school. He applied. After basic, Smith received his orders to the school at Harlingen, Texas.

Smith spent the next six months training at various stateside bases before heading to England in March 1943. There he underwent more training until being assigned to a B-17 unit, the 423d Bombardment Squadron, 306th Bombardment Group.

The first mission for Smith and his crew would be a bomb run against the submarine pens at Saint-Nazaire, France. In his ball turret, Smith made himself as comfortable as possible. Even at five feet, six inches, and 135 pounds Smith did not have much spare room. His twin .50-caliber machine guns hung ominously in the early morning air. He tested the hydraulics that moved the turret in circles. Above him, a stout metal plate separated him from the rest of the plane. Once airborne there was nothing below him.

"It was," Smith liked to say, "just like you're floating in the air."

On their way to the target the flight of heavy bombers was struck by more than fifty Focke-Wulf-190 fighters. Several dozen roared in on the formation from the front. Even more swooped down from the rear. Flak from antiaircraft guns burst in black puffs around the planes. Smith swiveled his turret back and forth, shooting at every enemy plane that came within range. Several B-17s began smoking or burning as the enemy fire found targets. But Smith was too busy to notice. Then his own plane took a hit.

An .88-caliber antiaircraft shell ripped into the Fortress's fuselage a foot from the radio operator. He was so scared he jumped right out of the plane. Without a parachute.

The shell not only destroyed the radio but, worse, it ruptured a four hundred-gallon fuel tank. Volatile, high octane fuel poured into the fuselage. Sparks from loose wires ignited the fuel. The plane's interior erupted in flames.

In his turret Smith pushed the hydraulic control that would release him from his ball. It didn't work. The backup system didn't work either. Fighting panic, he turned the manual crank and hoisted himself into the plane. A raging inferno greeted him.

By now the plane had plummeted to just two thousand feet over the Bay of Biscay. The second waist gunner had tried to bail out but caught his parachute harness on some equipment. Smith unhooked him. Then he opened the rear door and helped him bail out.

The feisty sergeant next turned his attention to the fire. He used every available fire extinguisher and put out most of the flames. He then poured the plane's water bottles on the fire until it was out.

By now separated from the formation, the B-17 was an easy target for the FW-190s. Smith alternated firing the two waist guns until the fighters withdrew. When all was quiet, he gave first aid to the wounded crew members and made repairs to the plane.

As the B-17 approached England, Smith decided to check up front. He found both the pilot and copilot wounded. He pulled the pilot from his seat, gave him and the copilot first aid, then climbed into the pilot's seat. Though he had no formal training he had watched the pilots enough to know the fundamentals. With the copilot coaching, Smith crossed the English coast, headed for the nearest RAF base.

He found it at Lands End. Somehow, Smith landed the wounded bomber. He bounced a few times, but they were safely on the ground. Ten minutes later the plane collapsed in the center, the huge wings folding together like a butterfly's.

Secretary of War Stimson, during a visit to England, presented the Medal of Honor to Sergeant Smith on July 16, 1943. He became the first of only three enlisted airmen to earn the high award in Europe.

Smith flew twelve more combat missions, sometimes as a waist gunner, sometimes down in the ball turret. The drama of his adventure over the Bay of Biscay and the added stress of the additional combat missions finally caught up with him in late October 1943. As he walked down the street of an English village his mind went blank. "I just forgot where I was," he said.

Several weeks of hospitalization followed, then Smith was assigned clerical duties with his squadron. He remained in that status until he returned to the United States and an honorable discharge in May 1945. He worked for the Treasury Department until 1970, when he started the *Police Officers Journal*, an independent newspaper devoted to police and community affairs. Five years later he retired to St. Petersburg, Florida. He died there on May 11, 1984.

The early months of America's daylight bombing raids were very costly. Through May 1943 General Eaker could barely muster a hundred bombers per day. Just six understrength bombing groups—four of B-17s and two of B-24s—carried the brunt of the Eighth Air Force's offensive against the Nazis. Very few new bombers and their valuable crews were making it to England.

To bolster his forces General Eaker bombarded Washington with requests for more planes, more men. He stressed that the continued bombing of Europe, especially aircraft factories, would be necessary to assure the success of the planned 1944 invasion of France. Unless he had the equipment, Eaker warned, he might not be able to keep Europe's skies clear of enemy fighters. That could spell disaster for the invaders.

Eaker's tactic worked. His Eighth Air Force received top priority on new planes and crews. By the end of May 1943 his available combat aircraft jumped from 100 to 215. New U.S. air bases sprouted up all over England. Eaker was promised another 800 bombers by summer's end, twice that many by year's end.

The American air campaign against Germany and the occupied countries slipped into high gear. In early June nearly 200 bombers returned to Saint-Nazaire. A few days later 235 bombers roared into the Ruhr, the heart of Germany's industrial area. At the same time another force of B-17s bombed armament factories in Antwerp, Belgium.

For the first three weeks of July rainy, foggy weather kept most of the Eighth Air Force on the ground. General Eaker used the time to plan his biggest effort to date. It would be the first concerted attempt at around the clock bombing in cooperation with the RAF. The main target would be the shipyards and submarine buildings at the German port city of Hamburg. Diversionary raids would be conducted against other significant targets, including a chemical plant in Norway.

"Little Blitz Week" began on the night of July 24, 1943. The RAF sent 740 bombers to Hamburg. Three thousand tons of high explosive bombs and incendiaries created huge fires. Over the next two days American B-17s continued hammering the city. On the third night the RAF returned with 722 bombers. More incendiaries created a firestorm that reached twelve hundred degrees centigrade, destroyed most of the old city, and killed forty thousand inhabitants.

Altogether, sixteen major industrial cities were hit during Little Blitz Week. Focke-Wulf fighter plants at Oschersleben, Warnemunde, and Kassel were hit. So were shipyards at Kiel. On July 26, 1943, the B-17s of the 407th Bombing Squadron, 92d Bombardment Group, headed for a rubber plant near Hannover, Germany.

JOHN C. MORGAN

Among the bombers departing Alcombury, England, that morning was the *Ruthie II*, piloted by Lt. Robert Campbell. As was his custom Campbell let his copilot, Flight Officer John C. Morgan, take off and fly the plane to the combat area. This was only Morgan's fifth mission as the copilot of a B-17. But he'd flown more than a dozen as a pilot sergeant with the Royal Canadian Air Force.

A big six-foot, two-inch, two hundred-pound Texan, Morgan had lived a full, adventure-packed life before enlisting in the RCAF in August 1941. A native of Vernon, Texas, where he was born on August 24, 1914, Morgan's yearning to fly began as a youngster. He first soloed at eighteen while a student at the University of Texas. But then his father put an end to that nonsense.

But Morgan's interest in flying did not wane. While attending a number of colleges and universities he secretly continued his flying lessons. By the time he received his pilot's license at age twenty, Morgan decided he wasn't cut out to he a scholar. So he did what seemed logical. He quit school and ran off to the Fiji Islands.

Morgan spent three years in the South Seas, working as an overseer for a pineapple plantation and in gold mines. When he returned to Texas in 1938 he tried to enlist in the army air force, but his academic record kept him out. He found work as a truck driver and warehouseman for an oil company. While there he broke his neck trying to stop a wayward fifty-five-gallon drum. His draft classification changed to 4-F.

But that didn't deter Morgan. Like a lot of Americans who wanted to fight the Nazis before their country entered the global conflict, Morgan went to Canada. "I didn't have any trouble with the physical," Morgan remembered years later in an interview. "They didn't ask me if I'd ever broken my neck and I didn't tell them."

Following flight training in Canada, Morgan went to England in the summer of 1942. When the Eighth Air Force arrived

Morgan, and most other Americans in the RCAF and RAF, were transferred to the U.S. Army Air Force. Morgan made the transition on March 23, 1943.

As they headed for Hannover, *Ruthie II*'s crew knew they'd have to make it past the German fighters waiting on the other side of the English Channel. The first wave of Focke-Wulfs hit them just as they crossed into Holland. Morgan saw an FW-109 coming straight at his B-17. There wasn't a thing he could do.

The first burst from the FW-109's 20-mm cannon ripped through the cockpit's windshield. One slug blew off the side of Campbell's head. Above Morgan, in the upper ball turret, another shell tore off the flight engineer's left arm at the shoulder. He fell through to the main section of the plane, blood gushing from his wound. More German fighters roared in. Their bullets destroyed part of the B-17's oxygen lines and most of its electrical system. Five crew members manning the bomber's machine guns slumped into unconsciousness from lack of oxygen.

Morgan, unable to see out of his shattered windshield, struggled with the dying pilot for control of the plane. But Campbell fought back wildly with all the delirium of a mortally wounded man. He smashed at Morgan with his fists, knocking some teeth loose, blackening both his eyes.

The grisly struggle continued as the bomber force flew on toward Hannover. Morgan realized the only way he could save the plane and its crew was to remain in formation. The guns of the other planes offered protection. If he dropped out he'd be destroyed in minutes.

Through an upper window Morgan focused on the belly of another B-17. He maintained his course by flying directly under it, guiding his plane with one hand, keeping his dying friend away from the controls with the other.

Incredibly, Morgan flew the B-17 all the way to Hannover. In the nose, the bombardier toggled his switch, sending his bombs into the mass of smoke that was the target. He then joined the navigator in manning one of the nose's .50-caliber machine guns. Not until the plane was fifteen minutes out from the enemy coast did the navigator decide to go up top and check with the pilot. What he saw shocked him.

In the after-action briefing the navigator said, "Morgan was flying the plane with one hand and holding the half-dead pilot with the other, and he had been doing so for two hours!"

Morgan calmly asked the navigator to get Campbell out of his seat. He couldn't land the plane from the copilot's seat because he couldn't see out of the shattered windshield. The bombardier and navigator pulled Campbell from his seat and secured him in the bombardier's compartment.

With all his fuel gauges reading empty, Morgan put his plane down at the first airfield he came to. Campbell died an hour and a half later. The B-17 never flew again. The five gunners all recovered, but with varying degrees of frostbite damage.

Five months later, on December 18, 1943, Morgan received his Medal of Honor. He remained on combat duty, flying in all twenty-five and a half missions. He would have liked it better had it been twenty-six. On March 6, 1944, during the first daylight raid over Berlin, Morgan was shot down. He spent the balance of the war in Stalag Luft 1. He is the only person to become a POW after receiving his Medal of Honor.

Morgan returned to active duty during the Korean War. He applied for combat duty, but the air force wouldn't let him go. He stayed in the States flying transports for two years. He retired as a full colonel.

Like most Medal of Honor recipients, Morgan has no delusions about his place in history. "There's no such thing as a hero," he says. "I was pushed into circumstances where I was forced to act. You can never say how you're going to react to something until it happens, but I think most people would have done the same."

When Little Blitz Week ended on July 29, 1943, the six days of ceaseless attacks had taken a severe toll. Eighty-eight bombers and their crews were lost. Dozens of other men succumbed to their wounds in England. All operations were called off for two weeks. The crews needed time to recover. The planes needed repairs. But the war went on. Thousands of miles to the south one of the bloodiest raids of the war was in its final stages of preparation.

A few weeks before Little Blitz Week began, Eaker had been ordered to send three of his B-24 bomber groups—the 44th, 93d, and 389th—to North Africa to join the Ninth Air Force. First organized in 1942 the Ninth Air Force helped the British Eighth Army battle General Rommel's Afrika Korps. With victory in the desert assured, the Ninth established a number of airfields around Benghazi, Libya. From there, the B-17s and B-24s of the Ninth supported the infantry fighting up the Italian boot.

Once U.S. bombers appeared on the European scene, Allied economic analysts began pushing for a strike against the German-controlled oil refineries at Ploesti, Romania. Since Germany possessed virtually no oil of her own, petroleum production was essential to her war economy. If the dozen Ploesti oil refineries could be taken out, Germany's potential for warmaking would be seriously crippled.

The planners for the Ploesti mission advocated the bold, novel concept of bombing the refineries from rooftop level. According to them, this extremely low-level bombing run would not only enhance the bombers' accuracy, but would reduce the effect of the defenders' antiaircraft guns. For several weeks the crews of the B-24s practiced maneuvering their sixty thousand-pound planes around just feet above the hot desert sands of Libya. The plan was daring, but seemed to have a better-than-average chance for success.

Unfortunately, the planners were working with erroneous information. Allied intelligence reported that Ploesti was only lightly defended by flak guns, and their crews were Romanians whose hearts were not really in the war. In reality, the local German commander, Brig. Gen. Alfred Gerstenberg, was a diehard Nazi who turned Ploesti into one of the most heavily defended cities in Europe. Deadly 88-mm flak guns, 20-mm and 37-mm rapid-fire cannon, and heavy machine guns ringed the target area. Their crews were not reluctant Romanians, but highly trained Germans.

Besides the antiaircraft weapons, Gerstenberg had at his disposal a half-dozen fighter squadrons at nearby airfields. Air raid wardens and more sophisticated early warning systems extended all the way to Axis-occupied Greece. Gerstenberg would know about any attack on Ploesti soon after the planes took off.

The 178 Liberators of Operation *Tidal Wave* began roaring down Benghazi's runways at dawn on Sunday, August 1, 1943. Things went wrong almost immediately. One B-24 crashed and burned on takeoff, killing the ten-man crew. As the bombers rendezvoused for their seven-hour, twenty-four hundred-mile flight, ten aborted, their engines fouled by the desert sand. Halfway across the Mediterranean the *Wingo-Wango*, the B-24 carrying the lead navigator, suddenly stood on its tail, flipped over backwards, and plunged into the water.

Over Albania unexpected cloud cover split the formation in two. The plan to have all five bombing groups hit their targets simultaneously began to fall apart. A little later the two lead groups misread a checkpoint and headed for Bucharest, southeast of Ploesti. The leader of them, Lt. Col. Addison E. Baker, 93d Group, soon realized his mistake. He turned toward Ploesti, but couldn't break radio silence to warn Col. Keith K. Compton, commanding officer of the 376th Group, of the error. Compton did not realize his error until he was on the outskirts of Bucharest.

Thus, the five bomb groups would hit Ploesti in three waves instead of one. And they would be approaching Ploesti from directions unfamiliar to them. To worsen matters, the German gunners had been warned the American bombers were coming in low. They fused their shells for point-blank range. A disaster was unfolding.

ADDISON E. BAKER
JOHN L. JERSTAD

The first group to arrive at Ploesti was Lt. Col. Addison E. Baker's ''Traveling Circus.'' Piloting the lead B-24, *Hell's Wench*, Baker drove hard and low for the target city. The twenty-two Liberators of the Circus tightened up their formation and dropped lower until they were skimming along just fifty feet above the well-tended farm fields leading to Ploesti. Next to Baker, his copilot, Maj. John L. Jerstad, strained to see through the haze enveloping Ploesti. Ahead of him barrage balloons, their tethering cables festooned with contact explosives, began to appear. Deadly black puffs of flak dotted the horizon.

Baker, a tall, stern-jawed resident of Akron, Ohio, was born on January 1, 1907, in Chicago, Illinois. He first enlisted in the army in 1929, serving for a year as an enlisted man before being accepted as a flying cadet. After successfully earning his wings and promotion to second lieutenant in February 1931, Baker served on active duty until February 1932, when he reverted to reserve status with the Ohio National Guard. Until he was recalled to active duty in November 1940, Baker ran his own service station in Detroit, Michigan.

After completing pilot training in the B-24 Baker, now a

major, took command of the 328th Bomb Squadron, 93d Group. He went to England in May 1942, served as operations officer of the 93d, then took command of the group in March 1943 after his promotion to lieutenant colonel.

Maj. John L. Jerstad, a slightly built, quick-witted man, was born in Racine, Wisconsin, on February 12, 1918. After graduating from Northwestern University in 1940, he taught school in St. Louis for a year before enlisting as an aviation cadet. Commissioned in February 1942, he went to England with the 93d Group in October 1942. An extremely dedicated officer, Jerstad flew every mission possible. When he reached the requisite twenty-five, he volunteered for more. He finally got so far past his quota he stopped counting.

When the 201st Provisional Combat Wing was established to organize the Ploesti raid its commander, Col. Edward J. Timberlake, the dean of the B-24 combat school and former commander of the Traveling Circus, picked Jerstad as his chief operations officer. Jerstad was understandably proud of his position. He wrote his parents, ''I'm the youngest kid on the staff and its quite an honor to work with colonels and generals.''

As operations officer, Jerstad didn't have to make the mission. But he couldn't let it pass. Colonel Timberlake tried to take him off the mission, but Jerstad declined. He told Timberlake, ''Don't worry, sir, Baker and I will make it all right.''

As *Hell's Wench* and the rest of the Circus raced towards Ploesti Jerstad called out the flak batteries to his gunner. ''Eight o'clock! Twelve o'clock! Five o'clock! Hell, shoot all over.'' On the ground haystacks popped apart to reveal flak batteries. Freight cars on railroad sidings collapsed to pour out 37-mm gunfire. More barrage balloons rose into the sky. Pits in farmers' fields opened and sprouted twin machine guns. The sky was literally filled with multicolored tracers from German guns.

Still, the Circus bore on. Several bombers began trailing smoke as the flak found targets. Men were bleeding and dying from shrapnel ripping through the planes' thin aluminum skin. Gleaming shards of aluminum and Plexiglas flitted down from the sky. First one, then two planes erupted in flames. They were too low for the crews to parachute to safety.

Hell's Wench held its course through all the fire. It seemed impossible for any plane to force its way through the nearly solid curtain of enemy fire, but Baker and Jerstad never wavered. They were determined to lead their group to its target.

Five miles out *Hell's Wench* hit a balloon cable. The B-24 continued on, the balloon wandering upward. Three miles out the bomber took a direct hit in the nose. In quick succession *Hell's Wench* took three more hits, in the wing, wing root, and a devastating blow in the cockpit. Flames erupted from the wing tanks.

Baker and Jerstad jettisoned their bombs to keep their plane in the air and continued to lead the way. In front of Baker were wheat fields where he could have put *Hell's Wench* down, but he didn't. Instead, the flaming B-24 flew on, headed for an opening between two tall refinery stacks. The flying torch that was now *Hell's Wench* took another hit just before the target. A witness in another plane said, "Their right wing began to drop. I don't see how anyone could have been alive in that cockpit, but someone kept her leading the force on between the refinery stacks. Baker was a powerful man, but one man could not have held the ship on the climb she took beyond the stacks."

Hell's Wench staggered awkwardly up to an altitude of about three hundred feet. Three or four of the crew tumbled out. She fell off on one wing, drifting toward another plane. That crew saw nothing but flames in the cockpit. The B-24, now a total mass of flames, crashed on her wing tip in a field. None of the crew, including those who bailed out, survived.

For their incredible gallantry in continuing to lead their group in their mortally wounded bomber, when they could have tried a crash landing, Baker and Jerstad became the first of five men to earn the Medal of Honor in the bloody skies over Ploesti.

Fifteen minutes behind the Traveling Circus came the final two groups. The Eight Balls of Col. Leon Johnson's 44th Group and the Pyramiders of Col. John R. Kane's 98th Group had made the correct turn and were headed for Ploesti on course.

Fully alert to the incoming bombers, the German gunners lusted for more blood. Kane's copilot said, "It was like flying through hell." Remarked Johnson, "it was indescribable to anyone who wasn't there. We flew through sheets of flame, and airplanes were everywhere, some of them on fire, others exploding."

Like Baker and Jerstad, Kane and Johnson ignored the savage

fire to lead their groups to their targets. The flak and machine-gun fire was so severe, one of Kane's echelons lost nine of sixteen planes, another five of six.

Both Kane and Johnson, who rose to four-star rank in the postwar air force, received the Medal of Honor for their intrepidity in leading their B-24s into the inferno of Ploesti.

Once past Ploesti, waves of enemy fighters set upon the surviving bombers. More planes went down. Some crippled bombers headed for neutral Turkey, where the crews were interned. Some made it to Allied-controlled Sicily, Malta, or Cyprus. Others headed for Libya, failed, and fell into the Mediterranean. Only eighty-eight B-24s made it back to Benghazi. The next day just thirty-three of those were declared fit to fly. The *Tidal Wave* force suffered 579 casualties, of which 310 were dead.

Though an estimated forty percent of Ploesti's capacity was damaged or destroyed, the refineries had sufficient reserve facilities to keep producing their monthly quotas until the Russians overran the fields in 1944.

Back in England the Eighth Air Force planners focused their attention on two new targets. Regensburg was the home of a Messerschmitt plant that produced forty percent of the Luftwaffe's single-engine fighters. Schweinfurt contained several factories that produced the precision ball bearings critical to the Luftwaffe. Both targets were in southeastern Germany farther than any Eighth Air Force planes had yet penetrated.

On August 17, 1943, Eaker sent 146 B-17s against Regensburg, while another 230 hit Schweinfurt. Once the short-range U.S. fighters left the bombers at the German border, Luftwaffe fighters tore into the B-17s. Sixty bombers went down; another 47 were so badly damaged they had to be scrapped. In turn, the American bombers destroyed over one-third of Schweinfurt's production capacity and hit every major Messerschmitt building in Regensburg with incendiaries or high explosives.

The Eighth Air Force B-17s went back to Schweinfurt on October 17. Again the lack of long-range fighter protection spelled disaster for the bombers. Of 291 B-17s on the mission, 60 failed to return. Eaker halted the bombing of Germany until his bombers had adequate fighter protection.

He started receiving the fighters he needed in late November 1943. The P-51 Mustang, equipped with long-range tanks, had an effective combat range of 950 miles. The planes 1490-horsepower Rolls-Royce liquid-cooled engine allowed the spunky little fighter to hit 440 miles per hour at thirty thousand feet. Performance tests indicated the Mustang could outspeed, outclimb, and out-dive any plane in the Luftwaffe's inventory. By the end of 1943, the P-51 was ready for action alongside the P-38 twin-fuselage Lightning and the P-47 Thunderbolt.

On January 11, 1944, the Eighth Air Force, now under the command of Lt. Gen. James H. Doolittle, launched the first large-scale American raid with fighter protection deep into the Reich. Three cities about a hundred miles west of Berlin, all producing components for planes of the Luftwaffe, would be hit by 663 B-17s and B-24s divided into three strike forces. Forty-nine Mustangs, all that were available, joined with the P-47s and P-38s to escort the bombers. Because of their longer range, only the P-51s would accompany the bombers all the way to the targets.

The Luftwaffe provided a reception every bit as deadly as they gave to the Schweinfurt-Regensburg raiders. Another sixty bombers would fall. The bombers inflicted heavy damage on their targets in spite of the resistance. Contributing to their success was the brilliant performance of the Mustangs. Against no losses of their own they shot down fifteen enemy fighters.

Four of the fifteen were knocked from the sky by thirty-year-old Maj. James H. Howard. Over Oschersleben Howard's flight spotted ME-109s and ME-110s below the bombers, climbing like a swarm of bees. In the wild dogfight that followed, Howard flamed one enemy fighter while the other Mustang pilots destroyed eight more. But in their eager, headlong dive the P-51s had left the bombers unprotected.

As soon as Howard realized this he put his plane into a steep climb. He reached the bombers to find them under attack by some thirty German fighters. He should have waited for his wingman and the others to join him, but Howard didn't want to waste the time. Single-handed he took on the entire force!

First, he flamed an ME-110. "I went down after him, gave him a couple of squirts, and watched him crash." Next he went after an ME-109. "I gave him a squirt, and almost ran into his canopy when he threw it off to get out." Next Howard zoomed in on a flight of four enemy fighters. Three of his guns jammed, but that didn't deter him. At least two of these planes fell under Howard's guns.

The action happened so quickly Howard never knew for sure how many enemy he knocked from the sky. Witnesses in the bombers claimed four to six. Headquarters credited him with four.

For his daring, Howard became the only P-51 pilot, and the only fighter pilot in Europe, to earn a Medal of Honor in World War II. He retired from the air force as a brigadier general.

General Doolittle's first major offensive against Germany's aircraft factories commenced on February 20, 1944. The operation called for coordinated attacks by the Eighth Air Force in England and the Fifteenth Air Force in Italy. The missions had originally been scheduled for early February, but bad weather over Germany postponed their launching. Finally, on February 19, meteorologists forecast a break in the weather.

Early the next morning, nearly the entire strength of the Eighth Air Force rose into the sky. More than a thousand bombers flew toward a dozen targets in central Germany and western Poland. Almost as many fighters accompanied them.

One of the planes that took off that morning was the *Mizpah*, a B-17 assigned to the 510th Bombardment Squadron, 351st Group. Their target was an aircraft plant near Leipzig. For the crew this was only their second mission. Two weeks earlier they had flown to Dijon, France, but that was really a "milk run" shakedown cruise. Leipzig would be their first real crack at the Germans.

WALTER E. TRUEMPER
ARCHIBALD MATHIES

Walter E. Truemper was born in Aurora, Illinois, on October 31, 1918, the eighth of ten children. As a high school student he was well-regarded for his prowess as a first baseman and as a golfer who consistently shot in the low seventies.

After attending Northwestern University and working part-time as an accounting clerk for several years, Truemper received his induction notice in June 1942. Following basic training he received an appointment as an aviation cadet in November 1942.

Truemper washed out of flight school in January 1943. He then received training as a navigator. When he finished that course in August 1943 he joined the crew of 1st Lt. Clarence Nelson, captain and pilot of the *Mizpah*.

A few days after Truemper reported to the *Mizpah* at Alexandria, Louisiana, the plane's ball turret gunner arrived. Sgt. Archibald Mathies was born on June 3, 1918, at Stonehouse, Lanarkshire, Scotland. When he was three his father brought the family to the coal mines of Pennsylvania. He graduated from high school in 1937, worked several years as a mechanic, then enlisted in the army air force on December 30, 1940.

Mathies trained as an aircraft mechanic and served with the 33d Pursuit Group at Mitchell Field, New York, before being assigned to gunnery school in February 1943. On September 15, 1943, he joined the crew of the *Mizpah*.

The next sixty days were hectic ones for Nelson and his crew. Every man was well-versed in his job, but it took a lot of tough training to weld ten individuals into the crew of a four-engine bomber headed for aerial combat over Europe. Day after day, flight hour after flight hour, the crew honed their skills to a razor-sharp edge. Their hard work paid off. *Mizpah* departed Dow Field, Bangor, Maine, on December 8, 1943, for the long transatlantic flight to England.

After the milk run to Dijon, the *Mizpah*'s crew felt they were veterans, but they still had twenty-four tough missions ahead of them before they could relax. Instinctively, they all knew that the first day of what would come to be known as "Big Week" would be one of tough combat for them. To a man, they knew they were up to it.

The flight to Leipzig was relatively uneventful. The escorting long-range P-51s caused the Luftwaffe to temper their attacks. Until the B-17s neared the target. Then the Luftwaffe attacked in earnest.

Fifteen minutes from their target, two ME-109s jumped the *Mizpah*. Two cannon shells exploded with deadly results in the cockpit. The copilot died instantly. Lieutenant Nelson drooped in his chair, unconscious from his severe wounds. *Mizpah* fell off on her right wing, dropped from the protective formation, and headed for the earth.

Reacting instantly to the impending doom, Truemper and top turret gunner Sgt. Carl Moore rushed to the cockpit. Together they pulled Nelson from his seat, grabbed the controls, and wrestled the plane back to a level attitude. With the windshield gone and the sub-zero air blasting into the compartment, Truemper pushed the control wheel forward. His pilot training told him the lower altitude would not only be warmer but would allow the crippled bomber to evade the Nazi fighters.

The next few hours were torturous. The three neo-pilots, Truemper, Moore, and Mathies, took turns in the open cockpit as they nursed the badly wounded *Mizpah* back toward England. With Mathies at the controls, the B-17 crossed into England's airspace.

Soon they were able to contact a control tower. Truemper, now at the controls, explained their situation and asked for directions to their home base. Once near that field, Truemper ordered all members of the crew to bail out. Minutes later only Truemper, Mathies, and the unconscious Nelson remained on board.

As soon as he learned of *Mizpah*'s predicament the 351st's commander, Col. Eugene Romig, took off in another B-17. He took a position off *Mizpah*'s wing to try and guide the novices to a landing—something neither Truemper nor Mathies had attempted before.

After the two planes circled the area several times Colonel Romig decided the crippled bomber was too badly damaged for the inexperienced pilots to land. He radioed the *Mizpah* and advised Truemper to head the bomber to sea, then bail out to safety. Truemper and Mathies held a hasty consultation, then radioed Romig.

"Sir, if that's a direct order, okay, but we'd rather try to bring her in. The pilot's still breathing."

Colonel Romig reluctantly agreed.

Twice the B-17 turned onto its final approach. Each time her erratic flight maneuvers caused the crewmen to abort. During each pass Romig talked to the two men. He was impressed by the coolness and determination of the officer and gunner.

Perhaps a trained pilot could have carried out the emergency landing. Truemper and Mathies could not. As *Mizpah* began her third approach to landing, she started descending. Truemper instinctively pulled back on the control wheel, raising the nose. The heavy wings lost their lift, the plane stalled, then nosed into the ground.

Four months later, on June 22, 1944, the army air force announced the awards of the Medal of Honor to the two men who valued their pilot's life more than their own.

Through February 25, Big Week bombers flew thirty-eight hundred sorties, thirty-three hundred by the Eighth Air Force and five hundred by the Fifteenth. Over ten thousand tons of bombs dropped on Reich targets. In all 226 U.S. Bombers and 28 fighters were lost.

Against this, the Germans lost 160 fighters. More importantly, Big Week destroyed or damaged more than half of Germany's aircraft manufacturing facilities. At Leipzig, 350 undelivered combat-ready ME-109s were demolished on the ground. Substantial damage was also done to ME-110 and Junkers factories at Gotha and Aschersleben.

The planners of Operation *Overlord*, the Allied invasion of Europe, had a special role for America's airpower. While the heavy bombers continued to focus their attention on Germany's war industries, medium bombers and fighters would conduct a systematic attack aimed at totally disrupting Germany's ground traffic. The main targets would be eighty railway marshalling yards and repair centers in Belgium and northern France. Their destruction, along with bridges, roads, and railway lines, would create a transportation desert in northern France, sealing off the German defenders from supplies and reinforcements.

LEON R. VANCE

As part of the overall plan, bombers attacked the port of Calais, France, on June 4, 1944, the day before the scheduled invasion. When adverse weather postponed D-Day for twenty-four hours, the bombers were sent back to Calais on June 5. The repeat attacks at Calais were necessary to deceive the Nazis as to the actual site of the invasion. If the *Overlord* chiefs did not send the bombers back, the Germans might guess the true landing site. The same unit that bombed Calais the day before, the 489th Bomb Group, was selected to go back. They knew the target area and had the best chance of success. The group's deputy commander, Lt. Col. Leon R. Vance, elected to accompany the mission in the lead B-24.

As the flight approached its target the lead bombardier bent over his bombsight. At the right moment he yelled ''Bombs away!'' Nothing happened. A malfunction in the bomb racks

kept all the bombs loaded. Not a single plane in the formation
dropped its bombs. Vance, standing on the flight deck between
the pilot and copilot, immediately issued orders to circle back
and approach the target again—at the same altitude and air-
speed. The Nazi flak gunners would be alert and waiting. But it
wasn't an unusual order for Vance. A 1939 West Point graduate
from Enid, Oklahoma, Vance was known as a daring and resourceful officer, possessed with a keen desire to complete his
mission.

The flak started hitting the B-24s as soon as they neared the
coastal batteries. Just minutes from dropping its bomb load,
Vance's plane, *Missouri Sue*, took several hits. The hydraulic,
electric, and fuel lines were all damaged or severed. The right
rudder and elevator were shot off. The radio room was destroyed. The nose turret had all its glass shattered. The top turret
was blown in half, and a large hole in the fuselage adjoined the
waist windows. Three of the engines ground to a halt.

The pilot died instantly. The copilot was badly wounded.
Vance, recovering from the stun of the exploding shells, saw
that one shell had nearly severed his right foot. The blast had
wedged the damaged limb under the copilot's seat.

Completely ignoring his intense pain, Vance struggled to an
upright position and took control of the plane. Totally in command, he led his formation over the target, bombing it successfully.

While the radio operator applied a tourniquet to his ankle,
Vance cut the fuel to the sole operating engine. He feared the
plane would catch fire and explode. He had enough altitude to
glide to England. At about this time Vance learned that an armed
five hundred-pound bomb had hung up in the bomb bay. As the
Liberator neared the English coast, Vance ordered the crew to
bail out. Before he could exit himself he thought he heard a cry
for help over the plane's intercom. Unwilling to evacuate the
plane if there was still an injured man aboard, Vance elected to
make a crash landing in the English Channel.

He banked the plane out to sea. While lying on the floor, able
to use only the ailerons and elevators for control, Vance made
a successful ditching. As the plane settled rapidly in the swells,
the bomb exploded, hurtling Vance free of the wreckage. After
inflating his life vest, Vance swam around searching for the other
crewman. Unable to find the man (he did not exist), Vance

started for shore. Fifty minutes later an air-sea rescue craft picked him up.

Once in the hospital Vance expressed his strong desire to return to active duty and combat flying. But Vance would be returned to the United States for rehabilitation. On July 26, 1944, he, along with other casualties of the air war, was loaded aboard a C-54 medical evacuation plane for the long flight back to America. On the leg between Iceland and Newfoundland, the plane disappeared.

Over two hundred thousand sorties were flown by the Eighth and Ninth Air Forces in support of the Normandy invasion. France's railroad lines were destroyed at numerous points. Over fifteen hundred locomotives were demolished. All twenty-four bridges over the Seine River from the sea to Paris were blasted into ruins. Throughout France rail traffic was thrown into chaos.

In addition, thirty-six German airfields, forty-one radar installations, and forty-five gun batteries were destroyed. So successful were the preinvasion bombings that only a handful of Luftwaffe fighters and bombers was able to answer the Allied invaders.

10
* * *

Central Pacific Combat

Ten days after the U.S. Marines invaded Bougainville, their long-awaited campaign in the central Pacific began. Sixteen transports carrying the combat-ready marines of the 2d Marine Division departed the New Hebrides on November 11, 1943. During the preceding weeks of training the marines had been shown maps of their target. The code name of the bird-shaped little island was *Helen*.

Admiral Nimitz's major objective in the central Pacific was Kwajalein Atoll in the Marshall Islands. Ruling the Marshalls since the 1920s under a League of Nations mandate had allowed the Japanese to turn the sixty-five-mile-long atoll into a well-fortified major air and naval base. Without the Marshalls the U.S. advance toward Japan would be stymied. But U.S. planners realized that before the Marshalls could be taken the Gilbert Islands, five hundred miles to the southeast, had to be wrested from the enemy.

Seized from the British early in World War II, the Gilberts had been used by the Japanese as their easternmost outpost. The presence of the Japanese on these coral islands not only hampered any attack on the Marshalls, but also threatened Allied communications between the central and southwest Pacific.

Central Pacific atolls presented very attractive objectives for the U.S. Navy. Their generally flat surfaces made good airfields. Their calm inner lagoons made excellent anchorages where vast armadas could escape the ravages of the sea.

The coral atolls did pose special problems for the ground forces. Their landing craft risked hanging up on the treacherous reefs ringing the atolls. Once ashore they had little, if any, cover.

The jagged coral formations provided hundreds of niches from which the Japanese defenders would have to be dug out one by one. Exploding artillery and mortar shells tore the coral into lethal chunks, multiplying injuries.

The key to the Gilbert Islands was Tarawa Atoll, located at the northern end of the chain. The largest of Tarawa's forty-seven islands was Betio, on the atoll's southwest corner; *Helen* to the invading marines. Just over two miles long and barely half a mile wide, Betio contained a Japanese airstrip and their major fortifications. Two thousand six hundred seasoned Japanese marines defended Betio. Fourteen huge coastal guns guarded the shoreline. No less than forty artillery pieces were sighted on the landing locations. Over one hundred machine guns covered every square inch of water approaching the island.

Twelve hundred Korean laborers had dug hundreds of deep holes in the coral, lined them with steel and concrete, covered them with logs and coral, then camouflaged them with scrub bushes. An intricate network of tunnels connected most of the positions and protected the defenders. The island's main command bunker was two stories high, with walls eight feet thick. Heavily reinforced with steel and concrete, the bunker could withstand a direct hit from an eight-inch shell. The Japanese commander, Rear Adm. Keiji Shibasaki, bragged, ''A million men cannot take Tarawa in a hundred years.''

He was wrong. Twelve thousand marines would take it in three days.

On maps, Betio resembled an upside-down bird. The invading marines would hit the bird's belly, or north coast, which faced the lagoon. Three battalions comprised the assault force. From east to west they were: 2d Battalion, 8th Marines; 2d Battalion, 2d Marines; and 3d Battalion, 2d Marines. Three more battalions would land in follow-up waves. Amphibious tractors (amtracs) would carry the initial waves across the coral reef to shore. They would then return to the reef to off-load marines from larger landing boats.

The invasion began early on the morning of November 20, 1943. Three battleships hurled their massive shells onto the tiny island. They were joined by dozens of cruisers and destroyers. Overhead, scores of carrier-based fighter planes dropped their bombs into the carnage. To observers, Betio seemed to disappear in smoke and flame.

Aboard the churning amtracs anxious marines prepared for what lay ahead. The massive barrage comforted many of the youngsters. They didn't think anyone could survive the brutal bombardment.

As the main assault waves crossed the line of departure, some Americans were already ashore. The division's scout-sniper platoon had the job of knocking out any Japanese on a long pier that jutted into the lagoon from Betio's north shore.

WILLIAM D. HAWKINS

Lean and lithe, 1st Lt. William D. Hawkins almost didn't make it into the military. Born April 18, 1914, at Fort Scott, Kansas, Hawkins moved with his family to El Paso, Texas, in 1919. There, he suffered a tragic accident. A neighbor accidentally spilled a large pot of boiling water on him.

A doctor saved Hawkins's life, but the child's future looked bleak. Scar tissue covered a third of his body. Its tautness left one arm crooked and his left leg drawn up. The doctor recommended surgery to cut the muscles of the afflicted limbs, but Hawkins's mother, the daughter of a doctor, refused. She knew such surgery would leave her son a cripple. Instead, she massaged his arm and leg for two hours every day. Amazingly, over the next year, the massage cured the damaged muscles. Within two years young Hawkins could walk without a limp and throw a baseball with his injured arm.

All through high school, and at the Texas College of Mines, Hawkins excelled in athletics, playing baseball and football. He spent his summer vacations working as a bellhop, ranchhand, and railroad section hand to help support his newly widowed mother.

With his engineering degree Hawkins took a job in Los Angeles. Like millions of other young men, Hawkins rushed to enlist right after Pearl Harbor. He tried the army and army air force, but they rejected him. The examining doctors took one look at his heavily scarred body and shook their heads. The scar tissue did not hamper him physically, but the regulations said he had too much of it, period.

The marines were not that strict. They were glad to have him. He signed up January 5, 1942. After basic training he attended scout and sniper school, then joined the 2d Marine Division. On November 17, 1942, after proving his courage and leadership abilities in several firefights on Guadalcanal, Hawkins received a battlefield promotion to second lieutenant. In rest camp in Australia on June 1, 1943, he received his silver bars. He also took command of the scout-sniper platoon.

On Betio, the 500-yard-long pier jutting into the lagoon contained a number of well-fortified Japanese positions. If they weren't eliminated they could send deadly enfilading fire into the marines storming the shore.

Aboard their amtracs Hawkins's men huddled low while enemy mortars crashed about them. At the pier Hawkins was the first out of the boat. Firing his carbine he drilled two Japanese machine gunners. Around him his men unlimbered flamethrowers. Down the pier Hawkins led his platoon. Throwing grenades, using a flamethrower, and firing his rifle, he wiped out one position after another, leaving the pier a smoldering wreck.

Ashore, literally dozens of Japanese automatic weapons sent a blizzard of lead flying over a four-foot-high coconut log seawall, pinning down the marines who had made it to shore. Hawkins disregarded the fire to lead the way in leaping the seawall. A round slammed into his lower leg, but he ignored it. He organized an assault squad from the few others who had ventured over the wall, then led it forward to wipe out a particularly pesky machine gun. With that done, he took the squad forward, fighting Japanese every inch of the way.

By nightfall that first day Hawkins had led his men in knocking out no less than four enemy machine-gun nests. He'd also been hit a second time, taking a sniper's bullet in his shoulder. While the corpsman bandaged him Hawkins cautioned the medic, "Don't pull it so tight that I'll have trouble shooting."

Hawkins took a third hit on the afternoon of November 21. Already that day he'd helped destroy three more machine-gun nests. When he was tagged for evacuation Hawkins refused to go. Under pressure to do so he radioed Col. David M. Shoup, commander of marines ashore on Betio.

"I came here to kill Japs," he said. "I didn't come here to be evacuated."

"All right," answered Shoup, "you can stay."

Stay he did. Before nightfall Hawkins moved the survivors of his platoon against a heavy cluster of enemy machine guns. While they laid down a base of fire, Hawkins dashed from gun to gun. He stood in full view of the Japanese to shoot point-blank into the slits of pillboxes. Then he tossed in grenades to finish off the occupants. A mortar shell erupted near him, killing three of his men and wounding him again.

But still Hawkins refused to quit. He moved out against a pillbox at the base of a small, sandy knoll. He tossed grenades at it. He'd thrown maybe six when a heavy machine gun fired directly at him. An explosive shell tore into his shoulder. Blood gushed from the hole. Seconds later Hawkins died.

The Marine Corps later named the airstrip at Betio in Hawkins's honor. On August 30, 1944, Hawkins's mother accepted his posthumous Medal of Honor. A few years later the El Paso city council voted to name one of the city's major streets after the gallant hero.

Many of the troop-laden amtracs hung up on the coral reefs lining the lagoon. There they were easy prey for the accurate Japanese artillery fire. A few were able to transfer their loads to a handful of battered amtracs that had made it across the reef. Of those amtracs, few made it all the way in to the beach. Most stopped hundreds of yards short, forcing the marines to wade the rest of the way through chest-deep water. Unable to return fire, they were slaughtered by the Japanese gunners. Hundreds died in the water. For days afterwards their swollen corpses bobbed grotesquely in the lagoon.

Those marines who made it ashore found temporary shelter behind the seawall. Though they were protected from machine-gun fire, blasts from enemy mortars killed and wounded more of them. Here and there small groups of men braved the heavy fire to crawl over the seawall to carry the battle to the Japanese. Occasionally a lone marine struck at the enemy.

One was S. Sgt. William Bordelon. He was one of just four men to survive the shelling of his amtrac five hundred yards from shore. The twenty-two-year-old San Antonio, Texas, native, a member of an assault engineer platoon attached to the 2d Marine Division, lost all but a few packs of dynamite in his struggle to reach the seawall. He busied himself gathering dynamite from those around him.

Then he sprang erect and went after the pillboxes. By charging them from the side he avoided their direct fire. Twice he tossed bundles of demolitions. Twice the pillboxes erupted in a thundering crash. He went after a third, but enemy machine-gun bullets knocked him down. He regained his feet, threw the dynamite, and knocked out the enemy position.

Back behind the seawall, instead of seeking first aid, Bordelon answered the cries for help from a wounded marine floundering in the surf. He saved another comrade, then, though bleeding badly, went after a fourth Japanese machine-gun nest. This time the enemy saw him coming and shot him dead.

For the first eighteen hours the situation on Betio was desperate. All along the thin beachhead, men were pinned down. Of the three assault battalions, only one landed intact. The 2d Battalion, 2d Marines, lost its commander just west of the pier. Half of the seven hundred men from the 3d Battalion, 2d Marines, were killed or wounded. Only about a hundred of its members made it ashore the first day. The rest, including the battalion commander, were still in amtracs hung up on the reef. That the entire assault didn't collapse in the face of the terrible resistance was primarily due to the courage and resourcefulness of the assault force's commander.

DAVID M. SHOUP

As a lieutenant colonel on the staff of the 2d Marine Division in 1942, David M. Shoup helped plan the assault on Tarawa. He had no idea he'd end up leading the assault. But then, during the practice landings in the New Hebrides, the assault commander took ill. The barrel-chested, bull-necked, cigar-chomping Shoup took his place.

The son of a farmer, Shoup was born in Battleground, Indiana, on December 30, 1904. After earning a degree in mathematics from DePauw University in 1926, Shoup took his ROTC commission as a second lieutenant in the Marine Corps. Years of foreign and shipboard duty followed.

In July 1942, Shoup joined the staff of the 2d Marine Division. He saw some action as an observer with the army's 43d Infantry Division on New Georgia, but Betio would be his first real combat experience.

Though he planned the operation, Shoup had some concerns about the plan. En route to Tarawa he expressed them to a correspondent. "The first wave will get in okay, but if the amtracs fail we'll either have to wade in with machine guns shooting at us, or the amtracs will have to run a shuttle service between the beach and the end of the shelf."

He was right on both accounts.

Shoup himself barely made it onto Betio that first day. His Higgins boat got stranded on a reef. Twice he hailed passing amtracs, but they didn't stop. Finally, about 10:00 A.M., he and his staff transferred to a boat that took them toward the fighting. On the way in Shoup took reports from his onshore commanders.

"Receiving heavy fire all along the beach. Unable to land. Issue in doubt."

Another message said, "Boats held up on reef of right flank Red Beach One. Troops receiving heavy fire in water."

Shoup radioed back: "Land Beach Red 2 and work west."

The reply stunned Shoup: "We have nothing left to land."

Shoup still hadn't reached the beach. Extremely heavy enemy fire kept driving them off. Twice they approached the end of the pier where Hawkins had done such a good job. Unfortunately, Japanese troops had swum back out to the pier and remanned their guns.

Finally one hundred yards from the pier, Shoup had enough of the delays. "Come on," he yelled to those with him, "we'll walk or swim in." Holding his map case and carbine over his head he jumped overboard. He made the pier. Shoup set up his command post in the waist deep water.

All around him chaos raged. Everywhere he looked corpses floated while wounded men painfully struggled to make the relative safety of the seawall. Here and there men disappeared when they stepped in submerged shell holes, their heavy equipment dragging them under.

Shoup finally made it ashore after commandeering a passing amtrac. He set up his command post in a sand-and-log bunker fifteen yards inland. A few minutes later, while he was outside his bunker giving orders, a mortar shell knocked him flat on his back. Jagged pieces of metal tore into his legs. He rose and hobbled on.

The leg wound proved worse than Shoup originally thought. He fell into a slight state of shock from the intense pain, but shook it off. He had to remain clearheaded to fight the battle.

Shoup worked frantically to communicate with his shattered command. He had to rely on runners to deliver his orders. He also had trouble reaching his superiors offshore. They did not know the true situation onshore. It would be many more hours before they did.

On the second morning Shoup learned his marines on Betio's western end had made remarkable progress. They had silenced the Japanese in their sector, actually driving to the edge of the airfield before nightfall forced a withdrawal.

Some reinforcements had made it to shore under cover of darkness. A handful of artillery pieces arrived, too. At daybreak, with communications reestablished, Shoup ordered his battered marines to attack. That was the only way to take the heat off the beachhead.

Except for a few catnaps during the night, Shoup had been on his feet for thirty hours. Since early morning he'd been on the radio asking for men, ammo, medical supplies, rations, and water. When asked by his superior if he had enough troops to do the job, Shoup answered, "No. We're in a mighty tough spot."

His marines made progress, though. Against stubborn resistance they fought as hard as they could. It was not easy. At one point a tearful young major stumbled into Shoup's command post.

"Colonel, there are a thousand goddamn marines on that beach, and not one will follow me across the airstrip."

Shoup spat in disgust. "You've got to say, 'Who'll follow me?' And if only ten follow you, that's the best you can do. But it's better than nothing."

By four that afternoon Shoup began feeling better about the fight. Reports from his combat units indicated they were overrunning the Japanese. More reinforcements poured ashore. A higher tide made it possible for the amtracs to carry the marines right to the seawall. Around six that night he radioed his command ship: "Casualties many; Percentage dead unknown; combat efficiency: we are winning."

At dusk, an entire battalion made it ashore without a single loss. That night the Japanese launched a desperate counterattack. They fell in droves in front of the marines' guns. In midmorning on the third day a navy Hellcat fighter landed on the airstrip. At 1:30 P.M. Betio was declared secure.

At 6:00 P.M. Shoup was relieved by Col. Merritt "Red Mike" Edson. "Dave," said Edson, "you look like you've been hit by a tank."

Shoup, bearded and blurry-eyed after sixty hours without sleep, grunted. "It's about time you showed up. Everything's downhill from here."

Following a few weeks in the hospital Shoup rejoined the 2d Marine Division as its chief of staff. He remained with the division through its campaigns in the Marianas Islands, then returned to the United States. He assumed duties at Headquarters, U.S. Marine Corps. On January 22, 1945, Navy Secretary James V. Forrestal presented Shoup his Medal of Honor.

Shoup had a brilliant postwar career. He received his first star in April 1953. Six years later he was nominated by President Eisenhower to be the twenty-second commandant of the Marine Corps. He began his four-year term on January 1, 1960. Shoup was a fiercely independent, strong-minded commandant who stirred considerable controversy by opposing the American buildup in South Vietnam. Even after he retired in 1964, Shoup continued to criticize America's involvement in Southeast Asia. He died on January 13, 1983.

Losses at Betio were shocking. In the seventy-six-hour fight for the tiny chunk of coral, 1,056 Americans died. Another 2,292 were wounded. Back home, the public recoiled in horror. Parents of dead marines flooded Congress with letters. Even Admiral Nimitz received letters from bereaved parents.

The casualty rates worried the navy. A study of the operation revealed the need for better information on enemy fortifications. The navy concluded that the preinvasion bombardment had been ineffective in destroying the well-built enemy positions. What was needed was a more accurate bombardment for a longer period of time with heavier shells.

Meanwhile, in the southwest Pacific, General MacArthur's leapfrogging along the coast of New Guinea and Admiral Halsey's move up the Solomons chain had finally neutralized the effectiveness of the major Japanese base at Rabaul. In accordance with their new strategy the two commanders agreed to bypass the base. Rather than needlessly risk American lives by invading eastern New Britain, the Americans would allow Rabaul to "wither on the vine" as the war pushed onward.

But that did not mean a complete end to the fighting in the area. The Japanese still possessed a considerable number of aircraft, planes that could be used to harass Allied shipping throughout the area. On nearly a daily basis American airmen clashed with Japanese. During this period a Marine Corps Corsair pilot secured a place in history as the marines' top air ace and created another legend.

GREGORY "PAPPY" BOYINGTON

Maj. Gregory Boyington was called "Pappy" because he was already an ancient thirty-one when he arrived in the South Pacific in the summer of 1943. The collection of oddball and misfit pilots he welded into VMF-214 called themselves the "Black Sheep." It reflected their perception of how the brass viewed them. A boisterous, caustic, cynical, hard-drinking man, Boyington whipped his young mavericks into a keen fighting unit in less than thirty days in mid-1943. Under his leadership the Black Sheep amassed an enviable combat record.

Boyington was born in Coeur d'Alene, Idaho, on December 4, 1912. The son of a dentist father and a music-teacher mother, Boyington grew up in Idaho and Tacoma, Washington. He majored in aeronautical engineering at the University of Washington, graduating in 1934. Always a keen athlete, he was a member of the college wrestling and swim teams.

Boyington took his ROTC commission in the army's coastal artillery corps, but what he really wanted to do was fly. In 1935 he finagled a transfer to the Marine Corps and their aviation training program. He earned his wings on March 11, 1937. Over the next four years he flew with the 2d Marine Air Group and the crack Marine Corps exhibition flying team. In 1941, while an instructor at the Naval Air Station, Pensacola, Florida, Boyington resigned his commission to accept a position with the Central Aircraft Manufacturing Co.

CAMCO was the cover name for an organization charged with finding pilots to fight the Japanese in China and Burma. It later became known as the "Flying Tigers." Boyington spent nearly a year with the group. In that time he flew over three hundred combat hours and shot down six Japanese planes.

When the Flying Tigers disbanded in July 1942 Boyington immediately requested reinstatement in the marines. To his amazement he found himself *persona non grata* for leaving the country in a "time of national emergency." After three months of rebuff Boyington fired off a last desperate telegram to the secretary of the navy. It worked. He gave up parking cars in a

Seattle city garage, slipped on the forest green of the marines, and headed to Guadalcanal.

By September 1943 Pappy had completed the training of his Black Sheep. From their base in the Russell Islands their Corsairs roared aloft on their first mission on September 16. They were to protect a formation of bombers headed for Ballale Airfield on Bougainville. When the bombers started down on their run Boyington and his nineteen Black Sheep started down, too. They ran smack into forty Zeroes coming through a cloud layer.

One Zero roared right up to Boyington, waggling its wings in a friendly gesture. Pappy squeezed his trigger. Nothing. He'd forgotten to arm his guns! Seconds later that problem was resolved, and he had his first victory as a marine.

Streaking downward to where the bombers were forming up for the flight home, Boyington flashed by another Zero. A quick burst of the trigger and the Corsair's six .50-caliber machine guns spat out a deadly spray that destroyed the enemy.

Boyington now found himself alone. The bombers and other Corsairs had headed for home. He turned back to the remaining Zeroes. He snuck up on one flying low and slow over the water. Sensing a trap, he pulled up just in time to meet another Zero coming at him head on. Boyington's bullets ripped into the plane. It fell seaward, smoking.

Low on fuel, Boyington turned for home. Then he spotted an unsuspecting Zero. A quick, single burst sent him down in flames.

This had been an impressive first mission. Boyington called it a day and, without enough fuel to make the Russells, set a course for the new airstrip at Munda. As he neared the airstrip he sighted an oil-smeared, bullet-scarred Corsair flying low over the water, a Zero hot on its tail. He roared down on the unsuspecting enemy, his guns chattering. The Zero stood on its tail. Boyington stitched a pattern of bullets up the plane's back. It exploded in flames.

When Boyington landed, his tanks were dry and he had thirty rounds of ammo left. He was also a double ace. In addition to his five victories, his squadron had downed another six Zeroes. The baaing of the Black Sheep was beginning to be heard.

In the next thirty-two days Boyington destroyed fourteen more Japanese planes. On December 23, 1943, Boyington led forty-eight Corsairs on a sweep to Rabaul. They caught forty enemy fighters in the air. A sky-filled dogfight broke out. When it was over, thirty of the enemy planes had gone down—twelve by the Black Sheep alone, of which Boyington flamed four. His score stood at twenty-four. Joe Foss's record of twenty-six was in danger for the first time in a year.

Two days after Christmas the Black Sheep flew back to Rabaul. The Japanese raced skyward to battle the Corsairs. Boyington tangled with a Zero. It went down. He was one victory away from tying Foss's record. He flashed eagerly among the remaining Zeroes, searching for a target. Then oil sprayed over his windshield. He tried three times without success to wipe away the film. Frustrated, he returned to his base at Torokina Airfield on Bougainville.

Bad weather kept him there for the next week.

The pressure on Boyington to beat Foss's record had been building in intensity. War correspondents badgered him incessantly. His Black Sheep were eager for him to take the lead as America's premier ace. Boyington himself wanted to get it over and done with. On January 3, 1944, Boyington got back into the air, leading a flight of forty-eight fighters toward Rabaul. His wingman, Capt. George Ashmun, told him, "You go ahead and shoot all you want, Gramps. All I'll do is keep 'em off your tail." Over Rabaul forty to sixty Japanese fighters rose to challenge the marines. "Let's get the bastards!" Boyington shouted over the radio.

"I poured a long burst into the first enemy plane that approached," Pappy later said. "A fraction of a second later I saw the pilot catapult out and the plane itself break into fire."

Boyington had no time to savor his victory. Too much was going on. He and Ashmun climbed. Twenty Japanese fighters jumped them. They scissored back and forth, protecting each other's blind spots. Ashmun flamed one Zero. Seconds later Boyington dropped another—number twenty-seven. But then he saw Ashmun's Corsair going down in a long, smoky glide, a dozen Zeroes on his tail.

Ignoring the odds, Boyington dove after the Zeroes. He kicked his rudder back and forth, spraying the enemy planes indiscriminately. Ahead of him, Ashmun's flaming Corsair crashed into the sea. Boyington drilled one of the enemy pursuers. It hit the water alongside Ashmun. Pappy Boyington had his twenty-eighth—and last—kill.

A pack of Zeroes chased Boyington across the water. He slammed his throttle forward, racing along at over four hundred knots, one hundred feet above the water. He could see the enemy rounds stitching patterns in his wing. All of a sudden his main gas tank blew up. He ejected. His parachute barely opened before he crashed into the water. The relief at being alive was short-lived. Four Zeroes zoomed down, strafing the water around Boyington. He dove repeatedly until the Japanese tired of the game and left. Then Boyington inflated his little life raft and climbed aboard.

He was hurt worse than he first thought. A piece of his scalp hung over his eyes. His left ear was nearly chewed off. His arms and shoulders had several shrapnel holes. A 20-mm round had shattered his left ankle. His left calf had a hole in it. Another bullet had torn a gash bigger than his fist in his left thigh. He gave himself what first aid he could. Eight hours later a Japanese submarine surfaced and took him aboard. Two hours later he was on a dock at Rabaul. His captors brutally tortured Boyington for several weeks. Blindfolded, he was kicked, beaten with ropes, and burned with lit cigarettes. For his entire six-week stay at Rabaul, Boyington suffered repeated indignation and torture.

Finally, after an intermittent stop at Truk, Boyington was sent to Japan. He languished in a Japanese POW camp near Yokohama until the war ended. After repatriation and hospitalization he received his Medal of Honor from President Truman in the Rose Garden of the White House on October 5, 1945. He also received a Navy Cross for downing three planes on his last mission.

Boyington's postwar life resembled a roller coaster. Ever the cynic, in his 1958 autobiography, *Baa Baa Black Sheep*, he downplayed his status as a hero, saying, ''Show me a hero and I'll show you a bum.'' He knew what he was talking about. Plagued by alcoholism, marital problems, and income tax difficulties, he was frequently down in the dumps. For a time he earned his living as a referee for professional wrestlers.

Boyington enjoyed a resurgence of popularity in 1976 when a TV series based on his exploits hit the screens. His last years were spent near Fresno, California, with his fourth wife. He painted for relaxation, turning out above-average desert and combat scenes.

As he grew older Boyington tired of recounting his wartime exploits. "The stuff is all gone, and I'd just as soon let it go and forget it," he said in a 1972 interview. "I rarely ever talk about it unless someone brings it up. I don't want to bore anybody or give the impression of being a bore."

One thing Pappy Boyington never had to worry about was being a bore. He died on January 11, 1988.

With the Gilberts in American hands it was now time to go after the Marshall Islands. Capturing them would accomplish two objectives: First, they would give the Americans an airbase within B-29 Superfortress range of Japan. Second, their capture would eliminate the need to assault Truk Island in the Carolinas. This massive Japanese base could then be bypassed, just like Rabaul.

The Japanese had airfields on six atolls in the Marshalls: Eniwetok, Kwajalein, Wotje, Maloelap, Jaluit, and Mili. Eniwetok sat farthest west. Kwajalein was in the center, Wotje and Maloelap were east and north, and Jaluit and Mili were east and south. Admiral Nimitz chose Kwajalein Atoll for his main thrust. By knifing into the heart of the Marshalls he could bypass the eastern atolls. Intelligence had also shown Kwajalein Atoll to be lightly defended.

The assault force consisted of the New York National Guard 27th Infantry Division and the 4th Marine Division. The 27th Division would assault Kwajalein Island on the south side of the atoll. The newly created 4th Marine Division (it had sailed directly to the Marshalls from San Diego) would send two regiments against the twin islands of Roi-Namur on the atoll's north side.

At 8:00 A.M., January 31, 1944, the naval bombardment of Roi-Namur began. Three battleships and two score of cruisers and destroyers pounded the little islands throughout the day and into the next morning. The 23d Marines were scheduled to hit the beaches of Roi at 10:00 A.M., February 1. Local squalls postponed the landing until noon. The untried marines raced rapidly inland against only minor opposition. The lengthy preinvasion bombardment had done its job.

After consolidating their positions, and with tanks ashore, the marines swept forward again at 4:00 P.M. Hundreds of minor skirmishes broke out. Dazed and leaderless, the Japanese fought desperately. Some hid in drainage ditches and fired into the rear of advancing marines. Others made frantic stands in the ruins of pillboxes. At one of these, twenty-two-year-old marine Pfc. Richard B. Anderson of Tacoma, Washington, jumped into a shell hole occupied by three marines. He pulled the pin of a grenade. As he prepared to throw it, the missile slipped from his hands. There was no time to retrieve it. It had been his fault. He compensated for it by leaping on the grenade as it exploded. The other three marines survived; Anderson died.

The marines reached the north shore of Roi at 6:00 P.M. The little island was in American hands.

Across the causeway, the 24th Marines were having a tougher time. Namur was more heavily defended than Roi. The rookie marines bogged down several times. Each time the gallantry of a few marines pushed the attack forward. One of them was 1st Lt. John V. Power of Worcester, Massachusetts. When his platoon was pinned down by devastating fire from a pillbox they tried to take it with grenades but were driven back. Power charged forward. He took a round in the belly. Covering the wound with his left hand and firing his carbine with his right, he continued forward. Hit twice more, he died in the entrance of the pillbox. His platoon swarmed up behind him, wiping out the enemy.

The surviving Japanese attacked that night. In the pale moonlight little knots of men fought viciously for survival. The individual fights raged through the night. With dawn, the marines spread out, hunting down and killing the remaining enemy. By noon, February 2, the battle for Namur was over. Roi-Namur was one of the shortest operations in the Pacific. Marine casualties came to 190 dead and 547 wounded. They buried over 3,400 Japanese and captured another 264.

Two days later the army's 27th Division completed the capture of Kwajalein Island. The American sledgehammer assault in the Marshalls smashed the outer layer of Japan's defensive perimeter. It opened the way for the thousand-mile advance to the Marianas Islands. From there the Japanese home islands would be even closer for the huge B-29 bombers.

An aircraft carrier attack on the fortress at Truk at the same time as the Marshalls assault resulted in 41 Japanese ships sunk and 200 planes destroyed. In two days of air raids, American planes sank 200,000 tons of enemy shipping. This loss seriously hampered the Japanese ability to resupply its other island bases. It also set off a serious debate in Japan between the army and navy chiefs as to how best to defend the home islands. One result was the sacking of the navy chief of staff, Admiral Nagumo, the Pearl Harbor architect. For the first time, the possibility of defeat occurred to the Japanese. The inner islands, the Marianas, Palaus, and Philippines, would have to be defended that much more resolutely.

In the southwest Pacific General MacArthur continued with his plans to leapfrog along New Guinea's north coast. With the isolation of Rabaul this area now became the core of Japanese strength in the theater. All along the 1,200-mile coastline the enemy had spotted their bases to cover every sector. MacArthur carefully selected his landing sites. Among them were Madang, Hansa Bay, Wewak, Aitape, and Hollandia.

While MacArthur prepared for these offensives General Kenney's Fifth Air Force continued its attacks on Japanese land bases and the ships supplying them. Weather permitting, Kenney's bombers and fighters went on missions every day. The attacks on Rabaul were nearly ceaseless, as were air strikes against Japanese airdromes along the north coast.

In late January 1944, the Fifth Air Force was assigned a supporting role for the last operation in the Solomons. Admiral Halsey was scheduled to occupy Green Island, just over a hundred miles east of Rabaul and off Bougainville's north coast. To protect the February 15 landing, Kenney's bombers would knock out the Japanese air bases at Kavieng, on the northwest tip of New Ireland, north of Rabaul.

Beginning on February 10, Kenney's bombers started hitting the air bases around Kavieng. B-25s pounded the area mercilessly for five days. On the last raid forty B-24s ruined the remaining Japanese airdrome, silenced three antiaircraft batteries, and set fires that blazed into the night. The Liberators were followed by sixty-five B-25s. They set fire to the tower area, destroyed the airplane and engine-repair facilities, destroyed ten patrol planes in the harbor, and blew up an ammo dump in a massive explosion. The enemy antiaircraft fire proved deadly, though. Several bombers were hit. One went down at the entrance to Kavieng Harbor. A call went out for an air-sea rescue plane.

NATHAN G. GORDON

Flying his PBY Catalina amphibious patrol plane a short distance from Kavieng was twenty-seven-year-old navy Lt. Nathan G. Gordon. A lawyer from Morrilton, Arkansas, Gordon enlisted in the navy's aviation cadet program in May 1941. Although he had never been in an airplane before, he decided he wanted to fly. He took his primary training in New Orleans, then headed to the PBY training school at Jacksonville, Florida. He earned his wings and an ensign's commission in February 1942.

Duty in the Caribbean flying antisubmarine patrols with VP-34 occupied Gordon's next year. From there he and his squadron mates served in Hawaii, at Midway Island, and near the Gilbert Islands flying a variety of missions. Eventually they ended up in Perth, Australia, patrolling the vast Indian Ocean for any signs of the Japanese navy.

At the end of December 1943, VP-34 headed for the seaplane base at Samarai, a small island off the southern tip of New Guinea's Papuan Peninsula. For the first time the squadron went on the offensive.

"We flew dozens of night missions against Japanese shipping in the Bismark Sea," Gordon said. "We executed low-level bombing and torpedo missions against their merchant ships. We'd leave our base in the late afternoon, fly to our operational area, spend the entire night searching for and bombing Japanese ships, then head back to Samarai at dawn.

"Our success is in the statistics. Four destroyers and one escort vessel damaged, over seventy-three thousand tons of shipping sunk, and between fifty and seventy-five barrages destroyed. It was a grueling job, but we did it well."

On February 14, Gordon was told his assignment the next day would be as a standby rescue plane for the strike on Kavieng Harbor.

The first call for help came soon after they'd taken up their assigned position. A B-25 had gone down about forty miles from Kavieng Harbor. Gordon raced to the site. He and his crew searched the area but could find no sign of a downed plane.

They had just departed the area when they received another message of a downed B-25. This one was right in Kavieng Harbor. They flew to the area, about a mile off shore. Gordon quickly spotted life rafts and dye markers but no survivors.

Though the sea was running in ten-to-fifteen-foot swells, making a landing particularly hazardous, Gordon opted to put down anyway in case there were survivors. The rough sea popped some rivets in the plane's hull, but Gordon still taxied around for several minutes. He could find no sign of life. He took off again.

A few minutes later he received a report of a third downed bomber. A fighter pilot said he'd circle overhead offering protection if the PBY would try a pickup. Gordon was apprehensive because the site was so close to the shore batteries, but headed for the scene anyway.

For the third time, Gordon flew back into Kavieng Harbor. Japanese shore batteries immediately took him under fire. As he landed, huge plumes of water danced around his plane. Shrapnel rattled against the PBY's thin aluminum skin. Oblivious to the danger, Gordon continued taxiing, his crew searching for the downed airmen. Suddenly, one of them spotted six men floating in a raft. They threw a rope to the occupants, but with the plane's two engines running they couldn't get the raft close enough to pull the men aboard.

"I realized to save them I'd have to cut my engines," Gordon said. "They were difficult to start under normal conditions, but I had no choice. If I didn't save those men they'd be captured and perhaps die."

He killed the twin engines. The PBY slowed to a standstill, a perfect target for the Japanese gunners. His crew started pulling the badly injured airmen aboard. All the while shells from the shore batteries dropped dangerously close. Only the up-and-down movement of the amphibious plane in the heavy sea prevented a direct hit.

With the men safely aboard, Gordon started the engines and took off. He was barely airborne when another call came. Another plane was down, this one even closer to shore. Would Gordon get them? He turned back. "A lot of enemy fire was hitting around us, but I had too many other things to worry about," Gordon said.

As before, Gordon landed, taxied up to the raft, the crew threw the three men a line, Gordon cut the engines, and the airmen were pulled aboard. Turning sharply to avoid an exploding shell, Gordon took off and started for home. He made twenty miles before the call came. Another plane was down. Six men were in life rafts only six hundred yards from shore. Would Gordon get them? He instantly turned around. As he flew over the raft he saw a new problem. In order to make the proper approach for the landing, parallel to the swells, Gordon would have to fly directly over the shore, completely exposed to Japanese fire. He never hesitated.

Skimming across the shore at just three hundred feet, his men firing every available weapon down at the Japanese, Gordon brought the PBY in for a perfect landing. A virtual cascade of enemy fire descended on the plane. Just five hundred yards from shore, Gordon calmly cut his engines while his crew pulled the airmen aboard. Turning sharply right and left to avoid the shells' splashes, he began his takeoff run. With the extra bodies aboard, the plane needed a much longer distance before it became airborne. Slowly, sluggishly, the heavy plane rose into the air. Gordon's incredible display of raw courage in defying the enemy gunners and his remarkable flying abilities saved fifteen men from certain capture. He headed for a seaplane base on New Guinea's coast. There he debarked the casualties, then headed for a well-deserved rest at Samarai.

Rear Adm. Thomas C. Kincaid, the chief of MacArthur's naval forces, presented Gordon the Medal of Honor on July 13, 1944, in ceremonies at Brisbane, Australia. At the same ceremony every one of Gordon's crew received a Silver Star.

After the war Gordon returned to his law practice in Morrilton. In 1947 he ran for lieutenant governor. He won that election, and each succeeding election for that office, until he retired in 1967. He then returned to the practice of law.

Before MacArthur began his move along New Guinea's north coast he decided on a side operation to capture the Admiralty Islands. Sitting like sentinels at the northern entrance to the Bismarck Sea, the Admiralties would not only prevent the Japanese from reinforcing Rabaul, but would give MacArthur another base from which to support his upcoming landings farther west on New Guinea. He set the landings for February 29, 1944.

Faulty intelligence convinced MacArthur the islands could be quickly conquered. He sent one thousand untried men of the 1st Cavalry Division's 5th Cavalry Regiment to invade Los Negros Island. By attacking the rear of the island rather than its harbor the cavalrymen took the Japanese defenders by surprise. Five hours after the landing the island's airport was in American hands.

On March 3, fifteen hundred more cavalrymen landed on Los Negros. They were just in time. The next night three thousand drink-crazed Japanese charged the American positions. While a loudspeaker blared "Deep in the Heart of Texas" at the Americans, wave after wave of suicidal Japanese, firing rifles and throwing grenades, charged straight at them.

Twenty-nine-year-old Sgt. Troy McGill's machine-gun position bore the brunt of one local attack. He and his eight-man squad faced two hundred enemy soldiers. They fought frantically until only McGill and one other man remained. The gutsy sergeant ordered the man to fall back, then turned to his machine gun. He blazed away, dropping enemy soldiers left and right until he ran out of ammo. With the Japanese sweeping down on him, McGill grabbed an M-1 and rose out of his foxhole. He bashed the enemy with the rifle until they overwhelmed him and killed him.

The American line held. The cavalrymen spent the next two days mopping up the remnants of the Japanese defenders. The Admiralties were declared secure on March 6.

On March 12, the Joint Chiefs of Staff formally approved MacArthur's plan for advancing along New Guinea's north coast. At the same time they ordered Admiral Nimitz to proceed with his plans to capture three more island groups in the central Pacific—the Marianas, Carolinas, and Palaus. The final drive to Tokyo had begun.

11

* * *

To the Marianas

The next stepping stones in Admiral Nimitz's drive across the Pacific were the Marianas Islands. Lying fifteen hundred miles east of the Philippines and only thirteen hundred miles southeast of Japan, the Marianas were key strongholds in the Japanese defensive chain. Possession of these islands would irrevocably cut off the Japanese base at Truk, pierce Japan's second line of defense, provide another base for the huge new B-29 bombers to bomb Japan, and might lure the remnants of the Japanese fleet into a decisive final battle.

Of the three major islands comprising the Marianas—Saipan, Tinian, and Guam—Guam was the major objective. A U.S. possession for over forty years, Guam had been easily overwhelmed in the early days of World War II. Retaking the island would have a larger symbolic than strategic effect. Guam would be the first American-held territory to be recaptured from the Japanese. Its occupation would be a major morale booster to all Americans, civilian and military.

To take Guam, Admiral Nimitz decided to attack Saipan first. Not only would Saipan's capture cut off Japanese air support to Guam, but Saipan also held the headquarters of Japan's Central Pacific Fleet and its 31st Army. Taking Saipan would cripple resistance on the other two islands.

Saipan was unlike any other single island the marines had so far assaulted. Fourteen miles long by six miles wide, it had numerous caves like those found on Tulagi, mountains and dense jungle like Guadalcanal's, a reef like Tarawa's, and swamps like Bougainville's. In addition, there was a city and a civilian population. The island's southern half had wide-open plains where large-scale military maneuvering would be subjected to heavy artillery fire. A fifteen-hundred-foot peak, Mount Tapotchau, dominated the center of the island. To the north, a series of high plateaus and rolling hills ended sharply in steep coastal cliffs that dropped hundreds of feet to the sea.

Saipan was defended by approximately thirty-one thousand Japanese troops. Most of them were soldiers of the 43d Division and the 47th Mixed Independent Brigade under Lt. Gen. Yoshitsugo Saito. Adm. Chuichi Nagumo, assigned to the Marianas after falling in disfavor with the Japanese military hierarchy, had 6,100 naval troops under his command.

To assault well-defended Saipan the Americans had two full marine divisions. The 2d and 4th Divisions would go ashore on Saipan's southwest coast on June 15, 1944. They would push inland until well established on the interior's high ground. The 2d Division would then turn north, capturing Mount Tapotchau. The 4th Division, meanwhile, would drive eastward, cutting the island in half, then clean out the lower half of the island. The two marine divisions, joined by the army's 27th Infantry Division, would then drive to Saipan's north coast, eliminating any Japanese they encountered.

The invasion got off to a bad start. Inexperienced naval gunnery officers wasted much of the preinvasion bombardment fire. As a result, the invaders' amtracs ran into a heavy barrage of Japanese artillery and mortar fire on their way to the beach. Ashore, the marines found well-prepared enemy positions. The fighting proved bitter and deadly. By the end of the first day the 2d Division had taken over five hundred dead; the 4th Division's losses exceeded its casualties at Roi-Namur.

Still, twenty thousand marines made it ashore. They were well enough established to throw back two suicidal banzai charges that first evening. The next morning the marines' advance continued.

Just after noon a battalion of the 4th Division ran into stiff resistance, supported by Japanese 75-mm artillery pieces. The battalion commander called for tanks. Gy. Sgt. Robert McCard, Company A, 4th Tank Battalion, brought his platoon of Shermans forward. Almost instantly, McCard's tank was cut off from the others and crippled by the converging shells of four enemy guns. He battled back with his tank's 75-mm gun and its machine guns.

But now the enemy had the range. The Sherman was finished. "Take off!" McCard ordered his crew. "Get out the escape hatch."

One by one, the crew lowered themselves through the hatch in the tank's floor, scurrying to safety while McCard hurled grenades at the advancing Japanese from the open turret. Japanese machine-gun fire rattled off the tank, wounding McCard. The Japanese charged. McCard, a veteran of the Marshall Islands fighting, seized a machine gun. He turned to face the Japanese alone. He got sixteen of them before they got him.

McCard's heroic stand allowed the other tanks to regroup. They advanced again, pushing the enemy back. By nightfall the 4th Division's lines were intact.

The 2d Division also made good progress. It was ready to turn north toward the town of Garapan. That night the 27th Infantry Division's 165th Infantry Regiment started coming ashore.

As soon as the American intent was clear the Japanese First Mobile Fleet was sent steaming toward the Marianas from near Borneo. The fleet commander, Vice Adm. Jisaburo Ozawa, had at his disposal nearly every remaining ship in the Japanese navy. Nine carriers, with 430 aircraft, 5 battleships, 13 cruisers, and 28 destroyers all headed for the decisive battle.

American submarines spotted the enemy flotilla the night of June 15–16. Adm. Raymond A. Spruance, commander of the Fifth U.S. Fleet, immediately dispatched a fast carrier task force west from the Marianas to intercept the Japanese. The two forces clashed on June 19, 1944. What followed was a day-long romp the American carrier-based pilots called "The Great Marianas Turkey Shoot."

The inexperienced Japanese pilots were completely outmatched by the navy fliers. Ozawa put 373 planes into the air; 130 returned. The U.S. Navy lost thirty planes. In addition, U.S. submarines sank two Japanese carriers.

The next day the forces met again. Another 65 Japanese planes fell from the sky. American dive-bombers sank the Japanese carrier *Hiyo*. The back of the Japanese navy was broken. Never again would its carriers venture forth to do battle.

By the end of eight days of fighting the southern half of Saipan had yielded to the might of the Marine Corps. To take the northern half a massive island-wide thrust was prepared. Three divisions, the 2d Marine on the left, the 4th Marine on the right, and the army's 27th Infantry in the center, started their attack on June 23. The movement initially made good progress. But soon the army troops, hampered by extremely rugged terrain and weak leadership, bogged down. The marines' flanks were dangerously exposed. The marine commanders were incensed. By nightfall of June 24, the marines had succeeded in effecting the removal of the 27th's commanding general.

Under fresh leadership the army troops got into line with the marines. By July 6 the troops had squeezed the remaining Japanese into the top one-third of the island. That day General Saito realized his battle was irrevocably lost. He ordered a last-ditch charge against the hated marines then slit open his belly. On another part of the island, Admiral Nagumo, also convinced of the disaster looming, shot himself in the head.

The suicide charge began late on the night of July 6. Between two thousand and three thousand Japanese, fueled with *sake*, swept down the coastal plain. Like stampeding cattle they thundered into the lines held by the 105th Infantry Regiment.

THOMAS A. BAKER

By the time of the massive banzai charge, Sgt. Thomas A. Baker had already proven himself to be a reliable combat soldier. His unit, Company A, 105th Infantry, 27th Infantry Division, landed on Saipan on June 17, 1944. They immediately went into the line on the right of the 2d Marine Division. They pushed inland across hot, steamy cane fields toward their objective, Nafutan Point on the island's southeast shore.

The dense foliage hampered their progress. With their combat fatigues drenched in sweat, the men of Company A were forced to stop every hundred yards or so to rest. Sporadic sniper fire added to their misery. On June 19 they crested Butterfly Ridge and for the first time saw the enemy. On the next ridge a 77-mm artillery battery, surrounded by machine-gun nests, peppered the ground around the advancing GIs.

Twice Company A stormed the ridge. Twice they were thrown back. During a lull Baker volunteered to bring up needed mortar shells. At the ammo point he found they were out of the shells. Instead, he picked up a bazooka and ammo bag and headed back for the front.

A few minutes later Baker's platoon leader was startled to see him worming his way across open ground toward the gun emplacement. There was absolutely no cover of any kind on the rocky ground. The enemy machine guns soon spotted Baker and began firing away at him.

Jumping up, Baker ran forward fifty yards until he could get a clean shot at the enemy. Dropping to one knee, he loaded the cumbersome weapon and, in rapid succession, fired four rounds into the gun positions. Miraculously unhit by the enemy fire, Baker's well-placed rounds destroyed the enemy strong point. The rest of the company surged forward, wiping out the remaining Japanese.

On July 2, Baker repeated his heroism. In a bold, single-handed charge on two well-concealed enemy positions, he wiped out three machine-gun nests and killed twenty Japanese soldiers.

Baker's gallantry could have stemmed from the deep sense of loyalty he felt for his unit—he'd been a member of Company A for nine years. After graduating from high school in his native Troy, New York, in May 1934, he found it hard to find steady work in a depression-plagued country. For a while he worked as a maintenance man at the local YMCA. But that didn't pay well. Then a friend tipped him off to the National Guard. For attending one drill a week he'd earn a dollar. To a YMCA handyman that dollar bill looked pretty good. He signed up with Company A, 105th Infantry, New York National Guard, in the fall of 1935.

Baker became a dedicated guardsman. He never missed a meeting. When his three-year enlistment ran out in 1938, he signed on for three more.

In October 1940, the New York National Guard was federalized as the 27th Infantry Division. They went to Fort McClellan, Alabama, to learn the intricacies of operating as part of an infantry division. They were still there when the Japanese attacked Pearl Harbor.

The 27th Division was rushed to the West Coast and then to Hawaii, the first combat division to leave the States. They garrisoned Hawaii for the next nine months, until the Japanese threat against the islands was eliminated. Then they headed deeper into the Pacific.

By the time the 27th Division reached the northern third of Saipan, it had assumed control of the western half of the island, the tapering terrain having squeezed out the 2d Marine Division.

On July 6, the 105th Infantry was pulled back just behind the front lines for a much-needed rest. As a result, they stood square in the path of the fanatical Japanese banzai attack.

The swarm of charging men slammed into the battle-weary GIs. They quickly called in artillery. It pounded into the swirling masses of Japanese, but still they came.

Sergeant Baker's squad occupied foxholes alongside railroad tracks leading south to the village of Makunsha. The full force of the suicide charge hit them at 3:00 A.M. As the Japanese poured over the tracks a grenade exploded in Baker's foxhole, seriously injuring his leg. He ignored the wound, calmly picking off Japanese with his rifle.

The sheer number of attackers nearly overwhelmed the intrepid sergeant. He pulled himself out of his foxhole, swinging his M-1 like a club. He bashed a few skulls before the first wave of attackers rushed past him.

Minutes later one of his squad found him crawling about, unable to stand on his damaged leg. That man, though wounded himself, picked Baker up and carried him 150 yards toward the rear of the perimeter.

Out of the darkness a sword-wielding Japanese officer appeared, slashing at Baker's rescuer until he fell, hacked to death. Baker fell to the ground. He was hit again, this time in the chest.

Ten minutes later Capt. Bernie Taft came across Baker and staggered along the railroad tracks with him until he, too, took a round. The next time someone stopped to help Baker he pushed him away, "Get away from me. I've caused enough trouble."

The last person to see Baker alive was Cpl. Carl Patricelli. At dawn he found Baker propped against a telephone pole. Patricelli tried to help him, but Baker raised his hand. "It's no use. I'm done for. Give me something to shoot with."

Patricelli handed Baker a loaded .45.

"I'll take some of them with me," Baker promised.

When the area was retaken later that morning Baker was still propped against the telephone pole. He lay dead, the empty pistol gripped in his hand. Around him were eight dead Japanese soldiers.

Baker's family accepted his posthumous Medal of Honor on May 27, 1945.

The fighting in Baker's sector raged well into the next afternoon. The heavy crush of Japanese broke through the American lines, hitting the rear echelon area. Baker's battalion commander, Lt. Col. William O'Brien, tried to rally his headquarters troops. He had already established himself as a bold front-line commander. On June 20, he had led three tanks in an assault on a Japanese strong point, fearlessly riding atop one tank, completely exposed to the enemy's vicious fire. Eight days later, he took command of an isolated platoon from one of his companies, led it forward in an attack on an enemy hill position, and personally captured five machine guns and one 77-mm artillery piece. When the Japanese banzai charge overran his headquarters on July 7, O'Brien roamed the front lines, firing at the swarming attackers with a pistol clenched in each hand. Though seriously wounded, O'Brien refused to withdraw. He died manning a jeep-mounted .50-caliber machine gun. Like Baker, his family received a posthumous Medal of Honor.

The Japanese who flooded the breached line raced all the way back to the artillery batteries manned by the 10th Marines. The gunners lowered their howitzers and fired point-blank into the howling mob. Still the enemy came on. The gunners fought as infantrymen, falling back as they battled, taking heavy casualties. Marines from nearby units rushed to help and evacuate the wounded. One of them, Pfc. Harold Agerholm, single-handedly saved forty-five men before he fell. Years later the residents of Racine, Wisconsin, voted to name a school after him and the town's other Medal of Honor hero, Maj. John Jerstad.

Not until nightfall of July 9 were the last of the marauding Japanese hunted down and killed. Over 2,500 enemy bodies were counted. The 105th Infantry suffered 668 casualties. That same day Saipan was declared secure. The island cost the Americans over 16,000 casualties. The Japanese lost 29,000 men. But the Americans now had an airbase within striking distance of Japan.

The Americans returned to Guam on July 21, 1944. Lying 125 miles south of Saipan, this largest of the Marianas Islands is thirty miles long and ranges from five to eight miles in width. It is a rugged island, studded with limestone ridges and deep ravines. Thick stands of jungle are only occasionally broken by rice paddies and sugar cane fields.

The island's principal town, Agana, and its harbor, Apra, lie on the western shores. Orote Peninsula, a heavily fortified rocky promontory, juts several miles westward below Apra harbor. To conquer the island the 3d Marine Division would land on beaches north of the harbor at Agana Bay, drive inland, and capture the high ground a short distance inland. The army's newly arrived 77th Infantry Division would send one of its regiments to join the marine's 1st Provisional Brigade on the beaches south of Orote Peninsula. Once they secured their beachhead they would turn north, choke off the peninsula, and link up with the 3d Marine Division.

The preinvasion bombardment softened up the beaches but did not knock out the Japanese artillery. Exploding shells dropped among the amtracs destroying twenty-four of them. On both beaches the fighting was heavy. American dead numbered 350 the first day.

But the troops resolutely pushed forward. South of Orote, the marines and soldiers gained two thousand yards before digging in for the night, sealing off the peninsula three days later. To the north, two battalions of the 3d Marine Division's 21st Marines made it to the top of Chonito Cliff overlooking their beachhead. On their right, the 9th Marines moved swiftly through open terrain, quickly overcoming relatively light resistance.

On the left flank the 3d Marines had the toughest fight. They suffered 815 casualties in 48 hours fighting up the cliffs in their sector. It was another two days before they finally tied in with the 21st Marines on their right and the beachhead was secure.

By July 25, the 3d Marine Division had expanded its beachhead to a depth of over a mile. Resistance had been tougher than expected. Casualties were high, thinning the line companies; only seven thousand riflemen manned the front lines.

That night Lt. Gen. Takeshi Takashina, the enemy commander, delivered his long-anticipated counterattack. Though his remaining troops were heavily plied with *sake* prior to the attack, Takashina did not plan for this to be a fanatical, suicidal banzai charge. Instead, it would be a "single stroke" that would "solve the issue of the battle." He sent patrols to probe the marines' lines looking of weak spots. They found them. An eight hundred-yard-wide gap existed between the 21st Marines and 9th Marines on their right. Japanese troops poured through the gap headed toward the Americans' rear. Support personnel found themselves fighting for their lives against Japanese racing through the rear area.

Takashina sent another column of his troops against the marines' left. Around midnight his 48th Independent Brigade slammed square into the section of the line held by the 2d Battalion, 9th Marines (detached from its parent regiment holding the right side of the line). The brunt of the attack fell on Company F, commanded by a young officer destined for Marine Corps greatness.

LOUIS H. WILSON

Capt. Louis H. Wilson, born February 11, 1920, in Brandon, Mississippi, enlisted in the Marine Corps Reserve in May 1941 after graduating from college. Officer candidate school at Quantico, Virginia, followed, with Wilson receiving his second lieutenant's commission on November 1, 1941. Several stateside commands occupied the next year and a half before Wilson went to the South Pacific in February 1943. Two months later he was promoted to captain.

Wilson took his company into battle for the first time at Bougainville. A no-nonsense, bull-chested man, Wilson learned to fight the Japanese in the thick jungles covering the island. At times he wasn't sure who was the greater enemy—the Japanese or the jungle. There were times when he moved his company through the foliage and was unable to see men ten feet away. The going was tough but Wilson was tougher. After some of the island's most difficult battles, Wilson brought his company back to Guadalcanal with a minimum of casualties.

That would change at Guam.

Company F came ashore in the initial waves. It took more casualties in the first day at Guam than it had in a month at Bougainville. On the afternoon of July 25, Wilson was ordered to take his company up Fonte Hill, a large hill behind Agana. After organizing his platoons, Wilson started forward.

The advance was made over three hundreds yards of rugged, wide-open terrain. Japanese machine-gun fire and mortars cut down the marines as they raced forward. Disregarding the intense fire, Wilson moved among his shattered platoons, urging his men forward in the best marine tradition. "Keep moving! Keep moving!" he shouted above the crash of the exploding mortars.

Several times Wilson moved out in front of his men, using his carbine to kill Japanese snipers. Finally, they reached the top of the hill. Wilson didn't waste any time. After sending his wounded back to the aid station, he assumed command of a reinforcing platoon and other disorganized units. He personally set his men in position, making sure his few remaining automatic weapons covered the most likely Japanese avenues of approach.

During this time the company took heavy fire from the enemy. Three times Wilson was hit. Three times he went down. Three times he got up. After five hours of fighting, Wilson finally moved back to his command post for medical attention. Once his wounds were treated, he called his platoon leaders together.

"We can expect to get hit tonight. Make sure your men are fully alert," he warned. "Get all the ammo you can. It'll probably be a rough one."

He was right. Two hours later, Takashina's men came up the hill. Chanting "Marine, you die!" over two thousand drunken, well-armed Japanese surged forward, firing rifles, throwing grenades.

As soon as the firing broke out, Wilson left his command post and joined his besieged platoons. Under incredibly heavy fire, Wilson moved about from platoon to platoon, issuing orders, leading by example, fighting alongside his riflemen. Wherever the fighting was heaviest, Wilson was there. He tossed grenades into the oncoming enemy, stopping them only yards away.

At one point he learned a wounded marine from one of his forward observations posts had been left outside the line. Concerned only with saving that man's life, Wilson dashed fifty yards directly into the Japanese, found his marine, hoisted him on his broad shoulders, and brought him back into the lines.

Seven times the Japanese charged. Seven times Company F, under Wilson's indomitable leadership, fought them off. Several times Wilson used his rifle as a club to beat off enemy soldiers who broke through the line. Under the flash of exploding mortar shells he witnessed his brave men wrestling the Japanese to the ground, using bayonets and knives to kill them.

The fighting raged for eight hours. Company F took over fifty percent casualties. But as the sun came up the marines held Fonte Hill. Stubborn enemy fire from a nearby hill still threatened the company. Determined to wipe them out, Wilson gath-

ered seventeen men. At their head he led them up the slope. The
defenders poured down a rain of mortars, machine-gun, and
rifle fire. Thirteen of Wilson's volunteers fell going up the hill.
Defying the odds, Wilson and the four remaining marines
stormed the enemy positions. With rifles blazing red-hot, tossing grenades left and right, they rolled over the Japanese, killing
all of them.

By 9:00 A.M. the battle for Fonte Hill was over. The 2d Battalion, 9th Marines, were nearly cut in half. Only the intrepid
stand of Wilson and Company F kept the Japanese from breaking through to the beach. Altogether some 3,500 of General
Takashina's men died that night, over 950 of them in front of
Wilson's company. The marines lost 200 men killed; another
645 were wounded.

Captain Wilson was among the wounded evacuated the next
day. He required three months of hospitalization before returning to duty. While serving at the Marine Barracks in Washington, D.C., he was summoned to the White House on October 5,
1945, where President Truman draped the blue ribbon of the
Medal of Honor around his neck.

Wilson's postwar career included a tour with the 1st Marine
Division during the Korean war, and several years at Headquarters, U.S. Marine Corps, in prestigious assignments. His service with the marines climaxed in 1975 with his appointment as
commandant of the Marine Corps. He retired to his native Mississippi in 1979.

The fighting on Guam dragged on for several more weeks.
Not until August 10 was the island declared secure. Taking Guam
cost the Americans seventy-eight hundred killed and wounded,
but Uncle Sam had come back to stay.

While the battle for Guam raged, the veterans of Saipan landed
on Tinian Island. Lying just three miles south of Saipan, Tinian
contained four airfields, with a fifth under construction. Marines
of the 4th Division landed on the island on July 24, 1944. By
nightfall over fifteen thousand marines had poured across the
shoreline.

Two marines earned Medals of Honor on Tinian, both for
covering grenades with their own bodies to protect their buddies. Pvt. Joseph W. Ozbourn, a BAR man with the 23d Marines, 4th Division, from Herrin, Illinois, had a live grenade

shot out of his hand on July 30. With no time to retrieve it, he fell on the deadly missile. On August 4, another Illinois marine, Pfc. Robert L. Wilson, jumped on a Japanese grenade thrown into the midst of his squad. Neither man survived.

Tinian was declared secure on July 31, 1944, although mopping up continued for several more weeks. The marines only suffered two thousand casualties—327 dead—in securing some of the finest airfields in the Central Pacific. It would have been better if none had died, but such is not the case in war.

After his success in the Admiralty Islands, General MacArthur decided to skip his next two scheduled targets on New Guinea's north coast, Hansa Bay and Wewak, and make a 500-mile leap to his principal target, Hollandia. This speedup in the timetable would bring him closer—both literally and figuratively—to his dearest aim, a return to the Philippines.

American GIs of the 41st Infantry Division came ashore near Hollandia on April 22, 1944. The landing there so surprised the Japanese, they put up only minor resistance. Most of the eleven thousand defenders fled into the hills behind the town. Within four days the GIs had captured the three Japanese airfields inland from Hollandia. Engineers quickly went to work to turn the area into a major supply depot. The Hollandia operation cost only 152 American lives versus 3,300 Japanese.

In spite of the success at Hollandia, there were still some six hundred miles of New Guinea coastline west of Hollandia, ending at the Vogelkip Peninsula. Unless the Japanese bases beyond Hollandia were neutralized they could threaten MacArthur's rear when he turned north to the Philippines. On May 27 he sent the 41st Infantry Division to Biak Island, in Geelvink Bay adjoining the Vogelkip Peninsula. Though MacArthur announced the imminent capture of the island within twenty-four hours of the landing, the Japanese mounted a stubborn resistance. Not until August 20 was Biak truly secure.

A regimental combat team went ashore at Noemfor Island, sixty miles west of Biak, on July 2. Though the landings were nearly unopposed, defenders inland put up a ferocious fight. A call for help went out. The 503d Parachute Infantry was dropped in to help. Fighting raged throughout the island until the end of July.

Sgt. Ray E. Eubanks, LaGrange, North Carolina, earned a

Medal of Honor on July 23 when he single-handedly maneuvered to within fifteen yards of a strong enemy position, supported by machine-gun, rifle, and mortar fire. As soon as he
opened fire on the position, the Japanese concentrated their fire
on him. He was hit and his rifle smashed from the flying lead.
Determined to destroy the enemy, he rushed forward, swinging
his useless rifle as a club, and killed four Japanese before he
was cut down. Behind him, his squad swept forward, swarmed
over the enemy emplacement, and killed forty-five Japanese.

After returning on July 30 from a conference with President
Roosevelt at Pearl Harbor, during which his plan to assault the
Philippines was confirmed, MacArthur sent the 6th Infantry Di-
vision ashore at Sansapor, at the far western end of the Vogelkip
Peninsula. Within days the moderate fighting was over. New
Guinea, the world's largest island, was conquered. Except for
one area.

Since late May, Japanese Lt. Gen. Hatazo Adachi had battled
American forces near Aitape, midway between Hollandia and
Wewak. On the night of July 10, he massed his troops on the
east bank of the Driniumor River, ten miles east of Aitape. Just
before midnight he launched a vicious attack against the Americans. Though the attack was fated to fail, for several days the
Japanese created havoc among the GIs.

GERALD L. ENDL

Gerald Endl was born in Fort Atkinson, Wisconsin, on August
20, 1915. He attended St. Joseph's Catholic School prior to entering the local high school from which he graduated in 1933.

Unable to find steady work in the midst of the depression,
Endl entered the Civilian Conservation Corps. He spent two
years building roads in the heavily forested regions of northern
Wisconsin. The pay only amounted to one dollar per day, but
the government did include three hot meals a day, and it was a
lot better than stocking shelves in the grocery store for ten cents
an hour.

By the time Endl returned to Fort Atkinson, the economy had
improved enough for him to find a job with a local manufacturing firm. His new financial security allowed him to take a wife
on January 11, 1941. He was up for a promotion at his factory
when his draft notice arrived in March 1941.

Endl reported for induction at Camp Grant, near Rockford,

Illinois, on April 16, 1941. A few days later he went to Camp Livingston, Louisiana, for basic training. From there he went to Camp Devens, Massachusetts. Endl expected to be home for good by Christmas because Congress passed a law granting a discharge to all draftees who had turned twenty-six by the end of the year. Pearl Harbor forced a change in his plans.

By coincidence Endl was sent as an infantry replacement to the 32d Infantry Division, Wisconsin National Guard. He found himself serving in the 128th Infantry Regiment with men from his hometown.

Endl's first taste of combat came during the bitter battle for Buna. Nothing in his life could have prepared him for the brutality of that fight. The savagery of the Japanese defenders was shocking. Endl didn't see the victory at Buna. He stopped a Japanese slug on December 16, 1942, resulting in a five-month convalescence in Australia. He returned to his outfit in May 1943.

On July 11, 1944, the 128th was on the front line near Anamo, New Guinea, fighting against General Adachi's fanatical troops. Endl moved up a jungle trail as the point man for his platoon. Suddenly, the Japanese opened up. Firing into the main body of the platoon from well-concealed positions, they killed the platoon leader and wounded a dozen more.

Sergeant Endl quickly assumed command of the survivors. Maneuvering through the dense jungle he deployed them in strong positions. The company commander sent another platoon out to flank the Japanese. They reacted by pressing their attack against Endl's platoon, forcing it back.

Seven of the original casualties were now in danger of being cut off. Endl wouldn't permit that.

He bounded forward, firing his M-1 from the hip. For ten minutes he held off the Japanese while others from his platoon rescued the casualties.

As Endl was withdrawing back to the relative safety of his platoon's new perimeter he came across four more wounded GIs lying in the tall grass alongside the trail. Selflessly, he hoisted one of the wounded on his shoulder and sprinted seventy-five yards down the trail to safety. Ignoring the pleas of his comrades, Endl voluntarily made three more trips through the enemy fire to rescue the others. He made it back safely with two of them. As he closed in on the American positions with the last man, a heavy burst of automatic weapons fire struck him, killing the two men instantly.

Endl's widow, Anna Marie, accepted her husband's posthumous Medal of Honor in ceremonies at the Janesville, Wisconsin, high school auditorium on March 27, 1945. Thousands of residents of Janesville and Fort Atkinson packed the hall to hear the gallant story of the local hero.

As part of Admiral Nimitz's overall plan for the U.S. invasion of the Marianas he deployed twenty-eight submarines to positions along the most likely avenues of approach for the Japanese fleet. Three of these boats took up patrols in Sibutu Passage, a narrow stretch of water between northeast Borneo and the island of Tawi Tawi in the Sulu Archipelago off Mindanao. For several months, Admiral Soemu Toyoda had been anchoring ships of his combined fleet at Tawi Tawi's harbor. If his ships headed for the Marianas, the subs would have plenty of targets.

SAMUEL D. DEALEY

One of the subs in the Sibutu Passage was the *Harder*. Since her commissioning in December 1942 *Harder*'s boss had been Comdr. Samuel D. Dealey. Under his astute leadership *Harder* had already sunk over a dozen Japanese ships on four war patrols. Dealey's aggressiveness in stalking enemy ships had already made him a legend in the Pacific.

The youngest son of a wealthy Texas family, Dealey was born in Dallas on September 13, 1906. An average student in high school, he was more interested in sports, mainly track and field, and in boxing. His grades weren't quite good enough to get him into college, so his family used their influence to finagle an appointment to one of the service academies. The one that had an opening was the Naval Academy. It didn't really matter to Dealey which one he attended, he was going mainly to please his family. He arrived at Annapolis in June 1925.

Dealey's lack of enthusiasm for his new surroundings soon became apparent through his poor grades and a large number of demerits for disciplinary problems. He was kicked out of the academy in February 1926. Deeply disgraced by his dilemma, Dealey arranged a meeting with his congressman. Usually, once you're bounced from a service academy, you're through, but

Dealey was able to talk his way back in. He'd start again in June 1926.

This time Dealey was successful. Though not a stellar aca-demician, Dealey did graduate in June 1930. For the next ten years he shunted from one dreary peacetime assignment to an-other, frequently talking of leaving the navy to work with his brothers in Texas. Then in late 1941 he took over command of the old sub *S-20*. He found a home. A year later he assumed command of the *Harder*.

Harder's first few patrols were relatively uneventful. Poor quality torpedoes resulted in just one Japanese ship sunk. Then in October 1943 *Harder* joined two other subs in a wolf pack near the Marianas. On this patrol Dealey finally came into his own.

On November 12, 1943, *Harder* sank a small freighter. Later that night, Dealey surfaced and sank one of the freighter's es-corts with gunfire.

A week later Dealey took on a convoy of three freighters and three escorts. *Harder* fired ten torpedoes, scoring seven hits. One freighter sank immediately, one sank later, and one es-caped. The destroyers attacked the sub, keeping her down until nightfall. Sixty-four depth charges rocked the submarine before the escorts broke contact. In his report Dealey wrote, "This was the most frustrated I have ever felt."

Dealey then surfaced. He spent three hours hunting for the freighter he missed, found her, then sank her. Out of torpedoes, he headed back to his base at Fremantle, Australia.

On the night of June 6, 1944, Dealey brought the *Harder* into Sibutu Passage. Radar contact was made with ships headed south. Soon afterwards three tankers and two destroyers rode into view. Needing speed to catch them, Dealey ordered his boat to the surface. A few hours later, as he closed in on his victims, the moon popped from behind a cloud bank. Seven miles away, a Japanese destroyer spotted the sub. She turned sharply toward the *Harder*.

Boldly, Dealey rode the surface, teasing the destroyer. Only at the last minute did he order, "Dive! Dive!" Once submerged, he ordered, "Left rudder," bringing *Harder*'s stern tubes to bear on the destroyer. When the enemy ship crossed astern one thousand yards away, Dealey barked, "Fire one! Fire two! Fire three!"

The torpedoes streaked toward the destroyer. One hit her under the bow, the second hit under the bridge, the third missed. Four minutes later the destroyer slipped under the waves.

Dealey returned to the surface and was spotted by the second destroyer. He tried to repeat his daring tactics, but only wounded the enemy.

The next day another destroyer spotted *Harder*'s periscope from just 3,000 yards' distance. She quickly hove over, bearing straight down on the *Harder*. Dealey waited until the oncoming bow wave was just 650 yards away. The crew in the control room sweated profusely. Wasn't Dealey going to fire? Did he have some trick up his sleeve?

Seconds later, as the destroyer approached to 500 yards, Dealey calmly spoke, "Fire one! Fire two! Fire three!" The torpedoes raced through the water toward the destroyer, straight down her throat.

Dealey later said, "Number four wasn't necessary. At a range of 300 yards we were rocked by a terrific explosion believed to have been the destroyer's magazine. In less than one minute after the first hit, and nine minutes after it was sighted, the destroyer sank."

Two nights later, June 9, Dealey spotted two enemy destroyers on patrol at the narrow northern neck of Sibutu Passage. At 3,000 yards the destroyers zigged to starboard and presented Dealey with a rare overlap. "It was just what the doctor ordered," Dealey said.

He fired four torpedoes in quick succession. He kept his eye glued to the periscope to witness the results.

The first torpedo missed. The second and third plowed into the closest destroyer, breaking her back. The fourth slammed into the second destroyer. Its explosion blew up the ship's boilers. When last seen by Dealey, the tail of the second destroyer was straight up in the air and the first had disappeared.

Aboard the *Harder* a cheer went up as the story of the tremendous victory spread among the crew. In just three days they'd sunk four destroyers and damaged another. It was an excellent score. But the patrol wasn't over.

The very next night Dealey spotted a huge task force of two battleships, several cruisers, and numerous destroyers. "Oh man, if we can get a shot at them, we'll really be cooking," he told his executive officer.

But it wasn't to be. A Japanese scout plane spotted the periscope and dropped a smoke bomb. A destroyer broke away from the force and bore dawn on the *Harder* at thirty-five knots.

"We had to hit him, or else," Dealey said. From fifteen hundred yards he fired a brace of three torpedoes straight down the destroyer's throat. "Two torpedoes struck with a detonation far worse than a depth-charging. By this time we were just passing eighty feet and were soon almost directly beneath the destroyer when all hell broke loose. Either his boilers, or magazines, or both, had exploded, and it's a lucky thing that ships' explosions are vented upward and not downward."

Harder's solo activities around Tawi Tawi convinced the Japanese a wolf pack was operating in the area. Accordingly, they stepped up their patrol activity, thus tying down ships that could have been used against the Allies elsewhere.

Back in Australia, *Harder* received a tumultuous welcome. General MacArthur sent his personal congratulations, and a DSC. The *Harder* received a Presidential Unit Citation. Since Dealey had already earned three Navy Crosses on previous patrols the Pacific submarine commander, Adm. Charles A. Lockwood, felt he deserved the Medal of Honor. He started the paperwork.

Harder's successful patrols were exacting a heavy toll on Dealey. His executive officer on the fifth patrol later said, "Sam was showing unmistakable signs of strain. He was becoming quite casual about Japanese antisubmarine measures. Once, on a previous patrol, I found Sam in a state of mild shock, unable to make a decision."

Dealey's local commander, Adm. Ralph Christie, didn't want him to go on a sixth patrol. But dealey insisted. "I've got to make this patrol." Christie yielded.

On August 24, 1944, *Harder* and *Hake* were on a two-submarine patrol in Lingayen Gulf, Luzon, Philippines. Spotted by a Japanese destroyer, both submarines dove. The *Hake*'s skipper later reported he counted fifteen depth charges erupt near the *Harder*. When he surfaced, he tried to reach the *Harder* by radio. He couldn't. She was never seen again.

On August 28, 1945, Dealey's widow, and their three children, solemnly accepted his Medal of Honor, and a fourth Navy Cross earned on his sixth war patrol.

* * *

With the Marianas in American hands and the massive Japanese navel and air base at Truk completely isolated, attention next turned to the Palau Islands in the western Carolinas. One thousand miles west of Truk and only five hundred east of Mindanao, the Palaus guarded the Philippines' eastern flank. However, based on MacArthur's success in New Guinea, the marines' capture of the Marianas, and the strategy of bypassing enemy strongholds, the question was raised about the necessity of invading the Palaus.

The key dissenter was Admiral Halsey. Fearing that an assault on the Palaus would be more costly than Tarawa, he proposed bypassing the islands and hitting the Philippines directly. Admiral Nimitz, on the other hand, felt the Palaus posed too great a threat to ignore. He was the ranking officer, so the invasion was on.

A few days before the scheduled invasion on September 15, 1944, Halsey's carrier-based fighters encountered only feeble resistance while striking Japanese air bases in the Philippines. It was obvious Japanese air power in the western Pacific was all but nonexistent. It seemed to Halsey like a perfect opportunity to strike directly at the Philippines. He recommended that the invasion of the Palaus and Mindanao be cancelled in favor of an immediate invasion of Leyte.

Nimitz agreed, with one exception. He still felt the Palaus were too important to ignore. The invasion of the key island, Peleliu, went forward.

Imperial Army Headquarters had ordered Lt. Gen. Sadae Inoue to hold the Palaus at all costs. To do so he had at his command between thirty thousand and forty thousand men. Most were on Babelthuap, at the northern end of the Palaus chain. Over eleven thousand were on Peleliu at the southern end. Unlike Japanese commanders on other islands who subscribed to the Japanese doctrine of annihilating the enemy on the beaches, Inoue was devoted to a new tactic. In his orders to his men he said, "If the situation becomes bad we will maintain a firm hold on the high ground."

Peleliu was custom-made for such a defense.

Six miles long north to south and two miles across at its widest, Peleliu was shaped like a lobster's claw. At its hinge, a wide, flat area in the south, lay an airfield. Two peninsulas stretched north and northeast. Rising just north of the airfield and running north about two miles was a low, wooded ridge riddled with caves. Maps called it Umurbrogal Mountain. The marines would call it Bloody Nose Ridge.

Bloody Nose Ridge was actually a coral ridge thrown above the water's surface by a long-forgotten volcanic eruption. It was an ungodly place, filled with nooks, crannies, and caves which Inoue used to construct a vast, interconnected network of fortified positions. Log and sandbag barricades protected most entrances. Deep within these caves the Japanese were almost invulnerable. Only the valor of individual marines would dig them out.

Th 1st Marine Division had been selected for the Peleliu landing. Based on naval intelligence the division's commander, Maj. Gen. William Rupertus, felt optimistic about the assault. To his officers Rupertus said, "We're going to have some casualties, but let me assure you this is going to be a short one, a quickie. Rough but fast. We'll be through in three days. It may take only two."

In reality, it would take nearly a month. Over twelve hundred marines would die; eight would earn Medals of Honor.

The marines hit Peleliu's western beaches on the morning of September 15, 1944. On the north were the 1st Marines, in the center the 5th Marines, and on the south the 7th Marines. As the preinvasion bombardment ended, Japanese artillery pieces came forth from their caves. Amtracs started exploding as the shells found targets. Both the 1st and 7th Marines suffered heavy casualties getting ashore; the 5th Marines landed nearly intact.

Once ashore, the marines, as a result of General Inoue's plan, were able to make rapid progress inland. The Japanese did launch a tank charge against the 7th Marines, but they easily repulsed it. By dark the 7th Marines had moved across the island, the 5th had driven nearly across the airfield, and the 1st Marines managed to keep its right flank tied into the 5th's left flank. The 1st's left-flank units were already being chewed up by Japanese emplaced in Bloody Nose Ridge's foothills.

The 7th Marines were the first to feel the full force of Peleliu's defensive fighters. With a blazing tropical sun beating on their heavy steel helmets, the men of its 1st and 3d battalions began their drive to clear out southern Peleliu's fortifications beginning on September 16.

Against pillboxes, casemates, bunkers, spider holes, trenches, and machine-gun nests the marines fought a bitter, brutal battle. Because of their connecting tunnels the Japanese could reoccupy positions the marines thought finished. Many a marine died from bullet wounds in his back.

The two battalions fought a grinding, three-day battle herding the enemy into two enclaves on the island's south shore. The pillbox-studded terrain might have cost even heavier casualties if it hadn't been for the actions of one man.

ARTHUR J. JACKSON

Born October 18, 1924, in Cleveland, Ohio, Arthur J. Jackson grew up in Portland, Oregon. In high school he played a good game of football, earning the respect of his teammates and coaches. After graduating in June 1942, Jackson worked locally until he was inducted into the Marine Corps in January 1943.

After basic training at San Diego, California, and advanced infantry training at nearby Camp Pendleton, Jackson joined the 3d Battalion, 7th Marines, 1st Marine Division, in Australia prior to its landing on Cape Gloucester, New Britain. After that campaign the division regrouped on Pavuvu in the Russell Islands. Then came the carnage that was Peleliu.

On the morning of September 18, Jackson's platoon, on the left flank of his company's position, was stopped by intense fire from a large blockhouse. Jackson and his buddies dropped to the ground with bullets whistling all around them. The sharp cries from other marines told Jackson some bullets found targets.

After carefully surveying the situation in front of him Jackson thought the saw a way to break the stalemate. "Cover me," he told the men around him. "I think I can get this pillbox."

With his buddies pouring out fire at the pillbox Jackson rushed forward. Amazingly, he reached the side of the pillbox unscathed. He slammed a fresh clip into his BAR. Then he stuck the BAR's barrel into one of the pillbox's gun slits and pulled the trigger. The heavy weapon bucked in his hands as the lethal rounds poured into the concrete pillbox.

Another marine brought forward a demolition charge. When Jackson had emptied the BAR's clip, he armed the charge and shoved it through the slit. A deep explosion rocked the ground under Jackson's feet. Enemy gunfire from the pillbox stopped. Mop-up troops counted thirty-five bodies inside the pillbox.

Convinced he could knock out more pillboxes, Jackson had the other marines lay down a base of fire while he went after two more emplacements. Once again he blew them up with demolition charges.

With a fresh supply of ammo and several more demolition charges, Jackson continued his one-man assault. Two squads of marines provided covering fire while Jackson went after more Japanese positions. Seemingly invincible, he scurried from one place to another, firing his BAR, throwing satchel charges and grenades. All this time the Japanese were throwing out all kinds of fire at him. They came close—Jackson's clothes and equipment were riddled with bullet holes—but Jackson escaped injury.

For over an hour Jackson roamed through the Japanese line, spreading death and destruction. When he finally ran out of targets Jackson collapsed against a pillbox. The sun and the fighting had physically drained him. Altogether Jackson wiped out a dozen Japanese positions and killed over fifty enemy soldiers. His actions permitted the 7th Marines' commander to radio General Rupertus, "The 7th Marines' mission on southern Peleliu is completed."

When the 7th Marines were fed into the line on Bloody Nose Ridge a few days later Jackson went with them. Within three days he was hit and evacuated. By the time he recovered the 1st Marine Division was ready for the Okinawa landings. Jackson, newly promoted to second lieutenant, was wounded again. This time his fighting was over for good.

In White House ceremonies on October 5, 1945, Jackson's parents and sister watched proudly as President Truman presented him with the Medal of Honor. When he had learned a few days earlier that he was to be so honored he humbly remarked, "This comes as a big surprise to me. I'd heard about nine months ago that I was going to be recommended for something, but I had forgotten about it."

Jackson remained in the Marine Corps after World War II. He had reached the rank of captain when he left the Marine Corps in 1961. He later went to work for the Veterans' Administration.

Once the marines solidified their hold on Peleliu's southern half, it was time to dig out the Japanese on Bloody Nose Ridge.

Under a roasting equatorial sun that sent daytime temperatures past 110 degrees, the 1st Marines started against Bloody Nose Ridge on September 17. Six days later they were finished as a fighting unit. The regiment suffered over seventeen hundred casualties; one battalion was down to seventy-four men. The survivors were pulled off the island.

General Rupertus next threw in his 5th and 7th Marine Regiments, and the Army's 321st Infantry. They, too, fought a battle of attrition, a slow, slugging, yard-by-yard struggle to blast the enemy from the high ground. Long-range flamethrowers mounted on tanks charred hundreds of caves and pillboxes. Cave mouths were sealed with explosives, but the Japanese would simply slither through their tunnels to another cave. Corsairs taking off from Peleliu's airfield, in the shortest bombing run in the war's history, dropped thousands of tons of bombs on the Japanese. But still they held. American casualties were so high, volunteers from the rear echelons were sought to help evacuate them.

One who volunteered on October 3, 1944, was eighteen-year-old Pfc. Richard E. Kraus from Chicago. A driver with the 8th Amphibious Tractor Battalion, Kraus joined three buddies to help evacuate a seriously wounded marine rifleman. After loading the casualty on a stretcher at the forward aid station the four men started the treacherous journey down the ridge to the hospital. As they neared the bottom of the trail in the gathering dusk, two men approached. They looked like marines. They proved to be Japanese. One tossed a grenade at the group. Kraus, intent only on saving the casualty and his buddies, jumped on the grenade. His young body absorbed the tremendous blast; he died instantly. His buddies hunted down and killed the intruders.

By the end of October the 5th and 7th Marines had driven the estimated one thousand remaining Japanese into a small packet in the heart of the Umurbrogal. The end was in sight, but the cost had been fearsome. Both regiments had suffered casualties amounting to nearly fifty percent of their strength. It would take the army's relieving 81st Infantry Division another three weeks of close-quarter fighting before it was all over.

General Inoue's men had caused the marines sixty-five hundred casualties, of which over twelve hundred died. They also killed 208 soldiers and wounded another 1,200. It would take the 1st Marine Division nearly six months to recuperate and rebuild its strength.

General MacArthur had his flank secured for his landings in the Philippines. Admiral Nimitz had his anchorage in the western Pacific. And the marines learned about a new enemy—one who would fight with more tenacity and daring the closer the Americans drove to Japan. The days of the suicidal, wasteful banzai charges were over. The individual Japanese soldier would have to be painfully dug out and ruthlessly slain.

12

★ ★ ★

D Day, the Invasion of France

Plans for the invasion of occupied Europe, the opening of the long-awaited Second Front, began in March 1943. A task of unprecedented, monumental proportions lay before the Allied staff. They had to plan not only where the invasion would take place but also who would carry out the task and how they would be supplied.

A process of elimination resulted in the Normandy coast west of Caen being selected as the invasion site. Not only were these beaches of high quality and somewhat sheltered from the prevailing winds, but the terrain inland was suitable for airfield development. Further, the port of Cherbourg, at the tip of the Cotentin Peninsula at the western edge of Normandy, was large enough to handle the massive quantities of supplies that the invasion troops would require.

The invasion would be carried out by five seaborne divisions and three airborne divisions. Beginning at Ste.-Mere-Eglise, at the east coast base of the Cotentin Peninsula, the U.S. 4th Infantry Division would go ashore on Utah Beach. Five miles east, the battle-tested U.S. 1st Infantry Division would storm Omaha Beach. Then came the British 50th Infantry Division on Gold Beach, the Canadian 3d Infantry Division on Juno, and finally the British 3d Infantry Division on Sword Beach, the easternmost landing zone. Behind Utah Beach two U.S. airborne divisions, the 82d and 101st, would parachute down in the hours of darkness prior to the seaborne invasion, seize the high ground, and secure the western flank. The British 6th Airborne Division would perform the same function behind Sword Beach.

Though the German High Command felt the anticipated Allied invasion would come at Calais, they still maintained a formidable force in Normandy. Six infantry and two panzer divisions under Field Marshal Rommel garrisoned the area. To thwart any invaders Rommel began constructing the Atlantic Wall in January 1944. Along the coast of Normandy, between the high-water and low-water points, he used slave laborers to build special devices designed to impede landing craft. Thousands of hedgehogs, tetrahedrons, dragon's teeth, curved rails, and sharpened stakes bristled along the shore. By the time of the Allied invasion the wall was nearly complete and would present a formidable obstacle to the invaders.

Millions of factors were considered in planning for the invasion. Though everything from ammunition to grave markers was accounted for, there was one factor over which the Operation *Overlord* planners had absolutely no control—the weather. Based on meteorological predictions, Eisenhower picked June 5 as the target date, with the sixth and seventh as alternates.

By June 3, all 170,000 assault troops were loaded aboard their transports for the brief trip across the English Channel. At airfields across England, paratroopers gave their equipment a final going over. Everything was ready for the invasion on Monday, June 5, 1944. Everything but the weather.

Heavy winds and overcast skies forced Eisenhower to postpone the launching of the invasion fleet for twenty-four hours. According to his chief weather forecaster, conditions over the channel would stabilize on June 6, allowing the invasion to proceed.

At 4:30 A.M., June 5, Eisenhower gave the word. After hearing a final weather briefing, the supreme commander told his staff, "O.K., we'll go."

The first Allies into France were airborne pathfinders. Beginning at 12:18 A.M., June 6, 1944, they parachuted into their drop zones behind Utah Beach to guide in the hundreds of paratrooper-laden planes behind them. Unfortunately, their work was for naught.

Thick clouds and exploding clumps of flak caused most of the planes to veer off course. Fully three-quarters of the thirteen thousand paratroopers were scattered far and wide. Many dropped into the sea. Others were dropped so far from their zones, it would be days before they rejoined their units. Nevertheless, small bands of men grouped together to fight the Germans as best they could. Amazingly, they were far more successful than anyone could have expected. Though disorganized they took key objectives that would help their brothers in arms coming to France on landing craft.

At the Normandy coast, salvo after salvo of high-explosive shells from American and British warships crashed into Utah Beach. Overhead, hundreds of bombers and fighters strafed and bombed the coastline. Offshore, thousands of infantrymen from the 4th Division, spray-soaked and seasick from three days aboard ship, prepared to hit the beaches. At precisely 6:31 A.M., the first landing craft deposited their charges on Utah Beach.

The GIs raced across five hundred yards of rocky sand, firing their rifles at targets in the hills above the beach. Behind them, tanks equipped with inflatable canvas covers rumbled ashore. They added the blast of their 75-mm cannons to the battle.

Surprisingly, German resistance was lighter than expected. Many of them had been killed in the preinvasion bombing; survivors were frequently too stunned to fight back. And the Americans had landed in the wrong place. The smoke and dust from the naval bombardment had obscured landmarks on the shore. A strong lateral current running off the beach contributed to the confusion by pushing the landing boats two thousand yards farther south than planned.

Among the first to realize the error was the 4th Division's assistant commander, fifty-seven-year-old Brig. Gen. Theodore Roosevelt, Jr. The son of one president and cousin to another, Roosevelt was the sole general officer to land in Normandy on D day. A truly remarkable and extraordinary man, Roosevelt fought in World War I with the 1st Infantry Division, earning both a DSC and a DSM.

He served again with the Big Red One in North Africa and Sicily during this war. Because of his fibrillating heart and troublesome arthritis, Gen, Omar Bradley, commander of the invading First U.S. Army, had taken Roosevelt off the list of those headed for Normandy. Roosevelt pleaded, telling Bradley he could help "to steady the boys." Finally Bradley relented, sending Roosevelt to the 4th Infantry Division.

Armed only with a small-caliber pistol and a walking stick, the wrinkled little general had a reassuring effect on all who saw him that blustery morning, moving among the troops, ignoring the enemy fire directed at him, and pointing out targets with his walking stick. Utterly fearless, he was an inspiration to everyone under fire that morning.

Now Roosevelt had to make a decision. Thirty thousand more men were scheduled to land at Utah that day. Only one road led inland. Should he take his men back north, where the resistance was stronger, and try to open up the exits there, according to the plan? Or should he keep this one road open and have the new arrivals go inland from here?

Gen. Roosevelt conferred briefly with his battalion commanders and made his decision. "Gentlemen," he announced, "we'll start the war from here."

The general's gamble paid off. His rapid movement inland deepened the beachhead and cleared the area for the fresh assault waves coming ashore. On July 12, just after General Eisenhower named him commander of the newly arrived 90th Infantry Division, General Roosevelt suffered a fatal heart attack. He was buried in the cemetery overlooking Utah Beach, only the second son of a president to earn the Medal of Honor (Rutherford B. Hayes's son, Webb C. Hayes, earned one during the Philippine Insurrection in 1899).

German resistance on Omaha Beach proved to be even more formidable than that found on Utah. Both ends of the beach were dominated by high cliffs, while behind the beach the ground sloped up to a plateau 150 feet high. The high ground gave the German defenders an unobstructed view of the beach, and they took full advantage of it. Every square inch of sand was covered by at least one automatic weapon or cannon.

The assault waves of the 1st Infantry Division faced a complex system of pillboxes, gun casements, mortar pits, firing trenches, and artillery pieces. Each of these was surrounded by barbed wire and mine fields. Most positions were connected to one another by tunnels and deep trenches.

The havoc these weapons wreaked upon the troops hitting Omaha was nearly indescribable. Huge explosions from artillery shells ruined landing craft and killed soldiers while they were still a half-mile offshore. Those who did land were cut down by the scythelike fusillade of German machine-gun fire. For those who survived that hell, mines planted on the beach waited to tear legs from torsos. Some of the infantry companies in the initial waves suffered casualties exceeding ninety percent.

Remarkably, here and there on the fire-swept beach men overcame their fear and the destruction around them to carry out their mission. First Lt. Jimmie W. Monteith, a twenty-six-year-old veteran of the 16th Infantry's war in North Africa and Sicily from Virginia, was in one of the first landing craft to touch shore. Finding himself among disorganized men from decimated units, he pulled them into his own platoon and got them moving off the killing ground of the beach. Unable to bring enough fire to bear on a pesky pillbox, he ran back to the water's edge where two tanks sat, buttoned up. On foot he led them through a mine field and into firing positions. Under his directions they wiped out the pillbox with cannon fire. Monteith crossed the open terrain several more times, knocking out two enemy machine guns during his forays. His luck ran out while leading his ragtag collection of soldiers against a local counterattack. Flanking fire from a Nazi machine gun ripped into his chest, killing him.

During the first few hours the situation on Omaha Beach was so bad General Bradley, offshore on the U.S.S. *Augusta*, seriously considered abandoning Omaha and sending the following waves ashore on the British beaches. In fact, at 9:00 A.M. he radioed Eisenhower asking for permission to do just that. The message never got through.

Amazingly, the valorous men on the beach pushed forward against incredible odds, overcoming the Nazi defenders. When reinforcing GIs and tanks started landing after midmorning the Americans began to win. By 1:30 P.M. Bradley had received an encouraging message from the beach: "Troops formerly pinned down on beaches now advancing up heights beyond beaches." The strength of the invaders was beginning to wear down the Germans. By dark the GIs held a beachhead six miles long and not quite two miles deep. It was a precarious hold, to be sure, but the fresh troops continuing to pour across the beaches would solidify it.

Farther east, British and Canadian troops fought their own fierce battle. But they, too, overcame tremendous odds and secured their beachhead by nightfall. Behind the assault beaches, the paratroopers, though still disorganized, kept German reinforcements from driving the Allies off their slender beach. By midafternoon, the 82d Airborne had linked up with 4th Infantry Division troops breaking out of Utah Beach. For the soldiers coming off Omaha Beach, the going was proving to be a lot tougher. Though Allied air power greatly reduced the German reinforcements that made it to the Normandy coast, some did get through, and the weary GIs had to fight their way through them.

WALTER D. EHLERS

Kansas farm boys Walter and Roland Ehlers enlisted in the army in 1940 to beat the draft. The brothers went to the 1st Infantry Division where they joined the same rifle company. Together, they fought the Nazis in North Africa and Sicily. When their unit, the 18th Infantry Regiment, went to England to prepare for the impending invasion, their company commander called them to his office.

"There's a big invasion coming up," he told them. "Casualties will be high. The two of you shouldn't be together."

He sent Roland to another company. On D day Roland's company landed a few hundred yards away from Walter's. A German mortar shell dropped on the ramp of Roland's landing craft as he was disembarking, killing him instantly.

Walter Ehlers and his twelve-man squad survived the D day landings. Three days later the twenty-three-year-old staff sergeant led his men against the Germans emplaced in Normandy's notorious hedgerows. The bocage was a patchwork of thousands of small fields enclosed by nearly impenetrable, centuries-old hedges. The hedges consisted of dense thickets of bushes, vines, and trees atop earthen revetments several feet thick and three or four feet high. A handful of German soldiers dug in among the hedges could hold off attacking troops with ease. The hedged fields had to be taken one at a time by the infantry.

At midmorning on June 9, a cool, overcast day, German rifle fire rang out as Ehlers took his men across one such field. Barking out orders, he led his squad forward to the base of a hedgerow.

"When I got to the hedgerow," Ehlers said, "I encountered a German patrol." He killed them all. Continuing forward alone, he spotted a German machine-gun nest and a mortar emplacement. Stealthily crawling on, he opened fire on the machine gunners, killing three and silencing the weapon.

Ehlers went farther, still out in front of his squad. "I came up to the mortar section. That's where my bayonet came in handy," he said. "It had a psychological effect on the Germans.

They looked horrified and started running." Ehlers pursued them, killing three. When another machine gun opened fire, the valiant Ehlers attacked it single-handedly. He killed the crew of that gun, too.

The next day, Ehlers's squad led their platoon deep into enemy territory. "We were so far ahead [of the rest of the Allied forces], we were practically nose-to-nose with the Germans," he said.

They were so far forward, in fact, they found themselves virtually surrounded by Germans as they moved across a field bordered by hedgerows. Enemy automatic weapons fire hit them from the front, both flanks, and the right rear. The platoon leader ordered a withdrawal. To cover the movement, Ehlers and a BAR man stood back-to-back, firing their weapons in a wide semicircle. Suddenly, the BAR man fell, badly wounded. Seconds later a sniper's bullet hit Ehlers in the back, spinning him completely around. He saw the sniper as he hit the dirt, fired his rifle, and killed him.

Despite his wound, Ehlers picked up the wounded man and carried him to the safety of the platoon. Then he darted back into the field, picked up the BAR, and brought it back. The platoon's medic patched up Ehlers's wound, then ordered him to an aid station. He refused, staying with his squad.

Of his heroism Ehlers later said, "Bravery? I used to consider it self-preservation. I felt we had a heck of a lot better chance in combat if we got things moving. I wasn't overly brave. I had the feeling that it might cost me my life if I *didn't* do it."

Ehlers received his Medal of Honor in the field on December 6, 1944. He also received the gold bars of a second lieutenant. He remained with his unit during the fighting across Germany and into Czechoslovakia. Along the way he earned a Silver Star, two Bronze Stars, and four Purple Hearts. Since the war he has worked almost continuously for the VA, helping other vets.

Though the Allies were clearly winning the battle the beachhead had not expanded as rapidly in some areas as had been planned. One of these areas was at the key road junction of Carentan. The German defenders clung doggedly to the area, preventing a linkup between the forces driving inland from Utah and Omaha Beaches. Rommel rushed reinforcements to the area. Elements of the 101st Airborne Division, finally organized after many of its troopers had fought incohesively for several days, moved toward the city from the north. To facilitate the city's capture they had to take four bridges over the river Douve.

ROBERT G. COLE

On June 11, 1944, some 250 members of the 3d Battalion, 502d Parachute Infantry Regiment, were moving on one of the bridges near Carentan. They advanced south down a long, exposed causeway. The causeway, about six to nine feet above marshes on either side, was utterly devoid of cover. It provided a perfect field of fire for German riflemen and machine guns hidden in the hedgerows bordering the far side of the marshes. During the advance, the column had suffered heavy casualties from the enemy fire. Still they continued forward, aware that capturing the Douve River bridge was critical to linking up with the GIs coming inland from the beaches.

Leading the column was the battalion commander, Lt. Col. Robert G. Cole. The son of an army veterinarian, Cole was born on March 19, 1915, at Fort Sam Houston, San Antonio, Texas. Growing up on an army base was a pleasant experience for Cole. As a youth, he spent many hours playing on the post's central parade ground while cavalrymen trotted past on their mounts.

Cole enlisted in the army in 1934 in order to attend the West Point preparatory school at Fort Sam Houston. He accepted an appointment to the academy in 1935, graduating in 1939. With his new gold bars in place, he joined the 15th Infantry Regiment at Fort Lewis, Washington, as an infantry second lieutenant.

While there he volunteered for a new venture for the army, the airborne infantry. Only the most capable officers were accepted for airborne training. Cole quickly proved to be one of the best. After jump training he joined the fledgling 502d regiment at Fort Bragg, North Carolina. Within two years he took command of its 3d Battalion.

The first combat mission for the 101st Airborne was the D day drop. Cole landed alone in the pitch dark that morning. Over the next few hours he gathered up seventy-five other lost paratroopers and headed for his battalion's objective. Along the way he led his small band against a convoy of German reinforcements racing to the beach. They wiped out the column, then continued on toward their objective. With more troopers joining his band, Cole led them toward Utah Beach, where they captured and held the inland end of one of the beach's exits. Cole's actions earned him a DSC.

One of Cole's men remembered him as a man who had that "rare combination of courage, integrity, a sense of humor, and, lastly, a deep understanding and concern for the men under his command."

Those qualities were evident outside Carentan. The enemy resistance increased without warning. Mortars and artillery shells added their mayhem to the rifle and automatic weapons fire falling on the paratroopers. The men scattered, seeking cover in the marshes.

Cole instantly started issuing orders, trying to move his weak forces against the enemy. The fire from the hedgerows, only 150 yards away, was so heavy any movement brought an immediate response. For nearly an hour the battalion lay pinned down, unable to move forward or backward. Cole knew something had to be done. They couldn't stay there. They'd all be wiped out.

During a lull in the artillery fire, Cole passed to his company commanders an order rarely heard in modern combat, "Fix bayonets!"

Around him he could hear the satisfying click of bayonets being fitted to rifle barrels. Brandishing his .45-caliber pistol, and completely oblivious to the enemy fire, Cole stood up in front of his men. He yelled a one-word command that would have stirred the blood of the old cavalrymen at Fort Sam Houston, "Charge!" Off he ran toward the hedgerow.

Behind Cole men watched in stunned silence. The officer was fifty feet away before the first man rose to follow him. Then others followed. First, single figures rose from the marshy ground. Then, small groups of two and three followed. In places, whole squads started running forward, bare steel visible at the ends of their rifles. Within minutes nearly the entire group of men was running toward the hedgerows, yelling as ferociously as they could.

German gunfire cut into the American line, dropping men along the line, but Cole's bold tactic worked. The paratroopers waded into the German emplacements, bayonets rising and falling as they slashed their way through the enemy.

It was over in minutes. German bodies lay sprawled around the hedgerows, most of them dead from bayonet wounds. Those Nazis who did survive fled to their rear. Sharpshooting paratroopers took them under fire, dropping dozens before they could reach safety.

Cole stood exhausted, surveying the battlefield. He could hardly believe it. They'd done it! Around him, men started cheering. Cole appreciated the jubilation, but had to quiet his men. There was still a lot of war to fight. He started issuing orders. Flankers were sent out, perimeter defenses set up. The Germans might counterattack.

They didn't. The bridge remained in American hands. The next day Cole's battle-weary 3d battalion was relieved by other 101st units who took Carentan on June 13. As a result, two Allied corps coming off the invasion beaches, the V and VIII, linked up. The Allied lodgement in Normandy now stood ten miles deep and sixty miles wide.

Cole's battalion spent another month fighting in Normandy before being returned to England for rebuilding preparatory to the next big jump. It came on September 17, 1944, when the 101st parachuted into Holland as part of Field Marshal Montgomery's Operation *Market Garden*.

On September 18, 1944, after requesting air support against a German target, Cole decided to personally lay orange identification panels out in front of his battalion's front lines. As he did so, a German sniper, hidden in a farmhouse just one hundred yards away, shot and killed him.

Sixteen days later the army issued General Order No. 79, awarding Cole the Medal of Honor for leading the first bayonet charge in the ETO. The presentation ceremony took place on October 30, 1944. On the parade ground at Fort Sam Houston where Cole had played as a child, his widow accepted his posthumous award. In her arms was the eighteen-month-old son Cole had never seen.

Despite successes such as Cole's, the Allied advance into France still moved more slowly than planned. Tenacious German defenders making skillful use of the terrain greatly reduced the American advance. Not until June 14, 1944, was Maj. Gen. Lawton Collins, of Guadalcanal fame, able to send his VII Corps up the Cotentin Peninsula toward Cherbourg. His three infantry divisions—4th, 9th, and 79th—encountered only token resistance as they fought their way north. That changed when they reached Cherbourg.

The twenty-five thousand Germans in Cherbourg turned the city and its suburbs into a massive fortress. Huge blockhouses, bristling with automatic weapons, were arranged in a semicircle five miles south of the city. Supported by artillery batteries within the city, the blockhouses covered every approach to Cherbourg. Collins called in a massive air strike on June 22. Over five hundred fighters and bombers pounded Cherbourg for hours. Over the next two days the GIs made substantial progress against the main German defenses. On June 25, the 79th Infantry Division faced Fort Du Roule, the strongest of Cherbourg's defensive positions. A multilevel fort built into the face of a promontory, the structure had mortars and machine guns in concrete pillboxes spaced across its face. Additional bunkers, fronted with barbed wire–filled antitank ditches, guarded the fort's approaches.

Two battalions of the 79th's 314th Infantry assaulted the fort on June 25. As they started forward, 1st Lt. Carlos C. Ogden's platoon of Company K was pinned down by a German 88-mm gun and two machine guns. "I knew we were going to get killed if we stayed down there," Ogden, of Paris, Illinois, said. So he fastened a grenade launcher to his rifle and started up the hill alone. Within minutes a German machine-gun bullet slammed into his head. Blood drenched his face. He stood, unwavering, and fired his grenade launcher at the 88. He knocked it out. Ogden then turned his attention to the machine guns. Still ignoring the merciless fire directed at him. Ogden knocked out both nests. Wounded again, he returned to his platoon and took it up the hill, wiping out the remaining enemy. Ogden survived the war and years later served as California's director of selective service under Gov. Ronald Reagan.

Cherbourg fell on June 26. The Allies finally had the port they so desperately needed. General Bradley next turned his forces south. His First Army's major objective was St. Lo, where four major and four secondary roads converged. Using ten divisions—the 82d Airborne, 79th, 90th, and 8th Infantry of the VIII Corps, the 83d, 4th and 9th Infantry Divisions of the VII Corps, and the 29th and 30th Infantry Divisions and the 3d Armored Division of the XIX Corps—Bradley launched his attack on July 3.

Under direct orders from Hitler, St. Lo's defenders put up a brutal defense. They counterattacked several times, nearly throwing the Americans back. Finally, units of the 29th Division took the little town on July 17. Bradley's First Army suffered more than forty thousand casualties in the two-week fight.

Though St. Lo was in American hands, the troops still needed to break out of Normandy. General Bradley's bold plan to do so, *Cobra,* called for a massive bombing by over a thousand bombers, after which two infantry divisions would burst through the German defenses near St. Lo. While they held the passage open, another infantry and two armored divisions would pour through, headed for Coutances, fifteen miles away.

Cobra began early on July 25. Wave upon wave of bombers roared over the waiting infantrymen, pounding the Germans into a stupor. The GIs stepped off. Their initial advance went smoothly as they quickly rolled over the stunned Germans. Then the resistance stiffened. The fighting got tougher. Out of the rough-and-tumble fighting in the hedgerows came one of the most remarkable stories of heroism in the entire war.

MATT URBAN

Five days after D day, the 9th Infantry Division came ashore at Utah Beach. At the head of the 60th Infantry Regiment's Company F was Capt. Matt Urban. A veteran of the 9th's campaign in North Africa and Sicily, Urban had repeatedly proven himself to be the epitome of an infantry officer.

Just a few days after landing in France Urban once again proved his mettle. On June 14, Company F attacked Renouf. Encountering heavy enemy small-arms and tank fire, the company's advance ground to a halt. Realizing his unit stood on the verge of decimation, Urban grabbed a bazooka. He told an ammo carrier to follow him, then worked his way through the hedgerows to a point near the two panzers. Brazenly exposing himself to the tanks' fire, he loaded and fired the bazooka. Within minutes he'd destroyed both armored vehicles.

Later that same day Company F led the attack into Orglandes. Urban took shrapnel in his leg from an exploding German 37-mm round. He refused evacuation. At 5:00 A.M. the next morning he led his company in yet another attack. An hour later he was hit again. This time there was no doubt; he'd have to be evacuated. By noon he was in the back of a truck, the first leg in his journey back to England.

Urban's story begins in Buffalo, New York, where he was

born on August 25, 1919. Though his family was not poor, money was scarce. Urban worked very hard through his high school years to contribute to the family's coffers. By saving extra money he was able to enter Cornell University in 1937. He earned good grades and excelled in boxing, winning his division in the collegiate championship of 1939.

As a member of Cornell's ROTC program, Urban received the call to active duty just after his graduation in June 1941. He attended officer candidate school, then joined the 60th Infantry Regiment at Fort Bragg, North Carolina. By the time the 60th Infantry received orders for overseas shipment in the summer of 1942, Urban held the post of executive officer in Company F.

In North Africa Urban quickly demonstrated his heroism and exceptional leadership traits. He earned two Silver Stars and the first of seven Purple Hearts. He also assumed command of Company F after its commanding officer became a casualty.

In mid-July 1944, while still recuperating from his wounds received near Orglandes, Urban was visited in the hospital by a wounded man from his company. Urban learned how the exceedingly brutal fighting in Normandy had reduced Company F from a first-class fighting machine to a frightened, frustrated, motionless mass of men. Determined to help his men, Urban deserted his hospital bed that very night. Over the next several days the determined captain hitchhiked his way back to France.

Still wearing his bandages Urban rejoined his demoralized company the morning of July 25. As a sergeant remembered, "The sight of him limping up the road, all smiles, raring to lead the attack, once more brought the morale of the battle-weary men to the highest peak."

Urban well remembers that day. "I was full of anger, remorse, and despair. I'd seen my men mutilated, chopped up. I was seeking revenge. I was like a tiger. It was all bubbling up inside of me, and it exploded."

Urban began his exploits that very afternoon by rescuing a wounded man from a burning tank. Late that evening his battalion's attack upon a well-entrenched German position located atop a prominent hill stalled under fierce fire. Two supporting tanks had been destroyed and a third, although intact, did not move. Urban located the lieutenant in charge of the supporting armor and laid out a plan of attack to reduce the hill position.

The lieutenant and a sergeant were killed by the intense enemy fire as they tried to climb aboard the immobile tank. Urban, though hobbling because of his leg wound, dashed through the unrelenting enemy fire and mounted the tank. As enemy rounds hit all around him, he ordered it forward. He armed the .50-caliber machine gun. While the tank fired its cannon into the enemy positions Urban followed up with well-aimed bursts of fire.

"I was crying as I went up that hill," Urban remembers. "I thought I was a goner, that I was headed for certain death."

But he didn't die. Unscathed, he reached the top of the hill. Alone, he had destroyed the enemy positions holding up his battalion.

Over the next five weeks Urban repeatedly displayed his fearless heroism. On August 2 he received his fifth wound. Against the battalion surgeon's advice Urban stayed with his company. Four days later the battalion commanding officer became a casualty. Over officers more senior in rank and age, Urban was selected to take his place. On August 15, while at the forefront of his battalion's attack, Urban was wounded for the sixth time.

Urban's battalion crossed the Meuse River near Heer, Belgium, on September 2. The lead elements immediately ran into a fierce barrage of enemy artillery, mortar, and small-arms fire. As was his custom, Urban left his command post to personally lead the disorganized GIs across the river. As he moved across open ground, an exploding mortar shell drove shrapnel deep into his throat. Although unable to speak above a whisper, he refused to leave the battlefield until assured his men had made it across the river. Only then did he agree to let the medics evacuate him.

The next day, while Urban sailed back to England aboard a hospital ship, the Germans counterattacked his battalion. Those GIs who weren't killed were captured. Among them was S. Sgt. Earl G. Evans who had served with Urban since North Africa. After Urban rode the tank into the German position in Normandy, Evans overheard a battalion officer say he was going to recommend him for the Medal of Honor. Unfortunately, that man died in the fighting at the Meuse.

When Sergeant Evans was repatriated in July 1945 he wrote a letter to the War Department, recommending Urban for a Medal of Honor. The War Department forwarded it to the commanding general of the 9th Division, on occupation duty in Germany. It never arrived. But a copy of Evans's letter was placed in Urban's personnel file.

In the meantime, Urban had recuperated from his wounds. He received a promotion to lieutenant colonel in October 1945. Five months later he received a medical discharge. Among his medals he counted two Silver Stars, a Legion of Merit, three Bronze Stars, and seven Purple Hearts. He knew nothing of Sergeant Evans's letter.

The postwar years passed peacefully for Urban. For sixteen years he served as executive director of the Monroe, Michigan, Community Center. In 1974 he became recreation director for Holland, Michigan.

At a 9th Division reunion in 1977, Urban learned of Evans's letter for the first time. He immediately began a campaign for the Medal of Honor. At the urging of the Disabled American Veterans the Pentagon began a review of Urban's story.

On July 19, 1980, thirty-six years after the fact, President James E. Carter hung the Medal of Honor around Urban's neck. Befitting the occasion, the presentation was made before veterans of the 9th Infantry Division at their reunion in Washington, D.C. An obviously moved President Carter said, "Matt Urban showed that moments of terrible devastation can bring out courage. His actions are a reminder to this nation so many years later of what freedom really means."

As President Carter turned to Urban, the heroic soldier struggled to maintain his soldierly bearing, but his face melted with emotion, his eyes shone with tears. The president also blinked back a tear. World War II was finally over for Matt Urban.

Though the fighting was tough and the casualties high, *Cobra* succeeded. Suddenly the breakout from Normandy was at hand. Armored units raced south with a previously unknown speed. The campaign marked a change from the slow and costly advances through the hedgerows of Normandy to dizzyingly fast thrusts against weakened Nazi defenders. One entire German corps had been smashed, another severely beaten.

Avranches, at the western base of the Cotentin Peninsula, fell July 31. The entire peninsula now belonged to the Americans. There was nothing to stop them from entering Brittany to the west or turning east toward Paris.

On August 1, 1944, General Bradley took command of the newly formed 12th Army Group. His First Army was taken over by Lt. Gen. Courtney H. Hodges. Lieutenant General Patton's Third Army was also activated that day.

In the hell-bent-for-leather tradition of his cavalry corps, Patton unleashed his Third Army with a lightning boldness never before seen in warfare. His armored divisions spearheaded his army's advance, often racing out of radio range. In just six days, Patton's armored columns covered the two hundred miles to the major port city of Brest. As at Cherbourg, the Germans stubbornly defended Brest. It held out until September 18.

While Patton's VIII Corps fought at Brest, he directed his XII, XV, and XX Corps south and east. By August 8, they had taken Le Mans, halfway to Paris. On August 18, they were only twenty miles from the Seine River, at Chartres, south of Paris.

Originally, General Eisenhower had planned to bypass Paris, with General Montgomery's 21st Army Group on the north and Bradley's 12th Army Group on the south. To attack Paris would be very costly in casualties and would also slow down the pursuit of the nearly broken German army. Political events took the decision out of Eisenhower's hands. The French 2d Armored Division, part of Patton's Third Army, triumphantly entered Paris on August 25, 1944.

South of Paris that same day, along the Seine River near Montereau, the 5th Infantry Division, part of the XX Corps of Patton's Third Army, battled German forces on the north side of the Seine. Since crossing the river the previous day the division had been fighting frantically to enlarge its bridgehead. Casualties were being ferried back to the south bank in rubber assault boats paddled by medics. Other medics on the south bank helped the casualties up the slippery bank to waiting ambulances. As one boatload of casualties reached midstream, a German machine gun suddenly opened fire on it from just one hundred yards away. All the casualties took to the water, except one man strapped to a litter. Two other patients, unable to swim, clung desperately to the boat's sides. Bullets from the machine gun kicked up water spouts around them. It looked as if they would die.

On the south bank, Pvt. Harold Garman, a medic with the 5th Medical Battalion, took in the scene in seconds. Without a moment's hesitation he dove fully clothed into the Seine. He swam directly into the machine-gun fire, intent only on saving the wounded. When he reached the boat he grabbed a rope dangling from its side and started towing it to the south shore. While machine-gun fire hit the water just inches from his exposed head, the Fairfield, Illinois, native towed the boat to safety. As he reached the south shore, riflemen knocked out the Nazi machine gun. Garman's inspiring action saved the three men. Garman, severely wounded in the fighting around Metz, France, in the fall, received his Medal of Honor from General Patton on April 6, 1945.

Ten days before Paris fell, and while Allied troops were still struggling through Normandy's murderous hedgerow country, a second invasion of France took place. On August 15, 1944, Operation *Anvil* put ashore ninety-four thousand troops on the French Riviera at St. Tropez. From there they would drive north up the Rhone River valley with all possible speed. At the very least, the southern France invasion would relieve German pressure on the forces in Normandy. If all went well, the forces from Normandy and those from southern France would link up and complete the liberation of France by autumn.

GIs of the 3d, 36th and 45th Infantry Divisions came ashore at the famed resort beaches beginning at 8:00 A.M. that morning. Though the Germans had ten divisions in the immediate area, the landings went surprisingly well. Within two hours the invaders had driven nearly one mile inland against light resistance.

Sgt. James P. Connor, of the 7th Infantry Regiment's Battle Patrol, proved instrumental in the success of his regiment's landing. Soon after coming ashore he was wounded and his platoon leader killed by exploding shrapnel from a hanging mine. Rather than seek aid, Connor assumed command of the platoon and continued forward, shooting a sniper hidden near a bridge. After advancing several thousand yards across a beach saturated with mines and under heavy enemy fire, the Wilmington, Delaware, native was wounded again, taking a round through his left shoulder. Again, Connor refused aid. "They can hit me, but they can't stop me," he said.

When the remaining men of the Battle Patrol hesitated under the Germans' fire, Connor prodded the soldiers forward. As he led his men against Nazi troops emplaced in a cluster of buildings just off the beach, Connor received a third wound, this time in his leg. Though he couldn't stand, he stayed in command of his men. Only after the Nazis had been wiped out did Connor relinquish command and seek treatment.

On August 28, Free French troops completed the capture of Marseilles, the Riviera's major port. From there, the invasion's commander, Lt. Gen. Lucian K. Truscott, sent his troops up National Highway 7 along the Rhone River toward Montelimar. Spearheaded by an armored task force, the GIs rushed north. Pausing only long enough to refuel or crush small German garrisons, Truscott's troops moved even faster than Patton's troops in Normandy.

Because Hitler had authorized the withdrawal of his armies from southern France, General Truscott wanted to close the gap at Montelimar through which the German Nineteenth Army was escaping. To help close the gap the 36th Infantry Division received the assignment of capturing the high ground commanding Highway 7 north of Montelimar. German troops fiercely resisted the GIs.

STEPHEN R. GREGG

Though born in the Bronx, New York, on September 1, 1914, Stephen R. Gregg grew up across the Hudson River in Bayonne, New Jersey. After graduating from high school in 1932, he worked in a New York art gallery for four years before deciding to attend trade school to learn welding. He was working on navy destroyers at Kearny, New Jersey, when he received his draft notice in January 1942.

After basic training, Gregg joined the 36th Infantry Division in training at Camp Blanding, Florida. A few months later they transferred to Camp Edwards, Massachusetts.

Gregg went ashore at Salerno with Company L, 143d Infantry, on September 9, 1943. He fought alongside Commando Kelly at Altavilla, being one of just twenty-eight men of their company to survive the vicious counterattack. Gregg earned a Silver Star for his gallantry in action at the disastrous Rapido River crossing. He was one of the last to withdraw, swimming back across the Rapido next to Commando Kelly. He also earned his first Purple Heart.

Gregg's survival of the 36th's numerous battles amazed him. "At San Pietro," he said, "we crawled through barbed wire while German tracers flew around. It was like the Fourth of July. Men in front of and behind me were killed in that fight. My overcoat had bullet holes through it in several places but, for some reason, none touched me."

Gregg's luck continued through the Anzio landing and the struggle to capture Rome. He didn't receive his second wound until August 27, 1944, the same day he earned the Medal of Honor.

Company L took up positions on a heavily wooded hill north of Montelimar on August 26. As the GIs watched, thousands of Germans moved up Highway 7, heading north. Some of them bivouacked in a valley below Company L's position. Recognizing the opportunity, Gregg's company commander called in the artillery. Nearly every piece of artillery under Truscott's command zeroed in on the area.

"It was a slaughter," Gregg recalled. "Everywhere we looked Germans were dying. Then our fighter planes zoomed in. Their rockets killed hundreds more. It was so bad I really felt sorry for them."

The next day, Company L, alone on the hill and mustering no more than one hundred effectives, began to move north. Unknown to them, Nazi troops had occupied positions higher up the slope. The first sign of trouble came without warning. Heavy rifle fire cut into the two leading squads. Men fell heavily, dead or badly wounded.

Several hundred yards to their rear, T. Sgt. Gregg heard the cries for help. "Why aren't the medics going up there?" he asked a nearby aidman.

"Firing's too heavy," the man replied.

"We can't leave them out there," Gregg said. "Cover me."

With that, he picked up a .30-caliber light machine gun and started up the hill. Firing from the hip in accurate, measured bursts, Gregg went up the hill, the aidman behind him. While Gregg kept the Germans pinned down, the medic pulled seven wounded men to safety. When all the casualties had been removed, Gregg started withdrawing. Then he ran out of ammo.

"All of a sudden four Germans stepped from behind trees," he remembered. "Why they didn't shoot me I'll never know. They motioned me to surrender and I did. What choice did I have? I put my hands up."

They had started moving toward the German lines when a

high-pitched scream warned of incoming artillery. All five men hit the ground. One of the Germans dropped a machine pistol. Gregg picked it up. Firing every which way, he dashed back to his company. Once Gregg rejoined his heavy weapons platoon, the company again started up the hill. Two hours later, they'd thrown the Germans off.

At dawn the next day the Nazis counterattacked; several Tiger tanks supported the attack. Gregg helped his company by acting as a forward observer for the 60-mm mortars. He called down more than six hundred rounds on the enemy that morning. His accurate directions caused heavy casualties among the attackers, preventing them from overwhelming the company's line.

Shortly after noon Gregg lost contact with the mortars. Believing the phone lines were cut he started tracing the wires back to the mortar emplacement. Through several hundred yards of woods, all under fire from enemy artillery and mortars, Gregg worked his way toward the mortars, emplaced in a ravine.

He had almost reached the ravine when an American soldier called out to him, "The Jerries got the mortars. They're dropping them on us."

Unwilling to concede the mortars to the enemy, Gregg ordered the soldier to cover him. "I'm going to drop a few grenades on them. Fire like hell, will you?"

Rushing from tree to tree, Gregg made his way undetected to within grenade-range of the ravine. He could see five Germans operating the American mortars. He pulled the pin on a grenade, then tossed it into the ravine. The explosion killed one German and wounded two. Gregg jumped into the pit and captured the remaining two Germans. When they were properly under guard, Gregg rounded up some nearby soldiers, gave them quick instructions on mortar operations, then started dropping rounds on the Germans.

A few hours later another company from the regiment reinforced the hill. With their help Company L held. Gregg's sustained gallantry served as an inspiration to the entire company.

Three months later, while fighting near the German border Gregg received a battlefield promotion to second lieutenant. Lt. Gregg remained with Company L throughout the brutal winter fighting in the Vosges Mountains. One day he was called to battalion headquarters. There he learned he would receive the

Medal of Honor for his actions near Montelimar. Gen. Alexander Patch made the presentation on March 14, 1945.

Gregg barely had time to realize what the decoration meant when his company commander slapped him on the back. "Better put that thing away," he advised Gregg. "We're going back in the lines tonight."

Within hours of receiving his medal, Gregg was in the back of a truck, heading toward the Siegfried Line. He battled the Germans for two more weeks before he received orders sending him home. He was one of just three remaining original members of his company.

Following his discharge in August 1945, Gregg joined the Hudson County, New Jersey, Sheriff's Department. He is still there.

Thousands of Germans died along National Route 7, but many survived. As the Americans continued pushing north the German resistance mounted. In spite of the odds against them, the Germans counterattacked whenever they could. One such attack came against the forward command post of the 3d Battalion, 7th Infantry, 3d Infantry Division, near Besançon, France, on the night of September 6–7, 1944.

ROBERT D. MAXWELL

Born October 26, 1920, Robert D. Maxwell called himself a "handcuffed volunteer"—a draftee, inducted into the army in July 1940 from his family's home in Larimer County, Colorado. He finished basic training, then joined the 3d Infantry Division at Fort Lewis, Washington.

Trained as a telephone lineman, Maxwell found himself frequently under fire as the 3d Infantry Division battled the Nazis across North Africa, Sicily, Italy, and Anzio. Linemen had to string their radio-telephone wires from front-line units to rear command posts, all the while exposed to the same enemy fire as the infantrymen. The job required daring men with nerves of steel. Maxwell was one of them. His coolness under fire at Anzio brought him his first Silver Star.

His second came on September 6, 1944, when he ignored intense enemy fire to string lines from one rooftop to another in Besançon. One of the witnesses to Maxwell's steadfastness said, "Technician 5th Grade Maxwell was the coolest customer I've ever seen. Tracer bullets were just barely clearing his head, yet he didn't seem to notice it.''

His commanding officer did, and recommended Maxwell for the Silver Star.

That same night a heavy force of Germans, supported by flak guns and automatic weapons fire, infiltrated through the battalion's forward companies. They made their way to within fifteen yards of the battered French farmhouse serving as the command post. The Germans raked the building with fire, their bullets ricocheting through doors and windows. Under this fire several Germans snaked to within ten yards of the building. They began throwing grenades at the defenders. Only a chicken-wire extension over the courtyard wall saved those inside. The grenades hit the wire, bounced off, and exploded harmlessly outside the wall.

Then a grenade cleared the chicken wire and dropped among a group of defenders. Maxwell saw it. He remembered what happened: ''It was cold that night, so I'd wrapped myself in a blanket when I went on guard. When the Germans attacked I used my .45 to fire back at them. When the grenade came in I realized it would go off in three seconds. I knew I couldn't get hold of it in the dark in time to throw it back.''

He grabbed his blanket and hurled himself on the grenade.

''It apparently went off between my feet while I was in a crouched position over it,'' Maxwell said.

A witness concurred. Pfc. James P. Joyce said, ''I lay still for a few seconds partially stunned by the blast. Then I realized I wasn't hurt. Maxwell had deliberately taken the full force of the explosion on himself in order to protect us and make it possible for us to continue at our posts and fight.''

''Part of my right foot was blown away,'' Maxwell said. ''I also got large shrapnel wounds on my left arm and temple, plus other wounds.''

A lieutenant helped Maxwell to a jeep. German rifle fire hit them both as they drove out of Besançon headed for an aid station. Quick actions by the doctors saved Maxwell's life. Within a few days he arrived at a hospital in Naples. His war was over.

After receiving his Medal of Honor on April 6, 1945, Maxwell settled in Eugene, Oregon, where his parents had moved during the war. He attended college, then became an automotive mechanics instructor at a local junior college.

A few days after Maxwell jumped on the grenade other elements of the 3d Infantry Division closed in on Vesoul, one of the last major German strong points in southern France. The French town fell on September 12, 1944. By straight line, Vesoul is more than four hundred miles from St. Tropez. That the Americans had covered this distance in less than a month, all the while fighting a vicious enemy, is truly one of the most remarkable feats of the war.

On the same day Vesoul capitulated, soldiers from Truscott's army linked up with men from Patton's army near Dijon. A few days later Truscott's Seventh Army was absorbed into Eisenhower's command. Nearly one-third of France had been freed. The Allied armies could now concentrate on smashing Hitler's western defenses and driving into Germany itself.

13

* * *

Into Germany

With the fall of Paris, the Germans apparently lost all incentive for a significant defense of eastern France. The Allies' original invasion plans called for a lengthy pause along the Seine to allow time to build their strength for the final thrust into Germany. But that halt had been predicated on a continuing, stiffer German resistance. With dispirited Nazi formations fleeing toward the safety of their homeland, such a pause was out of the question. The Germans had to be kept on the run. They could not be given the chance to strengthen any of their redoubts and build a co-ordinated defensive line across France.

As their first major target in Germany the Allies selected the Ruhr industrial area. An attack on this important area would force Hitler to commit his remaining armed forces to battle, whereupon the Allies would destroy them. To reach the Ruhr the planners selected two routes. The primary one would be northeast from Paris through Amiens, Maubeuge, and Liege. The secondary route would come from Metz and the Saar River basin to Frankfurt.

To crush the Nazi war machine the Allies amassed a land army that dwarfed all the world's previous armies. Three Allied army groups composed of seven armies were deployed in a grand arc reaching from the North Sea to Switzerland.

On the Allied left, or north, was the 21st Army Group consisting of the First Canadian and Second British Armies. Commanded by Field Marshal Montgomery, the army group had made great progress in their fight along the French coast. On August 30, 1944, the First Canadian Army captured Rouen, capital of Normandy. In the next seven days they rolled over the ports of Le Havre, Boulogne, Calais, and Dunkirk. To the Canadians' right the British Second Army liberated Amiens on August 31. Four days later the Tommies seized Brussels; the next day the major port of Antwerp fell. A few days later they stood poised on the Belgian-Dutch border northeast of Brussels.

The center of the Allied lines was held by General Bradley's 12th Army Group. Under his command, Bradley had the First and Third U.S. Armies advancing east; the newly formed Ninth Army was reducing Brest, far behind the front lines.

Since August 25, Lt. Gen. Courtney Hodges's First Army had made impressive gains. Heading northeast, they liberated Soissons and Laon, then crossed into Belgium near Mons. There they cut off the Fifth Panzer Army, capturing over twenty-five thousand Germans fleeing from coastal regions to their homeland.

General Patton's Third Army dashed rapidly eastward, reaching the Meuse River, 150 miles east of Paris, at Commercy on August 31. By noon that day his armored columns were across the river and headed toward the Argonne Forest of World War I fame. Patton's forces stood less than 60 miles from the German border.

On the south, or right, the First French and Seventh U.S. Armies comprised the 6th Army Group under Lt. Gen. Jacob Devers. They, too, pushed north and east, preventing German forces from reinforcing Nancy.

Altogether, over 2,500,000 men were under Eisenhower's command. Forty-nine Allied divisions—thirty-four infantry, fourteen armored, and one airborne—were available to throw against the Nazis. In addition, Eisenhower had four airborne divisions, two American and two British, and a Polish airborne brigade in reserve in England. Most of his units were at or near full strength. Exclusive of southern France, Allied casualties from D day to September 10 amounted to 224,569, or just about ten percent of total strength.

Against the Allies, Hitler's commander in the west, Field Marshal Gerd von Runstedt, had about forty-eight infantry and fifteen panzer divisions. However, hardly any of these were anywhere near full strength. Most had suffered severe losses in men and material. German casualties in northern France had exceeded half a million men. It would be nearly impossible to replace them.

The spectacular Allied run across France, with its brilliant successes, blinded many a commander's eyes to logistical and supply problems. Not only were the front-line troops exhausted, their vehicles required considerable maintenance. In spite of innovations like the famed Red Ball Express, only about half the required supplies reached the fighting divisions. Patton's Third Army burned up about four hundred thousand gallons of gas per day. On most days, he received only about a third of what he needed. The situation was the same all along the Allied front. By the end of the first week of September their advance was sputtering to a halt.

To help alleviate the shortage, and to capitalize on Montgomery's drive into Belgium and its vital port of Antwerp, Eisenhower decided to give supply priorities to Montgomery. In addition, he separated the U.S. First Army from General Bradley's 12th Army Group and temporarily assigned it to Montgomery. Patton's Third Army would drive into the Saar Basin alone, separated from its sister army by the dense Ardennes Forest.

As might be expected, Patton was furious with Eisenhower's decision. He felt that if given priority on supplies, he could have been inside of Germany in ten days or less. He called Eisenhower's decision "the most momentous of the war."

Montgomery's plans called for the U.S. First Army to move toward Germany along the best of the historic invasion routes through Charleroi, Namur, and Liege in Belgium to Aachen, Germany, on the West Wall. Hodges's most aggressive corps and commander, the VII Corps under Maj. Gen. J. Lawton Collins, led the First Army across the Belgian border on September 1. One of Collins's three divisions was the Big Red One, the 1st Infantry Division. They were put into position near Sars-la-Bruyere to contain German troops trying to escape Montgomery's forces moving up the French coast toward Dunkirk.

At 10:45 P.M. on September 3, a German infantry column preceded by an armored patrol vehicle came up the road. In their path stood Company H, 2d Battalion, 18th Infantry, and the machine gun of Pfc. Gino J. Merli.

As soon as he spotted the enemy column, Merli opened fire. His heavy slugs mowed down the Germans. Around him other GIs fired their M-1s at the scattering figures. The fight raged for over an hour before a bayonet attack by the Germans overran the American line, forcing most of them to retreat. Except for

Merli. Even as the Germans swept down on his position, the spunky twenty-year-old from Peckville, Pennsylvania, kept on firing. Grenades exploded all around him, lighting the dark night with brief flashes. Not until the Germans were right on top of him did Merli's machine gun fall silent. When they looked into the machine-gun pit all they saw was Merli's lifeless body. They moved on.

They had covered less than fifty yards when Merli's machine gun came to life. Spitting out thick slugs of lead, the gun turned in a complete circle, spreading death among the enemy. Another German assault wave bore down on Merli. More grenades flashed. When three Germans peered into the pit they, too, saw Merli's lifeless body. These Germans continued forward.

Merli popped up again, spraying his machine-gun bullets into the Germans. As each succeeding enemy wave rolled over the battlefield, Merli cut into them with his automatic weapon. When their grenades burst close to him, he'd feign death. As soon as they passed by, he'd be up again, firing away. The Germans never caught on to Merli's ploy. He kept it up until he ran out of ammo just before dawn. Then he again slumped at the bottom of his pit.

Reinforcing Americans swept the Germans off the battlefield that morning. They found Merli still alive. Around his position lay fifty-two dead Germans. His valiant stand had prevented the Germans from exploiting their breakthrough.

The continued success of the Allied forces throughout the first two weeks of September generated considerable optimism among the Allied commanders. Though the front-line infantryman was seeing and feeling increasingly stubborn resistance as he pushed closer to the German border, many senior Allied officers felt the collapse of Hitler's forces was imminent. The Allied Intelligence Committee in London went so far as to announce on September 8 that "organized resistance under the control of the German High Command is unlikely to continue beyond December 1, 1944, and it may end even sooner." The British War Office estimated, "If we go at the same pace as of late, we should be in Berlin by September 28."

To expedite the destruction of Germany, Field Marshal Montgomery proposed to Eisenhower on September 10 that he be allowed to make a concentrated push into Germany, capturing the Ruhr industrial area, thus forcing Germany's surrender. He argued that there were simply not enough resources available to keep all the armies advancing. Instead, he suggested, halt all but his British Second Army and the American First Army. With the full support of the supply system, these two armies, under Montgomery's direct command, would attack together through the Netherlands, cross the lower Rhine River, and seize the Ruhr.

Preparatory to his main attack, Montgomery further proposed a daring and innovative scheme to secure his left flank. Three Allied airborne divisions would drop behind German lines in Holland to secure a highway connecting three strategically vital Dutch cities: Eindhoven, Nijmegen, and Arnhem, on the north, astride the Rhine. The British 1st Airborne Division would jump on the north side of the Rhine and seize Arnhem. To the south, the U.S. 82d and 101st Airborne Divisions would land adjacent to the highway, seize a series of bridges that spanned canals and three large rivers, clear the highway, and hold it open. This phase of Montgomery's plan was code-named *Market*.

The second phase, *Garden*, called for the British XXX Corps, spearheaded by armored units, to race up the highway and link up with the airborne units. With the enemy forces thus split in half, the armored vehicles could then wheel to the east and drop into the Ruhr, essentially catching the Germans unaware.

Though Eisenhower vetoed Montgomery's main plan, he did approve *Market Garden*. He saw it as able to provide the impetus needed to get the Allies across the Rhine before the critical supply situation forced further halts.

Montgomery wasted no time in launching his attack. On September 17, 16,500 paratroopers and 3,500 glider-borne troops descended perfectly onto their landing zones. The 1st Airborne Division landed nine miles from Arnhem, as planned, and started their march to capture the city and its critical bridge. Unknown to them, two panzer divisions, the 9th and 10th SS, had recently bivouacked in the area for refitting. The ensuing battle decimated the British units. Only one battalion of five hundred men was able to fight their way to the north side of the bridge. There, the Germans cut them off, isolating them from help.

In the southernmost sector of *Market Garden*, the 101st Airborne Division landed north of Eindhoven between the Wilhelmina and Willems Canals. With great speed they captured four railway and highway crossings over the Willems Canal and the

Aa River at Veghel. They then turned south toward the vital highway bridge over the Wilhelmina Canal at Zon. As they approached the structure, German engineers blew it up.

Airborne engineers erected a wooden footbridge across the waterway, but a route for vehicular traffic would have to wait until the British ground forces arrived with the necessary materials. The paratroopers continued south, reaching Eindhoven the morning of September 18.

On the 101st's west flank that day, Company H, 2d Battalion, 502d Parachute Infantry, was sent to capture the rail and road bridges over the Wilhelmina Canal near the small Dutch village of Best. Not only would these bridges provide an alternate crossing site, but the site also controlled a road along which German reinforcements might try to reach Eindhoven.

En route to Best, Company H came under heavy fire from German infantry supported by several 88-mm cannon. Though pinned down, Company H's commander dispatched a reinforced platoon under 1st Lt. Edward L. Wierzbowski to the bridges. By the time they crawled the last few yards to a trench alongside the canal, Wierzbowski's force numbered only eighteen men, of whom three were wounded. They quickly dug in, Germans swirling around them. Soon they were surrounded.

JOE E. MANN

One of the men taking refuge with Lieutenant Wierzbowski was the platoon's lead scout, Pfc. Joe E. Mann. Born July 12, 1922, in Reardan, Washington, Mann grew up on his family's wheat ranch. During his high school years he not only played football, baseball, and tennis, but also excelled in debate and acted in several school plays.

In September 1942 Mann enlisted in the army, hoping to become a pilot. Unfortunately, a metal pin holding together a collarbone broken in a football game prevented him from entering the training program. Still desirous of being airborne, he volunteered for the paratroopers. By the time he'd completed his training, D day had come and gone. Mann sailed for England, where he joined the 101st Airborne Division.

Mann's first, and last, combat jump came on September 17, 1944. As lead scout for his platoon, he joined Wierzbowski in reconnoitering the bridges across the canal. Instead of finding a few sentries, they found a reinforced German regiment. Wierzbowski radioed his predicament to headquarters. They sent a battalion to help. It ground to a halt. A second battalion was dispatched. The German defenders brought it to a halt, too.

At the bridge, Mann and the others could hear their fellow paratroopers in the distance fighting to reach them, but they could not break through the ring of Germans.

At 10:00 A.M. on the second day, the stone bridge erupted in a violent explosion, destroyed by the Germans. Chunks of concrete and pieces of stone rained down on the stranded GIs, injuring several. The objective for which so many men had died no longer existed. But the little band of men was still trapped, and their comrades still fought to free them.

Early that afternoon Mann and another soldier crept from their position to check out the enemy's strength. About one hundred yards away they spotted an 88-mm gun, an ammo dump, and a stack of spare parts. Mann, an expert with a bazooka, destroyed the entire site with one round, then shot and killed six Germans who charged him.

All that day Wierzbowski sought a way out of his predicament. At one point an engineer lieutenant and a sergeant volunteered to try to return to the rest of the company. Within minutes of leaving, the lieutenant was captured, the sergeant shot. Mann twice tried to locate a route to safety. On his first foray he took a round in his left shoulder. The medic patched him up, put his arm in a sling, then tied it to Mann's side to prevent movement.

Undaunted, Mann continued to probe for an escape route. This time he took two hits in the right shoulder. Now both arms were tied to his side. Though unable to use a weapon, Mann insisted on being propped up at the edge of the trench so he could act as a sentry.

Mann maintained his vigil the entire night. As a misty dawn began to break, Wierzbowski spotted a small German patrol sneaking toward his position. He shouted a warning, but they were already too close. Several German grenades dropped into the trench. Able-bodied GIs tossed out two before they exploded. A third exploded under a machine gun, wrecking the gun and blinding the gunner. A moment later a fourth grenade landed by the gunner. With one eye blown entirely out, he groped madly until he found it, then tossed it from his hole seconds before it went off.

A fifth grenade fell behind Mann, who huddled with six other casualties. Helpless, with his arms tightly bound and useless, he yelled, "Grenade!" Then he lay back on the missile to take the explosion with his own body.

Wierzbowski reached Mann seconds after the blast. "Lieutenant, my back's gone," Mann said before dying.

A short while later, with all but three of his men casualties, Wierzbowski decided to surrender. The Germans sent the Americans to a German field hospital.

Later that day reinforcements finally reached the rest of Company H, still fighting near Best. Suddenly, the Germans began surrendering in droves. Wierzbowski convinced his captors to give up their arms. He escorted them to the airborne headquarters. Once there, he told the gallant tale of Joe Mann.

Joe Mann's father accepted his son's posthumous Medal of Honor on August 30, 1945. In 1956 the citizens of Best erected a memorial to Mann near where he died. Later, they named an amphitheater in his honor.

North of the 101st Airborne, the 82d Airborne Division landed near Nijmegen. Though they captured several bridges, the most important one, over the Waal River in Nijmegen, resisted numerous attempts to wrest it from the Germans.

In the meantime, the British ground column ran into much stiffer resistance than anticipated. They fell further behind schedule, reaching Eindhoven twenty-four hours late. Once at Nijmegen they were further delayed when they, too, were unable to shake the Germans loose from the vital bridge. In a desperate attempt to force the situation, the American paratroopers launched an impromptu river crossing. It succeeded, but at a fearful cost.

The British column continued north up the highway. By this time the Germans fully understood the Allied plan. They launched counterattacks at key American positions. One such attack hit an outpost of Company C, 504th Parachute Infantry, northeast of Nijmegen on September 21. German infantry, supported by two tanks and a half-track, threatened to annihilate the defenders.

The situation seemed desperate until a bazooka man, Pvt. John R. Towle, a cheerful eighteen-year-old from Cleveland, Ohio, told his buddies, "Today I get the Congressional Medal."

With that, he took his bazooka and moved forward two hundred yards along a roadside ditch. He damaged both tanks with well-placed rounds, causing them to withdraw. The youthful veteran of Anzio and Normandy then turned his attention to a house where nine Germans had holed up. With one round he killed all nine. He was pursuing the half-track when a German mortar shell exploded at his feet, killing him instantly. Towle's daring attack caused the German infantry to withdraw.

At Arnhem the British paratroopers continued their desperate battle. Unable to be reinforced, they were doomed. The armored column, traveling on a narrow two-lane road elevated above the surrounding, marshy lowlands, ran into one German roadblock after another. All day on September 22, fierce battles raged up and down the highway. A few armored vehicles reached the south side of the Rhine on the 23rd, but they were too little, too late.

On September 23, Montgomery ordered the survivors of the British 1st Airborne division to make their way across the Rhine. Of some ten thousand British paratroopers who landed on the north side of the Rhine, less than twenty-two hundred made it to safety. The 1st Airborne Division had ceased to exist.

In their bid to force a crossing into Germany the two forces of *Market Garden* had suffered over seventeen thousand casualties. The Allies had gained a sixty-mile-long corridor in Holland, but they failed to gain their Rhine bridgehead. The vision of a quick end to the war evaporated.

To the south of Arnhem, General Hodges's First Army penetrated the formidable defensive barrier running along Germany's border with Belgium known as the West Wall. The major objective in the area was the ancient city of Aachen.

Aachen had served as the seat of the Holy Roman Empire for eleven centuries. Charlemagne was born there and thirty-two subsequent kings and emperors received their crowns there. Hitler considered himself their successor. He issued personal orders to Aachen's commander to hold the venerable city to the last man.

Hodges sent his XIX Corps toward Aachen from the north. His VII Corps would assault the city from the south. Though over nineteen thousand artillery shells pounded the German fortifications the GIs ran into tremendous resistance. Casualties soared as the infantrymen pushed through the West Wall's fortifications with flamethrowers, bazookas, pole charges, tanks, tank destroyers, and sheer guts.

After five days and eighteen hundred casualties, the two corps were still three miles from their linkup. These three miles would prove to be the hardest yet.

Three key hill positions commanded the 1st Infantry Division's approach to Aachen from the south. The most formidable of the three was Hill 239. Called Crucifix Hill because of a large cross atop it, it was studded with concrete pillboxes, machine-gun nests, and mortar positions, all supported by several hundred German infantrymen. One of the units facing Crucifix Hill was Company C, 18th Infantry.

BOBBIE E. BROWN

The commander of Company C, Capt. Bobbie E. Brown, was a craggy-faced six-footer who, at age thirty-seven, already had twenty-two years in the army. Born in Dublin, Georgia, in 1907, Robert Evan Brown, Jr., left home in 1922; there were just too many mouths to feed and not enough money coming in. At the army recruiter's in Columbus, Brown told the sergeant he was eighteen. The army badly needed bodies in 1922, and Brown was big for his age. He was accepted. Because he filled out his first enlistment papers with his nickname "Bobbie," that's how the army knew him for the next three decades.

Brown instantly found a home in the army. Every aspect of military life appealed to him. He felt more motivated than he ever had before. "I always wanted to be tops in whatever I did," he once said.

And he was. He qualified as an expert with every weapon in the army's arsenal. He took up boxing and football, too. He scored thirty-nine victories in the ring. On the gridiron he made the all-army squad in 1927. Three universities offered him scholarships to play football for them, then they learned he'd only completed the seventh grade.

But that didn't matter to the army. By the time World War II began, Brown was the first sergeant in the headquarters company of General Patton's 2d Armored Division. After fighting across North Africa, Brown received a battlefield promotion to second lieutenant and a transfer to the 1st Infantry Division.

Brown led a platoon of Company C up Omaha Beach on D day. In the fighting across France his company commander was killed. Brown assumed command. A few days later the promotion became official when the battalion commander pinned the captain's bars on his collar.

At 4:00 A.M., October 8, 1944, Brown received his orders for the attack on Crucifix Hill. Of forty-three known pillboxes and bunkers, his company was responsible for numbers 17, 18, 19, 20, 26, 29, and 30. After a flight of P-47 Thunderbolts finished an air strike at 1:15 P.M., Brown led his company out of their positions in a graveyard at the foot of the hill. They made it about 150 yards to an antitank ditch in front of pillbox 18 before heavy German fire forced them to seek cover.

Brown turned to his platoon sergeant. "Get me a couple of flamethrowers, some pole and satchel charges."

Once armed with those, Brown had his riflemen lay down a base of fire. Then he started crawling alone toward pillbox 18. A bomb had blown a big crater alongside the pillbox. Brown jumped into it and prepared to drop a satchel charge through an aperture by a door. While he worked, a German soldier suddenly stepped out of the door.

Brown instantly leaped forward. He struck the man in the face with a full-fisted, powerful roundhouse punch. The young soldier dropped limply inside the door. Brown hurled in a satchel charge, slammed the steel door shut, then dove headfirst back into the crater.

The pillbox erupted, huge clouds of smoke billowing from its rifle ports. One down.

Brown wriggled his way back to his men, picked up some more charges, then went back uphill thirty-five yards past the still smoking bunker toward number 19.

Machine-gun bullets zipped past within inches of his head. Several mortar rounds crashed nearby, slamming his body to the ground. Under his company's covering fire he pushed forward. Snaking behind the concrete structure, Brown shoved a pole charge through a twelve-inch opening. That blew a gaping hole in the pillbox. For good measure Brown tossed a satchel charge. That took care of any survivors.

On his way back down the hill for more charges, Brown noticed blood covering one knee. Then his sergeant told him, "Sir, there's bullet holes in your canteen." Brown had no idea when he'd been hit.

Pillbox 20 was the largest and most heavily armed fortification on Crucifix Hill. A turret, mounting a cut-down 88-mm, revolved 360 degrees on the top. The walls were six feet of concrete. No less than six machine guns poked their barrels through firing ports. Later, it would be learned forty-five Germans manned the structure.

Brown had no idea how he'd knock it out. But he'd try.

He followed a communications trench the twenty yards from number 19 to 20. He studied the apertures, trying to decide which one to stuff a pole charge in, when nearby movement caught his eye. A German soldier was entering the bunker via a steel door, his arms filled with ammo.

As the German disappeared through the door, Brown acted. He lunged forward, pulled the door open, threw in two satchel charges, and dove for cover. Just as he landed on his face, the pillbox erupted.

With the destruction of pillbox 20, enemy resistance on Crucifix Hill crumbled. All that remained was mopping up. Brown's assault had secured the 1st Division's flank.

Brown was wounded during the street fighting in Aachen when an artillery shell landed practically beside him. Numb, blood streaming from his nose, ears, and mouth, Brown headed for an aid station.

He spent several months in a hospital in Belgium, then went home on thirty-day leave. He rejoined Company C in Germany and fought with it into Czechoslovakia. After the war ended, Brown flew home to receive his Medal of Honor on August 23, 1945.

The next two years were spent in and out of hospitals, as army doctors tried to repair the damage done by thirteen war wounds. He finished his thirty years of service to his country in 1952. Besides the Medal of Honor, Brown also held two Silver Stars and a Bronze Star.

Like many men who have faced the full horrors of war, Brown was plagued by painful memories of his wartime experiences. Unable to find a decent civilian job, he ended up as a janitor at the U.S. Military Academy.

Continually bothered by the horrible memories of war, and in constant pain from his injuries, Brown took his own life on November 12, 1971.

* * *

Aachen finally fell on October 21, the first major German city to be captured by the Americans. But it was an empty prize. The city had been pounded into a massive pile of rubble by bombers and artillery. The main drive to the Roer River now began in earnest. The U.S. Ninth Army took up positions on Hodges's left flank. To the south, General Patton's Third Army pushed through Metz and Nancy to the Saar. Farther south the Seventh Army moved toward the upper Rhine.

Though the VI Corps of the Seventh Army had advanced five hundred miles from mid-August through September, it had made only twenty-five more in October. The supply problem and increasing German resistance slowed the Americans to a near snail's pace. In the fighting near Cleurie, France, on October 9, 1944, 1st Lt. Victor L. Kandle earned a Medal of Honor for capturing fifty-five Germans and destroying three enemy strong points holding up his battalion of the 3d Infantry Division.

Time after time Kandle moved ahead of his men to attack German positions. At one point he braved enemy fire to storm a stout farmhouse held by the Nazis. He smashed his way through the building's front door, his M-1 carbine blazing. Within minutes he had slain several Germans and forced the surrender of thirty-two more. His actions allowed his unit to take its objective.

Kandle's victory was short-lived, though. Two months later, on December 31, 1944, he was killed in action.

General Patton's drive to the Saar River had been stalled by a lack of supplies and foul weather. Finally, on November 8, he started forward again. His Third Army had been battering at Metz since September. The renewed attack, an enveloping attack that sent one corps to the north and another to the south, pinched off the city. Metz fell to the Americans on November 17, Patton proud of himself for being the first to capture the historic city since Attila the Hun in 415.

In the fighting around Metz a GI from the 35th Infantry Division received credit for capturing a French town nearly single-handedly.

JUNIOR J. SPURRIER

While Bobbie Brown was undergoing basic training as a fifteen-year-old recruit, James I. Spurrier, Jr., was born in Castlewood, Virginia, on December 15, 1922. Deep in the heart of the economically depressed Appalachian area of western Virginia, life was very tough for the six Spurrier children. They lived in a shack in the woods outside of town. There was never enough food on the table. Young Spurrier left school in the seventh grade to work on a nearby farm. The few cents he made for his day's labor often made the difference between the family eating or not eating that day.

Spurrier's mother died in the summer of 1940. That September he enlisted in the army. Like Bobbie Brown, Spurrier had a hard time with the enlistment papers. He put his names in the wrong blanks on the form, so he became Junior J. Spurrier to the army.

Unlike Bobbie Brown, Spurrier did not take well to the army. Used to a wide degree of freedom, Spurrier bristled under the harsh discipline. He had a number of run-ins with the authorities resulting in several courts-martial and stockade time.

The army trained Spurrier as a baker and sent him to Jamaica. When his unit was returned to the States in the fall of 1943, Spurrier volunteered for duty as an infantryman. He joined Company G, 134th Infantry Regiment, 35th Division, in England as a replacement. The division landed in Normandy on July 6, 1944.

Beginning at St. Lo, Spurrier proved himself to be a superb combat soldier. To the officers and men of his company, he was utterly fearless in combat. His conduct off the line was another matter.

Maj. Frederick C. Roecker, Spurrier's battalion commander, considered him to be devoid of any discipline. "Staff Sgt. Spurrier was relieved of responsibility for any other men," he said. "He'd often leave his men unattended while he either went looking for liquor or to hunt down Germans. The latter may seem admirable, but a good NCO never leaves his men on their own."

Rather than command a squad, as his rank would have permitted, Spurrier simply served as a runner for his company commander, free to roam the battlefield as he desired.

The advance of Patton's Third Army across France and onto the battlefields of Lorraine gave Spurrier ample opportunity to display his knack for fighting. On September 16, 1944, near Lay St. Christopher, France, he earned the DSC when he spearheaded an assault upon a stubbornly defended hill position. Mounting a tank destroyer, Spurrier manned its .50-caliber machine gun as the TD made its way up the hill. In spite of heavy enemy fire directed at him, Spurrier killed over a dozen Germans and captured twenty-two prisoners. Twice he climbed down from his lofty perch to personally engage enemy bunkers with hand grenades and rifle fire.

Two months later, while approaching the Saar River east of Nancy, Spurrier's battalion assaulted the French town of Achain beginning at 2:00 P.M., November 13, 1944. To gain the village the attacking companies had to cross fifteen hundred yards of open ground. Halfway across the fields, heavy artillery fire fell on the advancing GIs. They ran to the nearest buildings. There, German resistance held them in check.

In the meantime, Spurrier, operating on his own, entered the town from the west. For the next four hours Spurrier roamed the town at will, engaging the Nazis whenever he encountered them. He used not only his M-1, a BAR, a tommy gun, and grenades, but captured German weapons as well to fight the enemy.

Several times during the afternoon Spurrier wandered into the battalion command post, prisoners in tow. He'd strip them of their personal belongings (one witness remembered Spurrier had dozens of watches by the time the day ended), then turn them over to the battalion officers. After replenishing his ammo supply he'd slip out a side door.

Various infantrymen reported spotting Spurrier well behind the German lines, creeping into enemy-occupied buildings. A grenade blast or two later, Spurrier would be back on the cobblestone street, gleefully making his way to the next building.

No one kept an accurate count of how many Germans Spurrier killed or captured. The best estimates indicate he was responsible for slaying about twenty-five Germans and capturing about sixty more. To those who fought in Achain with him, there is no doubt Spurrier was materially responsible for capturing the village. The men of his Company G started calling him "One Man Army."

Spurrier fought with the 35th through the Battle of the Bulge and into Germany. His undisciplined ways and excessive drinking continued to dampen his exploits. He became such a problem Major Roecker brought him back to battalion headquarters as a bodyguard.

Once Spurrier received his Medal of Honor from Lt. Gen. William H. Simpson on March 6, 1945, he went completely out of control. According to Roecker, "It was as if he felt the MH gave him complete protection."

It all came to a head just as the war ended. Spurrier threatened an officer with a shotgun. Roecker prepared court-martial papers. Before the court could convene, the war ended. All Medal of Honor men were ordered home.

Junior Spurrier's fighting had ended, but his war was only beginning.

He tried civilian life for a few years, but couldn't make it. He reenlisted. By the time of the Korean War, Spurrier's continued drinking had caused him to be busted to private. When he received orders to Korea he refused to go. He figured he'd seen enough combat. Rather than court-martial a holder of America's two highest decorations, the army gave Spurrier a general discharge in 1951.

Spurrier settled in Baltimore, Maryland. Over the next fifteen years he had a number of well-publicized run-ins with the police. He was jailed no less than three times. In 1961 he was convicted of attempted murder and given a two-year sentence.

He blamed alcohol for his problems, vowing to quit when he was paroled in 1963. But two years later he was back behind bars for defrauding a loan company. When released in 1969 he vowed to never touch alcohol again. "It's whipped me long enough," he told reporters.

This time he kept his promise. Spurrier retreated to an isolated cabin in eastern Tennessee. There he remained, working at odd jobs to pay his bills, avoiding liquor and the limelight. He died in obscurity on February 25, 1984.

On the First Army front General Hodges prepared to send the four divisions of his VII Corps toward the Roer River. But first, to protect his south flank, Hodges ordered an attack into the region south of Aachen known as the Huertgen Forest. It would not be an easy task. The 9th Infantry Division had tackled the forest in early October; it suffered forty-five hundred casualties in just over a week. Next Hodges sent the 28th Infantry Division to clear the forest and take the village of Schmidt, sitting astride a key ridge on the far side of the forest.

A belt of rolling, thick woodland covering an area twenty miles long and ten miles deep, the Huertgen Forest was a literal chamber of horrors. The battle for the forest combined all the worst elements of warfare, weather, and terrain. The entire area was teeming with German pillboxes, bunkers, and log-covered fortifications hidden under one-hundred-foot-tall pine trees.

The 28th Division started into the forest on November 2. By November 4 its men reached Schmidt. The next morning the Germans counterattacked and threw them out. It got worse from there. By mid-November the 28th was through. It moved south to the Ardennes area for rebuilding.

After the 28th came the 8th Infantry Division. Once it had been chewed up and withdrawn, division after division was fed into the meat grinder of the Huertgen Forest. In all, six infantry, one armored, and several smaller special units battled the forest. Not until December 13 would the Americans conquer Huertgen Forest. Over 120,000 Americans fought in the woods. More than 35,000 became casualties.

Ten men received Medals of Honor for their gallantry in the vicious killing ground of the forest. There were undoubtedly more who earned the high decoration, but there were not enough witnesses left alive to make the recommendations.

The 4th Infantry Division began its fight in the Heurtgen Forest on November 10, 1944. With its three regiments abreast, the division was given responsibility for a four-mile front just south of Schevenhutte, Germany. Like the divisions that had gone before it, the 4th found Huertgen a near-impossible task.

The thick woods provided excellent concealment for the Nazi defenders. The ground was thickly sown with mines, making every step a potential nightmare. German artillery safely emplaced to the east pounded the Americans unceasingly. The GIs never knew when the quiet of the forest would be broken by the sudden, crashing roar of exploding German artillery shells. Many exploded in the treetops, showering the ground below with lethal shards of red-hot metal. Not even a foxhole offered safety.

The weather only added to the infantryman's misery. Day after day, rain, sleet, and snow turned the ground into a nearly impassable mud. Nighttime temperatures dropped below freezing. Some winter clothing had reached the front, but the supply problems meant most GIs spent the night shivering in the bottom of a foxhole. Those men not killed or wounded by enemy fire ran a high risk of catching pneumonia.

The cloudy days meant the ground troops could not depend

on air support. While the planes sat on the ground, the riflemen had to push forward against a determined foe.

On the 4th's left flank, its 8th Infantry Regiment tried to break through the German line at Weh Creek. They made good progress, in spite of a severe pounding by a nasty 120-mm mortar, until they ran into a particularly diabolical German barricade.

The GIs called it the Thing. Sitting astride one of the few roads in that region, the Thing was a pyramid of three concertinas of wire, eight to ten feet high. Row after row of railroad ties, embedded in the frozen ground, supported the barbed wire. The ground all around the Thing was quickly sown with mines. A platoon of Sherman tanks learned the hard way that German antitank guns had the area zeroed in. The blackened hulks of several of the less fortunate tanks littered the roadside.

After numerous attempts to destroy the Thing on November 16 failed, the battalion pioneer platoon finally blew a gap in the wire during the early morning hours of November 17. But the daylight attempts to exploit the break were stymied. Three times the GIs of the 2d Battalion stormed the position; three times they were repulsed. Over two hundred men were killed or wounded by noon.

BERNARD J. RAY

One of the men huddled down in a damp foxhole was 2d Lt. Bernard J. Ray, a twenty-three-year-old platoon leader in Company F from Baldwin, New York. He'd watched his men get slaughtered as they tried to destroy the Thing. In the army for less than a year, Ray never expected the nightmarish horrors of the Huertgen Forest. He couldn't stand to see his platoon members killed or maimed.

Ray turned as his platoon sergeant dropped into his hole. "Can't we outflank this monster?" the sergeant asked.

"No," Ray replied, "The Old Man says we got to clear the road. That's the only way the tanks can move up."

The sergeant remarked that that seemed an impossible task. Ray said, "I've got a plan. I'm going to crawl up there and plant a charge under that thing. I'll blow it to kingdom come."

"Lieutenant, you're nuts."

Maybe so, but Ray was determined to get something going. He busied himself for the next few minutes preparing for his self-appointed task. Grenades hung from his web belt, his pockets bulged with percussion caps. A twenty-foot length of primer cord was wrapped around his waist. Across the lieutenant's back was a banded cluster of bangalore torpedoes. Under his arm he carried a bundle of dynamite.

"I'll sneak out there, set this stuff, then set a fuse," Ray told his sergeant. "You cover me."

On his belly he slithered across the cold, wet ground. Across fallen logs, around broken tree stumps, and through thick stands of brush Ray moved forward. As he drew closer to the Thing, the German fire picked up. Bullets smacked the ground all around him but somehow missed. His progress was slow because of all the explosives he carried. They not only weighed a lot, but the odds and ends kept catching on branches and tree limbs.

Once he reached the Thing Ray went to work. While mortar shells exploded near him and bullets snapped overhead, Ray pushed the dynamite ahead of him. Then he began setting up the wires to the detonator. It was slow, maddening work lying on his belly, so he rose to his knees. Almost instantly a blast from an exploding mortar shell knocked him flat.

Blood poured from a gaping hole in Ray's left side. A recon patrol, observing the lieutenant with binoculars, reported what happened next. "The lieutenant struggled back up and again started working on the charges. He grasped one end of the primer cord wrapped around his body and fastened it with fumbling hands to the dynamite. Then he attached the other end of the cord to the charger.

"Then he struggled to his knees, clutching the plunger with both hands. Suddenly, in an obviously premeditated move, he came down hard on the plunger."

With a shattering roar of red and orange flame, the Thing disappeared. With it went the main obstacle holding up the 8th Infantry Regiment and Lieutenant Ray.

When President Truman presented the posthumous Medal of Honor to Lieutenant Ray's father on December 12, 1945, he said solemnly, "The whole nation is proud of him."

Mr. Ray choked back tears as he said, "Bernie was a good boy, Mr. President."

Though most of the fighting in the Huertgen Forest fell on he infantrymen and junior officers of the line companies, the viciousness of the dense woods also consumed more senior officers. Lt. Col. George L. Mabry had assumed command of the 2d Battalion, 8th Infantry Regiment, 4th Infantry Division, on November 19, 1944. The very next day his leading assault companies bogged down when confronted by a mine field and heavy hostile fire. Sensing the need for direct action, Mabry went to the front lines and found a safe route through the mine field.

He then personally led his companies forward. At the vanguard of the advance he captured three Germans at bayonet point. A short time later he found himself confronted by nine Germans. He slugged it out with them, knocking one to the ground with the butt of his rifle and driving his bayonet into another. Before he could deal with the remaining seven, some other GIs came up behind him and helped him subdue them. Fortified by his courageous display, Mabry's battalion seized its objective, three hundred yards deeper in the woods, and held it against repeated counterattacks.

Mabry survived the war, eventually retiring from the army as a major general.

By late November the GIs finally broke through the hell of the Huertgen Forest. Ahead of them lay the Roer River plain. As they emerged from Huertgen, the attacking divisions still faced a formidable foe. Several fresh German divisions entered the line west of the Roer River near Duren. As the 83d Infantry Division broke out of the clutches of the forest on December 11, they found their way to several small villages blocked by the fresh Nazi divisions. In the three days it took to occupy these key crossroad hamlets, the division lost nearly one thousand men.

At Birgel the 83d's 329th Infantry Regiment forced the surrender of the remnants of a German grenadier division. At dusk on December 14, the Germans launched a counterattack to retake the village. One Tiger tank, supported by twenty infantrymen, approached Birgel on the road coming from the east.

RALPH G. NEPPEL

Manning a machine gun right in the tank's path was a twenty-one-year-old farm boy from Willey, Iowa. Ralph G. Neppel had been drafted in March 1943 off his family's farm in Carroll County, Iowa. At that time his goal in life was to marry, settle down on his own farm, and raise his family. His goal was postponed when his draft notice arrived; it was nearly shattered on December 14, 1944.

If the Germans rolled over Neppel's gun the rest of Company M, 329th Infantry, bivouacked in Birgel, would be slaughtered. Neppel held his fire until the enemy was less than 150 yards away. Then he opened fire.

The rounds from his .30-caliber machine gun tore into the German infantrymen, killing half a dozen. The others scattered, looking for cover on the snow-covered fields. Beside him, Neppel's squad members fired their rifles at the Germans.

The tank noisily ground forward. Thirty yards from Neppel it stopped. Its massive turret rotated slowly. When the 88-mm cannon was pointed dead on at Neppel and his crew, it fired.

Neppel never remembered much about the shot. "There was a tremendous roar," he said. "A blinding flash. The next thing I knew I was laying ten yards behind my gun. My crew was sprawled all over the road."

As he lay there on the cold dirt a tremendous pain gripped him. He looked down. His right leg was gone. His left leg was so severely slashed by shrapnel only strips of raw flesh held it together. Shock prevented Neppel from crying out in pain. He sat there in the road, too numb to move. Then his eye caught movement up ahead. The German infantrymen were coming out from behind their cover. Soon they'd be in the town.

Totally disregarding his debilitating injuries and the excruciating pain, Neppel started back to his gun. Inch by painful inch, he pulled himself forward on his elbows. Under cover of darkness he righted the weapon. His experienced fingers told him the gun was still in working condition. He fed in a belt of ammo. Then he pressed the trigger.

Neppel's fire caught the Germans completely by surprise. He mowed them down. He didn't stop firing until every one of the Germans lay dead in the snow. Without infantry support the tank turned and raced back to its own lines. Then Neppel collapsed alongside his smoking machine.

Doctors at a field hospital amputated what remained of Neppel's left leg. Then he went to a hospital in England. While there Neppel amazed everyone with his cheerfulness. He was determined not to let his severe injuries defeat him. A buddy from Iowa remembered Neppel's courage: "Although he lay next to me, and I knew he was in great pain, I never heard him com-

plain. Not once. And he was always cheering up everybody else
in the hospital, including me.''

Nine months of rehabilitation followed at McCloskey Army
Hospital, Temple, Texas. Absolutely determined to overcome
depression and his handicap, Neppel set to work learning to use
his prosthesis. He had to learn to walk again and perform the
daily routine activities most people take for granted. His stoi-
cism overcame all obstacles. He made remarkable progress.
Within a year of his injuries he could play golf, ride horseback,
climb ladders, drive an automobile, and play baseball.

Neppel's rehabilitation was briefly interrupted by a summons
to the White House. On August 23, 1945, President Truman
presented him the Medal of Honor.

When he received his discharge in February 1946, Neppel
returned to Carroll, Iowa. The townspeople gave him a rousing
welcome home. A short time later Neppel married his fiancée,
who provided the extra incentive he needed to surmount his
handicap. He worked at several sales jobs before he entered
college in 1949. Three years later he had his B.A. and had
entered graduate school. When he was offered a job with the
VA, Neppel took it.

For the next twenty-two years Neppel worked with disabled
veterans, setting an example for them to follow. When he heard
of a veteran who was depressed because of his injuries, Neppel
would pay him a visit. He'd pull up his pant legs, revealing his
artificial legs, and ask, ''What's this I hear you got a problem,
fellow?''

Neppel served for eight years on Iowa's Governor's Committee for the Employment of the Handicapped. He was a part-time
Disabled American Veterans service officer. In 1969 he was a
finalist for the President's Trophy for the Handicapped Person
of the Year. Along the way he also raised four children.

The attention Neppel received always made him uncomfortable. ''The attention makes me feel sort of funny,'' he said. ''I
really didn't do much. It was just a question of fighting on and
doing what a fellow could, or get killed.''

He also liked to say, ''Everybody's handicapped in some way.
In some of us it just shows more.''

As an outstanding example of how a person can overcome
severe handicaps, Neppel inspired countless others to meet the

challenges of their injuries. He died of cancer on January 27, 1987.

The six-week struggle for the Huertgen Forest would prove to be one of the most controversial battles of World War II. It was as if the battle became an end in itself, with the American commanders blindly making endless sacrifices.

General Hodges felt he had no choice. By bypassing the forest he would recklessly expose his flank to counterattack, at a time when he had no reserves to meet such a challenge. The offensive also battered six German divisions. And it forced the Germans to commit forces that could have been used to counter American advances elsewhere.

For all practical purposes the Allies had reached their objective of the Roer River by the end of December 16, 1944. Although the original objective had been the Rhine River, with the Roer only an intermediate target, by this time the Allies were pleased to have gotten as far as they had.

To renew the drive to the Rhine, Eisenhower met with Bradley and Montgomery on December 7. As a result of that meeting it was agreed to start again about the first of the year. Montgomery's 21st Army Group and the Ninth U.S. Army would sweep north of the Ruhr industrial area, while Bradley's First and Third Armies would continue their drive south of the Ruhr. The actual starting date was predicated on an improvement in the weather that would dry out the rain-soaked ground. Only then could the armored vehicles make progress.

Before the Allies could launch their new offensive, though, Hitler launched one of his own.

14
★ ★ ★
Battle of the Bulge

Adolf Hitler's grand plan to launch a massive counterattack against the Allies in the west began fermenting in his mind in July 1944. The Führer correctly reasoned that the Allies' rapid advance across France would overtax their supply lines. Further, the delaying actions fought by his retreating soldiers would force the Allies to pause to rest and refit before entering Germany. Such a delay would give him time to regroup his forces behind the barricades of the West Wall. Then he would unleash his masterful stroke against a weak spot in the Allied lines.

Hitler revealed his scheme to the high command of the Wehrmacht at his daily staff meeting on September 16, 1944. While his chief of operations staff, Gen. Alfred Jodl, discussed the situation on the Western Front, Hitler suddenly cut him short. Then he announced, "I have just made a momentous decision. I shall go over to the counterattack!" While the generals and their aides sat stunned, Hitler explained his plan.

A powerful German attack group would break through the thinly held American lines in the Ardennes Forest in Belgium. From there the panzer forces would break for the Meuse River and the port of Antwerp. This bold thrust would split the American and British armies, isolating the British in the north.

The Allies would be so stunned by the crushing blow, Hitler reasoned, they would be unable to react. He could then turn his armies to the east and smash the advancing Russians. If everything went according to his plan the Allies would sue for peace, leaving Hitler in control of central Europe.

The sector Hitler selected for cracking the American line was ideal for his plans. The Ardennes Forest, on Belgium's eastern border with Germany and south of Aachen and the Huertgen Forest, was thinly held. The 85-mile sector was used not only as a rest area for combat-worn divisions but also as a training ground for newly arrived units.

The 4th Infantry Division held the southern end of the Ardennes front. Like the 28th Infantry Division to its north, the division had been sent to the Ardennes area to recuperate from the bloodying it had taken at Huertgen. The 106th Infantry Division, which had arrived at the front on December 11, 1944, came next. The very northern end of the sector was held by the veteran 2d Infantry Division and another fresh division, the 99th Infantry.

Though it was originally scheduled to commence on November 1, logistical problems continually postponed the launching of Hitler's counteroffensive. The final date selected was December 16, 1944. Four German armies would attack the Ardennes. By expanding the draft to include all men from sixteen to sixty and combing all rear areas for able-bodied men, Hitler had amassed a force of three hundred thousand men in fifteen divisions. The were supported by nineteen hundred pieces of artillery. The meat of the attack were the nearly 1,000 tanks and armored assault guns, including 250 sixty-eight-ton behemoth Royal Tiger tanks. The entire success of Hitler's offensive hinged on these tanks forcing their way through the American lines, thus opening a route for the infantry.

Although the Allies had developed intelligence data that strongly suggested an attack in the Ardennes, their optimistic attitude caused them to ignore the clues. The first evidence the Allies had of the attack came at 5:30 A.M. on December 16. A sentry on the front lines reported over his telephone numerous pinpoints of light flickering along the German lines. Before the watch officer could reply, the crash of artillery shells filled the morning air. The sentry had witnessed the opening barrage of Hitler's nineteen hundred artillery pieces.

All along the eighty-five-mile Ardennes front Americans were stunned by the ferocity of the bombardment. Veterans remembered it as the worst of the war. Novices were shocked; no training could have prepared them for this. When the artillery barrage ended, German infantry and tanks poured out of the woods facing the Americans.

The Germans' main attack came on the northern flank opposite Elsenborn. Here SS Gen. Josef "Sepp" Dietrich's Sixth Panzer Army slammed into the rookie 99th Infantry Division. Ironically, two regiments of the veteran 2d Infantry Division has passed through the 99th's line the previous day to begin a small, local offensive. They had just reached their objective when Dietrich's panzers struck the 99th Division's positions. Between the rookies and the veterans the GIs were able to slow Dietrich's advance by twenty-four hours.

While the 2d Division's advance was being called off, its third regiment, the 23d Infantry, took up positions in front of Elsenborn near the small village of Krinkelt. All day on December 17 men of the 99th Infantry Division fell back through the 23d Regiment. No sooner had the retreating GIs passed than the leading German forces appeared in the woods and on the road. Soon Tiger tanks joined the Germany infantry.

A machine gunner from Company M, 23d Infantry, helped slow the German advance. Pfc. Richard E. Cowan set up his gun in support of Company I. Seven times the Germans threw themselves at the Americans. Six times they were repulsed. By the seventh attack the company had been reduced to about twenty-five effectives; all but three in Cowan's section were hit. He covered his company's withdrawal to a new line, then moved his machine gun into an exposed position in front of the new position.

When a Royal Tiger tank approached, Cowan cut down about half the eighty supporting infantrymen. Then the tank blew him out of his position with a shot from its 88. Amazingly, the youngster from Wichita, Kansas, survived the blast. Through continued blasts from the tank and numerous mortar bursts, Cowan kept up a steady fire against the advancing Germans. When the new position was also ordered to be abandoned, Cowan again covered the withdrawal, firing his machine gun from the hip while his buddies slipped into the town of Krinkelt. The next day he was killed, once again protecting his buddies.

All day on December 17, GIs of the 2d and 99th Division streamed back to Elsenborn Ridge under heavy pressure from the Germans. Many fled in panic, abandoning their gear and weapons. But not all of them. A good number fought valiantly, giving their buddies time to reach safety. Among them were three soldiers from Company K, 9th Infantry, 2d Infantry Division, holding an important crossroads just east of the hamlet of Rocherath.

WILLIAM A. SODERMAN

While other GIs fled past them, the three stubborn GIs busied themselves digging a pair of foxholes alongside the road. Pfc. Meredith Oliver remembered the scene: "It was just getting dark and it was foggy. There must have been three or four hundred of them, most of them without helmets and all of them without guns, and they kept shouting at us to run, too. They said they couldn't stop the Germans and nobody could and that we'd only get killed.

"After those guys ran through us," Oliver continued, "we kept digging but we hit shale and couldn't dig very deep. It was getting dark and then we heard the tanks coming, making a lot of noise."

In the foxhole just ahead of Oliver and Pfc. James J. Shutterworth, Pfc. William A. Soderman sat patiently, his bazooka lying beside him. Drafted from his job as a butcher in August 1943, the thirty-two-year-old had originally been trained as a radio operator. Then the huge casualties in the fight across France had resulted in him being switched to the infantry.

Huddled in their foxholes, the three men watched five German tanks roll up the road toward them. Soderman waited until the first tank clanked past him, then rose out of his hole, the bazooka across his shoulder. He fired. The rocket hit one of the tank's bogie wheels, disabling it. The other tanks rolled around it.

"The tank was so close," Oliver said, "I could have spit on it."

When the tank's crew abandoned their vehicle, Soderman and the others cut them down. American artillery started dropping around the crossroads, trying to stop the panzers. It didn't work. Twenty minutes later, three more tanks came down the road.

Again Soderman came out of his hole. He crawled fifty yards down the road. He leveled his bazooka and fired. Again he hit the lead tank's wheels. It ground to a halt. The other two tanks bypassed their disabled pal and headed into Rocherath.

No more tanks came that night. There was only the enemy artillery. It fell all night, killing and wounding some of the Americans holding positions behind Soderman.

Years after the war Soderman recalled his thoughts while he

spent that night in the snow-covered field. "I thought, 'This is a heck of a place to die,' " he said. "Then I thought somehow you expect a battlefield to look different. But it looked just like any old meadow around my home in West Haven, Connecticut."

Just when it was getting light the next morning the three men saw an enemy skirmish line coming at them about a hundred yards away. Disregarding his own safety, Soderman again came out of his hole. He put a bazooka round right in the middle of the Germans. Those who weren't killed or wounded ran. "We could hear their wounded screaming for a long time," Oliver said.

A few minutes later word reached the three GIs to pull back. The retreating Americans had finally established a defensive line in Rocherath. No sooner had that message been received than seventeen German tanks came down the road. Soderman started for them, armed with a single remaining bazooka rocket. Oliver yelled after him, "Bill, come back. You'll be killed!" Soderman ignored him.

Creeping down a roadside ditch, Soderman made it to within fifty yards of the lead tank. While its machine gun fired, missing him by scant inches, Soderman knelt and aimed his bazooka. The rocket flew true, knocking off the tank's tread. Out of ammo, Soderman turned to run back to his hole. Halfway there, a burst of machine-gun fire slammed into his shoulder. He staggered into the ditch. Painfully, he crawled back to his buddies. It was time to pull out.

Oliver and Shuttleworth grabbed Soderman and headed for the rear. Soderman described the eerie scene of the battlefield. "It was unreal," he said. "The early morning sun on the snow and those big tanks—some American ones, too—rolling around.

"Guns were firing all around. The tanks were shooting. But everybody seemed too busy to pay any attention to us as we walked out. I walked out of there upright. I guess I was too fuzzy to know exactly what I was doing."

Soderman was evacuated and ended up in a hospital in England. Of his deeds in the field outside of Rocherath, Soderman always maintained a modest air. "I just did what had to be done. A lot of men did the same. I just got lucky."

The army felt differently. It awarded him the Medal of Honor.

The tall, lanky hero received his award from President Truman on October 12, 1945.

After the war Soderman went to work for the VA. He remained with them, helping other veterans process claims and secure benefits, until his retirement in 1976. He always maintained a low profile, preferring not to capitalize on his distinction. He died on October 20, 1980.

The American high command was initially uncertain about the reports of the German attacks. They felt the fragmentary reports told only of localized enemy attacks. As more news reached headquarters, the overwhelming size of the German offensive became clear. Fresh units were rushed to the battlefield. The 1st and 9th Infantry Divisions took up positions along Elsenborn Ridge, blunting the German attack in that area. The panzers tried diverting around the American stronghold, but bogged down in soggy fields.

Eisenhower directed the deployment of two armored divisions from his reserves into the Ardennes. In the center of the front, where Lt. Gen. Hasso von Manteuffel's Fifth Panzer Army poured through a thirty-mile-wide gap between St. Vith and Bastogne, Eisenhower sent the 101st Airborne Division. To break the attack on the south flank he ordered elements of General Patton's Third Army to halt their attacks and head north for Bastogne. The American response was taking shape.

In spite of the Americans' best efforts, the Germans continued their successes. They rolled over the 7th Armored Division at St. Vith and surrounded the 101st Airborne at Bastogne. Just to the north, at Malmedy, the 30th Infantry Division, backed by the 82d Airborne Division, set up blocking positions. That put them on a crash course with the panzers of Dietrich's Sixth Army coming around to the south of Elsenborn Ridge.

In Malmedy the 120th Infantry Regiment, 30th Infantry Division, prepared to meet the enemy. On December 21, 1944, they struck. Quickly overrunning the American tank destroyers and antitank guns, they stormed into the town. The 3d Platoon of Company K found refuge in an abandoned factory. Sgt. Francis S. Currey discovered a bazooka in the building. A GI told him its ammo was in a building across the street. He braved the heavy enemy fire to cross the street and gather up the ammo. Then he calmly knocked out the lead panzer.

Taken under fire by three Germans in the doorway of a nearby house, he killed all three with a single burst from his BAR. A few minutes later he stumbled across five Americans pinned down by three panzers. Arming himself with antitank grenades he went tank hunting. Within ten minutes all three tanks were burning hulks. Next he climbed aboard a tank destroyer to man its .50-caliber machine gun. Under his withering fire the remaining German infantrymen withdrew. Currey, a nineteen-year-old from Hurleyville, New York, survived the war to wear his Medal of Honor.

With the 101st Airborne Division isolated at Bastogne, Eisenhower fed in other units to aid in the division's relief and stymie further German advances. One of the units was the 517th Parachute Infantry Regiment. After participating in the invasion of southern France, the paratroopers had been pulled out of the line in late November for some well-deserved R&R. While in a rest camp near Rheims, France, on December 21, 1944, they got the word to move into Belgium.

Trucks carried the paratroopers to Hotton, Belgium. They arrived on December 23, 1944. Their mission was to clear the three-mile area between Hotton and Soy, two small towns about ten miles northwest of Bastogne.

MELVIN E. BIDDLE

The lead scout for the entire 517th Parachute Regiment was twenty-one-year-old Pfc. Melvin E. "Bud" Biddle. As a youngster growing up in Anderson, Indiana, Biddle had frequently played soldier and dreamed of glory. Many times he and his friends would play "parachute" by jumping off stacked hay bales with an umbrella. He even dreamed of returning triumphantly to Anderson, a Medal of Honor around his neck. Few dreams have ever been as prophetic.

Two years after graduating from high school in June 1941, Biddle received his draft notice. Because it seemed exciting. Biddle volunteered for jump school. He joined the 517th at Naples, Italy, in March 1944. Four more months of intensive training preceded the 517th's participation in the invasion of southern France.

One of the reasons Biddle held the job of lead scout was because of his excellent vision. "I saw every German out in front before he saw me, which was a large part of keeping me alive," he said. His responsibilities as lead scout weighed heavily on his mind.

"I think I got so I would rather die than be a coward. I was terrified most of the time, but there were two or three times when I felt no fear. It's remarkable. It makes it so you can operate."

Biddle operated without fear on December 23, 1944. He crawled through thick, snow-covered underbrush toward a set of railroad tracks leading out of Hotton to Soy. After making his way to within ten yards of a German outpost, Biddle brought his M-1 to his shoulder. He killed two Germans and wounded a third. The wounded man escaped to warn his comrades of the approaching Americans.

"I should have got him," Biddle remarked years later. "He made it back to his machine guns and all hell broke loose."

Two previously unseen machine guns suddenly opened up on the Americans. While the GIs behind him took on the first gun, Biddle went after the second. Ignoring the stream of hot lead flying within inches of his head, Biddle worked his way to within grenade range. He tossed several of the missiles, killing the Germans and destroying the weapon.

That night, the paratroopers heard noise from a large number of vehicles. Because there were apparently so many trucks everyone assumed they had to be Americans. Biddle volunteered to lead a small party to contact them.

When they were several hundred yards from their lines, the little band was fired on. The noise had been generated by a column of German vehicles. The others fled back to the safety of their lines, but Biddle moved ahead alone, closer to the German encampment. He spent most of the night in the woods, developing information that greatly aided the American attack in the morning.

During the advance into Soy, Biddle spotted some Germans dug in along a ridgeline. He maneuvered himself unseen to an advantageous position. He then assumed a shooter's sitting stance and started firing at the line of Germans. He aimed at their heads, imagining their helmets were the targets on a stateside shooting range. One after another he mowed the enemy down. Altogether, he killed fourteen men, each with a bullet in the head.

For the next two weeks Biddle was too busy fighting Germans to give much thought to his actions between Hotton and Soy. In fact, when an exploding German 88-mm shell badly wounded him on January 3, 1945, that action was the last thing on his mind. Biddle was evacuated to England.

While in the hospital Biddle was unwittingly reminded of his heroic deeds. Another 517th paratrooper, unaware of who Biddle was, wowed the other casualties in the ward with the tale of Biddle's heroism. "Did you hear about that guy in the Bulge that shot all those Germans?" he'd start. "My God, between Soy and Hotton it was littered with dead Germans. I hear they're going to put that guy in for a Congressional."

The man proved correct. Though Biddle returned to his outfit in March 1945, the war ended before he again saw combat. The 517th was earmarked for participation in the invasion of Japan, but Japan surrendered before they debarked.

Back in the States, Biddle was on a well-deserved leave to Anderson when word reached him of the award of the Medal of Honor. He received the medal at the White House on October 12, 1945.

After the war, Biddle married his childhood sweetheart and fathered two daughters. He entered business for himself, but eventually went to work for the VA. He retired in 1984.

Though there was considerable action throughout the Ardennes campaign, the longest and most important fight occurred at Bastogne. Both sides recognized the importance of the crossroads town of 3,500 inhabitants. Through Bastogne passed the main east-west highway Hitler needed to reach Antwerp. Hitler directed his panzers to take the town.

Before they could do so, the 101st Airborne Division reached the town on December 19. Quickly setting up defensive lines, the Screaming Eagles resisted every German attempt to throw them out of the town. Though completely surrounded, the Americans refused a surrender demand from the German commander on December 22, 1944. It was the reply to the surrender demand that captured the imagination of the American public. It was a one-word response: "Nuts!" The siege continued.

To the south, the 4th Armored Division of Patton's III Corps spearheaded the relief of Bastogne. On December 26, after four days of heavy fighting, elements of the 4th Armored stood just four miles from Bastogne. The lead elements, the 37th Tank Battalion under Lt. Col. Creighton Abrams (later head of U.S. forces in Vietnam and army chief of staff), the 53d Armored

Infantry Battalion, and several miscellaneous artillery units formed Combat Command R.

On the afternoon of December 26, Abrams ordered his forty-ton Sherman tanks to make every effort to break through to Bastogne, regardless of resistance. They made good progress until they reached Assenois, a small town less than two miles from Bastogne held by the crack German 5th Parachute Division. Dusk was settling fast. Artillery crashed into the cluster of buildings. The Shermans started down a slope into the town, infantrymen riding on their decks.

In the town the GIs worked their way from house to house, clubbing, shooting, and bayoneting Germans. A freckle-faced nineteen-year-old from Lepanto, Arkansas, armed only with an M-1, went after the crews of two 88-mm artillery pieces pounding the tanks.

"Come on out!" Pvt. James R. Hendrix yelled to the gun crews. A German peeked over a parapet. Hendrix shot him. He then ran to a foxhole harboring another German soldier. Hendrix smashed him over the head with his M-1. Next he charged straight at the two guns. His bold attack so startled the Germans they surrendered.

Later that night, Hendrix knocked out two machine guns, saving the lives of two GIs pinned down by the weapons. Still later, just outside Bastogne, he braved the flames engulfing a half-track to pull a wounded soldier to safety. He survived the war to wear his Medal of Honor.

Before midnight that day the 4th Armored linked up with the 101st Airborne. The siege of Bastogne was broken. The final days of the Battle of the Bulge had begun.

Though the Germans had been halted, the Americans faced the formidable task of wiping out the remaining invaders. The badly weakened GIs faced not only a skillful and stubborn foe but also a harsh winter. Icy cold blasts of arctic air, combined with snow drifting more than five feet deep, made the Ardennes battlefield one of the worst of the war.

The final Allied drive to pinch off the bulge created by the Germans commenced on December 30. Hodges's First U.S. Army would attack from the north, while Patton's Third U.S. Army attacked to the north. The two armies planned to link up at Houffalize, some ten miles north of Bastogne.

The Germans fought with ferocity, blocking the Americans'

advance with sharp counterattacks of their own. They had eight
divisions in the area and still hoped to capture Bastogne. Their
frequent attacks greatly hampered the Third Army's progress.
Combined with the cold and snow, the Germans limited the
American advance to but two miles per day.

In spite of such difficulties, the Allies persisted. On January 8, 1945, Hitler authorized the withdrawal of his forces still
in the western tip of the bulge. At future staff briefings he displayed a noticeable lack of interest in events in Belgium.

The pincers of the two American armies closed on January 16,
when the linkup at Houffalize occurred. The Americans turned
east. St. Vith fell to the Americans on January 24. The Allied
front line had been restored to what it was on December 16,
1944.

The Battle of the Bulge officially ended on January 28, 1945.
Hitler's last, desperate attempt to save his Reich cost him over
100,000 casualties. His precious reserves of men and material
had been greatly reduced.

For the Americans, Hitler's offensive cost over 80,000 casualties, including 10,276 killed, 47,493 wounded, and more than
23,000 missing and presumed captured. Though the Americans
suffered severely, they had been able to contain Hitler's forces.
As Eisenhower stated at the beginning of the attack, this was a
great opportunity to shorten the war in Europe. For many days
in December there were those who doubted Ike's wisdom, but
in the end he was correct.

Eisenhower's declaration of the end of the Battle of the Bulge
did not mean the end of all hostilities in the sector. Numerous
pockets of Germans remained behind the American lines. They
would have to be hunted down and killed. Cut off from any
retreat, the surviving Germans fought with incredible tenacity.

LEONARD A. FUNK

Company C, 508th Parachute Infantry, 82d Airborne Division,
had taken heavy casualties in its weeks in Belgium. Committed
to the ground south of Malmedy, the paratroopers had helped
push the Germans back toward St. Vith. By January 29, 1945,
the company had been reduced to less than fifty effectives. When
the executive officer was killed, 1st Sgt. Leonard A. Funk not
only took over his duties, but also formed the company headquarters personnel into a fighting force.

Funk, born August 27, 1916, at Braddock Hills, Pennsylvania, enlisted in the army in June 1941. After basic training he volunteered for airborne training. When he'd won his wings he joined the newly formed 508th at Camp Blanding, Florida.

Funk served with the 508th throughout its stateside training, then went with them to England and the 82d Airborne Division. When the 82d jumped into Normandy, Funk was with them. He also jumped into Holland during the *Market Garden* operation. On September 17, 1944, he earned the DSC for leading his men in an attack on an enemy strong point. By the time of the Ardennes battle, Funk was serving as Company C's first sergeant.

Normally, a company first sergeant serves in an administrative position. But that wasn't Funk's style. All through the 82d's fighting in Belgium, Funk placed himself at the front lines. Though short in stature, five feet, five inches and 150 pounds, Funk was long on courage.

At daybreak on January 29, Company C boarded trucks in a driving snowstorm. It took them until late afternoon to reach their jumping-off point for an attack on the German-held town of Holzheim, Belgium. The paratroopers, wearing white smocks to help camouflage themselves, struggled through waist-deep drifts.

It was snowing so hard and the air was so cold, Funk had a hard time getting his tommy gun to work. He kept moving the bolt back and forth trying to keep it free. It was so cold, "everybody in my company had frostbitten feet," Funk said. "But since there were no replacements, we had to stick it out."

Under Funk's skillful leadership, his makeshift platoon of clerks joined the 3d Platoon in assaulting fifteen German-occupied houses in Holzheim. His little band of men captured thirty Germans; the rest of the company took fifty more. The prisoners were herded into a yard alongside a house. As understrength as his platoon was, Funk could only spare four riflemen to guard the POWs. Company B was due at any time. When they arrived they would assume control of the POWs. Funk returned to the fighting.

A short time later, after running into heavier-than-expected resistance, Funk started back through the town to advise the four guards to be ready to move out. Since the buildings he passed were held by other paratroopers, Funk slung his tommy gun over his shoulder.

Unknown to Funk, a force of Germans, wearing snow capes

similar to the Americans', had overwhelmed the four guards, releasing the prisoners. They were preparing to attack Company C from the rear when Funk, accompanied by a clerk, casually walked around the corner of the building into the yard.

"A guy I'd never seen before came up to me, talking in German," Funk said.

The Nazi officer stuck a machine pistol in Funk's stomach, ordering him to surrender. Funk was in a quandary. Almost one hundred Germans stood around him, their weapons pointed at the captive Americans. He couldn't allow the GIs to die. And he couldn't allow the Germans to hit his unsuspecting company. He had to act.

Pretending to comply with the surrender demand, Funk started unslinging his tommy gun from his shoulder. In a lightning swift movement, he whipped the weapon into a firing position, hoping it would work. It did. The Nazi officer fell, a startled look on his face. Funk emptied a full clip into the man. "I'd never seen a man take so many [bullets] in my life," Funk said.

As the officer hit the snowy ground, the other Germans opened fire. The clerk next to Funk fell dead. While Germans and Americans scattered, some heading for nearby houses, Funk slammed another clip into his weapon. He opened up on the Germans. In the chaos, the disarmed American guards seized fallen weapons, joining in the fight.

It all ended in less than a minute. When the firing died down, twenty-one Germans lay dead in the swirling snow. Another two dozen lay wounded. The remainder cowered on the ground. In the center of it all Funk stood tall, grimly holding his smoking tommy gun. He ordered the surviving Germans back into the yard. A little later Company B arrived. They took charge of the prisoners.

Funk's war continued into central Germany as the 82d fought across the Rhine River. By the time the war ended, the 82d stood on the Elbe River, waiting for a chance to enter Berlin. He returned to the states in June 1945. He received his Medal of Honor at the White House on August 23, 1945. In addition to that and the DSC, he earned a Silver Star, a Bronze Star, and three Purple Hearts.

After his discharge, Funk returned to his prewar job as a clerk at a local company. In 1947 he joined the VA. Twenty-five years later he retired as a division chief in the Pittsburgh Regional Office.

While his last-ditch efforts faltered in Belgium, Hitler had ordered another offensive far to the south in the Vosges Mountains. Not only did Hitler hope to lure Third U.S. Army troops away from Bastogne, he also planned for his troops to recapture the Alsatian city of Strasbourg, then link up with the Germans holding the pocket around Colmar, farther south in the Vosges.

The 6th Army Group commander, Lt. Gen. Jacob Devers, had considerable evidence the Germans planned to launch an attack. By Christmas Eve his intelligence sources revealed the Germans were massing in the Black Forest for an attack. The most likely dates seemed to be January 1–3, 1945. One hour before midnight, December 31, 1944, without artillery preparation, the Germans drove into the American lines.

The area they hit was where Hitler's West Wall barrier ran east and west, just east of Saarbrucken and north of Strasbourg. The heaviest blows, delivered by the XIII SS Panzer Corps, fell on the 44th Infantry Division. Sitting astride the road running from Sarreguemines to Rimling, the 44th guarded the critical Rohrbach Road junction.

Much as in the Ardennes, the battle seesawed. The 44th initially gave ground, counterattacked to recapture it, then lost it again. A small contingent of Company I, 71st Infantry Regiment, found itself trapped in a deep gully near Woelfling, France, on New Year's Day. Low on food and ammo, some of the men started talking about surrender. Their leader, Sgt. Charles A. MacGillivary, hushed them.

The Canadian-born NCO ordered the men to cover him while he tried to knock out four enemy machine guns preventing their withdrawal. While they fired, MacGillivary crawled up the gully's bank and into the hip-deep snow blanketing the forest. He made it to the first machine gun undetected. He lobbed grenades into it, killing the crew. Then he jumped up to attack German riflemen emplaced behind the nest.

After replenishing his ammo, he took out after the remaining three guns. MacGillivary boldly charged each position in turn, hurling grenades and firing his rifle. He was just rising off the snowy ground after hitting the last machine gun with his last grenade, when a wounded German gunner crawled behind the automatic weapon. Before MacGillivary could react, he fired. The slugs tore into the Canadian's chest and carved a line down his left arm, ripping it off.

MacGillivary killed the gunner with return fire. "When you're hit by bullets," he later said, "it's like a burn, as if you've been hit by a red-hot poker. To cool it off, I kept jamming the stump into the snow. When the medics finally got to me, they found a red cake of ice frozen to my upper arm." He survived the war to wear his medal, later joining the customs service as an investigator.

Just to the east of Rimling, another German assault struck the 14th Armored Division near Bitche, France. The German XC Corps, comprising the 256th and 361st Volksgrenadier Divisions, pushed ten miles south into the lower Vosges Mountains. Throughout the area, isolated bands of Americans fought desperate battles to stem the German onslaught.

GEORGE B. TURNER

When World War I ended on November 11, 1918, George B. Turner was a Marine Corps private on a ship in New York harbor waiting to go to France. He always regretted he'd never had the opportunity to serve his country.

A native of Longview, Texas, where he was born on June 27, 1899, Turner was the son of a distinguished state legislator and attorney. While Turner completed his four-year hitch in the marines, his family moved to Los Angeles. He went there after his discharge and worked in his father's law firm as an administrator. He settled into a comfortable life-style, all the while thirsting for the adventure denied him in 1918.

When it became apparent another global conflict was in the making, Turner tried to expedite his own involvement. None of the American military would take him because of his age. Twice he traveled to Canada to enlist in their army, but his age again proved to be a barrier. On the return from his second trip the Japanese attacked Pearl Harbor. Turner settled back to await the inevitable call.

It came on October 23, 1942. Turner married his girlfriend and reported to Fort MacArthur, California. He eventually found himself assigned to the 499th Armored Field Artillery Battalion, a part of the 14th Armored Division. His first question upon joining his new outfit was, "What section will see the most combat?" Told it would be a battery's forward observer's section, he instantly volunteered. He got his wish. He ended up as a machine gunner on a half-track and an observer for Battery C.

Because of his age, education, and work experience, Turner frequently received lectures on why he should go to officer candidate school and take a commission. Turner always declined. He knew an officer's commission would remove him from the front lines.

After landing at Marseilles, France, in November 1944, the 14th Armored and George Turner found plenty of opportunities to prove their worth. Before long both had developed reputations as hard-driving, dependable fighters. Turner constantly volunteered to accompany infantry patrols. He earned a Bronze Star in November 1944 for spending two hours in a church steeple spotting targets for his battery, all the while under enemy artillery fire.

The 499th Armored Field Artillery Battalion occupied the crossroads town of Phillipsbourg, France, on January 3, 1945. Infantry units of the 42d Infantry Division provided protection for the artillery pieces. Early on that bitterly cold morning German tanks, supported by experienced infantry, approached the town behind an intense artillery barrage. The guns of the 499th were ordered withdrawn to a more secure site. Everybody pulled back. Everybody but Pfc. George B. Turner. He wasn't about to leave this action.

Voluntarily attaching himself to a nearby infantry company, Turner picked up a casualty's rifle and joined the battle. Under pressure from two German tanks and about seventy-five German soldiers advancing down the town's main street, the U.S. infantry pulled back. Coming upon an abandoned bazooka, Turner picked it up and advanced alone under intense small-arms and cannon fire. Calmly moving to the middle of the street, he loaded the weapon, fired, and destroyed the lead tank. He fired a second time and blew the track off the remaining tank.

By now the sole target for the German infantrymen, Turner ran to a nearby abandoned half-track, removed a .30-caliber machine gun, and set it up in the middle of the fire-swept street. Alone and unaided, the gallant forward observer fought off the enemy infantry. He killed or wounded a great number of them, breaking up their attack.

Several hours later, the 42d Division units had reorganized and were ready for a counterattack. Still fighting as an infantryman, and given up for dead by the 499th, Turner joined in the attack.

When two supporting Sherman tanks took hits from a German antitank gun, Turner used his .30-caliber machine gun to cover the crew's escape. One of the tank commanders told Turner a man was still trapped in his tank.

Under a literal hail of enemy small-arms fire Turner ran to the burning tank. The vehicle's power traverse mechanism had become engaged causing the turret to revolve, but Turner still attempted the rescue. Just as he climbed up the tank's rear, it exploded in a rush of flames. Turner flew backwards, landing in a heap, his rescue attempt blocked.

Refusing to leave his new buddies, Turner remained with the infantry through the night and well into the next day. During this time he assumed the role of platoon leader, carrying out several missions against the Germans. Eyewitnesses report he drove off an enemy platoon, silenced a machine-gun nest, and led several patrols deep into German territory.

Late on January 4, a volunteer was sought to drive the wounded back to an aid station. Though he knew the entire route was under enemy fire, Turner unhesitatingly stepped forward. Well into the next day Turner made repeated trips with casualties. No one kept a record of how many trips he made, but a lot of men lived because of his fearlessness.

By the morning of January 5th the Phillipsbourg area had grown quiet. Turner decided it was time to return to the 499th. His commander, Capt. Clarence F. Graebner, remembered his arrival: "George was tired, dirty, and very hungry. What I especially remember was that his canteen had a bullet hole through it. Apparently, this was the closest the Germans came to hitting him as there was not a scratch on him!"

Graebner was too busy to do more than welcome Turner back and put him to work in the fire direction center. He didn't ask where Turner had been and Turner didn't say. Then Graebner received a visit from a 42d Division officer who wanted to confirm Turner's identity. The men of the 42d wanted to see Turner rewarded for his heroism.

He was. President Truman placed the Medal of Honor around his neck on August 23, 1945. Turner was the oldest enlisted man to earn the Medal of Honor in World War II.

With his quest for excitement at last fulfilled, Turner returned to Los Angeles. He settled with his wife in Bel Air, California, holding an executive position with Pepsi-Cola, Inc. He died of a heart attack on June 23, 1963.

Like his troops fighting in the Ardennes, Hitler's forces in the south lacked the resources to sustain their breakthrough. As a result, this offensive petered out in three weeks. The lines of Devers's 6th Army Group were soon restored to their original positions. The Allied troops under his command prepared to cross the Rhine and drive into Germany itself.

Before Devers could turn his forces loose, Eisenhower ordered the Germans holding out at Colmar to be destroyed. Devers assigned the French First Army to the task.

Centered on the Alsatian city of Colmar, south of Strasbourg on the eastern slopes of the Vosges, the German bridgehead west of the Rhine poked eighty miles wide and deep into Allied territory. Eight German divisions, over sixty thousand men, combined with brutal winter weather to deny the French a victory.

To reduce this threat the French First Army launched a two-pronged attack beginning on January 22, 1945. Driving up from the south, the French I Corps moved toward the Rhine River bridges at Breisach. On the north, the II Corps would drive south toward the same objective. Spearheading the II Corps would be the venerable 3d Infantry Division.

During this advance on Colmar the 3d Division would fight one of its toughest battles of the entire war. They would also produce a true American legend and the war's most decorated soldier.

AUDIE L. MURPHY

Born June 20, 1924, near Farmersville, Texas, Audie Murphy was the seventh of twelve children born into a dirt-poor share-cropper's family. Poverty was the family's mainstay. Life in agricultural central Texas was austere, even primitive, for itinerant farmers like the Murphys. They moved frequently during Audie Murphy's youth, finally settling in Celeste, Texas.

For a time they lived in a converted railroad boxcar on the edge of town; later they moved into a run-down house. Emmett Murphy, Audie's father, hired himself out to local farmers, working crops. Young Audie joined him so soon as he was able. Because of the need to work so much, young Murphy's education took a decided backseat. By 1939 he had only completed the fifth grade, so he quit for good.

The very next year Emmett Murphy deserted his family. He had disappeared for various periods all during Audie's youth, but now he was gone for good. As Audie once said, "My dad wasn't lazy, he just had a genius for not considering the future." Less than seven months later Murphy suffered the most traumatic experience of his life when his mother died on May 23, 1941. Always close to her, dependent upon her love and attention, he mourned her passing for months.

One of Murphy's greatest pleasures as a youngster was hunting. Those who knew him then considered him a natural marksman. He displayed an uncanny accuracy with a rifle. He possessed catlike reflexes, quick eyes, and an aggressive personality. All of these traits would later aid him during his two years in combat.

Murphy developed an interest in the military as a youngster, an interest fed by tales from two uncles who served in France during World War I. He frequently mentioned to friends his desire to enlist in the military. Perhaps he saw not only the glory and glamour but also the release it offered from poverty. Thus when the Japanese attacked Pearl Harbor, Murphy marched off to the local recruiters.

In the early days of the war, the military was fairly selective. Thus Murphy's slight stature (at age seventeen he stood five feet, five inches tall and weighed 110 pounds), combined with his delicate, babylike facial features, precluded any branch of the service from seriously considering him. Over the next few months Murphy improved his diet to put on weight. Armed with a letter from his sister attesting to his age, Murphy was accepted into the army on June 30, 1942.

By late fall 1942 Murphy had arrived at Fort Meade, Maryland, for advanced infantry training. As he had at basic, Murphy impressed his superiors there with his military bearing, leadership ability, and overall attitude. As a result, when he shipped to North Africa in February 1943 he wore the two stripes of a corporal. In North Africa he joined Company B, 1st Battalion, 15th Infantry Regiment, 3d Infantry Division. He would spend twenty-eight months with that unit, be promoted to its commander, and earn every combat decoration the army bestowed, two of them twice.

Murphy's first taste of war came on Sicily. There he killed for the first time, gunning down two Italian officers escaping on white horses. His cold-blooded attitude disturbed his platoon leader. "Why'd you do that?" he asked.

"That's our job," Murphy replied icily.

Malaria hospitalized Murphy on Sicily for several weeks. He rejoined his company at Salerno. Sicily had done much to dispel any lingering thoughts Murphy might have had that war was glamorous. Italy totally eliminated them. War was mud, mules, and mountains, not glorious cavalry charges. War was dark nights, rainy days, patrols, and hunger. War was grenades, rifles, and machine guns. But most of all war was pain and death. Murphy saw enough to last a lifetime.

Up the Italian boot, through Mignano, Monte Lungo, and Cassino, Murphy fought alongside his buddies. If he thought war in the mountains was bad, Anzio proved worse. Mere survival was a victory. Day after day artillery exploded around him. Attacks on key buildings brought more death. Murphy saw many of his longtime friends die at Anzio. "I began feeling like a fugitive from the law of averages," he said years later.

Murphy survived Anzio, miraculously one of the few men in his company not to hold the Purple Heart. The 3d Division was pulled from the line after the capture of Rome to prepare for the invasion of southern France. Rebuilt with replacements, the 3d Division hit the beaches on August 15, 1944. That same day Murphy earned his first combat decoration.

Company B landed east of Ramatoulle, south of St. Tropez. During the attack up "Pillbox Hill" behind the assault beaches, Murphy's best friend was killed by a sniper when he carelessly rose out of his foxhole to accept the surrender of a German soldier. Incensed at this treachery, Murphy advanced on a German machine-gun nest. After wiping out its crew, he picked up the automatic weapon and, firing from the hip, advanced up the hill. He shot at anything that moved. Determined to avenge his friend's death, Murphy killed no less than five enemy soldiers, wounded two, and forced the surrender of five more.

Murphy would receive the DSC on March 5, 1945, for this deed, but it never made up for the loss of his buddy. "I won the DSC," he said, "but all he got was death."

In the fighting near Besançon on September 15, a German

mortar shell exploded near Murphy, killing two men near him
and sending Murphy to the hospital.

He returned to his company less than a week later. In the
fighting around Cleurie, Murphy earned Silver Stars on October 2 and 5. A week later Murphy received a battlefield promotion to second lieutenant. His senior officers had recommended Murphy for the promotion several times, but he always
turned them down. He felt his lack of education would handicap
him in the administrative side of the job. Besides, army policy
was to rotate a newly commissioned officer out of his original
outfit. Murphy did not want to leave Company B.

When his battalion commander received a waiver on that policy and assured Murphy he would receive help on his paperwork, Murphy agreed to accept the promotion. The gold bars
were pinned on his tunic on October 14, 1944.

Twelve days after that, Murphy received his most serious
wound of the war. While attacking through the Montagne Forest
near Les Rouges Eaux, a sniper shot Murphy in the right hip.
Before the intense pain immobilized him Murphy killed his
assailant. This time Murphy spent two months in a hospital
recuperating.

Following several weeks' leave spent in Paris, Murphy rejoined Company B on January 14, 1945. The 3d Division was
in the final stages of training for the push on Colmar. Originally
in reserve, Murphy's battalion followed the lead units across
several rivers and through deep woods toward Riedwihr. On the
night of January 24, Murphy and his company dug in near the
Ill River. The weather was very cold, temperatures reaching ten
degrees to fifteen degrees above zero in the daytime and at night
falling to below zero. When Murphy awoke on January 25, he
found his hair frozen to the side of his foxhole.

That afternoon shrapnel from a German mortar peppered
Murphy's left leg. He hastily bandaged it, declining to visit an
aid station. That evening he posted his men in a finger of woods,
just west of Riedwihr and about one mile north of Holtzwihr.
The towns sat four miles northeast of Colmar.

Early the next morning Murphy assumed command of Company B after its commander fell wounded. There were eighteen
enlisted men left in the company; Murphy was the only officer.
His orders were to hold his position until reinforced. Besides
his handful of men he had two tank destroyers to support him.

About 2:00 P.M., January 26, six Mark VI Tiger tanks accompanied by between 200 and 250 infantrymen came north out of Holtzwihr toward Murphy's position. Murphy yelled to his men to get ready. In front of him one of the TDs slid into a ditch while trying to maneuver into a firing position. Its crew fled to the rear.

Spreading his map on the icy ground in front of his foxhole, Murphy called his supporting artillery battalion over the field telephone. "I need a round of smoke at coordinates 30.5–60. Make it fast."

At the same time that the first American rounds exploded among the Germans, a German round slammed into the remaining TD, setting it afire. The two surviving crewmen pulled out.

Murphy telephoned corrections to the artillery. Geysers of snowy dirt erupted among the enemy, hurling bodies in every direction, but didn't stop them. The German tanks rolled on, untouched.

Realizing the great danger to his men, Murphy turned to his platoon sergeant. "Get the men back, I'm going to stay here with the phone as long as I can." The sergeant hesitated. "Get the hell out of here," Murphy shouted. "That's an order!" Reluctantly, the sergeant pulled his men deeper into the safety of the woods. Lieutenant Murphy was all alone to hold back the attack.

"Let's have some more artillery!" he yelled into the phone.

Resting his carbine on the edge of his foxhole, Murphy began firing on the enemy infantry, now less than two hundred yards away. When he ran out of ammo, he headed for the burning TD and its perfectly good .50-caliber machine gun. Dragging his phone lines behind him, Murphy mounted the vehicle. After pulling the dead tank commander out of the way, he loaded the deadly weapon and started firing on the Germans.

Though he knew his heavy slugs would have no effect on the enemy armor, he hoped the loss of their infantry support would drive them off. And the artillery fire he continued to call in might knock out the tanks. After he called in one correction, the voice on the other end of the phone asked, "How close are they to you?"

"Just hold the phone and I'll let you talk to one," he responded. Then he pressed the trigger, letting go a long, chattering burst of fire. A line of Germans crumpled in the snow.

Several times the TD rocked with direct hits from the enemy cannon. Though Murphy nearly fell off twice, he caught himself and continued firing. Smoke from the fire provided good cover, preventing the Germans from getting a clear shot at him.

He called in another correction. "Drop fifty."

"That's awful close to you."

"Fire!" he ordered.

A few seconds later American artillery shells crashed to the ground a mere fifty yards in front of Murphy. By now most of the German infantry lay in grotesque positions in the open fields. Denied their protection, the remaining tanks started in retreat. Murphy called in one last correction. "Correct fire. Fifty over."

"That's right on your position," the voice warned.

"Let her go. I'm leaving," said Murphy as he leaped to the ground. He'd almost made the woods when the TD exploded, spewing flames into the air. The concussion sent him sprawling. His leg wound from the previous day started bleeding as he limped back to his men. Single-handedly, he had turned back an armored task force intent on wiping out the Americans.

In the woods, Murphy gathered up his company and led them in clearing the entire area of Germans. The next day he took Company B into Holtzwihr, capturing it by 10:00 A.M. Several more weeks of heavy fighting were required before the Colmar Pocket was cleared. The city itself fell on February 8, 1945. Murphy participated in all the fighting.

After being promoted to first lieutenant on February 16, 1945, Murphy served at battalion headquarters for several months. He missed most of his company's fighting across Germany and into Austria. He resumed command of Company B in late May.

Lt. Gen. Alexander Patch, commander of the Seventh Army, presented the Medal of Honor to Murphy on June 2, 1945, in ceremonies near Salzburg, Austria. In addition to the Medal of Honor, DSC, and two Silver Stars, Murphy earned the Legion of Merit, three Purple Hearts, and two Bronze Stars. With all the other campaign medals, unit citations, and foreign decorations Murphy returned to the States on June 13, 1945, and thirty-three medals and citations. Though not yet old enough to vote, he was America's most decorated hero of World War II.

Murphy received an incredible homecoming. His photograced the cover of *Life* magazine. The adulation heaped on the young warrior was nearly more than he could bear. Everywhere he went people sought him out. Some folks cried unashamedly when they met him. Weary from the constant attention and desperately needing a rest, Murphy accepted an invitation from actor James Cagney to retreat to his secluded home. That association led to a screen test, a Hollywood career, marriage to a young starlet, and a new life. Murphy made two critically acclaimed movies, *The Red Badge of Courage* and his autobiographical *To Hell and Back*. Most of the rest of the more than two dozen movies he appeared in were B-grade westerns.

As the years passed and the public's taste in movies changed, Murphy became involved in a number of business ventures. None of them succeeded. He found most investors were simply interested in trading on his name. He divorced his actress wife, then married again. He gave away his medals. The army replaced them. He gave them away again.

Plagued by financial problems Murphy got hooked on prescription drugs. He gambled heavily, losing thousands to unsavory bookies. Adverse publicity about his plight drove him into seclusion. The public's dissatisfaction with the politics of the Vietnam War made his status as a war hero uncomfortable.

On May 28, 1971, Murphy flew with four other people from Atlanta, Georgia, to Martinsville, Virginia. As a representative of an investment group, Murphy planned to visit a plant that produced prefabricated housing. The small plane went down in rain and fog near Galax, Virginia, just before noon. There were no survivors.

America's most decorated hero was buried at Arlington National Cemetery.

The reduction of the Colmar Pocket left only the northeast corner of Alsace, from near Sarreguemines on the west along the Moder River to where it joined the Rhine River north of Strasbourg, in German hands. Along with Montgomery and Bradley to the north, Devers planned a March offensive to breach the West Wall, cross the Rhine, and move into Germany.

15

* * *

Return to the Philippines

General MacArthur fulfilled his promise to return to the Philippines on October 20, 1944. On that date, the first of two hundred thousand men in the six divisions of Lt. Gen. Walter Krueger's Sixth Army began hitting the beaches on Leyte's northeastern coast. For over two and a half years MacArthur had plotted his every move with but one goal in mind: retaking the Philippines. But after spending over thirty months preparing for his triumphant reentry to the islands, MacArthur almost had his plans thwarted.

Admiral Nimitz, MacArthur's coequal in the Pacific and, like MacArthur, answerable only to the joint chiefs in Washington, preferred an invasion of Formosa. He felt that taking Formosa, just six hundred miles south of Japan, would not only cut off Japan from raw materials to the south but also allow the Allies to land on China's coast. From there, land-based bombers could easily attack Japan's home islands.

MacArthur argued that the capture of the Philippines would achieve the same objectives at a lower cost. Besides, he felt American honor and prestige dictated the liberation of the Filipino people, some of America's staunchest supporters.

In the end MacArthur won out. He was ordered to invade Leyte on October 20, 1944. At the heart of the Philippines, Leyte, with its broad, flat Leyte Valley, would be used for major airfields and supply bases to support operations elsewhere in the Philippines.

For the first time since Operation *Cartwheel*, MacArthur and Admiral Halsey worked in concert. Halsey's Third Fleet would protect the landing. With sixteen fast carriers, six fast new battleships, and eighty-one cruisers and destroyers, the Third Fleet was well equipped for its assigned task.

MacArthur's navy, the Seventh Fleet under Vice Adm. Thomas C. Kincaid, would provide direct support to the beachhead. Composed primarily of small escort carriers and slow old battleships, the Seventh Fleet would answer calls for help from Krueger's ground forces. Gen. George Kenney's Fifth Air Force, based on five Pacific islands bordering the Philippines, stood poised to challenge any air attackers.

The ground forces of the Sixth Army were divided into two corps. The X Corps consisted of the 1st Cavalry Division and the 24th Infantry Division. Both had been bloodied in MacArthur's campaigns in the islands guarding New Guinea's north shore. The 7th and 96th Infantry Divisions made up the XXIV Corps. The 7th had fought the Japanese in the Aleutian Islands and the Marshalls. The 96th was seeing its first combat. Two veteran infantry divisions, the 32d and the 77th, formed the reserve.

Following a heavy naval and aerial bombardment, ground forces started landing on Leyte just after 10:00 A.M. The X Corps went ashore at the Palo area, on the north. Its objective was to seize Palo and Tacloban and its airfield. Fifteen miles south, the XXIV Corps hit the beaches north of Dulag. Once ashore the four divisions would drive inland, capturing the fertile ground of the Leyte Valley.

The invading forces found only light resistance from the Japanese defenders. By the end of the day, all the assault divisions had made good progress; some units drove more than a mile inland, Casualties were light: 49 men killed, 192 wounded.

The 24th Infantry Division achieved its initial objectives. All assault units were dug in along Highway 1, which ran north out of Palo a mile inland. At 1:00 A.M. on October 21, three companies of Japanese from the 33d Infantry Regiment attacked north out of Palo. Under cover of darkness and aided by heavy machine-gun and mortar fire, the Japanese made a double envelopment of the American flanks while the main force came straight down the road. They fell on Company G, 34th Infantry, manning the lead positions near the village of Pawig. By 2:00 A.M. the attackers had pushed to within a few yards of the American perimeter. Everyone in Company G's 2d Platoon was killed or wounded except Pvt. Harold H. Moon.

Moon manned a machine gun right in the center of the action. The sole survivor in his nest, Moon's heavy fire attracted the full fury of the Japanese. Wounded by the enemy's concentrated fire, the twenty-three-year-old native of Albuquerque, New Mexico, refused to give up. Alone, he held off the enemy, firing burst after burst of machine-gun fire into the night.

For over four hours Moon succeeded in holding back the enemy onslaught. At dawn an entire Japanese platoon with fixed bayonets charged him. Moon calmly rose out of his hole and mowed them down. Eighteen fell dead, the rest retreated. A few minutes later he came out of his hole again to throw a grenade at a Japanese machine gun set up only twenty yards to his right. Before he could make the toss the machine gun shot him dead. The Japanese then attacked anew, but the remnants of Company G fixed bayonets, charged, and drove them off. In front of Moon's foxhole his platoon sergeant later counted over two hundred enemy bodies.

While the U.S. Army forces ashore on Leyte consolidated their beachhead and began the drive inland, the Japanese navy prepared for a final showdown with the U.S. Navy.

Adm. Soemu Toyoda decided on a three-prong reaction to the Leyte Gulf invasion. His center force, under Vice Adm. Takeo Kurita, approached from the west. It would sail east through the middle of the Philippines, transit the San Bernardino Strait between Luzon and Samar, and emerge onto the open sea. From there Kurita could fall on the invasion forces in Leyte Gulf to his south, beginning at dawn on October 25.

At the same time, Vice Adm. Shoji Nishimura's force would enter Leyte Gulf from the south. After transiting Surigao Strait north of Mindanao, Nishimura's fleet of seven warships would act as the southern arm of a great pincers movement.

The third portion of Toyoda's fleet was the northern arm under Vice Adm. Jisaburo Ozawa. Composed of four aircraft carriers, two battleships, and eleven cruisers and destroyers, the force had sailed from Japan with just 116 planes aboard its carriers. But they weren't really part of the plan. Ozawa was simply to act as a decoy, pulling Halsey's Third Fleet north, away from Leyte Gulf. Once Halsey was out of the way, Kurita and Nishimura would be free to destroy Kincaid's Seventh Fleet.

The Japanese plan began unraveling on October 23. American subs spotted Kurita's task force, giving Halsey his first hint of the enemy's plan. Halsey swung his fleet east and dispatched scout planes. The next morning the planes found Kurita still west of the San Bernardino Strait. An hour later another scout plane located Nishimura's force in the Sulu Sea west of Mindanao. Halsey ordered his carrier planes to attack the larger force, Kurita's.

At 8:30 A.M. while Halsey's dive-bombers and torpedo planes streaked westward, radar picked up a large group of planes headed for the Third Fleet. These planes were the remnants of the Japanese air force based on Luzon and Formosa. Only a thin line of U.S. fighters stood between them and Halsey's carriers.

DAVID McCAMPBELL

From the flight deck of the *Essex* seven F-6F Hellcats raced skyward, fighting for altitude. If the Japanese planes reached the carriers, it could mean disaster. Several of the other carriers were still launching torpedo planes and dive-bombers for a follow-up strike on Kurita's fleet. The leader of the Hellcats, Comdr. David McCampbell, boss of the *Essex*'s Air Group 15, spotted the enemy planes when he reached fifteen thousand feet. Sixty bandits—twenty bombers covered by forty fighters flying three thousand feet higher—appeared like black dots against the sky.

McCampbell keyed his microphone. "I have only seven planes. Please send help."

"Sorry," radioed the *Essex*. "None are available."

McCampbell swallowed. In over two and a half years of combat, this was his tightest moment. He gave the only order he could: "Let's go!"

McCampbell, a native of Bessemer, Alabama, where he was born on January 16, 1910, started his naval career with a discharge. Graduated from Annapolis in June 1933, in the depths of the depression, with the navy lacking funds, McCampbell received an honorable discharge along with his diploma. One year later he was recalled to active duty and commissioned an ensign. Two years later he received his first assignment involving aircraft: he was made gunnery observer for Scouting Squadron 11, aboard the cruiser *Portland*.

McCampbell had had an urge to fly ever since he was a youngster. He fulfilled that urge when he earned his naval aviator's wings in April 1938. McCampbell began World War II aboard the *Wasp*, serving aboard that famous carrier until she went down in September 1942 off Guadalcanal. After the sinking McCampbell returned to the United States where he took command of the new Fighter Squadron 15.

In February 1944, McCampbell was given command of Air Group 15, becoming the boss of all aircraft aboard the *Essex*. Under his brilliant leadership, Air Group 15 would amass an unparalleled war record. During their seven-month combat tour in the Pacific, Air Group 15 destroyed over six hundred enemy planes and nearly three hundred thousand tons of shipping, including the forty-five-thousand-ton battleship *Musashi*. During this tour McCampbell also became the navy's top-scoring ace, downing thirty-four enemy planes.

McCampbell's cool, calculating skill as a fighter pilot was strikingly demonstrated on June 19, 1944, during the Marianas Turkey Shoot. Leading his fighters against eighty Japanese aircraft, he personally knocked down seven. On October 24, he would flame nine more.

When the Hellcats reached twenty-four-thousand feet, amazingly unseen by the Japanese flight, McCampbell and his wingman, Ens. Roy Rushing, pushed their planes over into a dive. Pouring on the throttle, they dove into the formation. A Betty glided into McCampbell's sights. The Hellcat's six .50-caliber wing guns spat briefly. The twin-engined enemy bomber began pouring out smoke, then burst into flame. It tumbled down to the sea. Rushing also chalked up an enemy plane.

Rapidly regaining the altitude lost in the dive, McCampbell and Rushing again dove on the bombers. The enemy formation still held a course for the U.S. fleet. While McCampbell set his sights on an enemy fighter, a Zeke, he saw his other five planes zooming among the formation. Several long streaks of smoke attested to their stealth. McCampbell flamed the Zeke, then headed for a bomber. In seconds it was down.

For the next twenty minutes McCampbell and the six other pilots played hide-and-seek in the clouds with the bombers. Ignoring the bursts of fire from the bombers' machine guns, McCampbell jumped on another bomber as it slipped out of a cloud. He squeezed off a burst, leading the Betty by two lengths. The enemy plane flew right into the tracers. It fell off, trailing thick, oily smoke.

McCampbell had claimed four enemy planes, Rushing three.

The score stood at seven to nothing. The deadly toll continued. McCampbell zipped down again, missed, pulled up, and stitched a line of tracers into another bomber. Kill number five. He pounced on another fighter. His bullets ripped into the plane's fuel tanks. Number six.

The fearless pilot glanced at his fuel gauges. Because of the imminent threat he'd taken off with only half tanks. The tumultuous battle in the sky had used a lot of fuel. He'd have to watch his gauges.

Darting in and out of the formation the seven Hellcats took a heavy toll on the enemy. Still the Japanese fighters held their position, unwilling to tangle individually with the Americans. Suddenly, the surviving enemy bombers, still short of the American fleet, ditched their bombs. They turned tail and headed for home.

It was a weird, almost pathetic battle. Like wolves snapping at a herd of sheep, the Americans picked off the enemy planes. McCampbell lost track of his kills. He could only remember brief scenes. A bomber slipping away from the formation. His Hellcat bucking as he fired. Smoke. Flames. On to the next one. A fighter tried to save a bomber; McCampbell turned to face him head on. A huge explosion. Debris from the Zero slammed into McCampbell's plane.

McCampbell's fuel had run dangerously low. Beside him, Rushing had run out of ammo, but stuck with his skipper. Six Zeroes turned out of the formation to challenge the Hellcats. McCampbell responded. Twisting, turning, diving, climbing, he knocked down one, damaged another.

The running fight continued all the way back to Luzon's coast. At least two more bombers fell to McCampbell's deadly fire. McCampbell radioed his men, "Gas is running low. We'll be lucky to make it back to the *Essex*. Let's break it off."

Reluctantly, the Hellcats turned back. Someone counted the fleeing enemy planes. There were only nineteen fighters and bombers left—out of an original sixty!

Too low on fuel to make the *Essex*, McCampbell put down on the *Langley*. The official count for the day credited McCampbell with nine planes, Rushing with six, and the other five pilots with two apiece. If the final count of survivors was accurate it meant sixteen more enemy planes had been downed. Unofficial estimates credited McCampbell with six of those.

The seven pilots of Air Group 15 had performed a feat unmatched in warfare.

Besides fighting the Japanese Air Force to a standstill, McCampbell's efforts also allowed the American torpedo planes and dive-bombers to pound Kurita's fleet unmercifully. Deprived of his air cover, Kurita turned back. This movement allowed the Americans to concentrate on Nishimura's fleet to the south, preventing it from attacking the Seventh Fleet guarding Leyte's beaches.

The day following his incredible feat, McCampbell was assigned as target coordinator for three air groups attacking Ozawa's northern force. As a result of his "coolness, quick thinking, superior judgment, and outstanding leadership," one enemy carrier, one cruiser, and two destroyers were destroyed. McCampbell received the Navy Cross for this action, becoming the only person to earn the country's two highest awards on successive days.

McCampbell was flown back to the United States so President Roosevelt could present him with his Medal of Honor on January 10, 1945. McCampbell's combat days were over, but not his navy days. Among his postwar assignments were a berth as executive officer of the carrier *Franklin D. Roosevelt*; head of the Navy Flight Test Center at Patuxent River, Maryland; and command of the carrier *Bon Homme Richard*. He qualified as a jet fighter pilot in 1955. Before retiring as a captain in 1964, McCampbell served in the Joint Staff Office, Joint Chiefs of Staff.

Besides his Medal of Honor and Navy Cross, McCampbell also earned the Silver Star, Distinguished Flying Cross, Legion of Merit, and Air Medal.

Of his combat tour, McCampbell downplays his record. "The thing I hope to be remembered for is having the finest air group that ever hit the navy, Atlantic or Pacific. We sank more ships, shot down more planes, and our ship was never attacked while we were aboard and we never lost a bomber or torpedo plane through air-to-air combat. And," he adds, "I was never shot down, never had a forced landing, and never bailed out."

Kurita's retreat to the west had been only temporary. Though his losses were heavy, he was still determined to destroy the American fleet guarding the Leyte landings. As night fell on

October 24, Kurita was once again threading his way through San Bernardino Strait.

In the meantime, Halsey's scout planes spotted Ozawa's task force three hundred miles to the north. Halsey regarded Ozawa's four carriers as the major threat to the Leyte landings. He had no way of knowing Ozawa had only a handful of planes. Assuming Kurita was still steaming west, Halsey took the bait. He ordered his fleet north to do battle with Ozawa.

And he would have great success. From 8:00 A.M. through the afternoon of October 25, his planes filled the sky over the Japanese ships. By the time the day ended one Japanese carrier rested on the ocean floor and the three remaining carriers were badly damaged.

But Halsey had left San Bernardino Strait wide open.

By daybreak on October 25, Kurita was clear of San Bernardino Strait steaming down Samar's east coast, still undetected. When his lookouts spotted a group of carriers on the horizon launching planes, he was ecstatic. He thought he had caught Halsey's carriers at their most vulnerable. Kurita ordered his fleet to the attack.

What Kurita had actually come upon was a small group of escort carriers under Rear Adm. Clifton A. Sprague. As part of Kincaid's Seventh Fleet, the small fleet was providing air cover for the landing force and performing antisubmarine patrols. Lightly armed themselves, the six escort carriers had only seven destroyers to protect them.

Sprague's first warning of the approaching enemy came at 6:45 A.M., when a torpedo plane on antisubmarine patrol reported the approach of the Japanese battleships, cruisers, and destroyers. Sprague didn't believe it. He thought they must be part of Halsey's fleet. By the time the pilot confirmed his report, Sprague's own lookouts had sighted the pagoda-shaped enemy masts on the horizon.

Sprague wasted no time. He launched every available plane, turned south, and called for help. Heavy shells from the enemy battleships began dropping among the carriers, throwing up huge fountains of water. As the carriers ducked into a convenient rain squall, the seven small destroyers threw themselves between the enemy and the carriers. Zigzagging and laying great clouds of smoke, they plunged into the midst of Kurita's fleet, hoping to get close enough to bring their small guns in range. They kept firing torpedoes, few of which hit, but they did cause the Japanese ships to take evasive action, disrupting their attack.

One of the destroyers, the *Johnston*, was in the thick of the hectic fight all morning.

ERNEST E. EVANS

The commanding officer of the *Johnston* was Comdr. Ernest E. Evans, a thirty-two-year-old graduate of the Naval Academy's class of 1931. A Cherokee Indian from Oklahoma, Evans had taken command of the *Johnston* upon her commissioning on October 27, 1943. At the commissioning ceremony he told his 327-man crew, "This is going to be a fighting ship. I intend to go in harm's way, and anyone who doesn't want to go along had better get off right now."

Nobody moved.

The principal weapons of the twenty-two hundred-ton *Johnston* were five five-inch guns and ten torpedo tubes. Eighty-five percent of her crew was green. Only a third of her officers had ever been to sea. Less than twenty men had seen action. To whip his novice crew into shape, Evans drilled them relentlessly. The *Johnston* spent so much time at general quarters the crew nicknamed her "GQ Johnny."

Evan's diligence paid off. Three months after commissioning, the *Johnston* was bombarding the beaches of Kwajalein. The ship's gunnery officer remembered Evans from that engagement. "He was magnificent," said Robert C. Hagen after the war. "I can see him now: short, barrel-chested, standing on the bridge with his hands on his hips, giving out a running fire of orders in a bull voice. And once he gave us an order, he didn't ride us, but trusted us to carry it out the way he wanted it done. It was that quality of leadership which made us all willing to follow him to hell."

The *Johnston* plastered Eniwetok next, then spent three months on antisubmarine duty in the Solomon Islands. In August the *Johnston* participated in the invasion of Guam. Next she guarded escort carriers off Peleliu.

Evans and his crew were beginning to think they'd never see any real action. They'd been in four invasions and had never heard a return shot fired in anger. When Evans received orders to join the Seventh Fleet off Leyte to guard more escort carriers he could hardly mask his disappointment. It was just another baby-sitting job to him.

On the night of October 24 Evans spoke to Hagen of throwing a birthday party for the crew. He wanted ice cream and cake. It would help relieve the boredom. Hagen recalled Evans saying, "We're within three days of being one year old. It's been an uneventful year."

Less than eight hours later the *Johnston* would be smack in the middle of one of the toughest sea battles of the war.

When Kurita's fleet of four battleships, seven cruisers, and nine destroyers was spotted, Evans reacted instantly. The *Johnston* was the first to lay smoke, the first to start firing, and the first to launch a torpedo.

For the first twenty minutes the *Johnston* was too far away for her five-inchers to be effective. By 7:15 A.M. they'd closed the range. The *Johnston* fired at a cruiser. The hits angered the bigger ship. She returned fire and missed. Evans ordered his little ship to head for the cruiser. With shells splashing all around her the *Johnston* bore straight in at the twelve thousand-ton cruiser. At 7:20 Evans ordered, "Fire torpedoes!"

Ten torpedoes raced toward the enemy. Evans whipped the *Johnston* around, pouring out smoke. Three of the torpedoes hit, knocking the cruiser out of action.

At 7:30 the *Johnston* got hit. Three fourteen-inch shells from a battleship tore into her. Hagen said, "It was like a puppy dog being hit by a truck." Two shells knocked out all power to the steering engine and the after three five-inch guns. Dead men littered the decks.

One shell hit the bridge. Three officers standing near Evans were killed. Evans himself stood bareheaded and bare-chested, his helmet and shirt ripped off by the blast. The hair on his chest was singed; blood gushed from his left hand where shrapnel had ripped away two fingers. Shell fragments had peppered his neck and face. A corpsman rushed to him. Evans brushed him away. "Don't bother me now. Help some of the guys who are hurt." He then wrapped a handkerchief around the stumps of his fingers and returned to fighting his ship.

Evans headed for a nearby rain squall while the crew made hasty repairs. The ship had to be steered by hand, a backbreaking task. In spite of the devastation, the *Johnston* got off over a hundred more rounds at the enemy, hitting a cruiser and the lead Japanese destroyer.

At 7:50 Admiral Sprague ordered the destroyers to make a torpedo attack. Since she had only one engine giving power and no more torpedoes, the *Johnston* couldn't make the attack. But Evans wasn't done. He was going in harm's way.

"We'll go in with the destroyers and provide fire support," he boomed.

He went in, dodging salvos, firing back. The *Johnston* closed to within six thousand yards of one cruiser, pumping five-inch shells into her at a rapid rate.

At 8:20 Evans ordered his ship to attack a thirty thousand-ton battleship, only seven thousand yards distant. The little ship darted in, her guns firing shells as fast as they could. At least fifteen hit the battleship, but it was like a peashooter hitting a brick wall. The *Johnston* ducked back into her smoke.

Ten minutes later Evans saw the carrier *Gambier Bay* under attack from a Japanese cruiser. Evans turned to Hagen. "Commence firing on that cruiser, Hagen," Evans ordered. "Draw her fire on us and away from the *Gambier Bay*."

Evans conned the *Johnston* to within six thousand yards of the cruiser, scoring five hits. But the Japanese ignored the little ship. Evans broke off the attack when he sighted seven Japanese destroyers moving in on another group of carriers.

The *Johnston* took on all seven destroyers. Though she was hit several times, she was giving better than she received. The *Johnston* scored twelve devastating hits on the lead destroyer, sending her fleeing. Next the *Johnston* took on the second destroyer. After taking five hits, that destroyer also retired.

Johnston was nearly out of the fight now, but then an amazing thing happened: the other five destroyers all turned and headed after their leader. Evans, strutting around his shattered bridge like the captain of a battleship, was beside himself with elation. "Now I've seen everything," he said.

By 9:10 the *Johnston* had taken several more severe hits. One forward gun was knocked out, the other badly damaged. Fire crackled throughout the ship. An ammo locker exploded sending 40-mm shells hurtling throughout the ship. The bridge was so badly damaged, Evans moved to the fantail. He shouted his steering orders through an open hatch to the men turning the rudder by hand.

Twenty minutes later the *Johnston* was again being battered by enemy ships. Two cruisers off her port side, two ahead, several destroyers on her starboard, and a battleship astern fired point-blank at her. Hagen said it was like "a bunch of Indians firing on a prairie schooner."

By 9:30 *Johnston* was dead in the water. She had no more power. Fifteen minutes later Evans gave his final order. It was the saddest one he ever issued. "Abandon ship," he called.

At 10:10 the *Johnston* rolled over. A Japanese destroyer came up to one thousand yards and pumped a final salvo in her hull. That was the end of the *Johnston*.

Evans was seen climbing into a small boat with a group of men, but was not among the 141 survivors pulled from the sea two days later.

For his incredible fighting spirit, Evans was posthumously awarded the Medal of Honor on November 24, 1945.

Once he had been advised of the massive sea battle three hundred miles to his south, Halsey left two carrier groups to finish off Ozawa and raced south with his battleships. But he wouldn't be needed.

Although he held the upper hand, Kurita did not know it. Disorganized, low on fuel, and dismayed by the bold attacks by the *Johnston* and her sister ships, Kurita intercepted the message saying Halsey was coming to Sprague's rescue. Rather than be caught between the two forces, he decided to withdraw.

Sprague could not believe what he saw. Just when he thought he'd lost the battle it ended. His small force had outfought and outlasted a superior enemy fleet. As a result, he had protected the troop transports and MacArthur's beachhead.

It was a tremendous victory for the Americans. The Battle for Leyte Gulf cost the U.S. Navy one large carrier, two escort carriers, three destroyers, and less than three thousand men. The Japanese lost four carriers, three battleships, five heavy cruisers, four light cruisers, nine destroyers, and ten thousand men. Their navy was shattered, out of the war for good.

While the sailors of the U.S. Navy battled for superiority on the sea, members of the U.S. Army made good progress on Leyte. By the end of the second day the XXIV Corps had taken Dulag and San Jose. They moved into the Leyte Valley, intent on clearing it of the enemy. To the north the X Corps had easily overrun Tacloban, the provincial capital, and its nearby airfield. It turned to the northwest, its new objective the fishing port of Carigara, on Leyte's north coast.

Abnormally heavy rainfall delayed the opening of Tacloban's airfield. Until then MacArthur did not have control of the air. When most of the navy's carriers withdrew for refitting and damage repair, the enemy quickly took the advantage. Continuous bombardments by the Japanese slowed the engineers working on the airstrip. Not until October 27, 1944, were the first American fighters able to land at Tacloban.

Waiting to greet the pilots were both General MacArthur and General Kenney. One of the P-38 Lightning pilots they shook hands with was a twenty-four-year-old farm boy from northern Wisconsin.

RICHARD I. BONG

America's ace of aces was born in Poplar, Wisconsin, on September 24, 1920, the oldest of nine children. Life on the family farm was hard but not bleak. Dick Bong found plenty of time to hone his hunting and fishing skills between chores. He also worked hard in high school, graduating 18th in a class of 428 in 1938.

When Bong entered Superior State Teacher's College in the fall of that year his family assumed he'd pursue a career in engineering. But he had other ideas. As a youngster he'd been enamored of planes, building dozens of models of World War I fighters. Bong planned to attend Superior State for two and a half years, then enter the army air force's aviation cadet program. After a few years as an army pilot he'd go to work for one of the major airlines.

His plan almost worked. Bong had nearly completed his primary training as a pilot when the Japanese bombed Pearl Harbor. He had demonstrated such a natural ability for flying that after he earned his wings on January 9, 1942, the army retained him at Luke Airfield, Phoenix, Arizona.

Bong didn't like the assignment, but later he admitted the five months he spent instructing greatly improved his own flying skills. On May 2, 1942, Bong transferred to Hamilton Field, near San Francisco, where he learned to fly the new P-38 fighter. It was the beginning of a remarkable love affair.

Bong found the P-38 fighter to be much to his liking. Powered by a pair of 1,150-horsepower engines, the twin-fuselaged fighter could reach speeds of 395 miles per hour at 25,000 feet. At speeds above 300 miles per hour the P-38 outmaneuvered the fabled Zero. Her armament of four .50-caliber machine guns backed by a 20-mm cannon made the Lightning a formidable aerial opponent.

Dick Bong arrived at Port Moresby, New Guinea, on November 15, 1942, temporarily assigned to the 39th Fighter Squadron. He flew several combat missions in the Buna area, all without success. Then, on December 27, 1942, the 39th sent twelve P-38s against a flight of enemy aircraft headed for American shipping at Buna.

Bong later recalled what happened that day. After diving to throw off a pesky Zero sticking to his tail, Bong said:

> As I leveled off about two inches above the shortest tree in the Buna area, there was a Japanese dive bomber sitting right ahead of me. It was a perfect setup and even I couldn't miss. I gave him a short burst and he blew higher than a kite.
>
> I pulled up in a vertical turn and that's how I ran into the second one. Out of the corner of my eye I saw a Zero coming in a vertical turn that would conveniently put him right in my line of fire. I started shooting an impressive assemblage of .50-caliber dynamite, and it takes a lot more than a Zero to get through a solid burst of it in one piece. This particular Zero expired right in the middle of my sights and he never fired a single shot at me. He just rolled over on his back and went straight down.

For shooting down both planes, Bong received a Silver Star. By January 8, 1943, he'd downed his fifth enemy plane to officially earn the title "ace." Bong took a few weeks leave in Australia, then joined the 9th Fighter Squadron at Port Moresby.

Bong did his job extremely well. He racked up his score with impressive regularity. On March 3, he downed one enemy plane; on March 11, two; March 29, one; April 14, one; June 12, one; July 26, four; July 28, one; October 2, one; October 29, two; and November 5, two.

By the time he headed back to the States on November 10 for a well-deserved rest, Bong was the country's leading air ace with twenty-one confirmed kills.

Unlike other air aces who scored many of their victories in just a handful of vicious dogfights, Bong downed his through persistence and consistency. Though required only to fly every other day, he frequently volunteered for additional missions. He was a very competitive person who saw aerial combat as a way to improve his flying skills. He rarely thought about the deaths of the enemy pilots.

Bong returned to Poplar on November 18, 1943. In spite of a heavy snowstorm nearly the entire town turned out to greet him. In addition, he was besieged by reporters. As a clean-cut, good-looking young American fighter pilot, Bong was a natural media sensation. During his visit home Bong was constantly hounded by the press, badgered by inane questions, and followed wherever he went.

He soon tired of the attention. Though ordered to Washington for public relations work, Bong itched to return to the southwest Pacific. He finally got his wish: On January 29, 1944, he headed back overseas.

When he returned to New Guinea Bong didn't receive an assignment to a fighter squadron. Instead, General Kenney posted him to Fifth Fighter Command Headquarters at Nadzab. Along with Maj. Thomas J. Lynch and Col. Neel Kearby, Bong would be free to tag along on any mission he desired, in effect free-lancing as a fighter pilot.

Lynch and Kearby were two other hotshot pilots whose scores nearly equaled Bong's. Before he was shot down on March 5, 1944, Kearby had downed twenty-two enemy planes. He was posthumously awarded a Medal of Honor. Lynch never received a Medal of Honor, but probably should have. He claimed twenty kills before his death on March 8, 1944.

Though deeply saddened by the loss of his close friends, Bong nonetheless kept flying. On April 3, he downed his twenty-fifth enemy plane, only one away from equaling Eddie Rickenbacker's World War I record.

Bong broke Rickenbacker's record on April 12, 1944, doing so with a flair. He knocked down three enemy planes in one fifteen-minute blaze of combat. Not only did Bong receive congratulations from around the world, including Rickenbacker's, he was also promoted to major. And, to his chagrin, was grounded and ordered back to the States.

Bong arrived in Washington, D.C., on May 11, 1944. The

next day Bong met Eddie Rickenbacker. After a few days of press conferences, Bong went home on leave. During this time he proposed to his girlfriend Marjorie Vallendahl, whose college graduation picture graced the side of his P-38.

After completing advanced gunnery courses, Bong returned to New Guinea in September 1944. This time General Kenney assigned him as the Far East air forces' gunnery instructor. Bong would visit the various fighter squadrons teaching them new techniques. If he sometimes accompanied a squadron into combat to observe how the new methods worked, or to try out a new tactic himself, so much the better.

Bong arrived in New Guinea in the midst of a campaign against the oil refineries at Balikpapan, Borneo. He accompanied a flight of P-38s that attacked the area on October 10, 1944. He downed two enemy planes, raising his score to thirty, the first American pilot to do so. Along with more pesky press interviews, Kenney again grounded Bong.

That lasted until the opening of Tacloban. When Bong begged to join the first group flying into the newly won field, Kenney relented. Bong was so eager to duel the enemy that to keep him on the ground would border on cruelty.

Bong proved his worth that very same day by downing an enemy fighter. The next day he destroyed two more while damaging another pair. Things were quiet for several weeks, then Bong scored again on November 10 and twice more the next day.

In just over a month Bong had destroyed eight more enemy planes. His score stood at thirty-six, the highest for any American pilot. General Kenney decided Bong's record deserved the ultimate award. He prepared a Medal of Honor recommendation, specifically citing Bong's eight victories from October 10 to November 11, 1944.

Kenney should have waited a few more weeks to make his recommendation. On December 7, 1944, perhaps to remember Pearl Harbor, Bong got his 37th and 38th victories.

On December 12, 1944, at Tacloban, while a light rain fell, General MacArthur pinned the Medal of Honor to Dick Bong's tunic. As hundreds watched MacArthur said, ''Major Richard Ira Bong, who has ruled the air from New Guinea to the Philippines, I now induct you into the society of the bravest of the brave, the wearers of the Congressional Medal of Honor of the United States of America.''

Though a holder of the Medal of Honor, Bong returned to combat. Over Panubulon Island he downed his thirty-ninth plane on December 15. Two days later, over Mindoro, he bagged number forty. It would be his last.

General Kenney decided forty enemy planes destroyed was enough for one man. He first grounded Bong, then ordered him back to the States. Kenney said Bong should ''go home while he was still in one piece, marry Marjorie, and start thinking about raising a lot of towheaded Swedes like himself.''

On December 29, 1944, Dick Bong started home to do just that. Behind him lay two years of combat, over two hundred missions, forty, confirmed kills, seven probables, and eleven damaged enemy planes. It was a record that has never been broken.

After going through the obligatory public relations tour in Washington, Bong returned to Marjorie in Poplar. On February 10, 1945, the handsome couple was married in Superior's Concordia Lutheran Church. Following an extended honeymoon Bong reported to Wright Field, Dayton, Ohio, where he took a two-month course covering all the available information on the new jet-engine aircraft. Bong had requested duty as a test pilot for America's first jets at the Lockheed aircraft plant in Burbank, California.

Under study since October 1944, the P-80 Shooting Star jet represented the latest in America's aviation arsenal. Bong had learned about the craft during his previous visit to the States. He instantly decided this would be the perfect plane on which to sharpen his skills.

By August 6, 1945, Bong had logged just over four hours in the P-80. He was going up for a quick test of the plane at 2:30 P.M. that afternoon. He had a golf date that afternoon with Bing Crosby, so he couldn't fly for long. As it turned out, his flight lasted just about two minutes.

Seconds after takeoff the P-80 began emitting smoke. At four hundred feet altitude, sensing something was wrong, Bong started to bail out. Then he climbed back into the cockpit. The plane banked sharply to the right, then crashed. Major Bong was killed instantly.

* * *

MacArthur's drive across Leyte had stalled. Heavy rains and unexpected Japanese reinforcements from Luzon delayed the conquest of Leyte. By the end of October, though, elements of the 7th Infantry Division had crossed the island and reached the west coast. On the north the 1st Cavalry Division made an amphibious end run around the mountainous northeastern tip of Leyte and landed near Carigara.

At the same time the cavalrymen were making their landing, Japanese troops were digging in on a steep ridge southwest of the town. The struggle for Breakneck Ridge became the toughest clash of the Leyte campaign. It raged for weeks, the combatants fighting savagely, often hand to hand on the slick, muddy heights.

On November 3, 1944, Company A, 34th Infantry Regiment, 24th Infantry Division, went to the aid of a sister company pinned down by Japanese well-concealed on a thickly wooded slope. As the point squad started across a fast-running stream, its leader was killed. Sgt. Charles E. Mower, a nineteen-year-old from Chippewa Falls, Wisconsin, assumed command. As he started to lead his men across the stream, Mower was severely wounded.

Realizing his position in midstream provided the most advantageous point from which to bring fire on the enemy, Mower stayed where he was. Ignoring the fusillade of bullets filling the air around him, he directed his squad with shouts and hand signals in an attack on the enemy positions. Refusing to seek shelter or aid for his grievous wounds, Mower remained completely exposed to the deadly Japanese fire. Mower's squad destroyed two enemy machine guns and numerous riflemen under his skillful guidance. When they realized the half-submerged infantryman was the key to the assault on their lines, the remaining Japanese gunners concentrated their full fire on him. Again oblivious to the enemy's fire, Mower continued urging his men onward until he fell under a hail of fire.

Only the arrival of fresh GIs from the 32d Infantry Division broke the Japanese hold on Breakneck Ridge. The three-week battle cost the Americans fifteen hundred casualties.

Because of continued Japanese reinforcements pouring in through the west coast port of Ormoc, General Krueger boldly decided to land American troops there. In addition to eliminating the enemy reinforcements, the move would also split the defenders in two. Such a move could wrap up the campaign in short order.

At 7:00 A.M. on December 7, 1944, the 77th Infantry Division began landing south of Ormoc. Enemy resistance was so light that by 10:00 A.M. the entire division was ashore. Resistance stiffened the next day, and it took several more days of heavy fighting before Ormoc fell. From there the GIs started north up the Ormoc Valley, driving to link up with the X Corps still fighting near Breakneck Ridge.

The push north began on December 11. The assault battalions moved out at midmorning, but as they attempted to cross the Antilac River north of Ormoc, heavy fire pinned them down. The fire came from well-prepared enemy positions around the barrio of Cogon, astride Highway 2. Innumerable spider holes had been constructed in the waist-high grass. The principal defensive position was a three-story concrete building that had been converted into a blockhouse. An estimated battalion of enemy troops, supported by machine guns, antitank guns, and field artillery, held the redoubt. Until these positions were eliminated the Americans would be denied access to Highway 2.

Two regiments of the 77th Division butted against the enemy position for several days but only succeeded in reducing the stronghold, not destroying it. An intense artillery barrage on December 13 succeeded in further reducing the pocket, but the blockhouse remained. A two-company special assault force was finally organized to reduce the stubborn position.

Beginning at 9:30 A.M. on December 14, artillery and mortars laid their fire on the blockhouse and the surrounding area. The two companies, E and L, began the infantry attack just before 11:00 A.M.

ROBERT B. NETT

Leading Company E was twenty-two-year-old 1st Lt. Robert B. Nett. Born in New Haven, Connecticut, Nett had attended officer candidate school after being drafted in December 1942. Stateside assignments followed until he joined the 77th Infantry Division in time for the Guam invasion.

He survived the island campaign, earning a well-deserved reputation as a resourceful, nearly fearless leader. By the time of the Ormoc landings, Nett had taken command of his company.

As he led his company forward the Japanese resistance stiffened. His men bogged down under the withering small-arms and machine-gun fire. From his position at the rear of the assault line Nett could hear the cries for help from his wounded. It was time to act.

Nett, a tall, well-built man, bounded forward. Around him the GIs of his company were heavily engaged in hand-to-hand combat with the crafty foe. The Japanese were forcing the GIs back.

The young officer charged headlong into the fighting, his bayonet gleaming on the end of his rifle. He went straight for one enemy foxhole and jumped in, bayonet slashing. He killed the enemy rifleman. Nett spearheaded his company's assault, attacking the Japanese wherever he found them.

Time after time Nett went after individual Japanese soldiers. He used his bayonet with deadly effectiveness; seven enemy soldiers died under his blade.

Seriously wounded while encouraging his men forward, Nett ignored the numbing pain to continue his assault. He crept up to one coconut log- and earth-covered foxhole, dropped in a grenade, then emptied a full clip into the smoking hole.

Hit a second time, Nett directed his men in their fight. Several times he acted as a squad leader, personally leading the GIs. By now Company E had moved several hundred yards through the heavily foliaged area. Behind them, smoldering clumps of bushes attested to the deadly work of flame-thrower teams.

Only a few yards separated Company E from the blockhouse. Nett set his remaining troops into position for the final push. Just as he gave the order for the attack, he was struck for a third time. He knew now he was too badly wounded to continue forward. Calling one of his platoon leaders over, Nett calmly gave him instructions for the attack.

By 1:00 P.M. the blockhouse, or what was left of it, was secured. Nett's inspiring courage had provided the spark his men needed to overcome the determined enemy.

Nett received his Medal of Honor on February 16, 1946. He remained in the army, retiring as a colonel in 1973. He then began a teaching career in Columbus, Georgia.

* * *

As the 77th Division fought north up the Ormoc Valley, the 32d Infantry Division moved south toward them along Highway 2. The Japanese were entrenched on a series of ridges overlooking the road. A heavy rain forest covered the ridges and the deep ravines crossing them. The well-camouflaged enemy positions were nearly invisible from more than a few yards away. The Japanese counterattacked several times, driving the Americans back.

A position of Company K, 126th Infantry, was attacked by five Japanese tanks on December 15, 1944, near the hamlet of Limon. Pfc. Dirk J. Vlug took off after them, armed only with a bazooka and six rockets. As he said later, "This was my chance to get back at them for what they'd done to my buddies."

In the space of ten minutes, Vlug knocked out all five tanks. Vlug, a veteran of the New Guinea campaign, survived the war to return to his home in Grand Rapids, Michigan.

Not until December 22 did the 32d Division link up with troops from the south. The Ormoc Valley was securely in the hands of the Sixth Army. It would take several more weeks of bloody mopping up to wipe out various pockets of resistance, especially the resolute forces still holding out in the Breakneck Ridge area.

General MacArthur declared Leyte secure on Christmas Day 1944. Nearly sixty thousand Japanese troops died on the island. American casualties amounted to thirty-five hundred killed and twelve thousand wounded. Leyte was a resounding victory for the Americans. But its celebration was short-lived. Luzon lay ahead.

16

* * *

Luzon Invasion

General MacArthur's plan for invading Luzon nearly duplicated the successful Japanese invasion of three years earlier. Beginning on January 9, 1945, sixty-eight thousand men of General Krueger's Sixth Army would go ashore at Lingayen Gulf. From there the American army would drive 110 miles south to Manila. The broad central plain of Luzon favored the large-scale offensive maneuvers preferred by the U.S. Army.

The Japanese commander, Gen. Tomoyuki Yamashita, led more than 275,000 men, including one armored and six infantry divisions. Yamashita recognized he could neither prevent a U.S. landing nor afford to engage the Americans on Luzon's central plain. So he ordered most of his troops to pull back from the coastal areas and prepare for long delaying actions in the interior. He deployed 150,000 men into several mountain strongholds in the north; from there they could harass the Americans and tie down as many as possible. Another 80,000 held southern Luzon and the hills east of Manila. A third force of 30,000 were deployed in the mountains overlooking the Clark Field complex.

The 850-ship U.S. invasion fleet left Leyte on January 3 for the journey to Lingayen Gulf. When the fleet entered Lingayen Gulf on January 6, the Japanese launched a major kamikaze strike. Eleven vessels were badly damaged, one minesweeper was sunk, one cruiser crippled, and hundreds of sailors killed and maimed.

Just before noon that day, four Japanese suicide planes were detected flying low over the waters of Lingayen Gulf, headed straight for the destroyer *Walke*. Operating alone on a detached mission in support of minesweeping operations, *Walke* had no gun support from other surface ships.

Walke's CO, Comdr. George F. Davis, who had been born in Manila, instantly raced across the bridge to the exposed wing facing the attackers. Yelling orders to his gunnery officer, Davis directed his batteries in knocking down the lead plane. His guns caught the second one, sending it cartwheeling over the bridge to plunge into the sea on the *Walke*'s port side. They couldn't get the third plane, though. While Davis stood steadfast on the bridge, still giving orders, the kamikaze slammed into the bridge's after section.

Severely wounded in the blast, Davis still retained control of his ship. He called up the damage control parties, then turned his attention to the remaining suicide plane. He whooped with joy when his guns shot it down several hundred yards away. Davis ignored his fatal wounds, refusing lifesaving medical attention until he was sure his ship was out of danger. Only then did he consent to be carried below. Several hours later he succumbed to his injuries and burns.

The invading forces found Lingayen's landing beaches deserted by the Japanese. In the first few days the GIs quickly captured the coastal towns to secure a twenty-mile-long beachhead. The two divisions of Maj. Gen. Oscar Griswold's XIV Corps, the 37th and 40th Infantry Divisions, found the going easy as they pushed south from Lingayen Gulf. As they proceeded toward Manila, the liberated Filipinos gave the GIs a welcome rivaling the ones received by GIs in France. In a week the XIV Corps moved more than twenty-five miles south.

Maj. Gen. Innis Swift's I Corps, on the eastern edge of the beachhead, fought a much harder battle. The forward line of Yamashita's mountain stronghold put up a stubborn resistance. To aid the 6th and 43d Infantry Divisions General Krueger brought ashore one of his reserve units, the 25th Infantry Division, to help secure his southern flank.

The three divisions tackled the brutal job of dislodging the Japanese from the eastern foothills. They occupied a formidable array of caves, tunnels, and pillboxes. At the heart of their defenses were tanks—dozens of them. Not mobile tanks, though. Because of fuel shortages, most of the armored vehicles were buried to their turrets, acting as mini-pillboxes.

The 43d Infantry Division's 169th Infantry fought a particularly tough battle on January 12. Hill 318 stood on the east bank of the Bued River, four and a half miles east of San Fabian, right in the 169th's path. From its heights the Japanese commanded a stretch of Route 3, an important north-south road. The eventual capture of Hill 318 came largely through the efforts of one man.

ROBERT E. LAWS

By the time of the Luzon landings, S. Sgt. Robert E. Laws was a seasoned combat veteran. Born January 18, 1921, in Altoona, Pennsylvania, Laws had battled the Japanese on both New Georgia and New Guinea.

On the morning of January 12, Laws's company commander ordered him to take his squad along a narrow, seventy-yard-long finger of Hill 318 held by a reinforced Japanese company. At the end of the ridge was an enemy pillbox surrounded by rifle positions. Laws prepared his squad, remembering words of advice given to him by his father: "Don't ask others to do something you wouldn't do yourself."

"I looked at the hill," he said, "and was just thinking, 'Let's get this thing done so I can get back home.' They had the positions and the gun emplacements, but I had a mission. I wanted to accomplish it to the best of my ability. I was scared like hell, but I had a mission."

Laws set out on his mission. Ordering his squad to cover him, the veteran started moving toward the pillbox. Working his way forward, rushing from cover to cover, he made it to within grenade-range of the pillbox. He pulled the pins on several grenades, then hurled them up the hill toward the emplacement. None scored.

All the while the Japanese had him under fire. Small-arms fire hit near him; grenades exploded within arm's reach. Soon some of the hot steel ripped into his body.

"I think the first wounds were actually bullet wounds, then came the grenades," Laws recalled. "They hit in both legs. Until then, I thought it was just another battle like any of the others I'd been in.

"I was on the ridge," he continued, "and just looked down and saw the blood going down my pant leg. It didn't break any bones, though. It was just part of the job."

Laws persisted in his grenade assault. Finally, one found the mark. The pillbox erupted in smoke and flames. Joined now by his squad, Laws gathered up more grenades and started to work on the Japanese foxholes.

In the advance up the hill Laws took several more hits from grenade fragments. Suddenly, three Japanese riflemen with bayonets fixed rushed at him. Laws dropped two of them with pistol fire, then closed with the third. The two men grappled like street fighters. They fell to the ground, then rolled sixty feet down an embankment. When the dust cleared, Laws's squad members saw the lanky sergeant making his way back up the hill, a deep gash across his head. The Japanese soldier lay dead at the bottom of the slope.

A corpsman rushed up to Laws. He applied a hasty bandage, then led Laws back down the hill while the squad continued on to destroy the remaining enemy positions.

At the aid station an older doctor took one look at Laws, saw the exposed brain matter, and passed on to the next casualty. A younger doctor, who had witnessed the heroic action, felt he had to try to save Laws. He patched him up as best he could, then sent him to a hospital ship.

"I was in the hospital for about a year after that," Laws said. "It was a strange time because they kept moving me around to different hospitals. I would go to sleep and when I woke up I found some time had passed and I had been moved to a different hospital."

Along the way doctors worked feverishly on Laws. They removed most of the shrapnel from his limbs and put a steel plate in his head. Though still under doctors' care, Laws was well enough to travel to the White House on August 23, 1945 to receive the Medal of Honor from President Truman.

Laws remembered what Truman said to him that day. "He said I was a real tall one," said six foot, three inch, Laws. "He wanted me to bend over so he could put the medal around my neck."

The town of Altoona gave Laws a rousing hero's welcome. He worked for the Pennsylvania Railroad for ten years, then joined the post office. He stayed with them for thirty years, retiring in 1985. Along the way he raised three children.

Laws has always remained humble about his high honor. "When President Truman presented the medal, I accepted it for the men who served under me," he said. Of his numerous injuries Laws says, "I do have my bad days, mostly when the damp weather comes and when it gets too hot or cold. That plate in my head acts similar to a radiator in a car, absorbing the warmth or the cold.'' He died January 1, 1990.

The 6th Infantry Division encountered especially fierce resistance as it moved on the town of Muñoz. Not only did Muñoz occupy an important railroad yard, it also guarded the southern flank of larger San Jose, about five miles northeast. Flat and open, the approach to Muñoz offered only a few irrigation or drainage ditches as concealment for the attackers. Heat from a broiling tropical sun beat down on the infantrymen. In some platoons heat casualties equaled the dead and wounded.

When his platoon leader was evacuated, T. Sgt. Donald E. Rudolph took over the platoon. Two days later, on February 5, a line of enemy pillboxes held up the advance of Rudolph's unit, Company E, 20th Infantry. He worked his way across the open field, where he destroyed one pillbox by ripping a hole in its wood-and-tin roof and dropping in a grenade. After ordering a group of riflemen to cover him, Rudolph, from Minneapolis, Minnesota, took off toward another pillbox. This time he used a pickax to chop a hole in the roof before dropping in a grenade. In quick succession he wiped out six more pillboxes. Later, when an enemy tank came at them out of Muñoz, Rudolph charged it alone, dropping a white phosphorus grenade in the turret. Rudolph's deeds earned him a lieutenant's commission as well as the Medal of Honor.

The 25th Infantry Division had the assignment of capturing San Jose. The town was a major supply point for Yamashita. He planned a delaying action there until the supplies, mostly ammo, could be transported to his mountain positions farther north. Also, his 105th Division was retreating north through San Jose. Until they passed he couldn't relinquish the town.

With its three regiments abreast, the 25th jumped off on February 1. Like the 6th Division trying to push up from the south, the Tropic Lightning men ran into incredible resistance. A determined stand by the Japanese at Umingan ground the 27th Infantry Regiment to a halt. The 25th Division's commander tried a flanking movement by sending his 35th Regiment to the south. The maneuver worked, opening the way to San Jose. While the 27th and 161st Infantry Regiments continued toward San Jose, the 35th remained behind to take the bypassed town of Lupao.

Sitting astride Highway 8, Lupao was defended by two Japanese tank companies, two infantry companies, an artillery platoon, and other assorted units. Like other Japanese troops in the Pacific they would fight to the death.

CHARLES L. McGAHA

Charles L. McGaha was born February 26, 1914, in Cosby, Tennessee. A small hamlet in eastern Tennessee, overlooked by the Great Smoky Mountains, Cosby is the type of poor mountain town that has produced other war heroes, such as World War I's Alvin York. But they offer few economic opportunities for the young. Accordingly, in October 1937 McGaha traveled to Asheville, North Carolina, to enlist in the navy. Military service had deep roots in McGaha's family. One ancestor fought in the Revolutionary War. Others fought for the North in the Civil War; several relatives served in the trenches of France in World War I.

When McGaha arrived at the navy recruiter's he found the recruiter had filled his monthly quota. Undismayed, he traveled to Knoxville where he joined the army. The relationship would last for twenty-five years.

In 1941 McGaha joined the 25th Infantry Division at Schofield Barracks in Hawaii. On the morning of December 7, 1941, he was in the mess hall. "I had just finished breakfast," he recalled years later, "and had asked the sergeant who was relieving me for the morning paper when I heard a tremendous explosion. I ran to the door in time to see a low-flying plane with the rising sun insignia on it come out of a dive and drop bombs on some of our hangars two blocks away."

McGaha spent most of the next three years fighting the Japanese on a succession of islands in the Solomons. Along the way he picked up four Purple Hearts, but one enemy marksman who put a bullet in McGaha's side didn't live long enough to relish it. The Japanese soldier rose out of a foxhole to fire on McGaha. McGaha fired, too, but took a round himself.

And the enemy soldier?

"Well," said McGaha, "we didn't have any more trouble out of him."

But other Japanese near Lupao did bring him trouble. Soon after starting off toward the town on the morning of February 7, McGaha's unit, Company G, 35th Infantry, found its way blocked by five enemy tanks, ten machine guns, and a platoon of riflemen. The company was pushed back. McGaha's platoon and one other found refuge in a roadside ditch.

One of McGaha's men fell wounded about forty yards away across an open rice paddy. The man screamed for a medic. No one moved. There was just too much firing. It was sure suicide to go after him. Finally, McGaha could no longer stand the man's screams. He leapt from the ditch. Keeping low he ran to the man, hoisted him on his back, and started back. A Japanese bullet plowed a furrow down his arm, but he ignored it, carrying the man back to an aid station.

Rather than stay to have his arm tended to, McGaha returned to the ditch. There he found his platoon leader seriously wounded. McGaha, a master sergeant, assumed command of the platoon.

While he directed his men's fire against the Japanese he saw a litter party carrying a casualty to the rear. Seeing they were having trouble he went to help them. Just as he reached them a mortar shell exploded in their midst, killing two of the party, and tearing a gaping hole in his shoulder. Though suffering great pain, McGaha picked up the remaining man and carried him to cover.

Back at the ditch McGaha received an order to pull his men back. To give them protection, he deliberately exposed himself to the Japanese, drawing their fire so the platoon could withdraw. Only then did he move to the new position. There he collapsed from loss of blood and exhaustion.

While recuperating in the hospital McGaha received a meritorious promotion to second lieutenant. When the war ended McGaha returned to the United States where he joined the cadre at Fort Benning, Georgia. On March 27, 1946, he received his Medal of Honor from President Truman at the White House. A week later Cosby threw a huge welcome home party for its hero.

After retiring from the army in 1961 as a major, McGaha settled in Columbus, Georgia, outside Fort Benning, where he became a successful small business man.

One of McGaha's businesses was a local cab company which he ran out of an abandoned gas station. It was there the gutsy, seventy-year-old ex-GI met a brutal end on August 8, 1984. In an apparent robbery attempt, an assailant stabbed McGaha forty times, leaving him to bleed to death on the concrete floor of the station's bathroom.

* * *

While the I Corps fought its fierce battles east of Lingayen Gulf, the XIV Corps continued its relatively easy movement south toward Manila. The first major resistance they encountered came as they approached Clark Field, the former American airbase north of Manila. On January 23, they ran into the forward elements of Yamashita's thirty-thousand-man force.

The heights north of Clark Field were heavily fortified by the Japanese. Each cave had to be reduced with the help of tanks, flamethrowers, and demolition teams. Not until January 30 were Clark Field and the surrounding hills cleared of Japanese. The XIV Corps then continued the drive toward the main target: Manila.

At this time, General MacArthur launched two new offensive operations aimed at capturing Manila. On January 29, 1945, forty thousand troops of Maj. Gen. Charles P. Hall's XI Corps came ashore at San Antonio on the west coast of Luzon, just north of the Bataan peninsula. Their objectives were to capture an airfield, the naval base at Subic Bay, and seal off Bataan. MacArthur did not want the Japanese to repeat his own withdrawal onto the peninsula. By February 15, the XI Corps had established a line reaching from Subic Bay to Manila Bay. The right flank of the XIV Corps was now secure.

The second operation occurred on January 31, when two regiments of the 11th Airborne Division made an amphibious landing at Nasugbu Bay, fifty-five miles southwest of Manila. They easily overcame light resistance, then started toward Manila, moving along the shores of Manila Bay. On February 3, the 11th's 511th Parachute Regiment made an airborne assault on Tagaytay Ridge, east of Nasugbu Bay. They found the area clear of the enemy. They then linked up with the rest of the division, boarded trucks, and raced up the highway toward Manila.

To the north, the 37th Infantry Division entered Manila's northern suburbs on February 4. Ahead of them loomed a month of the most bitter fighting in the Pacific.

Manila was defended by sixteen thousand naval troops under Rear Adm. Sanji Iwabuchi and four thousand army troops caught in the city. Iwabuchi had ordered his men to defend Manila to the death. They fortified the city with barbed-wire entanglements and barricades of overturned vehicles. Buildings were turned into fortresses bristling with machine guns, artillery pieces, mortars, and riflemen. Nearly every major building in Manila—the city hall, the post office, the Manila Club, the University of the Philippines, the Manila Hotel, the train station and scores of others—teemed with fanatical Japanese desirous of dying for the emperor.

To slow the Americans, Iwabuchi ordered all bridges in the city destroyed. The blasts ignited fires, then shifting winds carried the flames into flimsy bamboo and wooden homes. The flames were visible more than fifty miles away. A thick pall of smoke blanketed most of the city, making the house-to-house fighting even more difficult.

The infantrymen of the 37th Infantry Division battled their way through the city's outskirts, then boarded landing craft to cross the Pasig River. At the same time, the 1st Cavalry Division swept around the city's eastern edge and entered Manila from that direction.

The street fighting in Manila rivaled any urban struggle found in Europe. Each time the GIs cleared one building, the next brimmed with even more weapons. Street corners were heavily defended by tanks, artillery pieces, and multiple machine-gun nests.

American casualties mounted at an alarming rate. Company A, 148th Infantry, 37th Division, took frightful casualties while assaulting the heavily fortified Manila Gas Works office complex on February 9, 1945. The intense enemy fire made evacuation of the wounded particularly tough. Volunteers were sought to help move the wounded to an aid station. Pfc. Joseph J. Cicchetti instantly volunteered. For the next four hours he led a litter team in carrying fourteen casualties across four hundred yards of fire-swept ground to the aid station. When he noticed a group of wounded in an open area exposed to enemy fire, Cicchetti fearlessly ran to their aid. As he approached them a shell fragment tore a gaping hole in his head. Though suffering excruciating pain he fearlessly persisted in his self-appointed mission. He picked up one casualty and carried him across his shoulders fifty yards to safety. The Waynesboro, Ohio, native then collapsed and died.

A few blocks away Company B of the same regiment had its hands full with the Paco Railroad Station. More than three hundred determined Japanese, backed by three 20-mm guns, one 37-mm gun, heavy mortars, and numerous machine guns manned the concrete structure. One hundred yards from its objective Company B was brought to a halt by the murderous fire. The attack seemed stymied until two GIs decided to take matters into their own hands.

JOHN N. REESE, JR.
CLETO RODRIGUEZ

A battered railroad shack stood about sixty yards from the railroad station, Pvt. Cleto Rodriguez, a twenty-one-year-old from San Antonio, Texas, and Pvt. John N. Reese, a Cherokee Indian from Pryor, Oklahoma, left the relative safety of their company to make their way through the rubble scattered across the rail yard to the shack. Once there they took turns firing out of the shack's windows at the Japanese in the station.

Both men had joined the 37th Division as replacements after the division had been bloodied on New Georgia Island. Reese grew up on the reservation in eastern Oklahoma where he learned the outdoor skills of his ancestors. Rodriguez, born in San Marcos, Texas, was raised in the tough barrios of San Antonio. He belonged to one of the city's street gangs and believes some of the things he saw as a gang member were as bad as what he endured during the war. "At least during the war, I knew the enemy was in front of me," he later said.

The two soldiers saw considerable combat during the division's year on Bougainville. Reese and Rodriguez were in the same company, but different platoons. They knew each other, but were not close buddies. When the division landed at Lingayen Gulf, the two faced more combat in the hills around Clark Field. Then came Manila.

When his company bogged down in front of the railroad station, Rodriguez saw a chance to break the Japanese defenders. His year of combat had given him a clear understanding of the brutal aspects of the war. "It's either you or them," he said. "I saw thousands of them coming at me, and I just knocked them off."

The two GIs held their exposed position for over an hour, firing away anytime a Japanese exposed himself. While one reloaded, the other manned the window position. At other times, one would spot targets for the other, calling out corrections in case of a miss. "A little bit more to the left, Johnny," Rodriguez would call out. Reese would shift his fire. "You got him, Johnny," Rodriguez announced.

Though an exact count was difficult, Company B's commander later estimated the gallant pair slew thirty-five Japanese in this area.

After discovering a group of Japanese attempting to reach a nearby pillbox, the two left the shack. Together they fired their BARs directly into the group. More than forty Japanese died under their combined fire. No further efforts were made by the enemy to man the emplacements.

Buoyed by their success, the pair pushed forward, reaching a spot just twenty yards from the station. Japanese fire filled the air around them as they scrambled for cover. During a brief lull in the firing, Rodriguez turned to Reese. "Cover me, Johnny."

With that he dashed right up to the building. Covered by Reese's accurate fire, Rodriguez tossed five grenades through an open doorway. The crippling explosions killed seven of the enemy, destroyed the 20-mm gun and a heavy machine gun.

By now the two had nearly expended their ammo. They started pulling back to their company's position. While one provided covering fire, the other would dart back a few yards to the nearest available cover. They leapfrogged back this way, taking nearly half an hour to cover a hundred yards.

They were within a few yards of safety when a Japanese slug zinged by Rodriguez's head.

"Watch it, Johnny," Rodriguez warned. "That one nearly hit me in the nose."

"I got the S.O.B. sighted," Reese replied over the noise. "Don't worry."

Seconds later Reese fell, shot between the eyes.

Rodriguez took one look at his friend and knew there was no hope. Alone, he continued his withdrawal, reaching his company unscathed. Together, in over two and a half hours of close, fierce, intense combat, the two killed more than eighty-two Japanese, completely disrupted their defense, and made the reduction of the train station strong point possible.

Rodriguez fought with his company throughout the horrible battle for Manila, earning a Purple Heart. He was wounded again when the 37th Division went after the Japanese holed up in northern Luzon. When the war ended Rodriguez was wearing the stripes of a sergeant and leading a rifle squad.

President Truman presented Rodriguez his Medal of Honor on October 12, 1945. A few days earlier, Reese's parents had accepted his posthumous decoration at a ceremony in Tulsa, Oklahoma.

Rodriguez made the army a career, retiring in 1969 as a master sergeant. He then joined the staff of a Texas state senator in San Antonio.

The battle for Manila raged throughout the entire month of February. Harsh fighting awaited the GIs on every street corner, in every building. If it could be defended, the Japanese did. The fighting was savage and was made more difficult by the presence of Manila's 700,000 residents. To protect them, MacArthur forbade the use of air strikes and artillery. The shockingly high American casualties caused MacArthur to relent on the artillery, but he clung to his prohibition on using air power.

During the 11th Airborne Division's drive into south Manila on February 13, 1945, its 511th Parachute Infantry Regiment hit heavy Japanese resistance at Fort McKinley. A dozen pillboxes blocked their advance. In the subsequent fighting to reduce eleven of the pillboxes Pfc. Manuel Perez, a twenty-one-year-old paratrooper from Chicago, Illinois, personally killed five Japanese. The last pillbox bristled with a pair of twin-mounted .50-caliber machine guns. Perez snuck around to the rear of the pillbox where he tossed in a grenade. As the Japanese fled, Perez calmly cut them down. He then entered the pillbox, using his bayonet and rifle butt to finish off the remaining enemy. Altogether, he killed eighteen Japanese in his drive to open a path for his company into Manila. Perez never knew he'd been recommended for the Medal of Honor because a Japanese sniper cut him down the next day.

Admiral Iwabuchi planned a last-ditch stand in the Intramuros, Manila's original walled city built by the Spanish in the sixteenth century. Intramuros was enclosed by stone walls up to forty feet thick and averaging sixteen feet high. For six days the Americans pounded the ancient citadel with seventy-eight 150-mm howitzers, a dozen 76-mm guns, twenty-four heavy mortars, and six tanks. Over eight thousand artillery shells blasted into Intramuros. Two regiments of the 37th Infantry Division assaulted the walled fortress beginning on February 23. Hundreds of Japanese had died in the bombardment, but the survivors fought on with a vicious resolve.

Not until February 25 did the last Japanese defender of Intra-

muros die. Over one thousand of his comrades lay in the smoldering ruins. Also scattered among the rubble were the remains
of hundreds of Filipino civilians ruthlessly executed by the brutal Japanese.

While the GIs struggled through the ruins of the once-great
city, another battle was taking place, a battle charged with emo-
tional significance for MacArthur. Corregidor Island had been
MacArthur's headquarters during the opening days of World
War II. From its Malinta Tunnel, followed by Gen. Jonathan
Wainwright, he had conducted the defense of the Philippines.

Both MacArthur and Iwabuchi recognized the strategic value of
the island. Its guns could prevent any ship from entering Manila
Bay. Iwabuchi put five thousand troops on the island. He stuffed
the tunnel complexes with ammo and explosives. He had his troops
sow the island with mines. The crafty Japanese admiral did all he
could to turn "the Rock" into an impregnable fortress.

MacArthur and Krueger decided on a combined airborne and
amphibious assault on the island. Paratroopers of the independent
503d Parachute Infantry Regiment would air assault onto the island's western high plateau, known as Topside. Once the high
ground was secure, the 34th Infantry Regiment, 24th Infantry Division, would come ashore near the center of the island at a point
known as Bottomside. The invasion was set for February 16.

Several days of aerial and naval bombardment preceded the
actual landing. More than a dozen destroyers ringed the island,
pumping shells at the Japanese defenders. The enemy did not
remain idle. They'd roll their guns out from hillside caves to take
potshots at the destroyers.

One shell tore into the veteran destroyer *Fletcher* on the morning of February 14. Red-hot fragments penetrated the number 1
gun's magazine, setting fire to several powder cases. Watertender 1st Class Elmer C. Bigelow, a twenty-four-year-old from
Hebron, Illinois, knowing a magazine explosion could destroy
his ship, reacted instantly. He picked up a pair of fire extinguishers, plunged through the billowing smoke, and started fighting
the fire. Though the acrid smoke seared his lungs, Bigelow remained in the magazine, using the fire extinguishers to put out
the blaze and cool the surrounding bulkheads. Because he had
not taken the time to don rescue-breathing apparatus, Bigelow's
lungs were damaged beyond repair. He died the next day know-

ing his selfless actions had undoubtedly saved the lives of dozens of his shipmates.

Starting at 8:30 A.M. on February 16, 1945, the paratroopers of the 503d Parachute Infantry Regiment began tumbling out of their C-47s over Corregidor. Landing on Topside, they quickly overcame scattered, light resistance. By noon the GIs of the 34th Infantry had made their landing, again against light resistance. They took up positions on top of Malinta Hill.

The Japanese on Corregidor planned a strange defense. Rather than face the Americans en masse, most of them holed up in Malinta Tunnel. Packed among them was a tremendous array of ordnance: more than thirty-five thousand artillery shells, two million rounds for small arms, eighty thousand mortar shells, over ninety thousand grenades, and a ton of TNT. The Japanese planned to sneak out of their hiding place at night to fall on the Americans under the cover of darkness.

The men of the 34th Infantry spent their days sealing off exits from the tunnels. The Japanese spent their nights breaking out of the tunnel, sometimes in considerable numbers. Late on the night of February 18 some six hundred Japanese Imperial Marines dug out of the tunnel and made their way to Topside.

The rifle companies of the 503d Parachute Infantry stretched in a rough circle around Topside. They waited anxiously in the inky blankness for the attack they all felt was coming. The soldiers had their weapons ready, grenades laid out in easy reach. Shortly before midnight the Japanese began a series of feints and probes against Company F. If they found a weak spot, they'd exploit it, force their way into the Americans' rear, and cause considerable casualties.

LLOYD G. McCARTER

When he heard the Japanese probing in front of his position, Pvt. Lloyd G. McCarter left his foxhole atop a small knob and moved downhill. From an exposed position there he could fire on any Japanese coming up the slight slope toward his platoon. McCarter was determined to keep the enemy from overrunning his unit.

McCarter and his twin sister were born in St. Maries, Idaho, May 11, 1917. A short, well-built, muscular youngster, McCarter excelled at sports, especially football, during his school years. He was so good, Gonzaga University in Spokane, Washington, offered him a full scholarship. McCarter took it, but not until he worked for a year as a logger after graduating from high school in 1936.

Before he graduated from Gonzaga, McCarter enlisted in the 148th Field Artillery, Idaho National Guard. When his unit was federalized in 1941, McCarter went with it to Fort Lewis, Washington. From there he answered the call for volunteers to join the paratroopers. McCarter earned his wings at Fort Benning, Georgia, then joined the newly formed 503d Parachute Infantry Regiment in training at Fort Bragg, North Carolina.

McCarter and the 503d got their first taste of combat when they jumped into Nadzab, New Guinea, in September 1943. They fought the Japanese on New Guinea for four long months before being pulled out of the lines for rebuilding and a rest in Australia. Then it was back to New Guinea and the airborne landing on Noemfor Island in July 1944.

From Noemfor the 503d went to Leyte and Mindoro in late 1944. McCarter earned a reputation as a terrific fighter during all this combat. He had an aggressive personality that thrust him into the thickest fighting. Because of that, he quickly earned his sergeant's stripes. But he also found himself frequently in trouble when not in the front lines. That's why, when he landed on Corregidor with nearly four years service, he had no stripes on his sleeve. He was a buck private. But his prowess earned him the position of company scout.

McCarter demonstrated his courage within minutes of landing on Corregidor. While the rest of his platoon lay pinned down by intense machine-gun fire, he charged alone across thirty yards of open ground to knock out the automatic weapon with a well-placed grenade.

During the daylight hours of February 18, McCarter hunted down and killed six enemy snipers who had infiltrated his battalion's area the night before. Late that night the Japanese snuck out of Malinta Tunnel, intent on killing as many Americans as they could before they died for their emperor.

From his position on the slope in front of his company, McCarter fired his Thompson submachine gun whenever he heard the Japanese in the brush around him. When he ran out of ammo for his tommy gun, he'd creep back up the hill for more. When that weapon jammed he used a BAR, then an M-1. Refusing to give up his forward position, McCarter kept calling out to his buddies behind him, "How ya doing?" At first, several dozen voices would answer him. Then, as the night wore on, fewer and fewer men were able to respond.

By 2:00 A.M on the 19th, everybody around McCarter had been wounded at least once. The Japanese kept trying to force McCarter out of his position, but he simply refused to budge.

The enemy sometimes rushed out of the darkness in bunches, sometimes in twos and threes. Some rushed forward tossing grenades, others were armed only with pointed sticks. McCarter blew them all away.

As dawn broke, the Japanese launched a last-ditch banzai attack. Screaming and chanting, they broke out of the surrounding brush. Still in his exposed position, McCarter stood up in his foxhole to spot the enemy's supporting machine guns. Suddenly, a burst of Japanese rifle fire tore into his chest. Blood gushed from the hole near his heart.

McCarter was on his back, desperately trying to stem the flow of blood. As he lay there he located the enemy weapons. He yelled their location to a mortar crew behind him. He watched in glee as the mortar shells dropped square on the enemy. Not until the attack had nearly ended did McCarter allow the medics to come to his aid.

While mopping up, McCarter's squad mates counted over thirty dead Japanese littering the landscape in front of McCarter's foxhole. Another hundred lay in a draw on which McCarter had called down mortar fire.

Six months of hospitalization followed for McCarter. The first few weeks were close for him. He'd lost so much blood he could barely remain conscious. At one point he awoke to find an MP at the foot of his bed. Though the soldier was there only to keep others from disturbing the hero, McCarter's past misdeeds were the first thought to pop into his mind. ''What have I done now?'' he asked plaintively.

Plenty, the army thought. It awarded him the Medal of Honor. While still recovering from his wound, McCarter received his decoration from President Truman on August 23, 1945.

Early in 1946 the hero joined the staff of the VA office in Boise. Two years later he took a wife. Life was never easy for McCarter after the war. He suffered both physical and mental pains from his wounds. The Japanese bullet still rested near his heart; the doctors had ruled it too dangerous to attempt its removal. McCarter's stress increased when his wife died suddenly in Decem-

ber 1954. A little over a year later the pain became more than
McCarter could bear. He ended his suffering on February 2, 1956.

Beginning on February 21, the GIs on Corregidor began their
drive eastward to rid the little island of Japanese. A massive
explosion that night in Malinta Tunnel killed all but six hundred
of the two thousand remaining enemy. The Americans spent
five more days squeezing the Japanese into the eastern corner of
the island. Then on the night of February 27, the Japanese det-
onated another cache of explosives. Debris landed as far as Malinta Hill, over a mile away. Fifty Americans died in the blast
and another 150 were injured.

But more than 200 Japanese also died. The explosion marked
the effective end of offensive operations on Corregidor. On
March 2, 1945, just nine days short of three years since he'd
departed, General MacArthur returned to Corregidor for the flag-
raising ceremony. The Americans lost 210 killed and another
1,000 wounded, nearly twenty-five percent of the entire force.
Japanese casualties came to 5,200; only 20 were taken alive.

While Corregidor was subdued, the fighting in Manila continued unabated. After the destruction of Intramuros, Admiral
Iwabuchi and several hundred of his men holed up nearby in a
complex of large, modern, government office buildings. Rather
than face them in the buildings the GIs dragged up their howitzers. Firing point-blank, they systematically destroyed the
buildings and the Japanese. Only then did the infantry and cavalrymen enter to kill the stunned survivors.

Not until March 3 were the last holdouts wiped out. Late that
day General Krueger received word that organized resistance in
Manila had ended. The liberation had been a brutal, costly affair.
Over a thousand GIs died, another fifty-five hundred were
wounded. Estimated Japanese deaths exceeded sixteen thousand.

Manila itself lay in shambles. Most of it was destroyed, damaged beyond repair, or repairable only at great expense. Millions
upon millions of dollars of damage had been done. Even worse,
in the sprawling ruins of the city lay the bodies of more than a
hundred thousand Filipinos who had died in the fight for Manila.

Following Manila's capture, the XIV Corps pushed south and
east, pursuing Yamashita's southern force, known as *Shimbu*.
Composed of nearly fifty thousand troops, *Shimbu* held the Si-
erra Madre Mountains and the important dams located there,

on the edge of Luzon's central plain. Before *Shimbu* would be conquered, more than four U.S. divisions would be thrown into the fight.

In northern Luzon, meanwhile, General Swift's I Corps had been involved in a series of grinding battles against General Yamashita's main force, *Shobu*. This 140,000-man army held strong defensive positions in the rugged Central Cordillera and Caraballo mountain ranges. Behind them lay the fertile fields of the Cagayan Valley, the Japanese's main food source.

Because the Americans lacked the shipping to make an amphibious landing on Luzon's north shore, they had to come after the Japanese the hard way: overland. The Japanese seemed to know this, so they paid particular attention to defending the few accessible mountain passes.

Late in February, I Corps launched a major attack against Yamashita's mountain stronghold. The 33d Infantry Division, on the left, began attacking toward Baguio, the site of Yamashita's headquarters. In the center, the 32d Infantry Division struck north along the Villa Verde Trail, a dusty, narrow track leading to the passes guarding the Cagayan Valley. On the right, the 25th Infantry Division also pushed north, along Highway 5, the main road leading over the mountains to the valley.

All along the line of advance, the war-weary Americans encountered serious resistance from the fanatical Japanese. Occupying cleverly concealed positions in the jungle-covered mountain heights, the enemy machine guns, mortars, and light artillery rained a constant fire down on the GIs. Each enemy strong point had to be eliminated through the courage of individual riflemen. It was war at its absolute worst.

The 25th Infantry Division snuck a regiment around the Japanese's left flank, falling on their rear. Unprepared for an attack from this quarter, the Japanese gave ground, falling back to the town of Lumboy. Here they occupied well-prepared positions and waited for the Americans.

RAYMOND H. COOLEY

Raymond H. Cooley was from the same area of Tennessee that produced famed cowboy star Tom Mix. Born May 7, 1914, in Dunlap, Tennessee, west of Chattanooga, Cooley was the son of poor farmers. He spent most of his youth migrating up and down the Tennessee River Valley while his father sharecropped or worked at odd jobs.

Cooley began working alongside his father at an early age. As a result he never received much formal education. At age twenty, Cooley hired on as a common laborer at the mammoth Penn-Dixie cement plant in Richard City, Tennessee.

Cooley was still working there when the Japanese bombed Pearl Harbor. Within a few months he'd enlisted in the army. After completing his training, Cooley joined Company B, 27th Infantry Regiment, 25th Infantry Division, in time to receive his baptism of fire on New Georgia Island. Following five months' combat duty in the central Solomons, the 25th Division was sent to New Zealand for rest and rebuilding.

The Tropic Lightning men spent nearly a year in New Zealand before sailing for Luzon. Attached to I Corps, the 25th operated in Luzon's northern half, fighting Yamashita's *Shobu* force. By the time of the Luzon landing, Cooley was a squad leader, wearing the stripes of a staff sergeant. His skill as a jungle fighter, learned on New Georgia and finely honed during hundreds of hours of training on New Zealand, brought him through the first two months of combat on Luzon unscathed.

On February 24, 1945, while attacking a camouflaged trench line near Lumboy, Cooley's squad went to ground under a withering fire from several Japanese machine guns. Cooley took it upon himself to crawl up to one machine gun, where he threw a hand grenade at the enemy. They promptly threw it back. Cooley rolled away from the explosion, escaping harm.

Arming a second grenade, Cooley calmly held it for several seconds of its safe period, then whipped it toward the enemy machine-gun nest. This time the Japanese couldn't throw it back. It destroyed the enemy weapon.

Determined to knock out the second automatic weapon, Cooley continued forward through the thick undergrowth. Several times he stumbled across Japanese foxholes. Each time he dropped a grenade on the Japanese, killing the enemy and relieving pressure on his company.

Inspired by his boldness and success, Cooley's squad moved up to join him in the attack on the second machine-gun nest. He pulled the pin on a grenade. As before, he held it for a few seconds. He drew his arm back. At that instant, six Japanese soldiers burst from hiding places. In seconds they had flung themselves at Cooley's squad.

Cooley couldn't throw his armed grenade. Everywhere he looked his men grappled with the Japanese. With less than five seconds to make a decision, Cooley acted. He tucked the armed grenade into his stomach and stepped away.

The blast tossed Cooley fifteen feet into the jungle. Fragments from the grenade tore into his stomach, spilling his entrails onto the jungle floor. His right hand was blown away. He lay there bleeding while his squad finished off the Japanese, knowing his actions had saved the lives of six Americans.

While his company surged forward through the gap in the enemy lines made by his actions, medics tended to Cooley's grievous wounds. Their quick action saved his life. Hospitalized back in the States, Cooley had recovered sufficiently to receive his Medal of Honor from President Truman at the White House on August 23, 1945.

Richard City held a "Cooley Day" on September 14, 1945, for the twenty-eight-year-old. Dignitaries in the parade included Tennessee's governor and one of its senators. Cooley turned his hero status into a springboard into local politics. In August 1946, he was elected a trustee of Marion County, Tennessee, as a Democrat. Cooley's chances of moving into state politics, perhaps as a state senator, appeared excellent. He probably would have made it, except for the dark side of his hero status.

Pain from his severe wounds continued to cause Cooley agony. The doctors at the VA hospital seemed unable to help him. He turned to alcohol to ease his suffering. Still the pain was nearly unbearable. He drank more. He had been drinking heavily when he started driving home in the early morning hours of March 12, 1947. He failed to negotiate a curve in the road. Cooley's car left the road, then overturned. He died at the scene before help could be summoned. Two days later he was buried with full military honors.

Initially, General Swift expected the 25th Infantry Division to face the toughest task as it pressed north up Highway 5. He was incorrect. The heaviest fighting fell on the 32d Infantry Division moving up the Villa Verde Trail.

The trail was actually an ancient dirt footpath. It ran over rugged, waterless heights into the Caraballo Mountains. For its first five miles, the trail twists up the east side of a rough, bare, mile-wide ridge bounded on the east by the Cabalisiaan River and on the west by the Ambayabank River. These first miles were negotiable by jeep, but beyond that the trail twisted and turned for another fifteen miles over terrain foot soldiers had much difficulty negotiating. From there the trail led to Baguio.

The Japanese hotly contested the Villa Verde Trail. As they had throughout the battle for Luzon, the enemy occupied well-fortified positions. Because of the heavy jungle growth, the Americans often walked smack into the middle of a Japanese strong point before they realized it. Day after dreary day, the GIs attacked. When stymied, they'd pull back, call for air strikes and artillery on the target, then charge back up the hill. As an official 32d Division report said, "This was combined mountain and tropical warfare at its worst."

In its six-week fight up the trail the 32d Division produced four Medal of Honor men. One of them was S. Sgt. Ysmael R. Villegas. His squad clashed with a well-entrenched enemy force occupying commanding ground on March 20, 1945, the day before his twenty-first birthday. Moving ahead of his men, Villegas, from Casablanca, California, systematically wiped out five enemy positions while ignoring the fusillade of Japanese fire directed at him. Though the enemy small-arms fire increased in intensity, Villegas continued his one-man mission. Before he could reach the sixth foxhole, he fell dead, riddled by enemy bullets. Incensed by their youthful leader's death, Villegas's squad rushed forward, overwhelming the enemy as they swept over the position. Later, seventy-five dead Japanese were counted in the area.

Baguio fell to the Americans on April 27, 1945. Yamashita pulled his remaining forces deeper into the mountains. Though most of Luzon had by now been liberated, considerable fighting remained in the pursuit of the remnants of *Shobu*. But while the battle for Manila flared, other battles were being fought by other Americans on other islands.

17

* * *

Bloody Iwo Jima

The B-29 Superfortress bombers which had been flying from the Marianas Islands to Japan since November 1944 had been incurring severe losses. In an effort to protect their homeland, the Japanese threw up savage blankets of antiaircraft fire. There were also many fighter planes left to defend the home islands, and if the pilots couldn't shoot down a Superfortress, they'd ram it.

A crippled bomber had a fifteen-hundred-mile trip before reaching its base. Many were too badly damaged to fly more than a few hundred miles from Japan. They fell into the sea, carrying their crews with them. Even if the crew were saved, the enormously expensive bomber was lost.

If the Americans had a base closer to Japan then damaged planes might be able to land there for repairs, as well as for medical treatment for injured crew members. In addition, fighter planes based on a close-in island could offer protection to the B-29s. Plus a closer island could be used as a regular fuel stop on the return flight, allowing the B-29s to carry greater bomb loads.

The island meeting all of the criteria was Iwo Jima. A part of the Bonin Islands, Iwo Jima lay just 760 miles from Tokyo. It was only four and a half miles long and two and a half miles wide, but it contained two operational airports, with a third under construction. They would easily accommodate the massive B-29s.

The importance of Iwo Jima was also obvious to the Japanese. The island commander, Lt. Gen. Tadamichi Kuribayashi, had twenty-one thousand men to defend the island. He would not fight for the beaches. Instead, he would go underground. Kuribayashi had his troops dig an extensive network of fighting positions. Most of his efforts were concentrated around Mount Suribachi, the 556-foot extinct volcano commanding the island's south end, and the boulder-strewn ridges and ravines of the north end.

By the start of 1945 Kuribayashi's men had completed their work. An intricate series of caves, bunkers, pillboxes, command posts, even medical stations, permeated Iwo. Sixteen miles of tunnels connected them all together. More than eight hundred gun positions, covered with several feet of Iwo's volcanic ash, dotted the island. Weapons for Kuribayashi's men ranged from rifles and machine guns to 320-mm spigot mortars. These bizarre weapons fired a 675-pound shell that was bigger than the firing cylinder and fit over and around it. Though it had a life of less than a dozen rounds, the erratic missile made a tremendous explosion on impact that spread death and injury in a wide swath.

Kuribayashi knew the invaders would have to come ashore on Iwo's southeastern beaches. This flatland of terraced volcanic ash offered the only opportunity for the amtracs to bring their loads ashore. Kuribayashi would concede these beaches to the Americans. Then, once they were ashore, with their vehicles and supplies piling up behind them, he would catch them in a vicious cross fire between his guns on Suribachi and those in the northern heights. The general ordered his men to refrain from banzai charges. Instead, they were to fight to the death from their positions, trading each of their lives for ten American ones.

Poised to strike this eight-square-mile island was the largest force of marines ever assembled—two full divisions with a third in reserve. The veteran 4th Marine Division, making its fourth island assault in thirteen months, would go ashore on Beaches Blue and Yellow, on the right, or north, side. The new 5th Marine Division, never before in combat although forty percent of its ranks were combat veterans, would land on Beaches Red and Green, the left flank of the beachhead, closest to Mount Suribachi. The 3d Marine Division stayed in floating reserve.

D day for Iwo Jima, February 19, 1945, dawned clear and calm. The bombardment force began pounding the island at 6:40 A.M. Out at sea the marines of the first wave boarded their landing craft. As the fire storm of shells and rockets roared overhead, they headed for shore. The first boat touched shore at 8:59 A.M., one minute ahead of schedule. Immediately, the am-trac drivers found themselves victims of Iwo's devilish terrain. Not only were the beaches steep, rising in a series of ten- to fifteen-foot-high terraces, but they were made of volcanic sand and ash so loose the vehicles' tracks could not get a grip in it. Instead of riding inland the marines were forced to disembark at the water's edge. From there they had to work their way up the terraces, slipping and sliding in the knee-deep sand.

At least the beaches were free of fire. Three waves of marines, twelve hundred men, landed before Kuribayashi's men opened fire. At first only scattered small-arms fire harassed the invaders. Then mortars began dropping among them. Then artillery shells. Then the 320-mm spigot mortars. The rapidly increasing enemy fire soon created a massive pileup on the beach. Men and equip-ment were everywhere, inviting targets for the Japanese.

The 1st Battalion, 28th Marine, 5th Marine Division, had been assigned the most dramatic mission of D day. They were to drive across the seven-hundred-yard width of Iwo Jima at this point and isolate Mount Suribachi from the rest of the island. Once that was accomplished, the entire regiment would turn its attention to reducing the formidable volcano. It would not be an easy task. Suribachi's defenders were well armed with a multi-tude of automatic weapons and artillery.

Companies B and C moved inland on a two-company front. Shellbursts ripped up and down the line, while small-arms fire whined overhead. Men died and men were wounded. Valiant marines wiped out pillboxes, only to have them come alive again as they moved past them. The Japanese could maneuver every-where by means of underground passages.

Company A was in reserve but soon found itself in the thick of battle as the heavy enemy fire took its toll on the lead com-panies.

TONY STEIN

Born September 30, 1921, in Dayton, Ohio, to immigrant par-ents, he was christened Anthony Michael Stein, but he never liked the formal name. He preferred to be called Tony.

A youth of unusual good looks, Stein dropped out of high school after the ninth grade. He served with the Civilian Con-servation Corps for a while, then worked construction. He finally settled in as an apprentice tool-and-die maker at the Delco Products plant in Dayton. Though he worked long, hard hours, he always found time for athletics. His favorite sport was boxing. He proved his proficiency in the ring by winning Dayton's Golden Gloves championship in February 1942.

Stein wanted to enlist in the marines right after Pearl Harbor, but his trade was considered critical to the war effort. Not until September 1942 was his occupation deemed nonessential. On September 22, 1942, he enlisted in the Marine Corps.

Following boot camp in San Diego, Stein volunteered for the paramarines. He went overseas with a marine raider battalion and fought with them in the closing phases of the battle of Guadalcanal. On Bougainville he served as a runner for his company commander. There he earned a reputation as a deadly hunter of Japanese snipers.

A national news release from Empress Augusta Bay quoted Stein as saying, "The snipers could hide everything but their eyes. They couldn't shoot with them covered, so I just waited 'til one raised his head and then I let fly with a burst before he could fire." On Bougainville, Stein killed five snipers this way, once dropping one at his company commander's feet.

After the marine raiders were disbanded following their capture of Villa Lavella Island in the Solomons, Stein returned home in early 1944. Assigned to the 5th Marine Division forming at Camp Pendleton, California, he was promoted to corporal and became an assistant squad leader. He married on July 21, 1944. He and his bride had a brief three-day honeymoon; then he shipped with his division for Hawaii.

On Hawaii Stein put his tool-and-die skills to good use. He pulled a .30-caliber, air-cooled machine gun from a wrecked navy fighter plane. In his spare time he fashioned it into a one-of-a-kind hand weapon fired from the hip in the swashbuckling style of an Old West gunfighter. He called it his "stinger." When he boarded the transport for the trip to Iwo Jima the stinger went with him.

Ashore at Iwo, Stein quickly placed himself and his unique weapon at the lead of his company's assault. With two marines covering him, he went after a pillbox holding up Company A's advance. Spewing bullets in rapid bursts, the stinger and its gung ho triggerman pinned the Japanese down while another marine finished them off with a demolitions charge.

In the next few hours Stein used his stinger to knock out nine other strong points. He fired his weapon so much he had to make eight separate trips back to the beach to pick up more ammo. He tore off his boots, whipped off his helmet, and sprinted rearward. Each time, he stopped to help a wounded marine to the beach.

On his ninth trip, the savage enemy fire finally caught up with Stein. Chunks of shrapnel slammed into his shoulder. His company commander ordered him to the beach for treatment and evacuation. Stein refused. He wanted to remain in the fight. For the rest of the day he stayed in action, attacking one pillbox after another. At the end of the day, when his platoon had to pull back to straighten the line, Stein covered the withdrawal with his stinger. Twice enemy fire knocked his weapon from his hand. Twice he retrieved it, using the machine gun with deadly effectiveness against the Japanese.

That night Stein finally consented to evacuation. He boarded a landing craft headed for a hospital ship. Ordinarily, Stein's war would have been over. But as news of the slaughter on Iwo reached him, he decided to rejoin his outfit. He climbed aboard an LST going ashore.

On March 1, 1945, Company A was embroiled in the fight for Hill 362A, in the center of the island. Bitter enemy fire had the whole company pinned down. Even tanks could not make progress. Every movement brought fire from the enemy emplaced in caves on the slopes of 362A. Stein volunteered to take a patrol and see what could be done to relieve the pressure. Nineteen men went forward with the gutsy corporal, ducking from shell hole to shell hole.

Tony Stein wasn't one of the nine men who made it back. A sniper killed him within minutes after he left.

When the Medal of Honor was presented to Stein's family on February 19, 1946, his mother spoke of her son. "Tony always had to do things, hard things. That's why he just had to be in the Marines. He wanted to see if he could do it."

He could.

On the beachhead's right flank, the men of the 4th Marine Division also found the going incredibly rough. The right flank battalion, the 3d of the 25th Marines, landed at the base of a ridge. Shells were whining and crashing as the marines pushed toward a rock quarry commanding the north beaches. The battalion commander, Col. Justice M. Chambers, "Jumping Joe" to his men, led them against the ridge. For three days Jumping Joe's marines fought for control of the ridge and its cliffs. Against pillboxes, trenches, caves, and other furiously active defenses, the thirty-seven-year-old veteran of Guadalcanal and the Marianas personally led his rifle companies in the gruesome battle. When they finally mounted the ridge, only 150 effectives of the original 900-man battalion remained. Chambers was still on his feet, though wounded, and the right flank of the invasion was at last secure.

On the left flank of the 4th Marine Division, the 1st Battalion, 23d Marines, fought to reach Airfield No. 1. By nightfall of the first day they had swarmed over the eastern edge of the airfield. Sgt. Darrell S. Cole, Company B, from Esther, Missouri, got them there as much as anyone else.

Cole led his machine-gun section against a set of sand-covered pillboxes blocking his platoon's progress. From their dark apertures a steady stream of small-arms fire and grenades flew toward the Americans. Cole cut loose at the pillboxes, knocking out two. The third resisted his efforts. Then his machine gun quit, jammed with sand. Angered and frustrated, Cole crawled forward, armed only with a pistol and grenade. At the rear of the pillbox he tossed his grenade in a slit. Screams following its explosion told of its effectiveness. Cole went back for more grenades. He repeated his heroic performance twice. On his third trip a grenade thumped at his feet. The twenty-four-year-old died in the blast, but he had cleared a path for his platoon to reach the airfield.

On the morning of the second day, February 20, the 28th Marines began the grim task of reducing Suribachi's defenses. Supported by artillery and destroyers the riflemen began flushing out the Japanese. The best way to attack their pillboxes was up close. Marines armed with rifles, bayonets, BARs, flamethrowers, and satchel charges had to take the positions one by one. Dozens of concrete pillboxes housed the enemy. Only by close-in fighting could they be destroyed.

By nightfall the marines had only gained a hundred yards, but they had reached the foot of the volcano. Behind the marines lay the smoldering ruins of over fifty pillboxes with their tenants dead inside. The third day was a repetition of the previous two.

The marines bounded forward, wiped out a strong point, moved on to the next. Casualties mounted; most companies fought at half-strength. Only the gallantry of individual marines made the advance possible.

DONALD J. RUHL

The main malcontent of Company E, 2d Battalion, 28th Marines, was twenty-one-year-old Pfc. Donald J. Ruhl. As much a maverick as the cattle he used to herd near his home in Joliet, Montana, Ruhl often grumbled about orders he considered unreasonable. Like wearing his helmet. It got in his way. He preferred a baseball cap. That frequently caused him trouble. His attitude earned him the disapproval of some of the men in his platoon, but he didn't seem to care. As far as he was concerned, they had no right to judge him until he proved himself in combat.

Company E came ashore with the ninth wave. They were the battalion's reserve, so they had no assignment the first day. Digging in a few hundred yards inland, they nervously eyed the heights of Suribachi looming ominously above them.

The company's status as battalion reserve didn't last long. At 5:00 P.M. they were ordered to follow the lead companies across the island, mopping up any overlooked Japanese. By dusk they were dug in near a large bypassed mound. Since it had been quiet all day, the marines assumed the mound was nothing more than an abandoned supply house.

After setting his men in position Ruhl's platoon leader took him to investigate the mound. As they approached it, a heavy door on its side rolled open and a three-inch field piece began pumping shells toward the beach. Another group of marines attacked the bunker, dropping thermite grenades into it. As the Japanese broke out of the smoking bunker, Ruhl dropped to his knee. He fired a full clip from his M-1, dropping eight enemy soldiers. When another rushed for freedom, Ruhl used his bayonet to finish him off.

The next day Ruhl ventured alone forty yards in front of his company's lines to rescue a fallen marine. He and a comrade then carried the casualty three hundred yards to the rear, all the while under enemy fire.

Back with his platoon, Ruhl volunteered to investigate an abandoned Japanese machine-gun nest seventy-five yards ahead of his platoon. Rather than run the risk of the enemy reoccupying the position under the cover of darkness and jeopardizing his platoon in the morning, Ruhl spent the night in the position, all alone.

By now Ruhl had silenced his critics. His aggressiveness and fearless manner had earned their respect.

At dawn of February 21, the three battalions of the 28th Marines renewed their assault on Suribachi. A forty-plane air strike combined with a naval bombardment preceded the movement. Ruhl, Sgt. Henry O. Hansen, and Lt. Keith Wells led the charge for Company E. At first it seemed the bombardment had silenced the Japanese. For the first fifty yards all the marines saw were enemy bunkers and pillboxes damaged by the bombs.

But as they passed the ruins they found there were still plenty of live Japanese left. Ruhl and Hansen mounted a silent, sand-covered pillbox. A trench full of Japanese behind the pillbox opened fire. The two marines emptied their rifles at the enemy. Wells was just climbing the bunker when a demolition charge came flying through the air.

Ruhl saw it first. "Look out, Hank!" he yelled and dove on the charge. The blast tossed him through the air onto his back. A gory cavity replaced his chest. Hansen reached for Ruhl to pull him to safety. Wells quickly ordered, "Leave him alone. He's dead."

Pfc. Donald Ruhl, Company E's rebel, had sacrificed himself to save two others. His posthumous Medal of Honor was presented to his parents on January 12, 1947.

The 1st Battalion, 26th Marines, came ashore the afternoon of February 19. They swarmed into a morass of destruction and heavy fire. It took them nearly two hours to negotiate their way inland. They spent their first night on Iwo Jima dug in a few hundred yards short of Airfield No. 1. The marines resumed the advance at 8:30 A.M. on February 20. Heavy fire from the Japanese quickly broke the assault line into little clusters of men. They moved forward in small units. One man at a time scampered forward, covered by his buddies. Every cluster of boulders seemed to hide a bunker or pillbox. At each sign of movement from the marines these erupted in a blast of machine-gun and rifle fire. Grenades flew through the air, exploding with fury into jagged shards that tore human flesh. By noon the marines had gained two hundred yards against resistance even more furious than that encountered on D day.

Under intense fire the marines scrambled for cover wherever they could find it. One group of four riflemen took refuge in a rock-strewn ravine. Among them was a marine who might have been the youngest combatant on Iwo Jima.

JACKLYN H. LUCAS

February 20, 1945, was Jacklyn H. Lucas's seventeenth birthday, though he barely took notice of the occasion as he fought his way inland. A bull of a youngster, carrying two hundred pounds on a well-muscled five-foot, eight-inch frame, in 1942 he had forged his mother's signature, claimed he was seventeen, and enlisted in his hometown of Plymouth, North Carolina.

The burly, loud-talking, smiling youth made it through boot camp and infantry training with no problems. Sent to a rear-echelon supply depot in Hawaii, Lucas rebelled at the assignment. He'd enlisted to fight the Japanese, and this wasn't his idea of a war. As a result, he often found himself in trouble.

Lucas saw the inside of the brig more than once, mostly as a result of fighting. His most serious offense came for being AWOL, in possession of a case of beer that wasn't his, and punching out the two marine MPs who sought to end his frolic. A thirty-day sentence on bread and water convinced Lucas he was in a chicken outfit.

In late January 1945 Lucas went down to the docks where he had a cousin boarding a transport with the Iwo Jima–bound 1st Battalion, 26th Marines. With all the confusion that existed during the boarding process, Lucas had no trouble sneaking aboard. His cousin and his buddies hid him among their combat gear, bringing him food and water. Back on Hawaii Lucas's outfit listed him as a deserter. But he couldn't have cared less. He was on his way to war.

After several days at sea, when there was no longer any chance of his being returned to Hawaii, Lucas turned himself in to the commander of Company C, Capt. Robert H. Dunlap. Dunlap had the good sense to welcome the feisty youngster into his company. Lucas was given equipment and a rifle and became a legal member of Company C. By revealing himself to Dunlap, Lucas avoided a desertion charge.

Once ashore Lucas quickly established himself as a good

combat marine. Moving at the front of his company, he waded
into the battle like a veteran. In the ravine Lucas and his three
comrades faced eight Japanese in a trench just a few feet away.
In the firefight that followed Lucas shot one of the enemy in the
forehead. "I saw the blood spurt from his head as he stared at
me," Lucas later recalled.

"Then my rifle jammed. A Japanese grenade landed in front
of me. I yelled a warning to the others and rammed the grenade
as hard as I could with my rifle butt into the volcanic ash soil."

Another grenade thumped in. Lucas fell forward, covering
both with his body. He began to think, "Luke, you're gonna
die." Then the bombs went off and his own hoarse scream rose
above the roar of the explosions.

"The force of the explosions blew me up into the air and onto
my back. Blood poured out of my mouth and I couldn't move,"
Lucas said. "I knew I was dying."

His comrades thought so, too. They stormed forward to wipe
out the Japanese. Then they returned to Lucas to collect one of
his dog tags. To their amazement he was not only alive but
conscious. They hustled him back to the beach for evacuation.

On the hospital ship *Samaritan* the doctors were stunned at
Lucas's survival. "Maybe he was too damned young and too
damned tough to die," said one surgeon. Then they began the
first of twenty-two operations to put Lucas back together.
Though he suffered myriad painful wounds and would retain
nearly two hundred pieces of shrapnel in his body, he was left
with a disability no more serious than a partly crippled arm.

Eight months after his brief foray into combat Lucas visited
the White House to receive his Medal of Honor from President
Truman. After the October 5, 1945, ceremony Secretary of the
Navy James Forrestal personally shook his hand and thanked
him. The Marine Corps forgave his past indiscretions and gave
him an honorable discharge. Nothing was too good for the
youngest Medal of Honor recipient of World War II.

After his discharge Lucas, who only had an eighth-grade education, completed high school. He then entered Duke University, eventually earning his degree in 1956. In 1952 he was
married on a national television program.

Unable to find a job to his liking, in 1961 Lucas accepted a
lieutenant's commission in the army. But peacetime military
service wasn't to his liking. There were several fights with other

officers and a lot of drinking. In 1965 the army quietly put him on inactive reserve and discharged him.

In 1966 Lucas started a home-delivery meat business in California. It prospered. Though he divorced his first wife, Lucas soon found another spouse. They moved to Maryland where they opened another meat business. Again they thrived. They lived in a mansion, drove fancy cars, and raised horses.

In 1973 Lucas discovered his wife was siphoning money from the business. He confronted her. He threatened her with divorce and said he'd cut her and her nineteen-year-old stepdaughter out of his will. At that point Erlene Lucas decided to have her husband killed.

With the help of her daughter's husband she procured the services of a hit man. In actuality, the hit man was a Maryland undercover cop. In June 1977 she and her son-in-law were arrested. By the time of the trial, though, the family had kissed and made up. Lucas sat next to his wife while she pled guilty to soliciting murder. She and her son-in-law received ten-year suspended sentences.

The marriage lasted only a few more years, then Lucas ran afoul of the Internal Revenue Service. In January 1983 they claimed he owed more than $135,000 in back taxes, interest, and penalties. They seized all his assets and garnished his income, including his $800.00 per month disability checks. He lost his business and his home.

Lucas and his eighteen-year-old son moved into a trailer. During this time Lucas was arrested for trespassing and carrying a concealed weapon in a futile attempt by him after his eviction to recover his possessions. In 1985 his trailer burned down. Uninsured, Lucas and his son moved into an old walk-in meat locker in an open shed on a neighbor's property. The Red Cross provided them with cots.

Misfortune continued to dog Lucas. In early August 1985 he volunteered to help a friend build a patio on his farm near Elkton, Maryland. He pitched a tent in a cornfield. After marijuana was discovered growing on the farm, Lucas was arrested and charged with possession of marijuana, possession with intent to distribute the drug, and manufacturing marijuana.

Lucas denied any involvement. "I don't even smoke cigarettes," he claimed. Maryland later declined to prosecute, citing Lucas's "heroic service to his country" as a factor in the decision.

Because of the publicity surrounding his case, Lucas received much-needed help. The VA agreed to intervene with the IRS to reach a solution to his tax problem. Job offers reached him. He remarried and moved away from Maryland to rebuild his life.

On the same day Jack Lucas jumped on the two grenades, his company commander also went above and beyond the call of duty. At the point of his battalion's advance, Capt. Robert H. Dunlap ran into heavy opposition at the base of a cave-studded cliff. The Japanese fire pinned Company C down. "Cover me!" Dunlap ordered as he sprinted forward to pinpoint the source of the fire. While bullets sang above him, the former paramarine crawled two hundred yards forward to the base of the cliff. From that vantage point he spotted half a dozen enemy positions. Machine-gun bullets kicked up a chain of geysers as he darted back to his company to relay the information to the artillery. Then he took off again, this time carrying a field telephone. Dunlap held his outpost for the next forty-eight hours, directing howitzer barrages on the enemy. His actions were primarily responsible for the clearing of the western beaches.

Five days later, again leading his company by example, Dunlap was cut down when a Japanese rifle bullet smashed into his hip. He survived his injuries and became a schoolteacher in his hometown of Monmouth, Illinois. During the Vietnam War his cousin, navy Capt. James B. Stockdale, earned a Medal of Honor while a POW in Hanoi, the only time in history that cousins have shared the glory of this honor.

Japanese resistance on Suribachi had grown weaker by the end of February 22. On the following day several small patrols succeeded in reaching the volcano's summit. The commander of the 2d Battalion, 28th Marines, Col. Chandler W. Johnson, summoned Donald Ruhl's executive officer, 2d Lt. Harold G. Schrier, and ordered him to take a patrol to the crest and secure it. "And put this up," he told Schrier as he handed him a small American flag.

Schrier took a forty-man patrol up Suribachi's side. Though the going was rough up the steep slope they ran into no Japanese. At the crater they found only a few enemy bodies. Somebody found a twenty-foot piece of pipe. The flag was lashed to the pole. While a Marine Corps photographer snapped pictures, the marines hoisted the flag into position.

Because this flag was too small to be clearly visible in the battle haze of Iwo Jima, Johnson ordered a larger one to be flown. When five marines and a navy corpsman raised that flag about two hours later, Associated Press photographer Joe Rosenthal was there to take the most famous photograph of World War II. Although two of the flag raisers later earned Navy Crosses for their actions on Iwo Jima, none of them received any decoration for their role on Suribachi.

With the securing of Suribachi, the marines turned their attention to the northern half of the island. This portion of Iwo contained the island's roughest terrain. Rocky outcroppings and fissured hills ran to the sea on both coasts. The natural obstacles would have been difficult enough, but it was here Kuribayashi concentrated most of his defenses. Countless tunnels, caves, dug-in tanks, pillboxes, and bunkers all zeroed in on the marines.

The main terrain feature in the area was Hill 382 and its smaller neighbor, the Turkey Knob. The marines of the 4th Marine Division called the area the Meatgrinder. They started chipping away at the Meatgrinder on February 24. The division paid dearly for it. On February 25 alone they took 792 casualties. Not until March 5 would the Meatgrinder be silenced.

On Iwo's left, or western half, the 27th Marines, 5th Marine Division, faced a similar situation at Hill 362A. Fifteen hundred Japanese manned the hill's defenses. The badly depleted marine rifle companies pushed off at 8:15 A.M., February 28. Accompanied by Sherman tanks, the advance made it up the side of the hill. The casualties were horrendous. In one spot ninety-four men were killed in less than an hour trying to cross an open space one hundred yards in front of a Japanese-held cave.

By 4:30 P.M. it was obvious the few marines remaining on Hill 362A could not hold their positions against the vicious cross fire the Japanese slung from caves higher up the hill. The marines were ordered to pull back. One of the corpsmen helping the wounded down the hill was Pharmacist Mate 1st Class John H. Willis of Columbia, Tennessee. All day he scrambled from one wounded marine to another with his satchel of lifesaving medicine and bandages. Shortly after 2:00 P.M. he caught a hunk of shrapnel in the shoulder and was ordered off the hill. At the aid station his wound was treated and dressed.

When he heard casualties had been overlooked during the pullback, Willis left the aid station to bring them in. Halfway back he came upon a badly wounded marine lying in a shell hole. There was time to jab a rifle, bayonet first, into the ground and rig a bottle of plasma to its stock. The next second a grenade dropped in the hole. Willis fielded the missile and hurled it back toward the Japanese. Seven more followed in quick succession. He tossed out all seven. The ninth one exploded in his hand, killing him instantly.

Hill 362A finally succumbed to the valor of the marines on March 2. Those Japanese who survived escaped through the area's network of tunnels to take up new positions on Nishi Ridge, three hundred yards west. Virtually the same elevation as Hill 362A, Nishi Ridge bristled with nearly one hundred caves packed with machine guns and mortars. The tunnels connecting the various caverns were so well constructed they even had electric lights.

Forty-five hundred marines in five battalions were in the push. As before, an artillery barrage preceded the advance. Then the marines crawled from their places of refuge to begin anew the struggle against the enemy and the terrain.

Fighting furiously against bitter resistance, the marines forced a wedge into Kuribayashi's defenses. That night, at 1:30 A.M. on March 3, 1945, the Japanese on Nishi Ridge launched a local banzai charge. For the next one and a half hours wave after wave of fanatical Japanese were beaten back with bayonets, knives, and entrenching tools in hand-to-hand combat. Two men on outpost duty in a foxhole twenty yards ahead of the main line shared the horrors of that night.

WILLIAM G. HARRELL

Born in the south Texas town of Mercedes on June 26, 1922, William G. Harrell enlisted in the Marine Corps in July 1942. When he completed boot camp he trained as an armorer at Camp Elliott, California. Harrell was a good marine. By the time he transferred to Company A, 1st Battalion, 28th Marines, 5th Marine Division, in February 1944 he wore corporal's stripes. One year later when he landed on Iwo on D day his sleeves bore the third stripe of a sergeant.

Early on the evening of March 2, Harrell's company commander sent him and his buddy, Pfc. Andrew J. Carter from Paducah, Texas, out on outpost duty. The two men, who had shared foxholes nearly every night since D day, made their way forward. A light rain had fallen during the day, turning the volcanic ash into a sticky paste. It also greatly added to the discomfort of the crisp night air.

The two marines took up positions in a long, narrow two-man foxhole on a little ridge forward of the depression where the company CP was established. Just beyond the foxhole the ridge fell off sharply into a ravine that was enemy territory. Because of the nearness of the Japanese, Harrell and Carter alternated one-hour watches.

Harrell was resting when Carter spotted shadows darting among the boulders in the eerie half-light of a parachute flare. He nudged Harrell with his foot. "They're coming out of the ravine," he whispered. He opened fire as Harrell got into position. "Got four," Carter announced quietly.

Harrell saw two shadows, fired twice, saw the shadows crumple. Carter slammed a fresh magazine into his M-1. He got off three rounds before it jammed. "Damned sand," he cursed. He started out of the foxhole. "I'll be right back, Sarge. I'll get another rifle and more ammo," he said, disappearing into the dark.

While Carter was gone Harrell maintained his lone vigil. Whenever he spotted an infiltrating enemy soldier he'd throw a grenade or blaze away with his M-1. An untold number of Japanese fell under his deadly fire. Harrell's determined stand prevented the enemy from overrunning his company's position. Then, while he slipped a new clip into his rifle, an unseen Japanese tossed a grenade into the foxhole. Harrell heard it hit. He fumbled for it in the dark. As he gripped it with his left hand it exploded in an ear-shattering blast.

Harrell sat on the bottom of the foxhole, momentarily stunned. He tried to stand. His left leg buckled. He looked at his left hand in the fading glare of a star shell. The limb hung from his wrist by a few tendons.

A few minutes later Carter dropped back into the hole to find Harrell trying to reload his M-1 with one hand. "What's wrong?" he asked.

"I'm hit bad. Grenade," Harrell muttered.

Suddenly two Japanese sprang from the ravine. One, an officer, swung a long saber. The other held a sputtering grenade. Carter fired his borrowed rifle at the sword bearer. It misfired. Reacting instantly, Carter lunged forward, driving the rifle's bayonet deep into the Japanese. Before he died, the enemy officer brought his saber down, nearly severing Carter's hand.

While Carter handled the officer, Harrell fired his .45-caliber pistol at the second enemy. The man's head exploded. Harrell leaned back against the foxhole wall. Carter had no weapon and was badly wounded. Harrell felt for sure he was dying. Around them the marine line erupted in a sustained roar as the firefight reached a crescendo. Mortars fell all along the line. Artillery shells slammed into Nishi Ridge. Overhead, flares contributed to the ghoulish night.

"I don't think I'll make it," Harrell told Carter. "There's no sense in both of us dying. Get back to the CP and stay there."

Carter didn't want to go, but knew he had no choice. "I'll be back with help," he promised. He clutched his nearly severed hand to his chest, pulled himself over the foxhole's lip, and disappeared into the darkness.

Harrell felt completely alone. Sharp waves of pain rippled up his injured arm. Blood poured from a dozen shrapnel wounds. He hoped the Japanese would leave him alone. But it was not to be.

Armed only with his .45, Harrell prepared himself to die. He had eight rounds in his clip. He figured he'd get eight Japanese before they got him. Suddenly, a Japanese soldier dropped into the hole. Harrell could smell the enemy's foul odor less than a yard away. A second Japanese crouched on the foxhole's rim, silhouetted against the night sky. The Japanese in the foxhole armed a grenade by rapping it on his helmet, set it at Harrell's feet, then started out of the hole. Harrell's pistol cracked. The intruder fell into the ravine with an agonizing scream.

Harrell grabbed the sputtering missile with his good right hand and shoved it toward the remaining Japanese. The blast killed the enemy and carried away Harrell's right hand. Harrell collapsed in the bottom of his hole.

At first light Carter returned, leading a team of stretcher-bearers back to his buddy. When they carried Harrell back the Japanese officer's saber lay next to him.

Harrell and Carter were nicknamed the "Two-Man Alamo" for their gallant stand. Carter received the Navy Cross for his efforts. Harrell, after months of hospitalization for his severe wounds, accepted his well-earned Medal of Honor from President Truman at the White House on October 5, 1945. The president looked grim as he draped the medal on the maimed marine whose arms both ended in bright steel hooks where his hands should have been. "All I can say, Sergeant," Truman said, "is that this medal is small enough tribute for what you have given for your country. America is most humble and grateful."

Harrell quickly overcame his handicap. He learned to light cigarettes, use a telephone, drive, take papers from files, and he even designed a special device that allowed him to fire a pistol; he could fire a rifle with no difficulty. He loved guns, shooting frequently at local ranges, and amassing a large collection of pistols and rifles.

After his discharge in 1946 he accepted a position with the VA. Harrell eventually became chief of the prosthetic appliance group, dealing with amputees, blinded, and deaf veterans. He married, fathering four children.

On August 9, 1964, as the result of an apparent love triangle, Harrell shot and killed a neighbor, the man's wife, then turned the M-1 on himself. Harrell's ten-year-old son found his father's lifeless body on the family front lawn after returning from a vacation in New York with his mother.

The value of Iwo Jima to the Americans became apparent on March 4, 1945. A B-29 bomber, the *Dinah-Mite*, running low on fuel after a bombing raid over Tokyo, made an emergency landing at Airfield No. 1. Within a few minutes a damaged fuel valve was repaired, and *Dinah-Mite* and her crew were safely on their way back to Saipan. By the time the war ended 2,250 additional distressed B-29s carrying 24,761 crewmen would land on Iwo.

By March 8, Iwo Jima's beaches teemed with sailors and marines, vehicles, and supplies. Though an occasional enemy artillery shell landed on the beach, it was now nearly a rear-echelon area. Up on the island's north end it was a completely different matter. On the front line the Japanese fought with an undiminished fury.

The remaining defenders, about four thousand men, had been squeezed into a few pockets along Iwo's rugged northern coast. Again, the numerous tunnels and caves gave the Japanese a tremendous advantage over the marine attackers. They had to be pried out, one at a time, by the marines.

On March 8, Company E, 2d Battalion, 27th Marines, 5th Marine Division, closed in on Kitano Point, Iwo's northernmost point. Only about three hundred yards separated the company from the sea, but every crag and crevice along the way contained fanatical Japanese. Company E's attack stalled.

One of its platoon leaders, 1st Lt. Jack Lummus, sprinted ahead. He knew all about gaining yardage. The Ennis, Texas, twenty-nine-year-old had been an all-American at Baylor University and an end for the New York Giants before joining the marines. When the concussion of a grenade knocked him down, he simply got up and charged the enemy position whence came the grenade. He killed the occupants with a single sweep of his tommy gun. Then a second grenade knocked him down, its shrapnel tearing a hole in his shoulder. Again he got up, rushed a second enemy strong point, and killed its occupants. He then motioned the company forward.

Lummus was twenty yards ahead of the surging marine line when he vanished from sight in the huge boom of an explosion. When the smoke cleared the marines could see Lummus. They thought he was standing in a shell hole. In reality the mine he'd stepped on had blown off both his legs. On the bloody stumps he urged his marines onward. "Keep coming. Goddammit! Don't stop! Keep coming." Several marines ran to his aid, tears streaking their dirt-caked faces. Lummus continued his shouting, "Keep moving! You can't stop now!"

The surgeons at the hospital could not save Lummus. All they could do was make his end a little easier. "I guess the New York Giants have lost a damn good end," he told one doctor. A short time later he died.

Near Airfield No. 1 on March 14, 1945, a ceremony was held to declare the capture of Iwo Jima from the Japanese. Many marines, ranking from private to general, later questioned the wisdom of this declaration. Several thousand Japanese still held out in three major pockets, one in the center of the island, and two near the north coast. Even Kuribayashi, deep in a cave near Kitano Point, questioned the premature announcement. He knew he was doomed, but still sent a message to his surviving troops exhorting them to resist as long as possible. The Japanese fervently carried out Kuribayashi's order. Six thousand additional

marine casualties were suffered before the volcanic island was
actually secure.

Elements of the 4th Marine Division worked to reduce one of
the hold-out pockets near Turkey Knob. Although the line companies had been drastically reduced—some companies contained less than twenty-five men and were commanded by
Pfcs.—the Japanese had to be wiped out.

FRANCIS J. PIERCE

It is more than a thousand miles in any direction from Earlville,
Iowa, to any salt water, and perhaps that is what attracted Frank
Pierce to the U.S. Navy. Growing up on a farm in northeast
Iowa made Pierce an avid hunter and a crack shot, but it also
produced a high level of monotony. He wanted to join the navy.
When he graduated from high school in June 1941 he was only
sixteen, so he had to wait six months before he could legally
enlist. That happened on his seventeenth birthday, December 7,
1941.

Several days later he was off to the Great Lakes Training Center for boot camp. Then he went to Portsmouth, Virginia, for
training as a hospital corpsman. From there he underwent combat infantry training with the marines at Camp Lejeune, North
Carolina, and Camp Pendleton, California.

Pierce's first taste of combat came at Roi and Namur Islands
in February 1944. No amount of training could have prepared
him for what he saw on the atolls: ripped-open chests, torn-off
limbs, gaping head wounds. Only nineteen years old, Pierce
saw sights that made older, more experienced men faint.

Though corpsmen are not supposed to carry weapons, Pierce
considered this foolish. It was too dangerous at the front to be
unarmed. Pierce carried a tommy gun slung over one shoulder.
His deadly effectiveness with the weapon earned him the nickname Angel with a Tommy Gun.

The invasions of Saipan and Tinian followed for Pierce and
the 4th Marine Division. Pierce spent most of his time at the
front lines, gathering the wounded for treatment at the rear. He
led a charmed life, surviving both islands. Then came Iwo Jima.

"Saipan and Tinian were strictly bush league compared with
Iwo," Pierce said. "That place was swarming with Japs, every
one of them dug in."

Pierce went ashore on February 19. For the next four weeks

he worked without letup. He made uncountable trips to the front lines to provide lifesaving aid to casualties. On these trips he made a mental map of enemy positions so he could plot the safest route from the front to the rear. On several occasions when Japanese infiltrators threatened his route, Pierce used his tommy gun to kill them.

By March 15, Pierce was one of the few original corpsmen still alive. His entire battalion contained only enough men to mount two understrength rifle companies. Just to the east of Airfield No. 2, they fought to wipe out the remaining enemy near Turkey Knob. The Japanese had no intention of surrendering; they fought to the death. Dozens of marine casualties littered the hard, rocky ground.

Pierce could find no safe way to evacuate the wounded. With one other corpsman, eight stretcher-bearers, and two badly wounded marines, he was caught in a vicious Japanese cross fire. To draw the enemy's fire from the bearers and the wounded, Pierce jumped into the open, spraying the enemy with his tommy gun. While he did this the bearers moved the casualties to a covered area.

As he worked on one of the casualties before moving on, an enemy sniper fired from close range, wounding the man again. Pierce stood up to provide a target for the sniper. He explained his action, "If I stood up, he'd be bound to make a motion. I was a good shot." Pierce's assessment of his ability was correct. The sniper moved, Pierce squeezed off a burst from his tommy gun, and the Japanese died.

The duel with the sniper used the last of Pierce's ammo. Determined to see his charges to safety, Pierce hoisted one of the casualties on his shoulder, carried him the final two hundred feet to safety, then returned for the remaining wounded marine.

By carefully marking a map Pierce had been able to pinpoint an especially pesky bunch of snipers. On March 16, Pierce led a patrol there. "I don't know if they found us or we found them. They were in a dugout covered with sand. It was very hard to spot. We were right on top of it when they opened fire. I remember tossing a firebomb into one of the openings, and somebody inside tossed it right back. It was a heck of a sensation."

The fight was short and sharp. As soon as the first marine fell wounded, Pierce reverted to his role of lifesaver. He crouched over the man. That's when the enemy finally got him. A rifle bullet tore a chunk of flesh from his shoulder. Shrapnel from a Japanese grenade peppered his back and left leg. Another corpsman moved to his aid. Pierce waved him back. His treatment could wait until the original casualty received aid. Only then did the plucky corpsman allow himself to be evacuated.

Discharged from the navy on December 1, 1945, Pierce returned to Earlville wearing a Navy Cross and Silver Star for his heroism on Iwo Jima. He remained in Iowa only a short time before moving to Grand Rapids, Michigan, where he hoped to meet a girl he'd been corresponding with for three years and get on the local police force. He succeeded on both counts. Within a year he'd married the girl and been appointed a patrolman.

In a postwar review of all Navy Cross awards a board of officers decided Pierce's feats on Iwo warranted a Medal of Honor. His record demonstrated a consistently remarkable performance under fire, though no one incident seemed to warrant the high honor.

His brother in Earlville advised him of the award. "I didn't believe him," Pierce said. "I had never heard of such a thing, and the war had been over for nearly three years. When I got the letter, I still didn't believe it until I read it two or three times."

Pierce donned his uniform one more time to visit the White House on June 25, 1948. Back in Grand Rapids the city threw a formal civic reception in his honor. Then he returned to his job as a patrolman.

During the years he was on the Grand Rapids police department Pierce frequently demonstrated the same fearlessness he'd shown in the Pacific. In 1955 he walked into an apartment and kicked a loaded big-game rifle from the hands of a man causing a disturbance. During a 1967 race riot he waded into a mob of rioters armed with a machine gun and sent them fleeing.

By the time he retired in 1982, Pierce had risen to the rank of deputy chief. He planned to enjoy his wife and four children. Four years later, on December 21, 1986, Pierce died after a long bout with cancer.

Fighting had diminished enough by March 19 to pull the survivors of the 4th Marine Division off Iwo Jima. They boarded transports for the long trip back to Hawaii. The division had suffered a casualty rate close to thirty percent. But that didn't tell the whole story. The average line company had a sixty-percent casualty rate.

Most of the 5th Marine Division departed the hell of Iwo Jima by March 27. Only the 3d Marine Division remained to fight the remaining Japanese. An estimated three thousand Japanese remained alive on the island. General Kuribayashi is believed to have died late in the battle, but his body was never recovered.

In the predawn darkness of March 26, several hundred drunken Japanese launched a local banzai charge against the 5th Pioneer Battalion, bivouacked near Airfield No. 2. About three hundred marines, army personnel, and air force supply troops slept peacefully in tents. After all, the island had been secured.

Moving grimly and silently, the Japanese struck from three directions. Within seconds, they were everywhere, slashing into tents, hacking at sleeping forms. First Lt. Harry L. Martin, from Bucyrus, Ohio, quickly organized a skirmish line from his black marines. In the dim light they coolly beat back one charge, then a second and a third. Armed only with a pistol, the thirty-four-year-old reservist went to the aid of two of his marines who lay wounded in a foxhole. He fended off a group of Japanese who tried to stop him, located the marines, then guided them to safety. Martin sustained two serious wounds a short time later, but attacked four Japanese manning a machine gun, killing all four with his pistol. Martin next rallied a small group of marines and led them in a countercharge. They had scattered the enemy when an enemy grenade exploded, killing Martin.

It was noon that day before the last of the Japanese attackers were hunted down and killed. Lieutenant Martin's actions brought him a posthumous Medal of Honor, the last of twenty-seven earned on Iwo Jima.

The capture of Iwo Jima cost the Americans 6,821 killed or missing and 19,217 wounded. Only 1,083 of the enemy survived the battle.

18

* * *

Defeat of Germany

As January 1945 passed into February, the grand Allied strategy that had been temporarily postponed by the Battle of the Bulge was once again put into motion. All along Germany's border, from Holland to Switzerland, the Allied armies stood poised for action. At the proper time they would smash into the West Wall, the steel and concrete barrier the Germans had built to seal their western border, cross the natural barrier of the Rhine River, then pour into the heartland of Adolph Hitler's Germany.

Rather than one massive movement into Germany Eisenhower's plan called for a staggered attack. The initial phase would belong to Montgomery's 21st Army Group, facing Germany on the northern end of the front. Beginning on February 8, two of his armies—the Canadian First and British Second—would drive southeastward from the Nijmegen area into the Rhine River lowlands.

Two days later General Simpson's U.S. Ninth Army would thrust northeastward from the Maastricht area of Holland to link up with the Canadians. The major obstacle in their path was the Roer River. Seven dams upstream, still in the hands of the Germans, could be opened, flooding the Roer River Valley and delaying Simpson's advance.

To capture the dams, the U.S. First Army of General Bradley's 12th Army Group would be used. Other than these forces, Bradley's army group would be held in check until Montgomery reached the Rhine. Then Bradley would go on the offensive, driving eastward from Belgium.

At the southern end of the front General Devers would remain on the defensive until Bradley reached the Rhine. Then Devers would hurl his Seventh Army into the sprawling region of the Palatinate.

Before the U.S. First Army, commanded by Lt. Gen. Courtney Hodges, could move on the Roer River dams, it had to finish its current operation. Elements of the First Army were still fighting to restore its front to its pre-Bulge position. Once the final salient was eliminated, priority would shift to Montgomery in the north. Bradley's armies would then begin preparation for their own drive to the Rhine.

Hodges put five divisions on the line to cross into Germany and attack the West Wall. In subfreezing temperatures, with the snow measuring at least two feet deep, the GIs stepped off on January 28. Resistance proved lighter than expected. In just four days the First Army advanced sixteen kilometers to the last high ground before the West Wall. A penetration of the Wall was made, but no breakthrough. Enemy resistance stiffened as the GIs moved farther eastward. The nearly unbearable weather made resupply almost impossible. Only the individual bravery of the soldiers on the front lines made the advance possible.

EDWARD A. BENNETT

One of the First Army units attacking the West Wall was the 90th Infantry Division of the VIII Corps. Pushing east directly through the Schnee Eifel, the 90th ran into heavy opposition as they neared the German village of Heckhuscheid at dark on February 1, 1945. Vicious machine-gun fire from a house sitting by itself on the outskirts of the town pinned down the men of Company B, 358th Infantry Regiment. GIs fell everywhere, some dying quietly, others screaming shrilly in pain.

The company commander called for artillery, but all it did was set fire to several other nearby houses. The light from their flames illuminated the soldiers seeking cover on the snow-covered ground. One of them began stealthily working his way to the edge of the open field.

It was Pfc. Edward A. Bennett. Born February 11, 1920, in Middleport, Ohio, Bennett's job at the Marietta Shipbuilding yard in Point Pleasant, West Virginia, had earned him an exemption from the draft. Until January 1944. Then the military's desperate need for manpower eliminated all but the most critical exemptions. Bennett reported for induction that month.

Infantry training followed at Fort McClellan, Alabama. When

he had completed his advanced training, Bennett shipped out for England in the fall of 1944. Once in England Bennett shuffled his way through the replacement pipeline. When he made it to France he was assigned to Company B, 358th Infantry. His regiment had fought across Normandy and into the Saar area, earning a reputation as a tough, dependable outfit.

Bennett joined Company B just before it moved into Belgium. None of his training had prepared him for the hardships of combat in the frozen land of central Europe. There were times when he couldn't remember not being cold. The Allies' rapid advance across France had outstripped the ability of the supply system to keep up. Not until late January did Bennett receive adequate winter clothing.

When the 90th Division pushed off, Bennett fought at the vanguard of the advance. Through the thickly wooded hills, cut by numerous water courses, he served as scout and point man for Company B. As they first approached Heckhuscheid there was no enemy fire. The GIs thought the town was unoccupied. They moved across an open field, silently hoping there were no Germans around. Those hopes were shattered when the sharp bark of enemy machine guns cracked across the still night.

Bennett hit the ground on the right flank of his company. After the artillery barrage he saw an opportunity to move through an adjacent wooded area to the house's blind side. He started crawling to the woods. The German gunners spotted him in the light of the burning buildings. Tracer rounds ripped overhead, missing him by mere inches. They followed him into the woods.

Once in the woods Bennett dodged from tree to tree in a circuitous route that brought him to the rear of the German-occupied farmhouse. A lone sentry guarded the rear door. His attention was focused on the firefight raging to the front of the building. He squatted there, shooting his rifle at the dark humps of Americans lying in the snow. Bennett pulled his trench knife from his scabbard.

The sound of the firing concealed the crunch of Bennett's boats on the snow. Just as he came up on the German the man turned, suddenly aware of the danger behind him. Bennett plunged his knife deep into the sentry's chest. Then Bennett turned his attention to the Germans within the house.

He raised his mud-encrusted boot, slammed it into the door, and stormed into the house. Seven Germans manned the first floor room. Bennett burst among them, his M-1 tucked under his arm. He fired, pulling the trigger as fast as he could. Three Germans flopped against the wall.

A fourth rushed at Bennett. The gutsy infantryman swung his M-1 like a baseball bat. The thunk of wood on bone filled the room. The force of the blow shattered the M-1's stock.

Three more Germans crouched in the corner. Bennett pulled a .45-caliber pistol from his hip. He emptied the eight-round clip into them. They sprawled in grotesque death positions.

As soon as Bennett's company realized the German threat had been eliminated, they swept into the town. By midnight Heckhusheid was firmly in American hands. Bennett's actions had allowed the 358th Infantry to continue its advance into Germany.

Bennett fought with the 90th Infantry Division across Germany and into Czechoslovakia. It was advancing into Prague's suburbs when the war ended. Bennett's continued daring earned him a Silver Star, Bronze Star, and four Purple Hearts. Because he had arrived late in the European theater, Bennett did not have enough points to return home at the end of the war. He stayed on occupation duty in Czechoslovakia. Then came word of the Medal of Honor. He flew home in early October 1945. On October 12, he received his award from President Truman. Bennett took his discharge a short time later. He returned to Middleport where he went to work for the VA. In September 1946 he reenlisted in the army. He spent a year on recruiting duty in Cincinnati, then transferred to Fort Ord, California, where he became an instructor at the army's leadership school.

After the Korean War began Bennett went there where he served as an advisor to several Republic of Korea divisions. He saw considerable action, performed with outstanding courage, and received a battlefield commission in June 1951.

Following his service in Korea, Bennett had routine assignments until October 1962 when a heart attack ended his military career. He moved his family to California where he went to work as a security advisor to a large corporation. He died on May 2, 1983.

The opening movement of the British and Canadian armies from Holland into northwest Germany began as scheduled on February 8. The crossing of the Roer River by General Simpson's Ninth Army on the British southern flank, due to begin two days later, was postponed because of problems on its southern flank.

Part of General Hodges's First Army was to jump off toward the Roer River dams on February 5. Resistance proved much more severe than anticipated. Not until the early morning hours of February 10 did they reach the largest of the seven dams, Schwammenauel. They found the Germans had damaged beyond repair the valves controlling the spillways. There was no way to stop the flood of water. In a few hours the Roer changed from a placid stream ninety feet wide, to a roaring river more than a mile across.

Simpson's movement adjacent to the British would have to wait for the flood waters to recede. That didn't happen until February 23. In the meantime, the British XXX Corps made remarkable progress. By February 23 they had breached the West Wall.

That same day Simpson's men finally began crossing the Roer. In spite of a rapid current that swamped many of the assault boats, by nightfall two and a half divisions were across the river. Within two days the Ninth Army held a salient six miles wide and three and a half miles deep. To the south, Hodges's First Army continued across the Roer, advancing on Cologne.

The linkup between the British and Americans of the Ninth Army occurred on March 2. Together they pushed east, headed for the Rhine. The Germans fought a desperate rear-guard action, buying time for the bulk of the Nazis to flee to the Rhine's east bank. Once the majority of the Germans had crossed the Rhine, their commander gave orders to destroy the nine bridges spanning the Rhine in that area. On the morning of March 10 the last two bridges, at Wesel, went up in a roar. The British came to a halt.

In Simpson's sector several of his divisions reached the Rhine as early as March 2. Resistance was almost nonexistent in some areas. At Neuss, on the Rhine's west bank across from Dusseldorf, Ninth Army GIs raced for the vital bridges. They came agonizingly close to winning their race. On one bridge Sherman tanks were clanking their way across when the Germans blew it. Simpson's army also halted before the Rhine.

Farther south General Hodges captured Cologne on March 6. Since early February, when his divisions had failed to capture the Roer dams, Hodges had operated in Simpson's shadow. But once the Ninth Army linked up with the British, Hodges was free to begin his own drive to the Rhine. The fall of Cologne was overshadowed by an event farther south in the First Army's zone of operation.

On March 7 a tank-infantry task force of the 9th Armored Division headed for the Rhine where the Ahr River flowed into it. Nestled at the junction was the small resort town of Remagen. Much to the Americans' surprise, the bridge at Remagen stood undamaged. Though the Nazis tried to blow the bridge they failed. By that afternoon thousands of GIs had poured across the structure.

Since Montgomery's forces were still two weeks away from crossing the Rhine in their sector, the offensive initiative passed to Bradley's troops. To further exploit the success at Remagen, Bradley proposed a coordinated attack into the Palatinate area by General Patton's Third Army and the Seventh Army of General Devers's 6th Army Group.

Patton's Third Army had officially been assigned a secondary role of "aggressive defense" in his section of the front along the Luxembourg border. Patton, as usual, interpreted his orders as liberally as possible. He unleashed his forces into the West Wall, capturing Prum and Bitburg. On March 1 they captured Trier. By March 7 they held Coblenz, where the Moselle River flowed into the Rhine. The next day Patton's forces linked up with the First Army, tightening the noose around the Germans caught in the Eifel.

Bradley now proposed that Patton, from his position along the Palatinate's northwest border, drive south and east. At the same time, from his positions along the area's southern boundary, Gen. Alexander Patch would send his Seventh Army north and east into the zone between the Saar River and the Rhine. Eisenhower approved Bradley's plan.

The giant squeeze-play began on March 13, 1945. The toughest resistance for Patch's army came on its extreme right flank along the upper Rhine. Where the Moder River flowed through the Haguenau Forest and the town of the same name, the Germans bitterly opposed the advance of the 36th Infantry Division.

MORRIS E. CRAIN

Company E of the 36th Division's 141st Infantry fought a desperate battle to enlarge the bridgehead across the Moder. Leading one of the platoons in the company was T. Sgt. Morris Crain of Bandana, Kentucky. Though only twenty years old Crain, who preferred to be known by his middle name of Eugene, had already been in the army for nearly three years. He enlisted on April 7, 1942, six months after his seventeenth birthday. His parents opposed the idea of so young a man entering the military, but Crain's patriotic arguments finally convinced them to sign the necessary papers.

Six months of infantry training followed Crain's enlistment. He then returned home for a seven-day furlough. While there he married his girlfriend. Then, in the summer of 1943, it was off to Italy and the 36th Infantry Division.

Crain saw considerable action in Italy at Salerno and in the battles up the Italian boot. While in a rest area in Italy in March 1944 Crain received word of the birth of his daughter, Morris Fay. From then on he fought the war with one purpose: to return home and see his baby. He read each letter from his wife over and over, memorizing the stories of his daughter's growth. He filled his letters with his plans for her future.

But first the war had to be won. After the landings in southern France Crain was wounded in the fighting around Montelimar. By the time he rejoined his company it was in the Vosges Mountains. A short time later he received a promotion to technical sergeant and took command of a platoon.

After crossing the Moder River on the morning of March 13, Crain spearheaded his platoon in taking its objective, a road junction just past the town of Haguenau. During its advance, the platoon killed ten Germans and captured twelve more. Shortly after his platoon had dug in, the Germans unleashed a furious barrage of artillery shells and mortars. Even during the heaviest firing Crain moved among his platoon, offering words of encouragement and urging them to stand firm.

As night fell the Germans increased their effort to throw the Americans out of Haguenau. Tiger tanks supported by German infantrymen moved on the town. In front of them, the artillery built in intensity. It finally got to be too much. Crain ordered his men to pull back into houses on the edge of town.

Using *panzerfausts* and cannon fire, the Germans systematically flushed the platoon from the buildings. Some of the squads pulled back.

Another platoon arrived to support Crain's. He braved the enemy fire to put them into position. Then he got word that five of his men were trapped in a house surrounded by Germans. Even though bursts from the enemy tanks' 88-mm cannons crashed into buildings around him. Crain went to their rescue.

Crain fought his way through the Nazi infantrymen to the rear of the house. From the back room the five GIs were holding off six Germans in the front room. Outside, less than fifty yards away, a Tiger tank methodically pumped one shell after another into the brick house.

Crain instantly took charge. "Get out of here," he ordered the men. "I'll cover you." Reluctantly, they did so.

With shells crashing through the walls and bullets hitting all around him, Crain turned to face the Germans. He killed three of the enemy before the house collapsed on him. He would never see his daughter.

In a solemn ceremony in Detroit, Michigan, Crain's widow's home, on March 7, 1946, two year-old Morris Fay accepted her father's posthumous Medal of Honor. A picture of the cute youngster, with the medal around her neck, ran in papers around the country.

Though the Germans continued to cling stubbornly to their defensive positions in front of Patch's Seventh Army, the enemy in front of Patton's men proved less formidable. The 80th Infantry Division fought its way into the Hunsruck Mountains, east of Trier. Despite forbidding terrain, muddy roads, and cold, rainy weather the 80th made three kilometers the first day.

Second Lt. Harry J. Michael of Milford, Indiana, led one of the rifle platoons in Company L, 318th Infantry, 80th Division. On March 13, before first light, he captured two enemy machine guns in a daring charge up a thickly wooded hillside. An hour later he led his platoon in an attack that netted twenty-five prisoners and three artillery pieces. Later that day he captured thirteen more prisoners during two lone reconnaissances into the forests. The next morning, while hunting snipers, Michael, who'd been drafted out of Purdue University in March 1943, was shot and killed. He'd been overseas less than one month.

By the evening of March 15 the Hunsruck Mountains had

been cleared, opening the way for Patton's armored units. Three
armored divisions, the 4th, 10th, and 11th, crossed the Moselle
River that day and the next. Their objective was the Nahe River,
twenty miles south of the Hunsruck Mountains. All three divisions made rapid advances. The 11th Armored Division made
the thirty-four kilometers to Kirn on the north side of the Nahe
in less than one day. On March 19, it headed south toward
Kaiserlautern.

In his inimitable style Patton demanded the most of his
men as they stormed into Germany. He got it. On the night
of March 22 six battalions of his 5th Infantry Division snuck
across the Rhine River ten miles south of Mainz, Germany.
Patton was ecstatic. Not only had he crossed the last natural
obstacle in his path, he'd done it before Montgomery had.

In the north, Montgomery was not set to begin his crossing
of the Rhine until 9:00 P.M. March 23. According to his plan,
the British Second Army would cross the Rhine north of Wesel.
Simpson's Ninth Army would make its crossing south of the
city. At the appointed hour British bombers pounded Wesel,
while British and American troops began their respective river
crossings. The Germans put up a fight, but there were simply
too many Allied soldiers coming at them.

By dawn on March 24 four divisions, two British and two
American, were solidly on the east side of the Rhine. Then,
beginning at 10:00 A.M., Montgomery unveiled his grand finale.
Sixteen hundred troop-carrying planes, followed by 650 tug
planes, each pulling two gliders, appeared in the western sky.
Under the watchful eye of Montgomery and his special guest,
Prime Minister Churchill, twenty-one thousand airborne troops
of the British 6th and the U.S. 17th Airborne Divisions began
landing north of Wesel.

The airborne troops encountered varying degrees of resistance. Some of the defenders quickly fled or surrendered.
Others fought on viciously with mortars, machine guns, and
sniper fire. Company G, 507th Parachute Infantry, came down
near Fluren, a suburb of Wesel. Ten men landed near Pvt.
George J. Peters, the platoon radio operator. While the other
paratroopers struggled to free themselves from their parachute harness, a German machine gun just seventy-five yards
away tore into them. Several of the airborne soldiers fell dead.

Knowing that the enemy automatic weapon would have to be

knocked out before the men could escape, Peters, experienced his first minutes of combat, charged headlong at the weapon. Knocked down by a burst of fire halfway to his objective, Peters arose and boldly started toward the gun once more. Again the enemy gun knocked him down. Unable to walk, Peters crawled toward the Nazi position. He kept going until he was close enough to toss grenades. His aim proved true. Two enemy gunners died in the blast. The protecting infantrymen retreated. Peters, from Cranston, Rhode Island, died knowing his actions allowed his comrades to complete their mission.

By nightfall the Allied troops had captured all their objectives and more. Both British and American troops had reached the Issel River, six miles east of the Rhine. Mopping-up operations in Wesel would continue for a few more days, but already combat engineers were constructing bridges across the river. Montgomery stood poised to head for Berlin.

But Berlin had ceased to be the major objective. As early as March 19, Eisenhower had assessed his army's next move. Once the Ruhr industrial area was surrounded the next major obstacle would be the Elbe River. From there, Berlin lay just fifty miles east across lowlands laced with lakes, rivers, canals, and tens of thousands of fanatical Nazis. When General Bradley offered an estimate of a hundred thousand casualties in taking Berlin, Eisenhower made up his mind. On March 28 he advised Premier Josef Stalin that he would halt his forces generally along the Elbe River. From there east, including Berlin, would belong to the Russians.

It was a momentous decision that would have political ramifications far into the future. The British were outraged at Eisenhower's unilateral decision. They appealed to General Marshall, but he backed his ground commander. Churchill even carried the appeal to President Roosevelt, but Roosevelt also declined to intervene. Eisenhower told his critics, "Berlin is nothing but a geographical location. They are not proper objectives in the war. The enemy is. That's what you go after."

With that decision made, Bradley turned his attention to the Ruhr. Though the Ruhr industrial area had lost much of its economic importance by the end of March 1945, the opportunity to trap the more than three hundred thousand German combat troops emplaced there excited Bradley. He planned to have the Ninth Army, on the north of the Ruhr, swing southeast once east of the region. Hodges's First Army, on the south, would swing northeast. The linkup was planned for the area near Paderborn, ninety miles east of Wesel.

The main force from the First Army would be spearheaded by Maj. Gen. J. Lawton ("Lightning Joe") Collins's VII Corps. He sent his 3d Armored Division racing for Paderborn. When they stalled against fervent resistance, Hodges responded by unleashing Maj. Gen. James A. Van Fleet's III Corps to assist Collins. The 7th Armored Division quickly took over the lead. It made good progress until it neared the German town of Ale-mart on April 5, 1945. An SS unit threw out a curtain of fire that forced the lead tanks off the road. Several companies of the 48th Armored Infantry Battalion tried to outflank the little town. Company C advanced down a small, open valley overlooked on either side by wooded slopes. The thick woods hid several companies of German riflemen reinforced by automatic weapons. Their murderous fire caught the Americans by surprise. In the confusion that followed the order to pull back, seventeen casualties were left behind. They lay three hundred yards away, along a path covered by the enemy's machine guns. It seemed like sure death to go after them.

THOMAS J. KELLY

One man weighed the risks involved against the lives of the seventeen Americans and decided he could not abandon them. Cpl. Thomas J. Kelly, a medic, approached his platoon leader. "If you give men enough covering fire," Kelly told the lieutenant, "I'll go out and get those guys."

The officer looked at Kelly as if he were crazy. "It's suicide to go out there," he warned. "Wait 'til I get some artillery laid down."

Kelly didn't want to wait. He felt that some of the wounded might die if he delayed too long. "Okay," the lieutenant offered, "we'll give you all the cover we can."

Kelly, born September 8, 1923, in Brooklyn, New York, and a veteran of the fighting in the Battle of the Bulge, began inching his way toward the group of wounded. By making skillful use of the available cover he was able to reach the depression sheltering the men without being hit by the enemy machine-gun fire.

Kelly took quick stock of the casualties. Ten of them were so badly wounded they couldn't walk. The others were ambulatory but suffering varying degrees of injuries. Kelly ordered those men to provide a base of fire while he treated the others.

After he was finished patching everyone up as best he could with the available medical supplies, Kelly made preparations to evacuate the most seriously wounded man. "I'll be back," he promised the others.

In an incredible display of superhuman strength Kelly, a husky man standing six feet, one inch, began the herculean task of dragging the casualty the full three hundred yards to safety. Unable to stand erect because of the enemy fire, Kelly crawled to the rear pulling the casualty behind him. When he reached the platoon he turned the man over to other medics.

Then he went back for the remaining men.

Kelly made ten trips across the bullet-swept valley, each time pulling a casualty with him. After his third or fourth trip two riflemen volunteered to help. Enemy fire cut them down before they were halfway back to the front. Kelly bound their wounds, then carried them one-by-one to the rear.

After he'd pulled the ten men to the rear, he returned for the remaining seven. They were just about out of ammo by the time Kelly got back. "We can make it out of here," he told them. "Just follow me. Stay low and keep spread out."

With him in the lead, sometimes crawling on all fours, sometimes on his belly, Kelly brought these seven men back to the platoon. By this time, the sheer physical effort of his heroic actions had nearly exhausted Kelly. Even though he was close to collapse due to fatigue, the brave medic declined to leave the platoon until the attack had been resumed and the objective taken.

Just over a month later the war ended. Kelly spent several months on occupation duty, then rotated home. He received his Medal of Honor from President Truman at the White House on October 12, 1945. Kelly then enrolled in college, using the GI Bill to earn his law degree from Fordham University.

Kelly then went to work for the VA as a contact representative. He later became a veterans' representative for the Civil Service Commission, retiring in 1978. He married in 1949, fathering one son and two daughters. He died on October 2, 1988.

The actual linkup between the Ninth and First Armies came on April 2, about twenty-five miles west of Paderborn. The

Germans were trapped. The fighting in the Ruhr continued at a feverish pitch for three more weeks. Not until April 18 did resistance end. Germany's Army Group B, under Field Marshal Walther Model, had been destroyed. Over 317,000 Germans surrendered. The Americans also liberated 200,000 displaced persons from forced labor and rescued 5,600 Allied POWs.

With the collapse of the Ruhr the Allies continued their drive east. In Holland troops of the Canadian First Army pushed north toward Arnhem and northeast toward Wilhelmshaven, Germany. Below them the British Second Army headed east toward the Elbe and northeast toward the port cities of Bremen and Hamburg. The main bodies of the U.S. Ninth and First Army swept east toward the Elbe and its main tributary, the Mulde.

In the south, below the Ruhr, the U.S. Third Army slanted southeast toward Chemnitz, Germany, just twenty miles from the Czechoslovakian border. The two armies of General Devers's 6th Army Group pushed deeper into southern Germany. His Seventh Army attacked toward the Austrian border, while the French First Army drove south into the formidable Black Forest.

While Eisenhower's great army overwhelmed Germany another, all but forgotten, phase of the war also drew to a close.

Ever since the invasion of Normandy had overshadowed the fall of Rome, subsequent events in France and Germany had pushed the war in Italy into the background. The GIs of the Fifth Army lacked a sense of purpose. They knew the war would be won in Germany. Yet their war went on.

After the fall of Rome, Field Marshal Albert Kesselring continued his policy of slowing the Allies via a series of temporary defense lines. The first of these came eighty-five miles north of Rome. It held the Allies for ten days. Thirty miles farther north the Germans regrouped behind yet another line. They held for another ten days before pulling back again.

While orchestrating these delaying actions Kesselring had his engineers working frantically to finish the Gothic Line. In the rugged northern Apennines 155 miles north of Rome, the Gothic Line would halt the Allies before they broke out onto the flat plains of the Po River Valley. The Gothic Line, winding through the mountains, was a wide belt of antitank mine fields, barbed-wire entanglements, artillery, and machine-gun fortifications carved into the rocky mountain faces.

Kesselring hoped to delay the Allies long enough to trap them in the mountains during another winter. Though Gen. Mark W. Clark's veteran troops broke the Gothic Line south of Bologna in October 1944, victory still eluded them. The Germans fought bitterly to retain their grip on their mountain positions. Clark's last push ended on October 22, just ten miles short of the Po Valley. Unable to maintain the momentum due to foul weather and vicious German counterattacks, the Fifth Army was doomed to spend another winter in the freezing mountains of Italy. The Allies would undertake no more offensive operations until the spring.

When Clark renewed his drive northward in early April 1945 one of the units he had on the line was the legendary 442d Regimental Combat Team. Organized in February 1943 at Camp Shelby, Mississippi, the 442d was composed of Japanese-Americans.

Despite the fact that their government had forcibly removed them from their homes and interned them in isolated camps, these American citizens were eager to prove their loyalty and courage. When the U.S. Army sought volunteers for a Japanese-American combat unit they were overwhelmed with volunteers.

After training in Mississippi, where they were treated to more racial inequities, the 442d went to Italy. Arriving in time to participate in the drive north of Rome, the GIs of the 442d quickly developed a well-earned reputation as an aggressive, able unit. Their regimental slogan, "Go for Broke," said it all.

In October 1944 the regiment transferred to France. There they fought in the Vosges Mountains as part of the 36th Infantry Division. When a seasoned outfit was needed to anchor Clark's offensive line along the west coast of Italy, he requested the 442d. They arrived back in Italy on March 25, 1945. On April 5, they launched an attack toward Massa.

SADAO S. MUNEMORI

He was born in Los Angeles, California, to parents who had emigrated from Japan to begin a new life in the United States. From the time he was old enough to understand, Sadao Munemori's parents praised the freedoms of their adopted country. Munemori grew up loving everything about America. He excelled at sports, loved baseball, ate hamburgers and hot dogs, and attended trade school to learn the art of auto mechanics.

When his father died in 1940, Munemori took over as head of the household, helping to support his two sisters and brothers.

After the attack on Pearl Harbor Munemori tried to enlist but was rejected because of his ancestry. Then came internment in the relocation camp at Manzinar, California. His family lost everything they had. Life in the barracks of Manzinar was austere and boring. The call for volunteers brought a quick response from Munemori.

Munemori survived the savage combat in Italy and France. On his first day back on the line in Italy on April 5, his unit, Company A, 100th Infantry Battalion, was assigned to take a key hill near Seravazza. Artillery pounded the German-held hill for ten minutes. Then Company A raced uphill, trying to reach the top before the Nazis could recover.

The enemy defenses were well planned. From a series of trenches they could cover all approaches. The German fire started. In the predawn darkness it wasn't very accurate, but it was backed up by grenades. Their explosions drove the Americans to cover.

A grenade fragment felled Munemori's squad leader. He took over, taking the squad through a mine field to within thirty yards of the first German trench. A heavy burst of machine-gun fire sent the GIs scurrying for cover in shell holes.

Munemori collected six grenades from his squad members. He then crawled forward alone. When he was fifteen yards from the gun he tossed his missiles. They landed true. With the explosions the gun fell silent. Munemori's squad started moving again.

A second machine gun opened up on them. Again the squad sought cover. Munemori went after his enemy position as before. His grenades knocked out this gun, too. He crawled back to a shell hole occupied by two of his men.

Just as he crawled over the edge of the crater, a German grenade bounced off his helmet and rolled to the bottom of the hole. Without hesitation Munemori vaulted forward, landing right on the grenade. The subsequent explosion killed him, but he saved the lives of his two men.

Munemori's frail mother accepted her son's Medal of Honor during a quiet ceremony on March 7, 1946. With his award the 442d Regiment became one of the most decorated regiments of World War II. Besides Munemori's Medal of Honor, the Nisei earned forty-seven DSCs, 354 Silver Stars, and more than 3,600 Purple Hearts. No one could ever again question their loyalty or courage.

Another unusual unit used during the last stages of the Italian campaign was the 10th Mountain Division. Composed strictly of volunteers, the 10th was recruited from among ski instructors, cross-country racers, forest rangers, fire jumpers, and winter-sports enthusiasts. The division also had a good share of mountain climbers, lumbermen, ranchers, and farmers from the Rocky Mountain states.

Trained to fight conventionally, as well as on skis, the 10th arrived in Italy in January 1945. In mid-February they took several peaks southwest of Bologna in a night operation that required an eight-hundred-man battalion to move by ropes and pitons up an ice-glazed cliff on three-thousand-foot Riva Ridge. Later the mountain troops took the heights of Monte della Torraccia and Monte Belvedere, setting the stage for the movement into the Po Valley. After these operations the 10th waited eight weeks for the main offensive to begin.

It started on April 14, 1945. Near Castel d'Aiano that day Company G, 85th Mountain Infantry Regiment, found itself pinned down by heavy mortar, artillery, and small-arms fire. Pfc. John D. Magrath rushed headlong into enemy fire, killing three Germans and capturing an enemy machine gun. Using his automatic weapon, Magrath, of Norwalk, Connecticut, wiped out two more enemy machine-gun nests and killed at least eight more Germans. Once Magrath had cleared a path through the enemy defenses, his company took its objective. Later that day, an exploding German artillery shell killed him.

On April 21, the U.S. Fifth Army on the western half of Italy and the British Eighth Army on Italy's east coast linked up north of Bologna. The Germans either fled northward or surrendered in droves. The Allies then crossed the Po River and, with the help of local partisans, easily took Milan, Turin, and Verona. Allied armored units raced to the Austrian and French borders to prevent German units from making their escape that way.

The campaign for victory in Italy, a grueling, twenty-month affair, was nearly at an end.

* * *

In Germany, the sweep to the Elbe River continued nearly unabated. There were pockets of resistance, but the determined GIs overcame them as rapidly as possible. They had only one goal in mind: Berlin. Through the Harz Mountains, Hameln, and dozens of not-so-famous German towns, the GIs rushed forward as fast as their vehicles could carry them.

Shortly after 8:00 P.M. on April 11, 1945, the Ninth Army's 2d Armored Division reached the Elbe River after a one-day push measuring seventy-three miles. Over the next forty-eight hours other American units drew up on the river's west bank. The Germans had destroyed all the river's bridges, so the GIs paused to regroup while preparations for the crossing continued.

Meanwhile, in a bunker deep beneath Berlin, Adolf Hitler reacted with glee to the news of President Roosevelt's death on April 12, 1945. He saw it as a sign his Nazi forces would prevail. He even thought his army might join with the British and Americans and turn east against the Russians. It was just one more of Hitler's delusions.

Not until April 15, 1945, did Eisenhower's decision concerning Berlin become known to his troops. Bradley advised General Simpson that day that he was to hold tight on the Elbe. Simpson was stunned. So were his division commanders when word filtered down to them. The disappointment was obvious everywhere. There was nothing for these GIs to do but sit tight and wait for the Russians to take Berlin and the war to end.

In the south the last major obstacle in front of General Devers's 6th Army Group was the city of Nuremburg. It was here that Hitler had held his immense prewar Nazi rallies. Devers knew the city would be defended to the bitter end.

His XV Corps closed in on the city on April 15. On Nuremburg's southside the 14th Armored and 45th Infantry Divisions took up blocking positions to prevent the city's defenders from escaping or being reinforced. The 3d Infantry Division stood poised to attack from the north; the 42d Infantry Division waited in the city's western suburbs. On April 16 these units began pushing toward the inner city, squeezing the defenders into an ever-smaller perimeter.

The Germans put up a fanatical resistance. Two divisions, the 2d Mountain and 17th SS Panzer Grenadier, provided most of the wallop. Some guardsmen, local police, and others all joined in the struggle for Nuremburg. The GIs were forced to take the city block by rubble-filled block in the worst kind of house-to-house fighting.

MICHAEL J. DALY

Combat heroism was no stranger to the Daly family of Fairfield, Connecticut. Paul G. Daly, an attorney with an army reserve commission, earned a DSC near Soissons, France, between July 19 and 22, 1918. After the war he returned to his successful New York City law practice. During World War II he volunteered for active duty and ended up fighting on Guadalcanal and in southern France. As a regimental commander fighting in the Vosges Mountains he was severely wounded and evacuated back to the States.

At about the same time one of his two sons, Michael J. Daly, was recovering from wounds he'd received fighting with the 1st Infantry Division near Aachen, Germany. Born September 15, 1924, young Daly entered West Point with the class of 1946. After his plebe year, though, he resigned to enlist in the infantry as a private.

Daly was sent to England after his training. The army pipeline funneled him to the 1st Infantry Division as a replacement for one of the thousands of casualties the Big Red One suffered on D day. Daly earned the first of two Silver Stars fighting across France.

When he was released from the hospital in England, Daly was reassigned to Company A, 1st Battalion, 15th Infantry Regiment, 3d Infantry Division. The division was heavily engaged in the reduction of the Colmar Pocket when Daly arrived. He quickly earned a second Silver Star for gallantry in action and a battlefield commission.

When the 3d Division bore down on Nuremburg Daly, though only twenty years old, was leading Company A. Unmindful of the tremendous volume of fire put out by the Nazi defenders, he led his weakened company into the city across the twisted wreckage of a railroad bridge. He was well ahead of his company, acting as a scout for the unit as they advanced along Bayreuthstrasse, the principal highway through the city. As 1st Sgt. Roy A Kurtz remembered, ''Lieutenant Daly had just begun to climb upon a low embankment along the railroad when a machine gun suddenly opened up on us from the other side of the

Leipziger Platz. We were caught out in the open by rapid traversing fire. Our men were killed left and right.''

Kurtz continued: ''Realizing that the whole company was threatened with annihilation, the lieutenant ran toward the machine gun, a conspicuous target as he crossed the tracks to a position in some rubble within fifty yards of the gun.''

Daly killed all the Germans with his carbine. He then pushed on alone until he sighted an enemy detachment entrenched in what remained of the house. S. Sgt. Ivan Ketron saw Daly signal for his men to halt, then move out alone. ''He was taking his life in his hands and we all knew it,'' Ketron said. ''I saw the lieutenant work his way forward to what was left of a house and open fire with his carbine.

''The Germans replied with a rain of automatic fire that sent up eddies of fine white dust from the building he was shooting from. Then *panzerfaust* rockets began to slam against the furthest wall of the building. Although all the Germans were concentrating on him, Daly kept firing his carbine until he'd killed all six of the Germans.''

After this strong point fell, Daly once again led his company forward. As he entered the grounds of a debris-filled public park two Nazi soldiers burst from cover. They set up a machine gun just ten yards from Daly. A nearby GI fell dead at the first burst. Daly seized the dead man's M-1 and killed both Germans.

In four separate firefights Daly killed fifteen German soldiers, destroyed three enemy machine-gun nests, and wiped out an entire German patrol. As his battalion executive officer said, ''His heroism during the battle for Nuremburg will never be forgotten by the officers and men who fought there.''

The day after his heroic adventure, Daly, again gallantly leading his company, took a burst of enemy fire full in the face. From the battlefield he went to army hospitals in England, then back to the States. Intensive treatment kept him under military doctors' care until September 1946.

Daly was able to attend the special White House ceremony on August 23, 1945, where President Truman placed the coveted medal around his neck. The next day Fairfield threw a rousing welcome for the young hero. He and his father, also recovering from his war injuries, rode together through town in a welcoming parade.

After the war Daly entered private business, forging a very successful career.

The battle for Nuremburg, the most German of all cities, raged in full fury until April 20, 1945. The brutal combat reduced the city to acres of rubbish. From Nuremburg the Seventh Army moved on to Munich and into Austria.

In the meantime, Russian troops broke through the German defensive barriers east of Berlin on April 23. Two weeks of savage fighting followed before the Nazi capital fell. On May 1, 1945, Adolf Hitler took his own life as Berlin burned around him. The next day the city surrendered. In Italy, German forces had surrendered on April 29, to be effective on May 2, 1945. With Hitler and his staunchest supporters out of the picture, Generaloberst Albert Jodl surrendered unconditionally to the Americans on May 7, 1945. VE-Day was officially held on May 8, 1945. Half of the world's most costly conflict was over. The conquest of Japan stood as the only obstacle to world peace.

19
★ ★ ★
The Last Battles

The last Pacific island on the long, deadly road to Japan was Okinawa. The largest of the Ryukyu chain situated just three hundred miles south of Japan, Okinawa was sixty times the size of Iwo Jima. Lying on a roughly southwest-northeast axis, Okinawa stretched sixty miles in length and averaged ten miles across, though its narrowest point measured but one and a half miles.

Like General Kuribayashi on Iwo, Okinawa's commander, Lt. Gen. Mitsuru Ushijima, knew he would be fighting a lost cause. Still, he proposed to make the capture of his island as expensive as possible for the Americans. His plan permitted the Americans to land virtually unopposed on the only feasible beaches, at Hagushi on Okinawa's west coast.

From there the invaders would move north and south. Okinawa's northern half was mostly mountainous, a jumble of pine-covered peaks and jungle-choked ravines from which defenders would presumably be hard to dislodge. But Ushijima planned only a light resistance in the north. He allocated only three thousand of his more than one hundred thousand troops to north Okinawa. A stronger defense over so vast a region would spread his forces too thin.

The Japanese would make their stand in the south. Their defensive line rested on the heights surrounding Shuri and Shuri Castle, in the center of Okinawa's southern third. The line's flanks swept back to the sea on either side, through a jungle of ridges to the chief city of Naha on the west, or left, through similar hills back to Yonabaru on the right. The bulk of the Japanese defenders occupied this area. Besides hundreds of

354

aboveground machine-gun emplacements, Ushijima also had his troops construct hundreds of fortified underground chambers. As on Iwo Jima, many of the chambers were connected by tunnels, some of which ran through the ridges from front to back.

To conquer Okinawa two corps of the Tenth Army under Lt. Gen. Simon Bolivar Buckner, Jr., were slated for the invasion. Maj. Gen. John Hodges's XXIV Corps consisted of the 7th, 27th, 77th, and 96th Infantry Divisions. All four army divisions had previously seen action in the Pacific.

The III Corps, led by marine Maj. Gen. Roy Geiger, had three marine divisions: the 1st, 2d, and the new 6th. The 1st and 2d Marine Divisions were blooded veterans of earlier brutal island campaigns. The 6th, though new in number, had seventy percent veterans in its ranks; only two of its battalions had not seen battle.

Altogether, 548,000 Americans of all services would have roles in the battle for Okinawa. Of these, 154,000 were in the combat divisions.

With the assault on Okinawa scheduled for April 1, the skies and seas around the island had to be swept clear of the enemy. To that end Vice Adm. Marc A. Mitscher took his Task Force 58 into Japanese home waters in mid-March 1945. Mitscher's targets were the forty-five airfields on the home island of Kyushu and the big naval bases at Kure and Kobe on the home island of Honshu. Mitscher was confident of his chances for success. Task Force 58 had sixteen fast carriers in four task groups, eight new battleships, two new cruisers, fourteen older cruisers, and more than two score destroyers to do battle with the Japanese.

Task Force 58 sent its first fighter sweeps to Kyushu at dawn on March 18. The pilots hit all forty-five airfields and claimed 387 enemy planes destroyed. That night Mitscher took Task Force 58 north for the strikes on Honshu.

The Japanese were not idle during these raids. Kamikazes by the score attacked the warships. Most were destroyed before they came within range of Task Force 58. Several did get through, though. On March 18 at least four carriers, the *Enterprise, Intrepid, Wasp*, and *Yorktown*, were hit by enemy bombs. Fortunately, they inflicted only relatively minor damage.

Shortly after 7:00 A.M., March 19, the carrier *Franklin* was in midst of launching her second strike of the day. Suddenly, from out of nowhere, a Japanese bomber flew directly over the *Franklin*'s bow and dropped two five-hundred-pound bombs. Both hit. They set off huge secondary explosions among the planes waiting to launch. Fires, fed by high-octane aviation fuel, quickly spread to racks of bombs and ammo. Violent explosions tore at the ship's insides, killing hundreds of men instantly and trapping hundreds more in smoke-filled corridors and rooms.

In the wardroom the forty-year-old Roman Catholic chaplain, Lt. Comdr. Joseph T. O'Callahan, a professor of mathematics at Holy Cross College prior to entering the navy in November 1940, had just finished breakfast when the first of the explosions slammed him to the deck. Shielding his head from the debris that filled the air, Chaplain O'Callahan made his way to his quarters where he grabbed the vials containing the holy oils needed to anoint the dying. He plopped his steel helmet on his head and headed to the flight deck "in search of my proper work."

The Jesuit priest found the deck littered with the bodies of the dead and dying. He immediately set to work tending to the physical needs of the wounded and the spiritual needs of the dying. At times he led fire-fighting crews to extinguish roaring flames. At other times he directed the efforts of the enlisted men in jettisoning overboard bombs, rockets, and ammo. He completely ignored the danger of the pyrotechnics filling the air to tend to the wounded. His coolness in a time of near disaster was instrumental in calming the crew. O'Callahan thus became the first priest to earn the Medal of Honor. He died on March 18, 1964.

In the *Franklin*'s main mess hall on the third deck Lt. (jg) Donald A. Gary found himself trapped with 288 men. A member of the navy since 1919, Gary had only been commissioned on November 1, 1943. As panic started to grip the apparently doomed seamen, Gary decided to find a way out. Alone, he found an escape path through dark, debris-filled corridors. Three times in the next five hours he returned through the thick, acrid smoke to lead groups of sailors to safety. Under his guidance all 288 men made it to safety. He then directed fire-fighting operations and, with the help of two others, got a boiler lighted and enough steam up to allow the *Franklin* to sail under her own power. Gary retired as a commander in June 1950, after thirty years' active service. He died April 9, 1977.

The *Franklin* made it to Pearl Harbor eight days later. Only 704 of her original 3,225-man complement remained aboard. The dead numbered 724, with another 1,797 wounded or injured seriously enough to have been evacuated from the carrier.

The Americans landed on Okinawa on Sunday, April 1, 1945, Easter Sunday, April Fool's Day. The 1st and 6th Marine Divisions landed abreast on the northern landing beaches. On the southern beaches of Hagushi, the army's 7th and 96th Infantry Divisions made the initial landing for XXIV Corps.

Although the American planners had not expected much resistance, what occurred that day was almost a lark. Against token resistance, sixty thousand Americans poured ashore. Within two hours of the 8:30 A.M. landing, patrols from the 7th Division had captured and moved beyond Kadena Airfield. An hour later the 6th Marine Division overran Yontan Airfield. By nightfall the American beachhead was five thousand yards deep and fifteen thousand yards wide. And, best of all, only twenty-eight men died that first day ashore.

By the end of the third day units of the 1st Marine Division crossed Ishikawa Isthmus, the narrow strip of land separating the northern two-thirds of Okinawa from the southern third. The assault troops had accomplished in just three days what the Tenth Army planners had figured would take three weeks. The two marine divisions now turned left for the drive north, while the 7th and 96th Infantry Divisions wheeled south.

Within twenty-four hours of beginning their movement south, the men of the XXIV Corps realized the real resistance was starting. The 7th Infantry Division, responsible for the east half of the island, took seven days to cover six thousand yards paying for the gain with 1,120 casualties.

On the west, the 96th Infantry Division also ran into Ushijima's first line of defenses. It took the GIs three days of deadly frontal assaults to overrun their first objective, Cactus Ridge. One thousand yards south of Cactus Ridge lay a rocky hogback, Kakazu Ridge, the western end of Ushijima's first line.

Four companies of the 96th's 383d Regiment went up against Kakazu Ridge before dawn on April 9. Within an hour two companies crested Kakazu Ridge and two more stood atop adjoining Kakazu West. Their victory was short-lived, however. At first light a thunderous artillery and mortar barrage poured down on the defenders. Almost immediately Japanese infantry counter-attacked.

Though ordered to hold the high ground at all costs, the two companies on Kakazu Ridge, their ranks depleted by casualties, started pulling back under a smoke screen at 10:00 A.M. Pfc. Edward J. Moskala, a twenty-three-year-old Chicagoan in Company C, volunteered to cover the withdrawal. He knocked off twenty-five Japanese before joining the withdrawal. Once at the bottom of the hill he learned two casualties had inadvertently been left behind. He went back for both, then was killed while fighting off four enemy infiltrators.

While the XXIV Corps ground to a halt against Ushijima's defenses B-29 bombers continued to pound the Japanese home islands. Day after day massive waves of the huge, shiny aluminum planes crowded the skies over Japan's major cities, dropping tons of bombs to the earth below. Though the few remaining Japanese fighter planes continued to harass the bombers, most of the time the bombing runs were routine. When danger did strike it sometimes came from within.

HENRY E. ERWIN

The *City of Los Angeles* was the lead B-29 for the 52nd Bombardment Squadron's attack on Koriyama, Japan, on April 12, 1945. As the lead plane it would give the signal at the Initial Point—the start of the bomb run—for the other B-29s to join in a tight formation. The signal was a white phosphorus bomb dropped from a release pipe in the B-29's belly.

Aboard the *City of Los Angeles*, S. Sgt. Henry E. Erwin, the radio operator, had the responsibility for launching the signal bomb. Encased in a steel canister approximately thirty inches long and four inches in diameter, the smoke bomb weighed about twenty pounds. Equipped with a six-second delayed-action fuse, once free of its release pipe the bomb would fall for about three hundred feet before igniting. It would burn at several thousand degrees Fahrenheit for about five minutes before going out.

Many of the B-29s crew felt the release pipe was too close to the ship's bomb bay for comfort. The *City of Los Angeles* carried more than three tons of incendiary bombs in its main bay that day. If the signal bomb should somehow reach the incendiaries the resulting explosion would obliterate the *City of Los Angeles* and any planes unfortunate enough to be near it.

Erwin had enlisted in the army air force for flight training on July 27, 1942, at age twenty-one, in his hometown of Bessemer, Alabama. Midway through aviation cadet training he washed out. Because he'd shown skill with the radio, the army sent him to radio school for further training. By April 1945 he was the senior radioman on the *City of Los Angeles*. He had ten missions under his belt. Fifteen more and he could go home.

Erwin relaxed as the pilot, Capt. Anthony Simeral, leveled the B-29 at altitude for the run to Koriyama. The farthest target yet for the Marianas-based bombers, Koriyama lay northeast of Tokyo. Because it hosted a complex of important chemical factories, Koriyama would be well defended by Japanese fighters and antiaircraft guns.

The flight was uneventful until they neared the Japanese coast. Then enemy fighters tore into the B-29 echelons, weaving in and out of the formation at speeds exceeding four hundred miles per hour. Soon the black clouds of exploding antiaircraft shells dotted the sky.

Captain Simeral maintained his position. Experience had taught him that evasive action offered no real protection against the enemy fighters. Besides, he had to fly straight and level to the IP.

Erwin prepared the signal bomb. He held it over the release pipe. His fingers found the triggering mechanism. Simeral spoke over Erwin's headphones, "Now, Sergeant Erwin." Erwin let the silver cylinder slide through his hands.

What happened next was a one-in-a-million unpredictable fluke. The signal bomb failed to clear the gate at the bottom of the release tube. Then it ignited. The blast blew the bomb back up the tube, full into Erwin's face. As he recoiled backwards, his nose melting off his face, the white-hot missile fell on the floor of the plane. It lay only feet from the incendiaries.

The other crewmen froze. Thick clouds of white smoke spewed forth from the burning bomb. At any minute it could ignite the firebombs.

Erwin, despite the pain engulfing his face, crawled toward the bomb. Through eyes nearly closed from white blisters he could just make out the blur of the super-hot bomb. As he reached it the *City of Los Angeles* suddenly lurched downward. The billowing smoke had filled the cockpit. Simeral and his copilot,

Lt. Roy Stables, choking on the smoke, were having a hard time controlling the plane. The heavy bomber dove toward the earth.

In the bomb bay Erwin reached for the bomb. His fingers rolled the missile toward him. He scooped up the blazing projectile, rose to his feet, and started toward the cockpit. Behind him, the other crewmen watched in frozen horror as Erwin, a mass of flames from the waist up, moved toward the copilot's window.

Erwin staggered forward, his once-wavy hair now singed off. His nylon life jacket melted into his skin. Flames burst forth from his trousers and shoes. The smell of roasting flesh filled the plane. The pall of smoke completely filled the narrow corridor. Erwin moved solely by instinct.

A few feet short of the cockpit Erwin found the navigator's collapsible table blocking his way. Incredibly, he tucked the white-hot projectile under his arm, fumbled for the table's latch with his free hand, found it, and folded the table out of his way.

Stables stood in shock as the flaming apparition stumbled into the cockpit. Simeral still fought to control the plane. The smoke blocked his view of the instruments and out the window. Behind him, Erwin screamed, "Open the window! Open the window!"

Stables lurched for the side window. As soon as he had it open Erwin lobbed the bomb through it, then collapsed in flames on the floor of the bomber. Stables and another crewman sprayed Erwin with the fire extinguishers until all the flames on his body were out. The once-handsome youth moaned quietly at first, then deep shrieks of pain escaped his burnt throat. His fifteen-second journey through hell had ended, but his real ordeal was only beginning.

Once the smoke cleared the cockpit, Simeral pulled the B-29 out of a dive just three hundred feet above the hills of Japan. Then, while Stables administered morphine to ease Erwin's horrible pain, Simeral set a course for the emergency strip on Iwo Jima.

Crash wagons met the *City of Los Angeles* as she ended her roll-out on Iwo's main strip. They rushed Erwin to the hospital. For the next several days doctors frantically worked on him. Nearly every inch of his body from the waist up was covered with third-degree burns. He received whole blood transfusions, injections against infection, internal surgery, and the first of hundreds of skin grafts. Though conscious throughout most of the ordeal, Erwin hovered on the brink of death. Few of the doctors expected him to live.

Because of the very real danger that Erwin would not survive his extensive burns the officers of his squadron prepared a Medal of Honor recommendation the very night of his deed. At 5:00 A.M. the next morning they hand-carried the documents to the headquarters of the Twentieth Air Force on Guam. Gen. Curtis LeMay was awakened. He read and signed the recommendation. The recommendation was flashed to Washington. Two days later word came back: Approved.

Erwin, in the meantime, had been flown from Iwo Jima to the more complete medical facilities on Guam. It was there, while he lay swathed in bandages from head to toe, that the Medal of Honor was pinned to his bandages on April 18, 1945. The award was one of the quickest on record. Because of the haste behind the ceremony, a Medal of Honor on display at army headquarters in Honolulu had been specially flown to Guam. General LeMay, who made the presentation, said to Erwin, "Your effort to save the lives of your fellow airmen is the most extraordinary kind of heroism I know."

Erwin answered simply, "Thank you, sir."

From Guam Erwin was flown to the burn unit at the army's Valley Forge Hospital outside Philadelphia. There he began the painful daily debridement baths necessary to wash away dead skin and commenced therapy and more skin grafts.

Miraculously, Erwin survived his severe burns. He was discharged from the hospital on October 8, 1947. At home again in Alabama Erwin went to work for the VA. He also married and raised a family.

Back on Okinawa the only good news came from General Geiger's marines in the north. Against scattered, light resistance the 6th Marine Division reached Okinawa's northernmost point, Hedo Misaki, on April 13, just eight days after jumping off. Most importantly, they sealed off the landward side of Motobu Peninsula, the one area of northern Okinawa where the Japanese made a stand.

Motobu, ten miles long and eight miles wide, was a tangle of densely wooded hills cut by deep ravines. The Japanese defenses centered on Mount Yae-dake, a twelve-hundred-foot-high peak on the peninsula's southern edge. The Japanese had every conceivable approach mined and pinpointed by artillery.

The 4th and 29th Marines began the assault on Mount Yae-dake on April 14. For three days they struggled up the steep slopes against stubborn resistance. The marines' losses were heavy. By the time Company A, 1st Battalion, 4th Marines, neared the crest of Yae-dake on April 16, sixty-five of its members were lost. In spite of the savage losses, Company A got to the top of Yae-dake but was thrown off under a hail of grenades and small-arms fire.

Cpl. Richard E. Bush was one of those wounded by the dozens of grenades that dropped among the marines. Several buddies pulled the twenty-one-year-old from Glasgow, Kentucky, to shelter under an outcropping of rocks. Prostrate under the care of a corpsman, Bush reacted instantly when a Japanese grenade landed between him and another casualty. Pushing the corpsman aside, he pulled the grenade to him and rolled on it. The explosion tore fingers off Bush's left hand and cost him an eye, but he survived the blast to receive the thanks of the men whose lives he saved.

Mount Yae-dake finally yielded to the marines on April 18. In the south, General Buckner renewed his attack against Ushijima's first defense line the next day. To bolster the offensive he moved the 96th Infantry Division eastward to the center of the front and brought the 27th Infantry Division in from reserve to attack the western end of the line. Even with the reinforcements Buckner's attack stalled under fierce resistance. Withering fire from all along the line halted the assault in its tracks.

Buckner's response was to throw in more manpower. Elements of the 77th Infantry Division were recalled from their successful attack on Ie Shima, an island off Motobu Peninsula.

Along the eastern end of the Japanese line the newly arrived 307th Infantry Regiment, 77th Infantry Division, faced the Maeda escarpment. A jagged limestone ridge fronted by a sheer cliff ranging from thirty to seventy feet in height, the escarpment was easily defended by Japanese well entrenched in uncountable caves and caverns. After bitter fighting the defenders were silenced. Next, the men of the 307th Infantry faced the challenge of scaling the cliff. The first troops up the cliff made it using fifty-foot ladders. They then hauled up cargo nets borrowed from the navy and draped them over the cliff's face for the following men to use. Once atop the cliff the GIs ran smack into the by-now-familiar Japanese tactic of attacking from the reverse slope. The fighting was especially fierce as the enemy used mortars, rockets, machine guns, satchel charges, and grenades to try and dislodge the Americans. Casualties mounted rapidly. Getting the men to safety was made particularly difficult by the sharp cliff.

DESMOND T. DOSS

As a strict adherent to the practices of the Seventh Day Adventist religion, Desmond T. Doss abhorred the idea of taking another's life. While the church encourages participation in the duties of citizenship, such as military service, it forbids its members to take a combat position. As a youngster in his hometown of Lynchburg, Virginia, Doss saw a picture of Cain killing Abel. "I looked at the picture," Doss recalled years later, "and I thought, 'How could a brother do such a thing?' That's probably one reason I was so much impressed about not wanting to kill."

When he was drafted on April 1, 1942, from his job in a shipyard in Newport News, Virginia, Doss registered as a conscientious objector. He was very willing to serve his country, but he wanted to save lives, not take them.

Assigned to the 77th Infantry Division as a medic, Doss endured a constant barrage of harassment and intimidation for his beliefs. When he knelt by his bunk to offer his evening prayers his first night in camp others in the barracks derided him and pelted him with boots. When he refused to pick up a gun during training and insisted on continuing his practice of observing Saturday as the Sabbath he was nearly kicked out of the army.

One of Doss's officers even filed Section Eight discharge papers for Doss, implying he had a basic instability that made him unsuitable for service. The effort was quashed when it was pointed out that Doss's work was exemplary. Another time he was placed on indefinite KP for refusing to stand inspection on Saturday. One particularly nasty barracks-mate made it a habit to tell Doss he'd kill him the first time they were in combat. Then he'd laugh.

The harassment continued during the 77th's deployment to the Pacific. Doss stoically endured it all, refusing to capitulate to his tormentors. It finally came to a halt when the division landed on Guam. Doss proved his courage time and time again, risking his life to go to the aid of the wounded. A skinny and somewhat awkward young man, Doss repeatedly left positions of safety to rescue casualties. The other soldiers and officers came to respect the noncombatant, and his visage became a welcome sight on the battlefield.

In spite of the agony he suffered at the hands of his comrades, Doss spoke highly of them. "I couldn't have worked with a better group of men," Doss said. "They trusted me, I trusted them, and we worked together as a team. And when I saw those men out there and knew their lives depended on me, I just couldn't let them go even though I knew it could cost me my life."

After experiencing more combat on Leyte in the Philippines, the 77th Division was called to the battle in Okinawa. Beginning on April 29, 1945, when the 307th Infantry went up the Maeda escarpment and continuing for the next three weeks, Doss performed a series of gallant rescues that saved the lives of well over a hundred soldiers.

When the men of the 307th Infantry topped the escarpment the relentless Japanese counterattack wounded nearly one hundred men. The able-bodied survivors began making their way back down the cargo nets to escape the fury of the enemy, leaving many casualties behind. At the cliff's base the men rested, bone weary from the frightening battle. Suddenly, a wounded and unconscious soldier, dangling from a rope sling, appeared before them. When they looked up, there was Doss, yelling over the roar of the gunfire, "Take him off. Send him straight back to the aid station."

For the next five hours Doss remained on top of the escarpment, gathering up the wounded and lowering them down the cliff. Under constant Japanese fire, Doss appeared oblivious to the danger while he single-handedly carried out his task. When he was through his company officers estimated he had rescued one hundred men. Doss figured it was fifty. They compromised on seventy-five.

On May 2 Doss again exposed himself to enemy rifle fire to rescue a wounded man two hundred yards forward of the main line. Two days later he went to the aid of four men cut down just eight yards from an enemy cave. After applying first aid he made four separate trips to carry them to safety. The next day he saved a wounded artillery officer, then went to the aid of a GI who had been severely wounded by Japanese holed up in a cave. Doss carried him one hundred yards to safety.

Doss credited his success to his Lord. "I didn't feel like I was going to be killed," he said. "I just said, 'Lord, help me.' I felt if I was going to be wounded it would be worth it if I could save one more man. I didn't feel like it was right for me to value my life above the lives of my buddies."

During a May 21 night attack, while treating a number of wounded, Doss took a load of shrapnel in his legs. Rather than call an aid man from cover, Doss remained in the open on the battlefield for five hours, treating his own wounds and comforting the wounded around him. When litter bearers finally reached him at dawn they started carrying him to the aid station. Along the way the trio got caught in an enemy tank attack.

Seeing a more critically wounded man, Doss crawled off the stretcher and directed the bearers to carry that man to the rear. While awaiting their return he was hit again, taking a rifle slug in the arm. Binding the shattered arm with a rifle stock he crawled three hundred yards over rough terrain to the aid station.

Doss faced a lengthy recovery from his wounds, but he was able to visit the White House on October 12, 1945, to receive his Medal of Honor. His injuries and the severe tuberculosis he contacted on Okinawa left him completely disabled.

On May 1, General Buckner started reinforcing his front line. The entire 1st and 6th Marine Divisions were called down from the north; the army's 27th Infantry Division would take over their garrison duty. By May 7, Buckner would have both of his corps prepared for a new offensive. From east to west the lineup would be: the 7th and 77th Infantry Divisions of the XXIV Corps, then the 1st and 6th Marine Divisions of the III Corps (the 96th Infantry Division formed the reserve).

In the 1st Marine Division's sector, local patrols scouted the proposed routes of advance for the upcoming offensive. The Japanese attacked them whenever possible.

ROBERT E. BUSH

First Lt. James Roach of the 2d Battalion, 5th Marines, 1st Marine Division, took out one such patrol before dawn on May 2. Eleven men accompanied him. One of them was Hosp. Apprentice 1st Class Robert E. Bush.

Born October 4, 1926, in Tacoma, Washington, Bush left high school to enlist in the navy in January 1944 when he was just seventeen years old. After boot camp, corpsman school, and a four-month apprenticeship in a naval hospital, Bush completed the field medical course at Camp Pendleton, California. Two days before Christmas 1944 Bush joined the 5th Marines in training on Pavuvu Island in the Russell Islands.

During his first thirty days on Okinawa Bush had more than ample opportunity to put his months of training to good use. When the call went out for volunteers to accompany Lieutenant Roach's patrol Bush stepped forward. As the patrol crested a small ridge a few hundred yards from its starting point, a deadly barrage of enemy mortars fell on the twelve men. Almost all of them were hit. One of the more seriously wounded was Lieutenant Roach. He lay supine at the top of the hill.

Bush instantly leapt to the officer's rescue. With his medical bag under one arm and a .45-caliber automatic in a shoulder holster under the other, Bush and two marines headed for Roach. Halfway up the hill enemy machine-gun fire dropped the two marines. Bush continued on alone.

At Roach's side Bush knelt and prepared a plasma bottle. As he slipped the needle into the officer's arm the Japanese came at him. Realizing Roach would die if he stopped the flow of life-giving fluid, Bush held the bottle with one hand and pulled his .45 free with the other. Silhouetted against the sky, Bush calmly took the attacking enemy under fire. The .45 proved inaccurate at that range, so when he emptied its clip he picked up Roach's M-1 carbine. Still holding the plasma aloft, Bush fired the rifle with his free hand. Several of the attackers fell.

An enemy grenade suddenly plopped onto the ground near the two men. Bush protectively crouched over Roach. The sharp explosion peppered Bush's backside with jagged chunks of shrapnel. He rose up, again firing the carbine. Three more Japanese fell to the ground. A second grenade hit the ground near Bush. He instinctively raised his left arm to shield his eyes.

This explosion drove shrapnel deep into Bush's left arm, shattering it. Pieces of hot steel also filled his right eye.

By this time surviving members of the patrol had joined Bush. Their combined fire drove the remaining Japanese off. Under his direction the marines carried Roach back to the company area. Bush started back under his own power. But he'd lost too much blood. Before he reached his company he collapsed.

When he came to, Bush was on a hospital ship bound for Guam. From there the casualty pipeline carried him to Pearl

Harbor, then to a naval hospital near Oakland, California. It was there he received his first glass eye.

Discharged in July 1945, Bush returned to Tacoma. His first priority was to resume his courtship with his girlfriend, Wanda Spooner. It wasn't long before Bush proposed and Wanda accepted. When word came that he was to receive the Medal of Honor at the White House on October 5, 1945, the young couple moved up their wedding date. They spent their honeymoon in Washington, D.C.

Back in Tacoma Bush finished his senior year of high school. He then used his GI Bill to complete college. In 1951 he became a partner in a lumberyard. Today he is a wealthy man who owns three lumberyards and a cement plant. His three sons work with him; his daughter has a family of her own.

With eighty-five thousand combat troops in five divisions at his disposal, Buckner launched his new offensive on May 7. All along the line ferocious Japanese resistance continued unabated. As one enemy unit was annihilated, another took its place. As on Iwo Jima, this was combat at its worst. Every Japanese position had to be dug out individually by riflemen.

To add to the misery Okinawa's incessant rain turned the battleground into a sea of mud. It was everywhere. It squeezed coarse and cold in boots. It got into a man's rifle. It added an unusual texture to a man's rations. It infected wounds. The ground became so boggy tanks could not move. Artillery pieces sank below their hubs.

Each division faced its own particular enemy strong point. For the 1st Marine Division it was Shuri Heights, guarding Ushijima's headquarters in Shuri Castle. On May 7, when the 1st Battalion, 5th Marines, was pinned down in a valley by a vicious blanket of enemy machine-gun fire from the ridge to their front, Pfc. Albert E. Schwab, a twenty-four-year-old from Tulsa, Oklahoma, took his flamethrower straight up the ridge. Before the Japanese cut him down, Schwab single-handedly wiped out two key enemy positions. His family accepted his posthumous Medal of Honor on Memorial Day 1946.

On Okinawa's east coast the Japanese defenders on Kochi Ridge and Zebra Hill chewed up two battalions of the 7th Infantry Division. The 96th Infantry Division's 382d Infantry replaced them on May 9. Two days later, after finally clearing

Kochi Ridge, the GIs turned their attention to Zebra Hill. Capt. Seymour W. Terry took his Company B forward until five pillboxes forced his men to ground. The twenty-six-year-old native of Little Rock, Arkansas, set off alone to wipe out the enemy positions. With grenades, satchel charges, and rifle fire he knocked out all five, killing twenty Japanese. Twice more that day Terry ventured ahead of his company to single-handedly wipe out a series of Japanese positions. He killed no less than twenty-five additional enemy during his bold charges. Later that night, while organizing his company to resist a counterattack, Terry died when a mortar shell burst at his feet.

The 6th Marine Division had its hands full with Sugar Loaf Hill, just on the northern outskirts of Naha, the large west coast city. Supported by two nearby hills, Sugar Loaf was the nerve center of the Japanese western flank. It would not yield easily. The 22nd Marines started attacking Sugar Loaf on May 12. Even though the marines were supported by tanks, the Japanese proved too strong. Three times that day the marines went up against the Japanese. Three times they were repulsed.

Again and again on May 13 the marines hit Sugar Loaf. Each time they met the same disastrous results. On May 14 two depleted companies from the 22d Marines and most of the 29th Marines tried again. Several batteries of artillery, flamethrowing tanks, and 4.2-inch mortars pounded the ground in front of the marines. By 3:30 P.M. they had secured a foothold on Sugar Loaf. An hour later the Japanese threw them back again.

At 7:30 P.M. the executive officer of the 1st Battalion, 22d Marines, Maj. Henry A. Courtney, approached the forty-three survivors of his two companies. "Men," began the twenty-nine-year-old Duluth, Minnesota, attorney, "if we don't take the top of this hill tonight, the Japs will be down here to drive us away in the morning. When we go up there, some of us are never going to come back down again. You all know what hell it is on the top, but that hill's got to be taken and we're going to do it."

To a man the marines followed Courtney up the hill. Heaving grenades every few steps, Courtney led the charge. By 11:00 P.M. they had gained the top. At midnight, Courtney heard the Japanese gathering on the reverse slope. "Take all the grenades you can carry," he whispered. When the Japanese were just one hundred yards away, Courtney ordered, "Charge!" Again leading by example, he took his marines right into the center of the enemy. Courtney died, but his men threw back the Japanese.

By dawn only fifteen marines remained alive on top of Sugar Loaf. Enemy machine gunners on the neighboring hills soon drove them off. Not until May 18 were the marines able to take and hold Sugar Loaf.

And so the battle for Okinawa continued through May and into June. Ushijima made the Americans pay a brutal price for each foot of ground. As the Americans battered against each obstacle, the Japanese bled them dry, then pulled back. On June 4, the 6th Marine Division made an amphibious assault on Oroku Peninsula, south of Naha. That caught the Japanese by surprise, allowing the 1st Marine Division to slice forward to the island's south coast. That proved to be the beginning of the end for Okinawa.

The campaign on Okinawa officially ended on June 21, 1945. There were several weeks of intense mopping up before the island was truly secure, but the worst was over. The Japanese lost 100,000 men on Okinawa, yet, amazingly, 10,000 more surrendered. American casualties topped 49,000, with 2,938 marines and 4,675 soldiers dying. Another 4,907 sailors also died, most as the result of kamikaze attacks on offshore shipping.

While the marines and soldiers of the Tenth Army slogged their way down the length of Okinawa, the Sixth and Eighth Armies continued their conquest of the Philippines. General MacArthur developed a plan to capture every major island he'd bypassed during the hop from Leyte to Luzon. He could have left these Japanese to wither on the vine, but MacArthur had come to retake all of the Philippine islands, not just a few of them. Anything less would breach his famous promise to the Filipinos. And there was the very real danger of leaving the islands' populations, and any American POWs, to the mercy of frustrated Japanese.

In a well-coordinated series of amphibious assaults, the Eighth Army began its sweep of the southern islands on February 28, 1945. First to fall was Palawan, then Panay, followed by Cebu and Bohol. On March 28, the 40th Infantry Division landed on Negros Island.

Negros, a rich island of sugar plantations, had been the headquarters of the Japanese Fourth Air Force, but now there were no planes on the island's eight airfields. As soon as the men of the 40th Infantry Division came ashore from neighboring Panay, most of the fourteen thousand Japanese pulled back into the interior mountains. They would hold out for two more months, meeting the GIs in short but vicious clashes.

JOHN C. SJOGREN

When he went for his induction physical in 1942 John C. Sjogren was rejected due to a bad back. He returned to his family's farm outside Rockford, Michigan, where he'd been born on August 19, 1916. The 4-F classification didn't bother Sjogren; there was plenty of work on the farm. But then Sjogren changed his mind.

"At first I didn't mind that I didn't have to go," Sjogren later said. "But then when all my friends were gone, patriotism started to take over and I realized that there was a job to be done."

It took some time for him to convince the military doctors that his bad back wouldn't get in the way of serving his country. "They eventually sent me to Camp McCoy, Wisconsin, for MP training, but I finally talked them into reclassifying me for the infantry," Sjogren recalled.

Following basic and advanced infantry training Sjogren volunteered to join the 40th Infantry Division completing its stateside training before shipping out for the Luzon invasion. He was assigned to Company I, 3d Battalion, 160th Infantry. Sjogren was with the 160th Infantry when it went ashore at Lingayen Gulf. During the subsequent attack on Clark Airfield north of Manila Sjogren was wounded. By the time he rejoined his outfit it was on Negros Island. Sjogren became a squad leader, wearing the stripes of a staff sergeant.

By late May the remaining Japanese had been squeezed into a few square miles in the north center of Negros Island. Near San Jose Hacienda a force of Japanese holed up on a steep hill commanding a broad plain. Two days of artillery and aerial bombardment had failed to dislodge them. They would have to be taken out one-by-one by the infantry. Sjogren's squad would lead the attack up the hill's narrow approaches.

"We were the point men," he said. "It was our job to clear the way for the rest of the soldiers. We knew we were in for a rough day. No one was naive enough to believe there wasn't going to be considerable loss of life."

Sjogren started his men. They pulled themselves uphill by grasping tree trunks felled by the artillery fire. Japanese machine-gun and mortar fire slowed Sjogren's squad. The enemy even fired antiaircraft guns straight down the hill. Sjogren saw his second-in-command take a machine-gun burst in the head. Ducking and dodging the whizzing gunfire, exploding grenades, and satchel charges, he pulled the man to safety and started administering first aid.

"I can still see him now," Sjogren recalled years later, "lying there. He had gone over a fallen tree trunk when he should have gone under it."

In spite of the medical efforts the man died. Sjogren realized they would all die if they stayed there. He ordered his men to pour rifle fire on the first enemy pillbox as he snuck uphill, loaded with grenades. "If they had hit me it would have been like hitting a barrel of gasoline," he said. "I had grenades in every pocket."

Using the shattered trees as cover, Sjogren made his way up the slope. Somehow he escaped the brutal fire from the Japanese to reach the first fortification. The men crawling behind him covered him by firing at the pillbox's gun slits, allowing Sjogren to crawl close enough to toss in a few grenades. That finished the position.

The squad started firing on the next enemy position. Again, Sjogren rushed up and dropped in a grenade. Led by the intrepid sergeant, the squad leapfrogged up the hill. While systematically attacking each enemy position Sjogren had several close calls. At one pillbox, enemy grenades landed at his feet. Sjogren turned and flattened himself against the concrete wall. Shrapnel ripped into his legs, causing flesh wounds. At another pillbox a Japanese rifleman had Sjogren square in his sights but inexplicably froze. Sjogren flipped a grenade in his direction.

At the last pillbox Sjogren burned his hand when he wrenched a machine gun out of a bunker by its barrel. Then he tossed in several grenades, killing the enemy gunners.

Sjogren always had a hard time explaining his actions that May morning. "I knew it was important that we take that hill. The pillboxes were holding up the progress of an entire division and . . . well, I suppose I just felt I had a job to do and went about doing it the best way I knew how."

He never could understand how he survived that day. "We were taking fire from all directions," he said. "It just didn't make any sense that we weren't all killed."

The Michiganer gave most of the credit for the success of his mission to his squad members. "I think every man in the squad came away with a medal. I sometimes think we were one of the most decorated squads in the whole war.''

After receiving his Medal of Honor from President Truman at the White House on October 12, 1945, Sjogren returned to his home in Rockford. He led a quiet life, marrying and raising a family. He built a successful career as a manufacturer's representative for fine furniture. He died on August 30, 1987.

On June 26, 1945, General MacArthur declared the end of the northern Luzon campaign. As were his other declarations of the cessation of hostilities, this one was also premature. Yamashita still had thousands of troops available to him in the mountains. For the next eight weeks he would masterfully elude three U.S. infantry divisions and several Filipino guerilla units.

Though the Allied units maintained the pressure on Yamashita, forcing him to move his headquarters several times, he inspired his men to fight bitterly for every ravine and ridge. In late July, Company D, 20th Infantry Regiment, 6th Infantry Division, supported two guerilla companies attacking up a ridge in the center of the Cordillera Mountains.

MELVIN MAYFIELD

Life in rural West Virginia had never been easy. For Melvin Mayfield, born March 24, 1919, at Salem, West Virginia, it was no different. His parents ran a dairy farm outside Salem. That meant long hours and plenty of hard work for everyone in the family. Consequently, education carried little importance. Melvin Mayfield ended his formal education before he reached the eighth grade.

In 1940 Mayfield moved to the small central Ohio town of Nashport. Even though a good portion of the country had started recovering from the Great Depression, such a recovery had not yet reached West Virginia. As Mayfield later said, ''We just up and moved to Ohio,'' seeking a better life.

The family settled on a small farm outside of town. Life was better, but there just wasn't enough income to support the entire family. As the oldest Melvin Mayfield left home first, enlisting in the army in the summer of 1941. Trained as a Signal Corps lineman, he joined the 6th Infantry Division in training at Fort Leonard Wood, Missouri, in the fall of 1941.

Nearly two years of stateside training preceded the 6th's shipment overseas in July 1943. The division spent six months in Hawaii before shipping out to New Guinea in January 1944. Mayfield, by now a corporal, and the 6th Infantry Division experienced their first combat in the Hollandia-Aitape area in the summer of 1944.

Mayfield survived the fighting on New Guinea to make the Lingayen Gulf landings on Luzon in January 1945. He participated in the fight down to Manila and in the mountains east of the capital. From there the division moved north to assist in the final annihilation of Yamashita's *Shobu* group.

The Japanese bitterly opposed the 6th Division's advance west from Kiangan to the Asin Valley in the Cordilleras. Instead of a simple mopping-up operation, the division found itself involved in mountain fighting as tough as any experienced during the Luzon campaign. Though the Japanese were chronically low on ammo, they made effective use of what they did have. In addition, movement of the 6th Division was severely hampered by torrential rains that fell day and night.

On the morning of July 29, two companies of Filipino guerillas attached to the 20th Infantry were assigned to take a circular ridge overlooking the regiment's advance. Thirty-four of the Filipinos made the military crest. From down below Mayfield decided to go with them. "I wanted to see what was on the other side of that hill," is how Mayfield later explained it.

Dodging from shell hole to shell hole, Mayfield made it to the guerillas. He joined them in laying down an effective suppressive fire on the Japanese, most of whom were farther up the rugged hill in four caves. Ninety minutes after the fight started one of the Filipinos was badly wounded. To Mayfield's amazement all the Filipinos started down the hill with the casualty. He was left there all alone.

Rather than wait for rescue Mayfield decided to go after the Japanese. Sneaking along from one outcropping of rocks to another, he made it to within grenade range of the first cave. Several well-tossed grenades silenced that position. Mayfield boldly went after the other caves, using his rifle and hand grenades with deadly effectiveness. Two more caves felt the sting of Mayfield's accuracy.

While working his way under fire toward the last cave an enemy round smashed into his M-1, ruining it and slashing a deep gash in his left hand. Disregarding the painful wound Mayfield crawled to where the departed Filipinos had left some gear. He stuffed his pockets with grenades and went back after the last enemy position.

Throwing grenades ahead of his path to keep the enemy down, Mayfield charged headlong at the enemy. Explosion after explosion crashed over the hillside. From a covered position below the cave Mayfield threw a half a dozen missiles into the small opening. At last the machine gun within fell silent.

Mayfield's gallant one-man assault, the last Medal of Honor action in World War II, cleared the way for the 20th Infantry to move into the Asin Valley. Before the advance could be fully exploited, however, the war ended. A few months later Mayfield received his honorable discharge, shed his uniform, and returned to renew his life as a dairy farmer.

Word of the Medal of Honor award reached Mayfield in early May 1946. A quiet, unassuming man, he preferred not to receive his award in the limelight of the White House. Instead, a simple ceremony was held on Memorial Day 1946 in Columbus, Ohio. Mayfield stayed around for the banquet that night in his honor, then returned to his farm. He had chores to do in the morning. He married a few years later, fathering four children. He died on June 19, 1990.

Eight days after Corporal Mayfield went up that hill on Luzon the B-29 bomber *Enola Gay* lifted off from the long runway on Tinian Island. Secured in its belly was the prototype of a truly awesome weapon. The *Enola Gay* flew to Hiroshima where it dropped its deadly cargo. The huge mushrooming cloud not only killed eighty thousand Japanese but ushered in a new era of warfare. On August 9, 1945, a second atomic bomb was released over Nagasaki.

Five days later Japan surrendered. Formal surrender ceremonies were held aboard the battleship U.S.S. *Missouri* in Tokyo Bay on September 2, 1945. The most costly war in world history was over at last.

Appendix: World War II Medal of Honor Recipients

Name Rank, Branch	Home State	Unit	Place	Date
Adams, Lucian S. Sgt., USA	Tex.	3d Inf. Div.	France	Oct. 28, 1944
*Agerholm, Harold C. Pfc., USMC	Wis.	2d Mar. Div.	Saipan	July 7, 1944
Anderson, Beaufort T. T. Sgt., USA	Wis.	96th Inf. Div.	Okinawa	Apr. 13, 1945
*Anderson, Richard B. Pfc., USMC	Wash.	4th Mar. Div.	Roi-Namur, Marshall Is.	Feb. 1, 1944
*Antolak, Sylvester Sgt., USA	Ohio	3d Inf. Div.	Italy	May 24, 1944
Antrim, Richard N. Lt., USN	Ind.	U.S.S. *Pope*	Celebes Is.	Apr. 1942
Atkins, Thomas E. Pfc., USA	S.C.	32d Inf. Div.	Luzon, P.I.	Mar. 10, 1945
*Bailey, Kenneth D. Maj., USMC	Ill.	1st Mar. Raider Bn.	Guadalcanal	Sept. 12–13, 1942
*Baker, Addison E. Lt. Col., USAAF	Ohio	Eighth Air Force	Ploesti, Romania	Aug. 1, 1943
*Baker, Thomas A. Sgt., USA	N.Y.	27th Inf. Div.	Saipan	June 19– July 7, 1944
Barfoot, Van T. T. Sgt., USA	Miss.	45th Inf. Div.	Italy	May 23, 1944
Barrett, Carlton W. Pvt., USA	N.Y.	1st Inf. Div.	France	June 6, 1944
Basilone, John Sgt., USMC	N.J.	1st Mar. Div.	Guadalcanal	Oct. 24–25, 1942
*Bauer, Harold W. Lt. Col., USMC	Nebr.	VMF-212	Solomon Islands	May 10– Nov. 14, 1942
*Bausell, Lewis K. Cpl., USMC	D.C.	1st Mar. Div.	Peleliu	Sept. 15, 1944

*Posthumous award

Name Rank, Branch	Home State	Unit	Place	Date
*Beaudoin, Raymond O. 1st Lt., USA	Mass.	30th Inf. Div	Germany	Apr. 6, 1945
Bell, Bernard P. T. Sgt., USA	N.Y.	36th Inf. Div.	France	Dec. 18, 1944
Bender, Stanley S. Sgt., USA	Ill.	3d Inf. Div.	France	Aug. 17, 1944
*Benjamin, George, Jr. Pfc., USA	N.J.	77th Inf. Div.	Leyte, P.I.	Dec. 21, 1944
Bennett, Edward A. Cpl., USA	Ohio	90th Inf. Div.	Germany	Feb. 1, 1945
*Bennion, Mervyn S. Capt., USN	Utah	U.S.S. *West Virginia*	Pearl Harbor	Dec. 7, 1941
*Berry, Charles J. Cpl., USMC	Ohio	5th Mar. Div.	Iwo Jima	Mar. 3, 1945
Bertoldo, Vito R. M. Sgt. USA	Ill.	42d Inf. Div.	France	Jan. 9–10, 1945
Beyer, Arthur O. Cpl., USA	Iowa	603d Tank Dest. Bn.	Belgium	Jan. 15, 1945
Bianchi, Willibald C. 1st Lt., USA	Minn.	45th Inf. (PS)	Luzon, P.I.	Feb. 3, 1942
Biddle, Melvin E. Pfc., USA	Ind.	517th Para. Inf. Rgt.	Belgium	Dec. 23–24, 1944
*Bigelow, Elmer C. WT 1, USN	Ill.	U.S.S. *Fletcher*	Corregidor Island, P.I.	Feb. 14, 1945
Bjorklund, Arnold L. 1st Lt., USA	Wash.	36th Inf. Div.	Italy	Sept. 13, 1943
Bloch, Orville E. 1st Lt., USA	N.Dak.	85th Inf. Div.	Italy	Sept. 22, 1944
Bolden, Paul L. S. Sgt., USA	Ala.	30th Inf. Div.	Belgium	Dec. 23, 1944
Bolton, Cecil H. 1st Lt., USA	Ala.	104th Inf. Div.	Holland	Nov. 2, 1944
Bong, Richard I. Maj., USAAF	Wis.	Fifth A.F.	S.W. Pacific Area	Oct. 10– Nov. 15, 1944
*Bonnyman, Alexander 1st Lt., USMC	N.Mex.	2d Mar. Div.	Tarawa	Nov. 20–22, 1943
*Booker, Robert D. Pvt., USA	Nebr.	34th Inf. Div.	Tunisia	Apr. 9, 1943
*Bordelon, William J. S. Sgt., USMC	Tex.	2d Mar. Div.	Tarawa	Nov. 20, 1943
*Boyce, George W. G. 2d Lt., USA	N.Y.	112th Cav. RCT	New Guinea	July 23, 1944
Boyington, Gregory Maj., USMC	Wash.	VMF-214	Solomon Islands	Sept. 12, 1943– Jan. 3, 1944

Name Rank, Branch	Home State	Unit	Place	Date
Briles, Herschel F. S. Sgt., USA	Iowa	899th Tank Dest. Bn.	Germany	Nov. 20, 1944
Britt, Maurice L. 1st Lt., USA	Ark.	3d Inf. Div.	Italy	Nov. 10, 1943
*Brostrom, Leonard C. Pfc., USA	Idaho	7th Inf. Div.	Leyte, P.I.	Oct. 28, 1944
Brown, Bobbie E. Capt., USA	Ga.	1st Inf. Div.	Germany	Oct. 8, 1944
Bulkeley, John D. Lt. Comdr., USN	Tex.	Torpedo Boat Squadron 3	Luzon, P.I.	Dec. 7, 1941– Apr. 10, 1942
Burke, Frank 1st Lt., USA	N.J.	3d Inf. Div.	Germany	Apr. 17, 1945
*Burr, Elmer J. 1st Sgt., USA	Wis.	32d Inf. Div.	New Guinea	Dec. 24, 1942
Burr, Herbert H. S. Sgt., USA	Mo.	11th Armrd. Div.	Germany	Mar. 19, 1945
Burt, James M. Capt., USA	Mass.	2d Armrd. Div.	Germany	Oct. 13, 1944
Bush, Richard E. Cpl., USMC	Ky.	6th Mar. Div.	Okinawa	Apr. 16, 1945
Bush, Robert E. HA 1st Cl., USN	Wash.	1st Mar. Div.	Okinawa	May 2, 1945
*Butts, John E. 2d Lt., USA	N.Y.	9th Inf. Div.	France	June 14, 16, & 23, 1944
*Caddy, William R. Pfc., USMC	Mass.	5th Mar. Div.	Iwo Jima	Mar. 3, 1945
*Callaghan, Daniel J. Rear Adm., USN	Calif.	U.S.S. *San Francisco*	off Savo Island	Nov. 12–13, 1942
Calugas, Jose Sgt., USA	P.I.	88th F.A. (PS)	Luzon, P.I.	Jan. 16, 1942
*Cannon, George H. 1st Lt., USMC	Mich.	6th Defense Bn.	Midway Island	Dec. 7, 1941
*Carey, Alvin P. S. Sgt., USA	Penn.	2d Inf. Div.	France	Aug. 23, 1944
*Carey, Charles F., Jr. T. Sgt., USA	Wyo.	100th Inf. Div.	France	Jan. 8–9, 1945
Carr, Chris Sgt., USA	N.H.	85th Inf. Div.	Italy	Oct. 1–2, 1944
*Carswell, Horace S. Maj., USAAF	Tex.	Fourteenth Air Force	over South China Sea	Oct. 26, 1944
Casamento, Anthony Cpl., USMC	N.Y.	1st Mar. Div.	Guadalcanal	Nov. 1, 1942
*Castle, Frederick W. Brig, Gen., USAAF	N.J.	Eighth Air Force	over Germany	Dec. 24, 1944

Name Rank, Branch	Home State	Unit	Place	Date
Chambers, Justice M. Lt. Col., USMC	D.C.	4th Mar. Div.	Iwo Jima	Feb. 19–22, 1945
*Cheli, Ralph Maj., USAAF	N.Y.	Fifth A.F.	New Guinea	Aug. 18, 1943
Childers, Ernest 2d Lt., USA	Okla.	45th Inf. Div.	Italy	Sept. 22, 1943
Choate, Clyde L. S. Sgt., USA	Ill.	601th Tank Dest. Bn.	France	Oct. 25, 1944
*Christensen, Dale E. 2d Lt., USA	Iowa	112th Cav. RCT	New Guinea	July 16–19, 1944
*Christian, Herbert F. Pvt., USA	Ohio	3d Inf. Div.	Italy	June 2–3, 1944
*Cicchetti, Joseph J. Pfc., USA	Ohio	37th Inf. Div.	Luzon, P.I.	Feb. 9, 1945
Clark, Francis J. T. Sgt., USA	N.Y.	28th Inf. Div.	Luxembourg & Germany	Sept. 12 & 17, 1944
Colalillo, Mike Pfc., USA	Minn.	100th Inf. Div.	Germany	Apr. 7, 1945
*Cole, Darrell S. Sgt., USMC	Mo.	4th Mar. Div.	Iwo Jima	Feb. 19, 1945
*Cole, Robert G. Lt. Col., USA	Tex.	101st Abn. Div.	France	June 11, 1944
Connor, James P. Sgt., USA	Del.	3d Inf. Div.	France	Aug. 15, 1944
Cooley, Raymond H. S. Sgt., USA	Tenn.	25th Inf. Div.	Luzon, P.I.	Feb. 24, 1945
Coolidge, Charles H. T. Sgt., USA	Tenn.	36th Inf. Div.	France	Oct. 24–27, 1944
*Courtney, Henry A., Jr. Maj., USMC	Minn.	6th Mar. Div.	Okinawa	May 14–15, 1945
*Cowan, Richard E. Pfc., USA	Kans.	2d Inf. Div.	Belgium	Dec. 17, 1944
Craft, Clarence Pfc., USA	Calif.	96h Inf. Div.	Okinawa	May 31, 1945
*Craig, Robert 2d Lt., USA	Ohio	3d Inf. Div.	Sicily	July 11, 1943
*Crain, Morris E. T. Sgt., USA	Ky.	36th Inf. Div.	France	Mar. 13, 1945
*Craw, Demas T. Col., USAAF	Mich.	Western Task Force	Morocco	Nov. 8, 1942
Crawford, William J. Pvt., USA	Colo.	36th Inf. Div.	Italy	Sept. 13, 1943
Crews, John R. S. Sgt., USA	Okla.	63d Inf. Div.	Germany	Apr. 8, 1945

Name Rank, Branch	Home State	Unit	Place	Date
*Cromwell, John P. Capt., USN	Ill.	U.S.S. *Sculpin*	near Marshall Islands	Nov. 19, 1943
Currey, Francis S. Sgt., USA	N.Y.	30th Inf. Div.	Belgium	Dec. 21, 1944
Dahlgren, Edward C. Sgt., USA	Maine	36th Inf. Div.	France	Feb. 11, 1945
Dalessondro, Peter J. T. Sgt., USA	N.Y.	9th Inf. Div.	Germany	Dec. 22, 1944
Daly, Michael J. 1st Lt., USA	Conn.	3d Inf. Div.	Germany	Apr. 18, 1945
*Damato, Anthony P. Cpl., USMC	Penn.	4th Mar. Div.	Eniwetok, Marshall Is.	Feb. 19–20, 1944
*David, Albert L. Lt. (jg), USN	Mo.	U.S.S. *Pillsbury*	South Atlantic	June 4, 1944
Davis, Charles W. Maj., USA	Ala.	25th Inf. Div.	Guadalcanal	Jan. 12–13, 1943
*Davis, George F. Comdr., USN	P.I.	U.S.S. *Walke*	Luzon, P.I.	Jan. 6, 1945
*Dealey, Samuel D. Comdr., USN	Tex.	U.S.S. *Harder*	near Luzon, P.I.	June 6– July 3, 1944
DeBlanc, Jefferson J. 1st Lt., USMC	La.	VMF-112	Solomon Islands	Jan. 31, 1943
*DeFranzo, Arthur F. S. Sgt., USA	Mass.	1st Inf. Div.	France	June 10, 1944
*DeGlopper, Charles N. Pfc., USA	N.Y.	82d Abn. Div.	France	June 9, 1944
*Deleau, Emile, Jr. Sgt., USA	Ohio	36th Inf. Div.	France	Feb. 1–2, 1945
Dervishian, Ernest H. T. Sgt., USA	Va.	34th Inf. Div.	Italy	May 23, 1944
*Diamond, James H. Pfc., USA	Miss.	24th Inf. Div.	Mindanao, P.I.	May 8–14, 1945
*Dietz, Robert H. S. Sgt., USA	N.Y.	7th Armrd. Div.	Germany	Mar. 29, 1945
Doolittle, James H. Lt. Col., USAAF	Calif.	—	over Japan	Apr. 18, 1942
Doss, Desmond T. Pfc., USA	Va.	77th Inf. Div.	Okinawa	Apr. 29– May 21, 1945
Drowley, Jesse R. S. Sgt., USA	Wash.	American Div.	Bougainville	Jan. 30, 1944
Dunham, Russell E. T. Sgt., USA	Ill.	3d Inf. Div.	France	Jan. 8, 1945

Name Rank, Branch	Home State	Unit	Place	Date
Dunlap, Robert H. Capt., USMC	Ill.	5th Mar. Div.	Iwo Jima	Feb. 20–21, 1945
*Dutko, John W. Pfc., USA	N.J.	3d Inf. Div.	Italy	May 23, 1944
*Dyess, Aquilla J. Lt. Col., USMC	Ga.	4th Mar. Div.	Roi-Namur, Marshall Is.	Feb. 1–2, 1944
Edson, Merritt A. Col., USMC	Vt.	1st Mar. Raider Bn.	Guadalcanal	Sept. 13–14, 1942
Ehlers, Walter D. S. Sgt., USA	Kans.	1st Inf. Div.	France	June 9–10, 1944
*Elrod, Henry T. Capt., USMC	Ga.	VMF-211	Wake Island	Dec. 8– 23, 1941
*Endl, Gerald L. S. Sgt., USA	Wis.	32nd Inf. Div.	New Guinea	July 11, 1944
*Epperson, Harold G. Pfc., USMC	Ohio	2nd Mar. Div.	Saipan	June 25, 1944
Erwin, Henry E. S. Sgt., USAAF	Ala.	Twentieth A.F.	over Japan	Apr. 12, 1945
*Eubanks, Ray E. Sgt., USA	N.C.	503d Para. Inf. Rgt.	New Guinea	July 23, 1944
*Evans, Ernest E. Comdr., USN	Okla.	U.S.S. *Johnston*	off Samar, P.I.	Oct. 25, 1944
Everhart, Forrest E. T. Sgt., USA	Tex.	90th Inf. Div.	France	Nov. 12, 1944
*Fardy, John P. Cpl., USMC	Ill.	1st Mar. Div.	Okinawa	May 7, 1945
*Femoyer, Robert E. 2d Lt., USAAF	Fla.	Eighth A.F.	over Germany	Nov. 2, 1944
Fields, James H. 1st Lt., USA	Tex.	4th Armrd. Div.	France	Sept. 27, 1944
Finn, John W. Avn. Ord. Mate, USN	Calif.	Naval Air Station	Kaneohe Bay, Oahu, Ha- waii	Dec. 7, 1941
Fisher, Almond E. 2d Lt., USA	N.Y.	45th Inf. Div.	France	Sept. 12–13, 1944
*Flaherty, Francis C. Ens., USN	Mich.	U.S.S. *Oklahoma*	Pearl Harbor	Dec. 7, 1941
*Fleming, Richard E. Capt., USMC	Minn.	VSB-241	near Midway Island	June 4–5, 1942
Fluckey, Eugene B. Comdr., USN	Ill.	U.S.S. *Barb*	off China coast	Dec. 1944– Feb. 1945
Foss, Joseph J. Capt., USMC	S.Dak.	VMF-121	Guadalcanal	Oct. 9– Nov. 19, 1942

Name Rank, Branch	Home State	Unit	Place	Date
*Foster, William A. Pfc., USMC	Ohio	1st Mar. Div.	Okinawa	May 2, 1945
*Fournier, William G. Sgt., USA	Maine	25th Inf. Div.	Guadalcanal	Jan. 10, 1943
*Fowler, Thomas W. 2d Lt., USA	Tex.	1st Armrd. Div.	Italy	May 23, 1944
*Fryar, Elmer E. Pvt., USA	Colo.	11th Abn. Div.	Leyte, P.I.	Dec. 8, 1944
Funk, Leonard A., Jr. 1st Sgt., USA	Penn.	82d Abn. Div.	Belgium	Jan. 29, 1945
Fuqua, Samuel G. Lt. Comdr., USN	Mo.	U.S.S. *Arizona*	Pearl Harbor	Dec. 7, 1941
Galer, Robert E. Maj., USMC	Wash.	VMF-244	Solomon Islands	Aug.– Sept. 1942
*Galt, William W. Capt., USA	Mont.	34th Inf. Div.	Italy	May 29, 1944
*Gammon, Archer T. S. Sgt., USA	Va.	6th Armrd. Div.	Belgium	Jan. 11, 1945
Garcia, Marcario S. Sgt., USA	Tex.	4th Inf. Div.	Germany	Nov. 27, 1944
Garman, Harold A. Pvt., USA	Ill.	5th Inf. Div.	France	Aug. 25, 1944
Gary, Donald A. Lt. (jg), USN	Ohio	U.S.S. *Franklin*	off Japan	Mar. 19, 1945
Gerstung, Robert E. T. Sgt., USA	Ill.	79th Inf. Div.	Germany	Dec. 19, 1944
*Gibson, Eric G. Tech. 5, USA	Ill.	3d Inf. Div.	Italy	Jan. 28, 1944
*Gilmore, Howard W. Comdr., USN	La.	U.S.S. *Growler*	near Rabaul, New Britain	Jan. 10– Feb. 7, 1943
*Gonsalves, Harold Pfc., USMC	Calif.	6th Mar. Div.	Okinawa	Apr. 15, 1945
*Gonzales, David M. Pfc., USA	Calif.	32nd Inf. Div.	Luzon, P.I.	Apr. 25, 1945
Gordon, Nathan G. Lt., USN	Ark.	VPB-34	Bismarck Sea	Feb. 15, 1944
*Gott, Donald J. 1st Lt., USAAF	Okla.	Eighth A.F.	over Germany	Nov. 9, 1944
*Grabiarz, William J. Pfc., USA	N.Y.	1st Cav. Div.	Luzon, P.I.	Feb. 23, 1945
*Gray, Ross F. Sgt., USMC	Ala.	4th Mar. Div.	Iwo Jima	Feb. 21, 1945
Gregg, Stephen R. T. Sgt., USA	N.J.	36th Inf. Div.	France	Aug. 27–28 1944

Name Rank, Branch	Home State	Unit	Place	Date
*Gruennert, Kenneth E. Sgt., USA	Wis.	32nd Inf. Div.	New Guinea	Dec. 24, 1942
*Gurke, Henry Pfc., USMC	N.Dak.	3d Mar. Raider Bn.	Bougainville	Nov. 9, 1943
Hall, George J. S. Sgt., USA	Mass.	34th Inf. Div.	Italy	May 23, 1944
*Hall, Lewis Tech. 5, USA	Ohio	25th Inf. Div.	Guadalcanal	Jan. 10, 1943
Hall, William E. Lt. (jg), USN	Utah	VS-2	Coral Sea	May 7–8, 1942
*Hallman, Sherwood H. S. Sgt., USA	Penn.	29th Inf. Div.	France	Sept. 13, 1944
*Halyburton, William D. PM 2, USN	N.C.	1st Mar. Div.	Okinawa	May 10, 1945
Hamilton, Pierpont M. Maj., USAAF	N.Y.	Western Task Force	Morocco	Nov. 8, 1942
*Hammerberg, Owen F.P. BM 2, USN	Mich.	Salvage Unit, Pacific Fleet	Pearl Harbor	Feb. 17, 1945
*Hansen, Dale M. Pvt., USMC	Nebr.	1st Mar. Div.	Okinawa	May 7, 1945
*Hanson, Robert M. 1st Lt., USMC	Mass.	VMF-215	Bougainville New Britain	Nov. 1, 1943 Jan. 24, 1944
*Harmon, Roy W. Sgt., USA	Calif.	91st Inf. Div.	Italy	July 12, 1944
*Harr, Harry R. Cpl., USA	Penn.	31st Inf. Div	Mindanao, P.I.	June 5, 1945
Harrell, William G. Sgt., USMC	Tex.	5th Mar. Div.	Iwo Jima	Mar. 3, 1945
*Harris, James L. 2d Lt., USA	Tex.	756th Tank Bn.	France	Oct. 7, 1944
*Hastings, Joe R. Pfc., USA	Ohio	97th Inf. Div.	Germany	Apr. 12, 1945
*Hauge, Louis, J., Jr. Cpl., USMC	Minn.	1st Mar. Div.	Okinawa	May 14, 1945
Hawk, John D. Sgt., USA	Wash.	90th Inf. Div.	France	Aug. 20, 1944
*Hawkins, William D. 1st Lt., USMC	Tex.	2d Mar. Div.	Tarawa	Nov. 20–21, 1943
Hawks, Lloyd C. Pfc., U.S.A.	Minn.	3d Inf. Div.	Italy	Jan. 30, 1944
*Hedrick, Clinton M. T. Sgt., USA	W.Va.	17th Abn. Div.	Germany	Mar. 27–28, 1945
Hendrix, James R. Pvt., USA	Ark.	4th Armrd. Div.	Belgium	Dec. 26, 1944

Name Rank, Branch	Home State	Unit	Place	Date
*Henry, Robert T. Pvt., USA	Miss.	1st Inf. Div.	Germany	Dec. 3, 1944
Herrera, Silvestre S. Pvt., USA	Ariz.	36th Inf. Div.	France	Mar. 15, 1945
Herring, Rufus G. Lt., USN	N.C.	LCI (G) 449	Iwo Jima	Feb. 17, 1945
*Hill, Edwin J. BMC., USN	Penn.	U.S.S. *Nevada*	Pearl Harbor	Dec. 7, 1941
Horner, Freeman V. S. Sgt., USA	Penn.	30th Inf. Div.	Germany	Nov. 16, 1944
Howard, James H. Lt. Col., USAAF	Mo.	Ninth A.F.	over Germany	Jan. 11, 1944
Huff, Paul B. Cpl., USA	Tenn.	509th Para. Inf. Rgt.	Italy	Feb. 8, 1944
*Hughes, Lloyd H. 2d Lt., USAAF	Tex.	Eighth A.F.	Ploesti, Romania	Aug. 1, 1943
*Hutchins, Johnnie D. S1c., USN	Tex.	LST 473	New Guinea	Sept. 4, 1943
*Jachman, Isadore S. S. Sgt., USA	Md.	513th Para. Inf. Rgt.	Belgium	Jan. 4, 1945
Jackson, Arthur J. Pfc., USMC	Oreg.	1st Mar. Div.	Peleliu	Sept. 18, 1944
Jacobson, Douglas T. Pfc., USMC	N.Y.	4th Mar. Div.	Iwo Jima	Feb. 26, 1945
*Jerstad, John L. Maj., USAAF	Wis.	Eighth A.F.	Ploesti, Romania	Aug. 1, 1943
*Johnson, Elden H. Pvt., USA	Mass.	3d Inf. Div.	Italy	June 3, 1944
Johnson, Leon W. Col., USAAF	Kans.	Eighth A.F.	Ploesti, Romania	Aug. 1, 1943
*Johnson, Leroy Sgt., USA	La.	32d Inf. Div.	Leyte, P.I.	Dec. 15, 1944
Johnson, Oscar G. Pfc., USA	Mich.	91st Inf. Div.	Italy	Sept. 16–18, 1944
Johnston, William J. Pfc., USA	Conn.	45th Inf. Div.	Italy	Feb. 17–19, 1944
*Jones, Herbert C. Ens., USN	Calif.	U.S.S. *California*	Pearl Harbor	Dec. 7, 1941
*Julian, Joseph R. Plt. Sgt., USMC	Mass.	5th Mar. Div.	Iwo Jima	Mar. 9, 1945
*Kandle, Victor L. 1st Lt., USA	Wash.	3d Inf. Div.	France	Oct. 9, 1944
Kane, John R. Col., USAAF	La.	Ninth A.F.	Ploesti, Romania	Aug. 1, 1943
Kearby, Neel E. Col., USAAF	Tex.	Fifth A.F.	New Guinea	Oct. 11, 1943

Name Rank, Branch	Home State	Unit	Place	Date
*Keathley, George D. S. Sgt., USA	Tex.	85th Inf. Div.	Italy	Sept. 14, 1944
*Kefurt, Gus S. Sgt., USA	Ohio	3d Inf. Div.	France	Dec. 23–24, 1944
*Kelley, Jonah E. S. Sgt. USA	W.Va.	78th Inf. Div.	Germany	Jan. 30–31, 1945
*Kelley, Ova A. Pvt., USA	Mo.	96th Inf. Div.	Leyte, P.I.	Dec. 8, 1944
Kelly, Charles E. Cpl., USA	Penn.	36th Inf. Div.	Italy	Sept. 13, 1943
*Kelly, John D. T. Sgt., USA	Penn.	79th Inf. Div.	France	June 25, 1944
Kelly, Thomas J. Cpl., USA	N.Y.	7th Armrd. Div.	Germany	Apr. 5, 1945
*Keppler, Reinhardt J. BM 1, USN	Wash.	U.S.S. San Francisco	off Savo Island	Nov. 12–13, 1942
Kerstetter, Dexter J. Pfc., USA	Wash.	33d Inf. Div.	Luzon, P.I.	Apr. 13, 1945
*Kessler, Patrick L. Pfc., USA	Ohio	3d Inf. Div.	Italy	May 23, 1944
*Kidd, Isaac C. Rear Adm., USN	Ohio	U.S.S. Arizona	Pearl Harbor	Dec. 7, 1941
*Kimbro, Truman Tech. 4, USA	Tex.	2d Inf. Div.	Belgium	Dec. 19, 1944
*Kiner, Harold G. Pvt., USA	Okla.	30th Inf. Div.	Germany	Oct. 2, 1944
*Kingsley, David R. 2d Lt., USAAF	Oreg.	Fifteenth A.F.	Ploesti, Romania	June 23, 1944
*Kinser, Elbert L. Sgt., USMC	Tenn.	1st Mar. Div.	Okinawa	May 4, 1945
Kisters, Gerry H., Sgt., USA	Ind.	91st Recon. Squadron	Sicily	July 31, 1943
Knappenberger, Alton W. Pfc., USA	Penn.	3d Inf. Div.	Italy	Feb. 1, 1944
*Knight, Jack L. 1st Lt., USA	Tex.	124th Cav. Rgt.	Burma	Feb. 2, 1945
*Knight, Raymond L. 1st Lt., USAAF	Tex.	Twelfth A.F.	Italy	Apr. 24–25, 1945
*Kraus, Richard E. Pfc., USMC	Minn.	8th Amphib. Tractor Bn.	Peleliu	Oct. 5, 1944
*Krotiak, Anthony L. Pfc., USA	Ill.	37th Inf. Div.	Luzon, P.I.	May 8, 1945
*La Belle, James D. Pfc., USMC	Minn.	5th Mar. Div.	Iwo Jima	Mar. 8, 1945
Lawley, William R., Jr. 1st Lt., USAAF	Ala.	Eighth A.F.	over Europe	Feb. 20, 1944

Name Rank, Branch	Home State	Unit	Place	Date
Laws, Robert E. S. Sgt., USA	Penn.	43d Inf. Div.	Luzon, P.I.	Jan. 12, 1945
Lee, Daniel W. 1st Lt., USA	Ga.	117th Cav. Recon. Squad- ron	France	Sept. 2, 1944
Leims, John H. 2d Lt., USMC	Ill.	3d Mar. Div.	Iwo Jima	Mar. 7, 1945
*Leonard, Turney W. 1st Lt., USA	Tex.	893d Tank Dest. Bn.	Germany	Nov. 4–6, 1944
*Lester, Fred F. HA 1, USN	Ill.	6th Mar. Div.	Okinawa	June 8, 1945
*Lindsey, Darrell R. Capt., USAAF	Iowa	Ninth A.F.	over France	Aug. 9, 1944
Lindsey, Jake W. T. Sgt., USA	Miss.	1st Inf. Div.	Germany	Nov. 16, 1944
*Lindstrom, Floyd K. Pfc., USA	Colo.	3d Inf. Div.	Italy	Nov. 11, 1943
*Lloyd, Edgar H. 1st Lt., USA	Ark.	80th Inf. Div.	France	Sept 14, 1944
*Lobaugh, Donald R. Pvt., USA	Penn.	32d Inf. Div.	New Guinea	July 22, 1944
Logan, James M. Sgt., USA	Tex.	36th Inf. Div.	Italy	Sept. 9, 1943
Lopez, Jose M. Sgt., USA	Tex.	2d Inf. Div.	Belgium	Dec. 17, 1944
Lucas, Jacklyn H. Pfc., USMC	N.C.	5th Mar. Div.	Iwo Jima	Feb. 20, 1945
*Lummus, Jack 1st Lt., USMC	Tex.	5th Mar. Div.	Iwo Jima	Mar. 8, 1945
Mabry, George L. Lt. Col., USA	S.C.	4th Inf. Div.	Germany	Nov. 20, 1944
MacArthur, Douglas Gen., USA	Wis.	U.S.A.F.F.E.	Luzon, P.I.	Dec. 1941– Mar. 1942
MacGillivary, Charles A. Sgt., USA	Mass.	44th Inf. Div.	France	Jan. 1, 1945
*Magrath, John D. Pfc., USA	Conn.	10th Mountain Div.	Italy	Apr. 14, 1945
*Mann, Joe E. Pfc., USA	Wash.	101st Abn. Div.	Holland	Sept. 18, 1944
*Martin, Harry L. 1st Lt., USMC	Ohio	5th Mar. Div.	Iwo Jima	Mar. 26, 1945
*Martinez, Joe P. Pvt., USA	Colo.	7th Inf. Div.	Attu, Aleutian Is.	May 26, 1943
*Mason, Leonard F. Pfc., USMC	Ohio	3d Mar. Div.	Guam	July 22, 1944

Name Rank, Branch	Home State	Unit	Place	Date
*Mathies, Archibald Sgt., USAAF	Penn.	Eighth A.F.	over Europe	Feb. 20, 1944
*Mathis, Jack W. 1st Lt., USAAF	Tex.	Eighth A.F.	over Germany	Mar. 18, 1943
Maxwell, Robert D. Tech. 5, USA	Colo.	3d Inf. Div.	France	Sept. 7, 1944
*May, Martin O. Pfc., USA	N.J.	77th Inf. Div.	Ie Shima	Apr. 19–21 1945
Mayfield, Melvin Cpl., USA	Ohio	6th Inf. Div.	Luzon, P.I.	July 29, 1945
McCall, Thomas E. S. Sgt., USA	Ind.	36th Inf. Div.	Italy	Jan. 22, 1944
McCampbell, David Comdr., USN	Fla.	Air Group 15	Philippine Sea	June 19 & Oct. 24, 1944
McCandless, Bruce Lt. Comdr., USN	Colo.	U.S.S. San Francisco	off Savo Island	Nov. 12–13 1942
*McCard, Robert H. Gy. Sgt., USMC	N.Y.	4th Mar. Div.	Saipan	June 16, 1944
McCarter, Lloyd G. Pvt., USA	Idaho	503d Para. Inf. Rgt.	Corregidor, P.I.	Feb. 16–19, 1945
McCarthy, Joseph J. Capt., USMC	Ill.	4th Mar. Div.	Iwo Jima	Feb. 21, 1945
McCool, Richard M., Jr. Lt., USN	Okla.	LSC (L) (3) 122	Okinawa	June 10–11, 1945
McGaha, Charles L. M. Sgt., USA	Tenn.	25th Inf. Div.	Luzon, P.I.	Feb. 7, 1945
McGarity, Vernon T. Sgt., USA	Tenn.	99th Inf. Div.	Belgium	Dec. 16, 1944
*McGee, William D. Pvt., USA	Ind.	76th Inf. Div.	Germany	Mar. 18, 1944
*McGill, Troy A. Sgt., USA	Tenn.	1st Cav. Div.	Los Negros, Admiralty Is.	Mar. 4, 1944
*McGraw, Francis X. Pfc., USA	N.J.	1st Inf. Div.	Germany	Nov. 19, 1944
*McGuire, Thomas B. Maj., USAAF	N.J.	Fifth A.F.	over Luzon, P.I.	Dec. 25-26, 1944
McKinney, John R. Pvt. USA	Ga.	33d Inf. Div.	Luzon, P.I.	May 11, 1945
*McTureous, Robert M. Pvt., USMC	Fla.	6th Mar. Div.	Okinawa	June 7, 1945
*McVeigh, John J. Sgt., USA	Penn.	2d Inf. Div.	France	Aug. 29, 1944
*McWhorter, William A. Pfc., USA	S.C.	32d Inf. Div.	Leyte, P.I.	Dec. 5, 1944

Name Rank, Branch	Home State	Unit	Place	Date
Meagher, John T. Sgt., USA	N.J.	77th Inf. Div.	Okinawa	June 19, 1945
Merli, Gino J. Pfc., USA	Penn.	1st Inf. Div.	Belgium	Sept. 4–5, 1944
*Merrell, Joseph F. Pvt., USA	N.Y.	3d Inf. Div.	Germany	Apr. 18, 1945
*Messerschmidt, Harold Sgt., USA	Penn.	3d Inf. Div.	France	Sept. 17, 1944
*Metzger, William E. 2d Lt, USAAF	Ohio	Eighth A.F.	over Germany	Nov. 9, 1944
Michael, Edward S. 1st Lt., USAAF	Ill.	Eighth A.F.	over Germany	Apr. 11, 1944
*Michael, Harry J. 2d Lt., USA	Ind.	80th Inf. Div.	Germany	Mar. 14, 1945
*Miller, Andrew S. Sgt., USA	Wis.	95th Inf. Div.	France & Germany	Nov. 16–29, 1944
Mills, James H. Pvt., USA	Fla.	3d Inf. Div.	Italy	May 24, 1944
*Minick, John W. S. Sgt., USA	Penn.	8th Inf. Div.	Germany	Nov. 21, 1944
*Minue, Nicholas Pvt., USA	N.J.	1st Armrd. Div.	Tunisia	Apr. 28, 1943
*Monteith, Jimmie W. 1st Lt., USA	Va.	1st Inf. Div.	France	June 6, 1944
Montgomery, Jack C. 1st Lt., USA	Okla.	45th Inf. Div.	Italy	Feb. 22, 1944
*Moon, Harold H., Jr. Pvt. USA	N. Mex.	24th Inf. Div.	Leyte, P.I.	Oct. 21, 1944
Morgan, John C. 2d Lt., USAAF	Tex.	Eighth A.F.	over Europe	July 28, 1943
*Moskala, Edward J. Pfc., USA	Ill.	96th Inf. Div.	Okinawa	Apr. 9, 1945
*Mower, Charles E. Sgt., USA	Wis.	24th Inf. Div.	Leyte, P.I.	Nov. 3, 1944
*Muller, Joseph E. Sgt., USA	N.Y.	77th Inf. Div.	Okinawa	May 15–16, 1945
*Munemori, Sadao S. Pfc., USA	Calif.	442d Rgt. Combat Team	Italy	Apr. 5, 1945
*Munro, Douglas A. SM 1, USCG	Wash.	—	Guadalcanal	Sept. 27, 1942
Murphy, Audie L. 2d Lt., USA	Tex.	3d Inf. Div.	France	Jan. 26, 1945
*Murphy, Fredrick C. Pfc., USA	Mass.	65th Inf. Div.	Germany	Mar. 18, 1945

Name Rank, Branch	Home State	Unit	Place	Date
Murray, Charles P. 1st Lt., USA	N.C.	3d Inf. Div.	France	Dec. 16, 1944
*Nelson, William L. Sgt., USA	Del.	9th Inf. Div.	Tunisia	Apr. 24, 1943
Neppel, Ralph G. Sgt., USA	Iowa	83d Inf. Div.	Germany	Dec. 14, 1944
Nett, Robert B. 1st Lt., USA	Conn.	77th Inf. Div.	Leyte, P.I.	Dec. 14, 1944
*New, John D. Pfc., USMC	Ala.	1st Mar. Div.	Peleliu	Sept. 25, 1944
Newman, Beryl R. 1st Lt., USA	Wis.	34th Inf. Div.	Italy	May 26, 1944
*Nininger, Alexander R. 2d Lt., USA	Fla.	57th Inf. (PS)	Luzon, P.I.	Jan. 12, 1942
*O'Brien, William J. Lt. Col., USA	N.Y.	27th Inf. Div.	Saipan	June 20– July 7, 1944
O'Callahan, Joseph T. Lt. Comdr. (Chap), USN	Mass.	U.S.S. *Franklin*	off Japan	Mar. 19, 1945
Ogden, Carlos C. 1st Lt., USA	Ill.	79th Inf. Div.	France	June 25, 1944
O'Hare, Edward H. Lt., USN	Mo.	VF-3	Near Rabaul, New Britain	Feb. 20, 1942
O'Kane, Richard H. Comdr., USN	N.H.	U.S.S. *Tang*	Philippine Islands area	Oct. 23 & 24, 1944
*Olson, Arlo L. Capt. USA	S.D.	3d Inf. Div.	Italy	Oct. 13–27, 1943
*Olson, Truman O. Sgt., USA	Wis.	3d Inf. Div.	Italy	Jan. 30–31, 1944
Oresko, Nicholas M. Sgt., USA	N.J.	94th Inf. Div.	Germany	Jan. 23, 1945
*Owens, Robert A. Sgt., USMC	S.C.	3rd Mar. Div.	Bougainville	Nov. 1, 1943
*Ozbourn, Joseph W. Pvt., USMC	Ill.	4th Mar. Div.	Tinian	July 30, 1944
Paige, Michael Plt. Sgt., USMC	Penn.	1st Mar. Div.	Guadalcanal	Oct. 26, 1942
*Parle, John J. Ens., USN	Neb.	LST 375	off Sicily	July 9–10, 1943
*Parrish, Laverne Tech. 4, USA	Mont.	25th Inf. Div.	Luzon, P.I.	Jan. 18–24, 1945
*Pease, Harl, Jr. Capt., USAAF	N.H.	Fifth A.F.	over Rabaul, New Britain	Aug. 6–7, 1942

Name Rank, Branch	Home State	Unit	Place	Date
*Peden, Forrest E. Tech. 5, USA	Kans.	3d Inf. Div.	France	Feb. 3, 1945
*Pendleton, Jack J. S. Sgt., USA	Wash.	30th Inf. Div.	Germany	Oct. 12, 1944
*Peregory, Frank D. T. Sgt., USA	Va.	29th Inf. Div.	France	June 8, 1944
*Perez, Manuel, Jr. Pfc., USA	Okla.	11th Abn. Div.	Luzon, P.I.	Feb. 13, 1945
*Peters, George J. Pvt., USA	R.I.	17th Abn. Div.	Germany	Mar. 24, 1945
*Peterson, George S. Sgt., USA	N.Y.	1st Inf. Div.	Germany	Mar. 30, 1945
*Peterson, Oscar V. WTC, USN	Wis.	U.S.S. *Neosho*	Coral Sea	May 7, 1942
*Petrarca, Frank J. Pfc., USA	Ohio	37th Inf. Div.	New Georgia	July 27, 1943
Pharris, Jackson C. GMC, USN	Calif.	U.S.S. *California*	Pearl Harbor	Dec. 7, 1941
*Phelps, Wesley Pvt., USMC	Ky.	1st Mar. Div.	Peleliu	Oct. 4, 1944
*Phillips, George Pvt., USMC	Mo.	5th Mar. Div.	Iwo Jima	Mar. 14, 1945
Pierce, Francis J. PM 1, USN	Iowa	4th Mar. Div.	Iwo Jima	Mar. 15–16, 1945
*Pinder, John J., Jr. Tech. 5, USA	Penn.	1st Inf. Div.	France	June 6, 1944
Pope, Everett P. Capt., USMC	Mass.	1st Mar. Div.	Peleliu	Sept. 19–20, 1944
*Power, John V. 1st Lt., USMC	Mass.	4th Mar. Div.	Roi-Namur, Marshall Is.	Feb. 1, 1944
*Powers, John J. Lt., USN	N.Y.	VB-5	Coral Sea	May 4–8, 1942
Powers, Leo J. Pfc., USA	Mont.	34th Inf. Div.	Italy	Feb. 3, 1944
Preston, Arthur M. Lt., USN	Md.	Torpedo Boat Squadron 33	Halmahera Island	Sept. 16, 1944
*Prussman, Ernest W. Pfc., USA	Mass.	8th Inf. Div.	France	Sept. 8, 1944
*Pucket, Donald D. 1st Lt., USAAF	Colo.	Fifteenth A.F.	Ploesti, Romania	July 9, 1944
Ramage, Lawson P. Comdr., USN	Vt.	U.S.S. *Parche*	near Luzon, P.I.	July 31, 1944
*Ray, Bernard J. 1st Lt., USA	N.Y.	4th Inf. Div.	Germany	Nov. 17, 1944

Name Rank, Branch	Home State	Unit	Place	Date
*Reese, James W. Pvt., USA	Penn.	1st Inf. Div.	Sicily	Aug. 5, 1943
*Reese, John N., Jr. Pfc., USA	Okla.	37th Inf. Div.	Luzon, P.I.	Feb. 9, 1945
*Reeves, Thomas J. Radio Elec., USN	Conn.	U.S.S. *California*	Pearl Harbor	Dec. 7, 1941
*Ricketts, Milton E. Lt., USN	Md.	U.S.S. *Yorktown*	Coral Sea	May 8, 1942
*Riordan, Paul F. 2d Lt., USA	Mo.	34th Inf. Div.	Italy	Feb. 3–8, 1944
*Roan, Charles H. Pfc., USMC	Tex.	1st Mar. Div.	Peleliu	Sept. 18, 1944
*Robinson, Jame E. 1st Lt., USA	Tex.	63d Inf. Div.	Germany	Apr. 6, 1945
Rodriguez, Cleto Pvt., USA	Tex.	37th Inf. Div.	Luzon, P.I.	Feb. 9, 1945
*Roeder, Robert E. Capt., USA	Penn.	88th Inf. Div.	Italy	Sept. 27–28, 1944
*Rooks, Albert H. Capt., USN	Wash.	U.S.S. *Houston*	Java Sea	Feb. 4–27, 1942
*Roosevelt, Theodore, Jr. Brig. Gen., USA	N.Y.	4th Inf. Div.	France	June 6, 1944
Ross, Donald D. Mach., USN	Colo.	U.S.S. *Nevada*	Pearl Harbor	Dec. 7, 1941
Ross, Wilburn K. Pvt., USA	Ky.	3d Inf. Div.	France	Oct. 30, 1944
Rouh, Carlton R. 1st Lt., USMC	N.J.	1st Mar. Div.	Peleliu	Sept. 15, 1944
Rudolph, Donald E. T. Sgt., USA	Minn.	6th Inf. Div.	Luzon, P.I.	Feb. 5, 1945
*Ruhl, Donald J. Pfc., USMC	Mont.	5th Mar. Div.	Iwo Jima	Feb. 19–21, 1945
Ruiz, Alejandro R. R. Pfc., USMC	N.Mex.	27th Inf. Div.	Okinawa	Apr. 28, 1945
*Sadowski, Joseph J. Sgt., USA	N.J.	4th Armrd. Div.	France	Sept. 14, 1944
*Sarnoski, Joseph R. 2d Lt., USAAF	Penn.	Fifth A.F.	Solomon Islands	June 16, 1943
*Sayers, Foster J. Pfc., USA	Penn.	90th Inf. Div.	France	Nov. 12, 1944
Schaefer, Joseph E. S. Sgt., USA	N.Y.	1st Inf. Div.	Germany	Sept. 24, 1944
Schauer, Henry Pfc., USA	Mont.	3d Inf. Div.	Italy	May 23–24, 1944
Schonland, Herbert E. Lt. Comdr., USN	Maine	U.S.S. *San Francisco*	off Savo Island	Nov. 12–13 1942

Name Rank, Branch	Home State	Unit	Place	Date
*Schwab, Albert E. Pfc., USMC	Okla.	1st Mar. Div.	Okinawa	May 7, 1945
*Scott, Norman Rear Adm., USN	Ind.	U.S.S. *Atlanta*	off Savo Island	Nov. 12–13, 1942
*Scott, Robert R. MM 1, USN	Ohio	U.S.S. *California*	Pearl Harbor	Dec. 7, 1941
Scott, Robert S. 1st Lt., USA	N.Mex.	43d Inf. Div.	New Georgia	July 29, 1943
Shea, Charles W. 2d Lt., USA	N.Y.	88th Inf. Div.	Italy	May 12, 1944
*Sheridan, Carl V. Pfc., USA	Md.	9th Inf. Div.	Germany	Nov. 26, 1944
*Shockley, William R. Pfc., USA	Calif.	32d Inf. Div.	Luzon, P.I.	Mar. 31, 1945
Shomo, William A. Maj., USAAF	Penn.	Fifth A.F.	over Luzon, P.I.	Jan. 11, 1945
*Shoup, Curtis F. S. Sgt., USA	N.Y.	87th Inf. Div.	Belgium	Jan. 7, 1945
Shoup, David M. Col., USMC	Ind.	2nd Mar. Div.	Tarawa	Nov. 20–22, 1943
Sigler, Franklin E. Pvt., USMC	N.J.	5th Mar. Div.	Iwo Jima	Mar. 14, 1945
Silk, Edward A. 1st Lt., USA	Penn.	100th Inf. Div.	France	Nov. 23, 1944
Sjogren, John C. S. Sgt., USA	Mich.	40th Inf. Div.	Negros, P.I.	May 23, 1945
Skaggs, Luther Pfc., USMC	Ky.	3d Mar. Div.	Guam	July 21–22, 1944
Slaton, James D. Cpl., USA	Miss.	45th Inf. Div.	Italy	Sept. 23, 1943
*Smith, Furman L. Pvt., USA	S.C.	34th Inf. Div.	Italy	May 31, 1944
Smith, John L. Maj., USMC	Okla.	VMF-223	Solomon Islands	Aug.–Sept., 1942
Smith, Maynard H. Sgt., USAAF	Mich.	Eighth A.F.	over Europe	May 1, 1943
Soderman, William A. Pfc., USA	Conn.	2d Inf. Div.	Belgium	Dec. 17, 1944
Sorenson, Richard K. Pvt., USMC	Minn.	4th Mar. Div.	Roi-Namur, Marshall Is.	Feb. 1–2, 1944
*Specker, Joe C. Sgt., USA	Mo.	48th Eng. Combat Bn.	Italy	Jan. 7, 1944
Spurrier, Junior J. S. Sgt., USA	Va.	35th Inf. Div.	France	Nov. 13, 1944

Name Rank, Branch	Home State	Unit	Place	Date
*Squires, John C. Pfc., USA	Ky.	3d Inf. Div.	Italy	Apr. 23–24, 1944
Stein, Tony Cpl., USMC	Ohio	5th Mar. Div.	Iwo Jima	Feb. 19, 1945
Street, George L. Comdr., USN	Va.	U.S.S. *Tirante*	off Korea	Apr. 14, 1945
Stryker, Stuart S. Pfc., USA	Oreg.	17th Abn. Div.	Germany	Mar. 24, 1945
Swett, James E. 1st Lt., USMC	Calif.	VMF-221	Solomon Islands	Apr. 7, 1943
*Terry, Seymour W. Capt., USA	Ark.	96th Inf. Div.	Okinawa	May 11, 1945
*Thomas, Herbert J. Sgt., USMC	W.Va.	3d Mar. Div.	Bougainville	Nov. 7, 1943
*Thomas, William H. Pfc., USA	Mich.	38th Inf. Div.	Luzon, P.I.	Apr. 22, 1945
*Thomason, Clyde Sgt., USMC	Ga.	2d Mar. Raider Bn.	Makin Island, Gilbert Is.	Aug. 17–18, 1942
Thompson, Max Sgt., USA	N.C.	1st Inf. Div.	Germany	Oct. 18, 1944
*Thorne, Horace M. Cpl., USA	N.J.	9th Armrd. Div.	Belgium	Dec. 21, 1944
*Thorson, John F. Pfc., USA	Iowa	7th Inf. Div.	Leyte, P.I.	Oct. 28, 1944
*Timmerman, Grant F. Sgt., USMC	Kans.	2d Mar. Div.	Saipan	July 8, 1944
*Tomich, Peter WTC, USN	N.J.	U.S.S. *Utah*	Pearl Harbor	Dec. 7, 1941
Tominac, John J. 1st Lt., USA	Penn.	3d Inf. Div.	France	Sept. 12, 1944
*Towle, John R. Pvt., USA	Ohio	82d Abn. Div.	Holland	Sept. 21, 1944
Treadwell, Jack L. 1st Lt., USA	Okla.	45th Inf. Div.	Germany	Mar. 18, 1945
*Truemper, Walter E. 2d Lt., USAAF	Ill.	Eighth A.F.	over Europe	Feb. 20, 1944
*Turner, Day G. Sgt., USA	Penn.	80th Inf. Div.	Luxembourg	Jan. 8, 1945
Turner, George B. Pfc., USA	Calif.	14th Armrd. Div.	France	Jan. 3, 1945
Urban, Matt Capt., USA	N.Y.	9th Inf. Div.	France	June 14– Sept. 3, 1944
*Valdez, Jose F. Pfc., USA	Utah	3d Inf. Div.	France	Jan. 25, 1945

Name Rank, Branch	Home State	Unit	Place	Date
*Vance, Leon R. Lt. Col., USAAF	N.Y.	Eighth A.F.	over France	June 5, 1944
Vandegrift, Alexander Maj. Gen., USMC	Va.	1st Mar. Div.	Guadalcanal	Aug. 7– Dec. 9, 1942
*Van Noy, Nathan, Jr. Pvt., USA	Idaho	532d Eng. Boat & Shore Rgt.	New Guinea	Oct. 17, 1943
*Van Valkenburgh, Franklin Capt., USN	Wis.	U.S.S. *Arizona*	Pearl Harbor	Dec. 7, 1941
*Van Voorhis, Bruce A. Lt., Comdr., USN	Wash.	VB-102	Solomon Islands	July 6, 1943
*Viale, Robert M. 2d Lt., USA	Calif.	37th Inf. Div.	Luzon, P.I.	Feb. 5, 1945
*Villegas, Ysmael R. S. Sgt., USA	Calif.	32d Inf. Div.	Luzon, P.I.	Mar. 20, 1945
Vlug, Dirk J. Pfc., USA	Mich.	32d Inf. Div.	Leyte, P.I.	Dec. 15, 1944
Vosler, Forrest T. T. Sgt., USAAF	N.Y.	Eighth A.F.	over Germany	Dec. 20, 1943
Wahlen, George E. PM 2, USN	Utah	5th Mar. Div.	Iwo Jima	Mar. 3, 1945
Wainwright, Jonathan M. Gen., USA	N.Y.	U.S.A.F.P.I.	Luzon, P.I.	Mar. 12– May 7, 1942
*Walker, Kenneth N. Brig. Gen., USAAF	Colo.	Fifth A.F.	over Rabaul, New Britain	Jan. 5, 1943
*Wallace, Herman C. Pfc., USA	Tex.	76th Inf. Div.	Germany	Feb. 27, 1945
Walsh, Kenneth A. 1st Lt., USMC	N.Y.	VMF-124	Solomon Islands	Aug. 15 & 30, 1943
*Walsh, William G. Gy. Sgt., USMC	Mass.	5th Mar. Div.	Iwo Jima	Feb. 27, 1945
*Ward, James R. S1c., USN	Ohio	U.S.S. *Oklahoma*	Pearl Harbor	Dec. 7, 1941
Ware, Keith L. Lt. Col., USA	Calif.	3d Inf. Div.	France	Dec. 26, 1944
*Warner, Henry F. Cpl., USA	N.C.	1st Inf. Div.	Belgium	Dec. 20–21, 1944
Watson, Wilson D. Pvt., USMC	Ark.	3d Mar. Div.	Iwo Jima	Feb. 26–27, 1945
*Waugh, Robert T. 1st Lt., USA	Maine	85th inf. Div.	Italy	May 11–14, 1944
Waybur, David C. 1st Lt., USA	Calif.	3d Inf. Div.	Sicily	July 17, 1943

Name Rank, Branch	Home State	Unit	Place	Date
*Weicht, Ellis R. Sgt., USA	Penn.	36th Inf. Div.	France	Dec. 3, 1944
*Wetzel, Walter C. Pfc., USA	Mich.	8th Inf. Div.	Germany	Apr. 3, 1945
Whiteley, Eli 1st Lt., USA	Tex.	3d Inf. Div.	France	Dec. 27, 1944
Whittington, Hulon B. Sgt., USA	La.	2d Armrd. Div.	France	July 29, 1944
Wiedorfer, Paul J. Pvt., USA	Md.	80th Inf. Div.	Belgium	Dec. 25, 1944
*Wigle, Thomas W. 2d Lt., USA	Mich.	34th Inf. Div.	Italy	Sept. 14, 1944
Wilbur, William H. Col., USA	Mass.	Western Task Force	Morocco	Nov. 8, 1942
*Wilkin, Edward G. Cpl., USA	Mass.	45th Inf. Div.	Germany	Mar. 18, 1945
*Wilkins, Raymond H. Maj. USAAF	Va.	Fifth A.F.	near Rabaul, New Britain	Nov. 2, 1943
*Will, Walter J. 1st Lt., USA	N.Y.	1st Inf. Div.	Germany	Mar. 30, 1945
Williams, Hershel W. Cpl., USMC	W.Va.	3d Mar. Div.	Iwo Jima	Feb. 23, 1945
*Williams, Jack PM 3, USN	Ark.	5th Mar. Div.	Iwo Jima	Mar. 3, 1945
*Willis, John H. PM 1, USN	Tenn.	5th Mar. Div.	Iwo Jima	Feb. 28, 1945
*Wilson, Alfred L. Tech. 5, USA	Penn.	26th Inf. Div.	France	Nov. 8, 1944
Wilson, Louis H. Capt., USMC	Miss.	3d Mar. Div.	Guam	July 25–26 1944
*Wilson, Robert L. Pfc., USMC	Ill.	2d Mar. Div.	Tinian	Aug. 4, 1944
Wise, Homer L. S. Sgt., USA	La.	36th Inf. Div.	Italy	June 14, 1944
*Witek, Frank P. Pfc., USMC	Ill.	3d Mar. Div.	Guam	Aug. 3, 1944
*Woodford, Howard E. S. Sgt., USA	Ohio	33d Inf. Div.	Luzon, P.I.	June 6, 1945
Young, Cassin Comdr., USN	Wis.	U.S.S. *Vestal*	Pearl Harbor	Dec. 7, 1941

Name Rank, Branch	Home State	Unit	Place	Date
*Young, Rodger W. Pvt., USA	Ohio	37th Inf. Div.	New Georgia	July 31, 1943
Zeamer, Jay, Jr. Maj., USAAF	Maine	Fifth A.F.	Solomon Islands	June 16, 1943
*Zussman, Raymond 2d Lt., USA	Mich.	756th Tank Bn.	France	Sept. 12, 1944

Bibliography

Adleman, Robert H, and Walton, George. *The Champagne Campaign.* Boston: Little, Brown and Co., 1969.

Allen, William L. *Anzio—Edge of Disaster.* New York: Elsevier, 1978.

Appleman, Roy E., et al. *Okinawa: The Last Battle.* Rutland, Vt.: Charles E. Tuttle Co., 1960.

Beck, John J. *MacArthur and Wainwright.* Albuquerque, N. Mex.: The University of New Mexico Press, 1971.

Birdsall, Steve. *Log of the Liberators.* Garden City, N.Y.: Doubleday, 1980.

_____. *Saga of the Superfortress.* Garden City, N.Y.,: Doubleday, 1980,

_____. *Flying Buccaneers.* New York: Doubleday, 1977.

Bong, Carl, and O'Connor, Mike. *Ace of Aces.* Mesa, Ariz.: Champlin Fighter Museum, 1985.

Breuer, William B. *Devil Boats.* Novato, Calif.: Presidio Press, 1987,

_____. *Retaking the Philippines.* New York: St. Martins Press, 1986.

Bulkley, Robert J., Jr. *At Close Quarters.* Washington, D.C.: Government Printing Office, 1962.

Carter, Ross S. *Those Devils in Baggy Pants.* New York: Bantam Books. 1985.

Costello, John. *The Pacific War.* New York: Rawson, Wade Publ., Inc., 1981.

Crocker, Mel. *Black Cats and Dumbos.* Ridge Summit, Penn.: Tab Books, 1987.

Dugan, James, and Stewart, Carroll. *Ploesti.* New York: Ballantine Books, 1962.

Editors, Boston Publishing Co. *Above and Beyond.* Boston: Boston Publishing Co., 1985.

Flanagan, E. M. *Corregidor, The Rock Force Assault.* Novato, Calif.: Presidio Press, 1988.

Frank, Bemis M. *Okinawa: The Great Island Battle.* New York: Elsevier-Dutton, 1978.

Gailey, Harry A. *Peleliu, 1944.* Annapolis, Md.: The Nautical & Aviation Publ. Co. of America, 1983.

Glines, Carroll V. *The Doolittle Raid.* New York: Orion Books, 1988.

Gregg, Charles T. *Tarawa.* New York: Stein and Day, 1984.

Hess, Gary R. *The United States at War, 1941–1945.* Arlington Heights, Ill.: Harlan Davidson, Inc., 1986.

Hess, William N. *Pacific Sweep.* Garden City, N.Y.: Doubleday, 1974.

Jablonski, Edward. *America in the Air War*. Alexandria, Va.: Time-Life Books, 1982.

_____.*Flying Fortress*. Garden City, N.Y.: Doubleday, 1965.

Johnston, Stanley, *Queen of the Flattops*. New York: E.P. Dutton & Co., Inc., 1942.

Kenney, George C. *General Kenney Reports*. New York: Duell, Sloan, and Pearce, 1949.

Kurzman, Dan. *Race for Rome*. Garden City, N.Y.: Doubleday, 1975.

Leckie, Robert. *Strong Men Armed*. New York: Bantam Books, 1963.

Lord, Walter, *Day of Infamy*. New York: Henry Holt and Co., 1957.

MacDonald, Charles B. *The Battle of the Huertgen Forest*. Philadelphia: J.B. Lippincott Co., 1963.

_____.*The Last Offensive*. Washington, D.C.: Government Printing Office, 1972.

_____.*The Siegfried Line Campaign*. Washington, D.C.: Government Printing Office, 1963.

Manchester, William. *American Caesar*. Boston: Little, Brown and Co., 1978.

Maurer, Maurer, editor. *Air Force Combat Units of World War II*. Washington, D.C.: Government Printing Office, 1961.

Morin, Raul. *Among the Valiant*. Alhambra, Calif.: Bordon Pub. Co., 1963.

Morrison, Wilbur H. *Point of No Return*. New York: Times Books, 1979.

Morton, Louis. *The Fall of the Philippines*. Washington, D.C.: Government Printing Office, 1952.

O'Leary, Michael. *United States Naval Fighters of World War II in Action*. Poole, Dorset, England: Blandford Press, Ltd., 1980.

Ross, Bill D. *Iwo Jima, Legacy of Valor*. New York: The Vanguard Press, 1985.

Ryan, Cornelius. *The Longest Day*. New York: Simon and Schuster, 1959.

Schott, Joseph L. *Above and Beyond*. New York: G.P. Putnam's Sons, 1963.

Schultz, Duane. *Hero of Bataan: The Story of General Jonathan M. Wainwright*. New York: St. Martins Press, 1981.

Schuon, Karl. *.U.S. Marine Corps Biographical Dictionary*. New York: Franklin Watts, Inc. 1963.

_____.*U.S. Navy Biographical Dictionary*. New York: Franklin Watts, 1964.

Sherrod, Robert. *History of Marine Corps Aviation in World War II*. Baltimore: Nautical & Aviation Publ. Co., 1987.

_____.*Tarawa*. New York: Bantam Books, 1983.

Simpson, Harold B. *Audie Murphy, American Soldier*. Dallas: Alcor Publishing Co., 1975.

Sims, Edward H. *Greatest Fighter Missions*. New York: Harper & Bros., 1962.

Smith, S. E., editor. *The United States Marine Corps in World War II*. New York: Random House, 1969.

Starr, Chester G. *From Salerno to the Alps*. Washington, D.C.: Infantry
    Journal Press, 1948.
Toland, John. *But Not in Shame*. New York: Random House, 1961.
Vedder, James S. *Surgeon on Iwo*. Novato, Calif.: Presidio Press, 1984.
Weigley, Russell F. *Eisenhower's Lieutenants*. Bloomington, Ind.: Uni-
    versity of Indiana Press, 1981.
Wheeler, Richard. *Iwo*. New York: Lippincott & Crowell, 1980.
_____.*A Special Valor; The U.S. Marines and the Pacific War*. New
            York:
Harper & Row Publ., 1983.

A special thanks to these Medal of Honor recipients whose interviews,
help, and friendship over the years made this book possible: Edward
A. Bennett (now deceased); Melvin E. Biddle; Maurice L. Britt; Francis
S. Currey; Charles W. Davis; Walter D. Ehlers; Leonard A. Funk; Nathan
G. Gordon; Stephen R. Gregg; Gerry H. Kisters (now deceased); Gino J.
Merli; John C. Morgan; Ralph G. Neppel (now deceased); Robert E.
Nett; Carlos C. Ogden; Cleto Rodriguez; Donald E. Rudolph; and Junior
J. Spurrier (now deceased).

Index

About the Author

Edward F. Murphy, a military historian, is one of the foremost authorities on the Medal of Honor and its recipients. As founder and president of the Medal of Honor Historical Society, a nonprofit research organization, he edits and publishes their journal, *Medal of Honor Annals*. An Army veteran himself, Mr. Murphy is the author of *Vietnam Medal of Honor Heroes*. He is currently working on a volume of Medal of Honor recipients from the Korean War. He and his wife, Kay, reside in Mesa, Arizona.